PUBLIC
MANAGEMENT

MAYFIELD PUBLISHING COMPANY

PUBLIC MANAGEMENT:

Public and Private Perspectives

EDITED BY

James L. Perry

Kenneth L. Kraemer

UNIVERSITY OF CALIFORNIA, IRVINE

To Jacqueline, Jennifer,
Kim, and Kurt

Library of Congress Catalog Card Number: 82-073742
International Standard Book Number: 0-87484-564-5

Manufactured in the United States of America
Mayfield Publishing Company
285 Hamilton Avenue, Palo Alto, California   94301

Sponsoring editor: Chuck Murphy
Manuscript editor: Nancy Blumenstock
Managing editor: Pat Herbst
Art director: Nancy Sears
Cover designer: Michael Rogondino
Production manager: Cathy Willkie
Compositor: Auto-Graphics, Inc.
Printer and binder: George Banta Company

■ CONTENTS

350
P976

■ **PART SIX**
MANAGEMENT TOOLS

■ **PART SEVEN**
PERFORMANCE CRITERIA: IS THERE A
"BOTTOM LINE" IN GOVERNMENT?   **329**

■ PREFACE

Although we were both educated in traditional schools of public administration (Syracuse University and the University of Southern California), we have spent the entirety of our academic careers, a total of twenty-three years, in a generic school of management. The educational philosophy of a generic school differs markedly from that of either a school of business or a school of public administration. The central organizing principle of generic schools is that the knowledge, techniques, and skills necessary for effective administration or management are similar for organizations in a variety of sectors of society. This philosophy contrasts with the uniqueness that many public administration scholars claim for public administration. Since our training familiarized us with the latter philosophy and our experience familiarized us with the former, we have had the opportunity to evaluate both views—and we have become increasingly aware of the inadequacies of each.

In our experience of the generic viewpoint, good management typically meant good business management. We became aware, however, that the subject matter in our colleagues' course syllabi frequently touted techniques that failed miserably when applied to government. Furthermore, our generic curriculum, until very recently, neglected to develop in students a skill highly regarded in the public sector—the ability to interact with and manage diverse, external, and mainly political interests. Were these inadequacies in the generic viewpoint evidence of its inaccuracy—evidence that public administration is different? They might have been so regarded if our educational backgrounds had not raised similar doubts about the alternative viewpoint.

As public administration students, we often were exposed to techniques from business or to research on business organizations. Yet it was seldom mentioned that those techniques or ideas might have to be modified before they could be applied to government organizations. In the absence of any appreciable body of knowledge about public organizations per se, assertions and anecdotal evidence that public administration was different from business administration were used to make the case that public administration was unique. It was not a strong case.

We believe the term "public management" represents a new approach that has grown naturally from weaknesses in the other prevailing educational philosophies. Public management is a merger of the normative orientation of traditional public administration and the instrumental orientation of generic management. Normative public administration has traditionally been concerned with the relation between democracy and administration, illustrated by such seemingly unanswerable questions as these: "What are the appropriate goals of public administration in a democracy?" "How should such goals be derived?" "How should these goals be implemented to be consistent with democratic principles such as equality of access, opportunity, and outcome?" Public administration traditionally has emphasized "process" approaches to answering these questions and has focused on the principles of equal access and opportunity as guidelines. However, experience and research have increasingly shown that equality of access and opportunity do not always result in equality of outcomes, and attention has shifted to normative consideration of the appropriate conditions for achieving equal outcomes in the management of public affairs.

In contrast, the instrumental orientation of generic management has focused largely on strategies and tactics for aligning organizational structures with specific goals, motivating individuals and groups toward goal compliance, and allocating resources to reinforce authority structures and goal-oriented behavior. To an increasing extent, generic management has also emphasized the use of tools and techniques to determine strategy and tactics and to evaluate individual, group, and organizational performance.

When we say that public management is a merger of these normative and instrumental orientations, we mean that it recognizes the normative context of management as important, but it presupposes that, whatever the context, management strategy and tactics will usually depend on pragmatic and organizational considerations as much as on political philosophies. Public managers need tangible administrative competence to manage organizations successfully in a political environment. The public management approach emphasizes that the individual manager must be able not only to understand and analyze the unique institutional and organizational systems in which he or she is embedded, but must also be able to bring an array of techniques and skills to bear in directing that system. This book is intended to fill a void in available teaching resources on the public manager as a professional and on public management as a field.

Since Woodrow Wilson wrote his classic essay exhorting reformers to help make the business of government "less unbusinesslike," the field of public administration has been seeking to differentiate itself from business administration. But comparisons between government and business are inevitable. In fact, they are important to understanding how management ideas from the private sector have been imposed on public administration and how this process affects what is actually done in public organizations. A key question is, How appropriate are these ideas, and how well has their transfer worked? This book is aimed at enhancing a future manager's competence to ask such questions, to make comparisons between business and government, and to reach informed judgments about the applicability and utility of their ideas.

As the foregoing suggests, this book focuses on the context and behaviors that confront public managers and the management techniques and processes available to cope with that environment. The book is designed to examine the theory and explore the practice of public management. We use a comparative approach, focusing on identifying the differences and similarities between public and private organizations in order to define both the generic and the unique aspects of public management.

Although no one can yet claim to be able to identify conclusively the distinguishing features of this nascent field called public management, some of its emerging characteristics are readily identifiable:

1. Its primary purpose is to develop an understanding of how public, primarily governmental, organizations may accomplish the missions charged to them. What characterizes "public" organizations and those hybrids of concern to public management is that they are subject, both intensively and extensively, to political direction, constraint, and control in their operation. This fact has implications not only for the roles of managers in public organizations but also for their self-concept and motivations, their knowledge and skills, and their tools and techniques.

2. The executive function, in contrast to legislative and judicial functions, is the focus, and executives and managers in public organizations are the predominant clientele of this applied field.

3. The discovery of differentiated knowledge, tools, and techniques for more effective executive management is a key to developing tangible administrative competence among public executives and managers.

4. Intersector and interorganization comparison is a critical method for definition and advancement of the field.

In this book we have brought together twenty-seven articles that convey these generic and unique features of public management; define the boundaries of the knowledge, skills, and tools available to public managers; and raise issues for research and for continuing practitioner-academic dialogue. The readings are grouped into seven sections. Each section is preceded by a general introduction to its subject matter, a synopsis of the key issues in the articles, and an explanation of how the articles relate to one another.

The ordering of the readings provides a logical progression for someone who is becoming familiar with public management, but you may wish to sequence the readings differently, depending on your interests. The text begins by addressing the motivations underlying the definition and study of public management. In Part One, "The Roots of Public Management," it is argued that the heritage of ideas found in Woodrow Wilson's seminal essay is an integral part of this newest identity for public administration. Part Two, "Views of Well-Traveled Practitioners," presents case studies of individuals who have been managers in both the public and the private sectors and who have found that managing in the public sector presents unique problems. Parts One and Two together make a convincing case, on both normative and experiential grounds, that the development and acquisition of differentiated knowledge about public management is a useful endeavor.

The external and internal dynamics that make public organizations similar to or different from other types of organizations are explored in Parts Three,

Four, and Five. Part Three offers several different views on the general similarities and differences between public and private organizations and management. In Part Four, the distinguishing features of public organizational environments are discussed. The articles in Part Five examine the conceptual and empirical bases for differences in the job-related behaviors of public employees. The essentially comparative orientation of these three sections illustrates the approach that we believe is necessary for the development of a truly public management.

Following this thorough comparative assessment of the context of public management, the tools and techniques available for public managers are discussed in Part Six. This section considers the adaptations that must be made in management tools such as finance, personnel, marketing, and collective bargaining when they are transferred from private organizations to the public sector.

In the concluding section, "Is There a 'Bottom Line' in Government?," we look at the predominant criteria on which the performance of public organizations is judged. Still using a comparative approach, the readings in this section assess the differences between the public and private sectors in terms of organizational performance criteria such as efficiency, effectiveness, innovativeness, and organizational survival.

We emphasize that this book is only a beginning in the effort to define public management. Many of the later articles reporting personal experiences, reviewing current research, or critically examining some aspect of public management reflect the fact that thinking about public management is preliminary and developing. Therefore, we strongly believe that continued attention to the subject, especially through systematic comparative research in public and private organizations, is warranted.

We hope these readings will not only broaden and deepen your understanding of this field but will also stimulate your interest. If we are able to pique your curiosity, we will have succeeded in fostering the critical thinking essential for the continuing development of a body of knowledge about public management.

J.L.P.
K.L.K.

Return

OCLC FirstSearch: Display
Your requested information from your library UNION INST & UNIV

SHIPPED - Lender

4424323232

GENERAL RECORD INFORMATION

Request Identifier:	44243232	Status:	SHIPPED
Request Date:	20080710	Source:	FSILLSTF
OCLC Number:	9464587		
Borrower:	**KSG**		
Receive Date:			
Due Date:	**20080815**		
Lenders:	*VCO, MDP, VVV, FBM, MLB		
Request Type:	Loan	Need Before:	20080731
		Renewal Request:	
		New Due Date:	

BIBLIOGRAPHIC INFORMATION

 Search the Gary Library Catalog

Call Number:	
Author:	Perry, James L.; Kraemer, Kenneth L.
Title:	Public management : public and private perspectives /
ISBN:	9780874845648 (pbk.)
Edition:	1st ed.
Imprint:	Palo Alto, Calif. : Mayfield Pub. Co., 1983
Verified:	WorldCat Desc: xiv, 390 p. : Type: Book

BORROWING INFORMATION

Patron:	KELMAN
Ship To:	ILL/Kennedy Sch Libr/79 JFK St./Harvard University/Cambridge MA/02138
Bill To:	Same FEIN #421103580
Ship Via:	Library Rate
Electronic Delivery:	
Maximum Cost:	IFM - 20.00
Copyright Compliance:	CCG
Fax:	(617) 495-1972
Affiliation:	NELINET ILL Code Signer
Borrowing Notes:	Thanks!

LENDING INFORMATION

■ ACKNOWLEDGMENTS

This book has benefited from the encouragement, support, and creative efforts of our colleagues, co-workers, and families. At the forefront of the many individuals who have contributed to this book are the authors whose work is published here and the editors of various journals who have kindly granted us permission to reprint copyrighted articles. We wish to thank these authors and editors for the wealth of stimulating material they have made available to us.

The Graduate School of Management and the Public Policy Research Organization, our professional homes for many years (both at the University of California at Irvine), engendered the intellectual climate in which this book emerged and have provided us with the resources to see the project through. In particular, we wish to express our appreciation to Linda Guillen, who typed the introductions, to Laurel Ferejohn, who proofread and edited the manuscript, and to Rod Jenks, who constructed the index.

We have also benefited from our association with a dedicated professional staff at Mayfield Publishing Company. Chuck Murphy's interest in a book on public management provided the impetus for this effort. Along the way, he has helped us to prepare a thorough manuscript by arranging for a peer review of our original proposal and our final draft. During the review process, we received valuable comments from many of our colleagues around the country. We are especially grateful for the advice of Hal Rainey, of Florida State University; Charles Levine, of the University of Maryland; Larry Mann, of the University of Arizona; Hal Angle, of the University of Minnesota; and for reviews by Ross Clayton, of the Sacramento Public Affairs Center; Myron D. Fottler, of the University of Alabama; Elliot Kline, of the University of the Pacific; Naomi B. Lynn, of Kansas State University; Eugene B. McGregor, of Indiana University; H. Brinton Milward, of the University of Kentucky; and Alan Saltzstein, of California State University at Fullerton.

Pat Herbst, managing editor at Mayfield, has ably led us through the maze of the production process. Pam Trainer helped guide us through one of the most difficult tasks—obtaining and compiling letters of permission from au-

ACKNOWLEDGMENTS thors and publishers. Nancy Blumenstock did a thorough job of copyediting, and Laraine Etchemendy-Bennett has done a fine job of advance marketing.

We reserve our final acknowledgment for our families. They experienced our various moods and expectations during the preparation of this book and frequently had to exercise patience and tolerance. We feel that the book has been worth our effort, and we hope it has been worth theirs.

J.L.P.
K.L.K.

Public
Management

PART ONE

THE ROOTS OF PUBLIC MANAGEMENT

Public management as a special focus of modern public administration is new. But its roots extend back to the founding of the field of public administration, usually credited to Woodrow Wilson's essay "The Study of Administration," which appeared in 1887 and is reprinted here.

In his essay, Wilson calls for establishing a new science of administration that would make the business of government more businesslike, improve the quality of personnel in government, and improve the organization and methods of government. The focus of this new science of administration was to be on the executive function in government, because this function was "outside the proper sphere of politics." The primary objective of administrative study was to "rescue executive methods from the confusion and costliness of empirical experiment and set them upon foundations laid deep in stable principle." Basic to Wilson's perspective of the study of administration was the comparative method, for "without comparative studies in government we cannot rid ourselves of the misconception that administration stands upon an essentially different basis in a democratic state than that on which it stands in a non-democratic state."

Thus, Wilson laid four foundations for the study of administration that characterize public management today: (1) government as the primary organizational setting; (2) the executive function as the proper focus; (3) the discovery of principles and techniques for more effective management as a key to developing administrative competence; and (4) comparison as a method for study and advancement of the field.

Since Wilson's classic essay first appeared in 1887, the science of public administration has periodically shifted its primary focus in a search for identity, but it has recently returned full circle to the foundation laid by Wilson. The extent to which its focus has shifted over time can be seen by examining four paradigms that have characterized the evolution of public administration (Henry, 1975): the politics/administration dichotomy, the principles of administration, public administration as political science, and public administration as administrative science. Underlying this evolution is a fundamental tension between the two basic approaches to the study of public administration—that of political science and that of general administration.

As the writings of Wilson and other early scholars in the field suggest, public administration began as a subprovince of political science and was primarily concerned with government reform. The first paradigm of public administration, *the politics/administration dichotomy*, characterized the period from 1900 to 1926 and established public administration as a discipline. It began with Frank J. Goodnow's *Politics and Administration* (1900) and reached its apex in Leonard D. White's *Introduction to the Study of Public Administration* (1926). The early thrust of this paradigm was on distinguishing administration from politics—the central concern of political science. Goodnow wrote that there were two distinct functions of government: Politics "has to do with policies or expressions of the state will," and administration "has to do with the execution of these policies" (pp. 10–11). The functions of politics and administration, however, were not firmly equated with particular branches of government; both the legislative and the executive branches performed these functions, and Goodnow felt that the "assignment of such functions to separate authorities is impossible" (pp. 21–22).

Consistent with this early thrust, White (1926) accepted the politics/administration dichotomy and used the term "management" to refer to the distinctive content of public administration in what is described as "the first textbook devoted in toto to the field" (Henry, 1975, p. 379). Although White's work was based largely on the ideas discussed by Wilson and Goodnow, it was also concerned with what he re-

garded as special problems, such as personnel recruitment, examination, classification, promotion, discipline, and retirement, in "the management of men and materials in the accomplishment of the purposes of the State" (1926, p. 5). Moreover, White maintained that the conduct of public administration is much like that of commercial, philanthropic, religious, or educational organizations. But he also argued that it is different from the conduct of American business because of its greater emphasis on public accountability and its "gigantic struggle to loosen the grip of the politician" (1926, p. 6). Nevertheless, White felt that the business model was a good one for government to emulate.

The *principles-of-administration* paradigm characterized the period from 1927 to 1937. The primary focus of public administration was the search for, and articulation of, basic principles of administration that could be considered to be universal. This line of development in public administration stemmed from general administration, which also had given rise to business administration. Practitioners, consultants, industrial administration specialists, sociologists, and other scholars and executives wrote in general terms about "organizations," "management," and "administration" as comparable categories. These writers were concerned with all kinds of organizations, not just governmental, and with management or administration as a universal, generic process substantially the same in military, governmental, religious, voluntary, business, industrial, or other applications.

W. F. Willoughby's *Principles of Public Administration* (1927) was the first full-fledged text to articulate such principles for public administration, and Luther Gulick and Lyndall Urwick's *Papers on the Science of Administration* (1937) represented the "high noon" of the new orthodoxy in public administration. As suggested by the emphasis on principles, human organization was the primary focus of this paradigm, irrespective of the political, institutional, or value systems in which it occurred. Principles of administration could be arrived at indirectly from the study of arrangements for human association of any kind.

Thus, the gap between the political-science and general-administration approaches was not extremely wide. Although the political scientists confined their central interests primarily to government, they looked outside government for ideas and methods that might be useful. In their search for administration unencumbered by politics, these political scientists were akin to the generalists in their concern with universally applicable organizational and managerial ideas and techniques. Both groups of writers emphasized structural as opposed to behavorial aspects at the formal, technical, and executive levels of organizations and sought to develop a science of administration based on principles.

The period from 1937 to 1950 was one of basic challenge to the principles of administration and, in a sense, to much of what had gone before. Herbert Simon demolished both the principles of administration and the politics/administration dichotomy—the foundations of the science of public administration—in his book *Administrative Behavior* (1947). He offered a new paradigm centered on the concept of decision making, with a split between the factual and normative aspects of public administration, grounded in empirical sociopsychological research. For a variety of reasons, Simon's paradigm never caught on, and public administration once again sought its paradigm in political science.

Public administration as political science characterized the period from 1950 to 1970. Some political scientists sought a broader understanding of administration by viewing the administrative process as a phase of contemporary civilization (Morstein Marx, 1946), as an ecology of people, places, technologies, and problems (Gaus, 1947), and as unique social, governmental, and ideological facts (Waldo, 1948). Others focused on the behavior of organizational participants as part of the general "behavioral persuasion" that swept the social sciences (Simon, Smithburg, & Thompson, 1950; Dimock & Dimock, 1953). Still others focused on public policy making and the intermingling of politics and administration (Appleby, 1949), or reintroduced the case study, with its detailed examination of organizational and executive behavior (Stein, 1952). The result of these varied intellectual directions was that public administration lost any unifying focus and, as a corollary, its identity as a distinct discipline. The field was again ripe for a change, which, as it turned out, was a move in the direction of general administration.

Public administration as administrative science, the fourth paradigm, characterized the period from 1956 to 1970, competing with the political-science paradigm. The creation of the School of Business and Public Administration and the *Administrative Science Quarterly* at Cornell University marked the formal institutionalization of the concept of management as a generic process. Although the general-administration approach had existed since the early 1900s, its reemergence evolved from a widely shared belief, in universities and among practitioners, that the concepts of human relations, communications, behavioral science, operations research, and statistical decision theory presented an imminent prospect for developing an administrative science (Litchfield, 1956). Organization theory, organization behavior, and management science thus became the focus of the new paradigm.

With this fourth paradigm, the generic approach to administrative education achieved its clearest articulation (Hinderaker, 1963). The approach starts with the observation that administrators in business and government have shifted increasingly from one sector to another during their professional careers. It is reinforced by the perception in academic and professional circles that there exists a body of knowledge about management and organizations and a set of tools and techniques that are common to the business and government sectors. Therefore, knowledge, tools, and skills can be packaged and delivered through a single academic vehicle that will prepare students to function in either business or government.

The generic concept attained full expression in only a few (most of them new) educational programs. But, for a while, it swept through programs in business and public administration alike—until public administrationists began to ask: If the administrative-science route were selected as the sole perspective of public administration, could one continue to speak of "public" administration? Would there be any future role for schools of public administration, or would their roles be absorbed by the relatively larger and more successful business schools? And, would profit-conscious "business-school types" appreciate the value of the public interest as an important aspect of administrative science? As Nicholas Henry (1975) notes, the answers to these and other questions were "less than comforting" to public administrationists. Thus emerged the public-

management paradigm.

Basic to all of the foregoing paradigms has been a polarity of perspectives. One perspective is of management as a generic activity, involving knowledge, techniques, and skills common across institutional, political, and value systems; the other perspective is of public administration as a special activity, involving public interest values, public goods, and social affairs. This book, with its use of the name *public management*, is an attempt to define a new intersection of these dichotomous perspectives.

The context of public management is primarily the government sector, including its interactions with the private sector. The focus of public management is on public administration as a profession and on the public manager as a practitioner of that profession, rather than as a politician or a statesman. Essential to both the profession's and the manager's credibility are certain knowledge bases, techniques, and skills in the management of public organizations and their interorganizational relationships. Knowledge and techniques may be drawn from a variety of disciplines and institutional settings, but the essential aim of administrative study is to determine by empirical and comparative analysis: what is alike and what is different about public and private management; what similarities and differences are important; and what is the appropriate special content of public management. Implicit in this task is an assumption, reasonably borne out by the remainder of this book, that, although there is much that public management potentially shares with private management, it also has a unique content. This book aims to explore and define the boundaries and special focus of the profession of public management.

REFERENCES

Appleby, P. H. *Policy and administration.* University, Ala.: University of Alabama Press, 1949.

Dimock, M. E., & Dimock, G. O. *Public administration.* New York: Rinehart, 1953.

Gaus, J. M. *Reflections on public administration.* University, Ala.: University of Alabama Press, 1947.

Goodnow, F. *Politics and administration.* New York: Macmillan, 1900.

Gulick, L., & Urwick, L. (Eds.). *Papers on the science of administration.* New York: Institute of Public Administration, 1937.

Henry, N. Paradigms of public administration. *Public Administration Review,* July/August 1975, *35,* 378–386.

Hinderaker, I. The study of administration: Interdisciplinary dimensions, *Western Political Quarterly,* September 1963, *16,* 5–12.

Litchfield, E. H. Notes on a general theory of administration. *Administrative Science Quarterly,* June 1956, *1,* 3–29.

Morstein Marx, F. (Ed.). *Elements of public administration.* New York: Prentice-Hall, 1946.

Simon, H. A. *Administrative behavior.* New York: Free Press, 1947.

Simon, H. A., Smithburg, D. W., & Thompson, V. A. *Public administration.* New York: Alfred A. Knopf, 1950.

Stein, H. *Public administration and policy development: A case book.* New York: Harcourt, Brace, 1952.

Waldo, D. *The administrative state.* New York: Ronald Press, 1948.

White, L. D. *Introduction to the study of public administration.* New York: Macmillan, 1926.

Willoughby, W. F. *Principles of public administration.* Washington, D.C.: Brookings Institution, 1927.

1 | The Study of Administration

Woodrow Wilson

I suppose that no practical science is ever studied where there is no need to know it. The very fact, therefore, that the eminently practical science of administration is finding its way into college courses in this country would prove that this country needs to know more about administration, were such proof of the fact required to make out a case. It need not be said, however, that we do not look into college programmes for proof of this fact. It is a thing almost taken for granted among us, that the present movement called civil service reform must, after the accomplishment of its first purpose, expand into efforts to improve, not the *personnel* only, but also the organization and methods of our government offices: because it is plain that their organization and methods need improvement only less than their *personnel*. It is the object of administrative study to discover, first, what government can properly and successfully do, and, secondly, how it can do these proper things with the utmost possible efficiency and at the least possible cost either of money or of energy. On both these points there is obviously much need of light among us; and only careful study can supply that light.

Before entering on that study, however, it is needful:

I. To take some account of what others have done in the same line; that is to say, of the history of the study.
II. To ascertain just what is its subject-matter.
III. To determine just what are the best methods by which to develop it, and the most clarifying political conceptions to carry with us into it.

Unless we know and settle these things, we shall set out without chart or compass.

I

The science of administration is the latest fruit of that study of the science of politics which was begun some twenty-two hundred years ago. It is a birth of our own century, almost of our own generation.

Reprinted with permission from the *Political Science Quarterly*, June 1887, 2, 197–222.

Why was it so late in coming? Why did it wait till this too busy century of ours to demand attention for itself? Administration is the most obvious part of government; it is government in action; it is the executive, the operative, the most visible side of government, and is of course as old as government itself. It is government in action, and one might very naturally expect to find that government in action had arrested the attention and provoked the scrutiny of writers of politics very early in the history of systematic thought.

But such was not the case. No one wrote systematically of administration as a branch of the science of government until the present century had passed its first youth and had begun to put forth its characteristic flower of systematic knowledge. Up to our own day all the political writers whom we now read had thought, argued, dogmatized only about the *constitution* of government; about the nature of the state, the essence and seat of sovereignty, popular power and kingly prerogative; about the greatest meanings lying at the heart of government, and the high ends set before the purpose of government by man's nature and man's aims. The central field of controversy was that great field of theory in which monarchy rode tilt against democracy, in which oligarchy would have built for itself strongholds of privilege, and in which tyranny sought opportunity to make good its claim to receive submission from all competitors. Amidst this high warfare of principles, administration could command no pause for its own consideration. The question was always: Who shall make law, and what shall that law be? The other question, how law should be administered with enlightenment, with equity, with speed, and without friction, was put aside as "practical detail" which clerks could arrange after doctors had agreed upon principles.

That political philosophy took this direction was of course no accident, no chance preference or perverse whim of political philosophers. The philosophy of any time is, as Hegel says, "nothing but the spirit of that time expressed in abstract thought"; and political philosophy, like philosophy of every other kind, has only held up the mirror to contemporary affairs. The trouble in early times was almost altogether about the constitution of government; and consequently that was what engrossed men's thoughts. There was little or no trouble about administration—at least little that was heeded by administrators. The functions of government were simple, because life itself was simple. Government went about imperatively and compelled men, without thought of consulting their wishes. There was no complex system of public revenues and public debts to puzzle financiers; there were, consequently, no financiers to be puzzled. No one who possessed power was long at a loss how to use it. The great and only question was: Who shall possess it? Populations were of manageable numbers; property was of simple sorts. There were plenty of farms, but no stocks and bonds: more cattle than vested interests.

I have said that all this was true of "early times"; but it was substantially true also of comparatively late times. One does not have to look back of the last century for the beginnings of the present complexities of trade and perplexities of commercial speculation, nor for the portentous birth of national debts. Good Queen Bess, doubtless, thought that the monopolies of the sixteenth century were hard enough to handle without burning her hands; but they are not remembered in the presence of the giant monopolies of the nineteenth century. When Blackstone lamented that corporations had no bodies to be kicked and no souls to be damned, he was anticipating the proper time for such regrets by full a century. The perennial discords between master and workmen which now so often disturb industrial society began before the Black Death and the Statute of Laborers; but never before our own day did they assume such ominous proportions as they wear now. In brief, if difficulties of governmental action are to be seen gathering in other centuries, they are to be seen culminating in our own.

This is the reason why administrative tasks have nowadays to be so studiously and systematically adjusted to carefully tested standards of policy, the reason why we are having now what we never had before, a science of administration. The weightier debates of constitutional principle are even yet by no means concluded; but they are no longer of more immediate practical moment than questions of administration. It is getting to be harder to *run* a constitution than to frame one.

Here is Mr. Bagehot's graphic, whimsical way of depicting the difference between the old and the new in administration:

> In early times, when a despot wishes to govern a distant province, he sends down a satrap on a grand horse, and other people on little horses; and very little is heard of the satrap again unless he send back some of the little people to tell what he has been doing. No great labour of superintendence is possible. Common rumour and casual report are the sources of intelligence. If it seems certain that the province is in a bad state, satrap No. 1 is recalled, and satrap No. 2 sent out in his stead. In civilized countries the process is different. You erect a bureau in the province you want to govern; you make it write letters and copy letters; it sends home eight reports *per diem* to the head bureau in St. Petersburg. Nobody does a sum in the province without some one doing the same sum in the capital, to "check" him, and see that he does it correctly. The consequence of this is, to throw on the heads of departments an amount of reading and labour which can only be accomplished by the greatest natural aptitude, the most efficient training, the most firm and regular industry.

There is scarcely a single duty of government which was once simple which is not now complex; government once had but a few masters; it now has scores of masters. Majorities formerly only underwent government; they now conduct government. Where government once might follow the whims of a court, it must now follow the views of a nation.

And those views are steadily widening to new conceptions of state duty; so that, at the same time that the functions of government are every day becoming more complex and difficult, they are also vastly multiplying in number. Administration is everywhere putting its hands to new undertakings. The utility, cheapness, and success of the government's postal service, for instance, point towards the early establishment of governmental control of the telegraph system. Or, even if our government is not to follow the lead of the governments of Europe in buying or building both telegraph and railroad lines, no one can doubt that in some way it must make itself master of masterful corporations. The creation of national commissioners of railroads, in addition to the older state commissions, involves a very important and delicate extension of administrative functions. Whatever hold of authority state or federal governments are to take upon corporations, there must follow cares and responsibilities which will require not a little wisdom, knowledge, and experience. Such things must be studied in order to be well done. And these, as I have said, are only a few of the doors which are being opened to offices of government. The idea of the state and the consequent ideal of its duty are undergoing noteworthy change; and "the idea of the state is the conscience of administration." Seeing every day new things which the state ought to do, the next thing is to see clearly how it ought to do them.

This is why there should be a science of administration which shall seek to straighten the paths of government, to make its business less unbusinesslike, to strengthen and purify its organization, and to crown its duties with dutifulness. This is one reason why there is such a science.

·   ·   ·

II

The field of administration is a field of business. It is removed from the hurry and strife of politics; it at most points stands apart even from the debatable ground of constitutional study. It is a part of political life only as the methods of the counting-house are a part of the life of society; only as machinery is part of the manufactured product. But it is, at the same time, raised very far above the dull level of mere technical detail by the fact that through its greater principles it is directly connected with the lasting maxims of political wisdom, the permanent truths of political progress.

The object of administrative study is to rescue executive methods from the confusion and costliness of empirical experiment and set them upon foundations laid deep in stable principle.

It is for this reason that we must regard civil-service reform in its present stages as but a prelude to a fuller administrative reform. We are now rectifying methods of appointment; we must go on to adjust executive functions more fitly and to prescibe better methods of executive organization and action. Civil-service reform is thus but a moral preparation for what is to follow. It is clearing the moral atmosphere of official life by establishing the sanctity of public office as a public trust, and, by making the service unpartisan, it is opening the way for making it businesslike. By sweetening its motives it is rendering it capable of improving its methods of work.

Let me expand a little what I have said of the province of administration. Most important to be observed is the truth already so much and so fortunately insisted upon by our civil-service reformers; namely, that administration lies outside the proper sphere of *politics*. Administrative questions are not political questions. Although politics sets the tasks for administration, it should not be suffered to manipulate its offices.

This is distinction of high authority; eminent German writers insist upon it as of course. Bluntschli, for instance, bids us separate administration alike from politics and from law. Politics, he says, is state activity "in things great and universal," while "administration, on the other hand," is "the activity of the state in individual and small things. Politics is thus the special province of the statesman, administration of the technical official." "Policy does nothing without the aid of administration"; but administration is not therefore politics. But we do not require German authority for this position; this discrimination between administration and politics is now, happily, too obvious to need further discussion.

There is another distinction which must be worked into all our conclusions, which, though but another side of that between administration and politics, is not quite so easy to keep sight of: I mean the distinction between *constitutional* and administrative questions, between those governmental adjustments which are essential to constitutional principle and those which are merely instrumental to the possibly changing purposes of a wisely adapting convenience.

One cannot easily make clear to every one just where administration resides in the various departments of any practicable government without entering upon particulars so numerous as to confuse and distinctions so minute as to distract. No lines of demarcation, setting apart administrative from non-administrative functions, can be run between this and that department of government without being run up hill and down dale, over dizzy heights of distinction and through dense jungles of statutory enactment, hither and thither around "ifs" and "buts," "whens" and "howevers," until they become altogether lost to the common eye not accustomed to this sort of surveying, and consequently not acquainted with the use of the theodolite of logical discernment. A great deal of administration goes about *incognito* to most of the world, being confounded now with political "management," and again with constitutional principle.

Perhaps this ease of confusion may explain such utterances as that of Niebuhr's: "Liberty," he says, "depends incomparably more upon administration than upon constitution." At first sight this appears to be largely true. Apparently facility in the actual exercise of liberty does depend more upon administrative arrangements than upon constitutional guarantees; although constitutional guarantees alone secure the existence of liberty. But—upon second thought—is even so much as this true? Liberty no more consists in easy functional movement than intelligence consists in the ease and vigor with which the limbs of a strong man move. The principles that rule within the man, or the constitution, are the vital springs of liberty or servitude. Because dependence and subjection are without chains, are lightened by every easy-working device of considerate, paternal government, they are not thereby transformed into liberty. Liberty cannot live apart from constitutional principle; and no administration, however perfect and liberal its methods, can give men more than a poor counterfeit of liberty if it rest upon illiberal principles of government.

A clear view of the difference between the province of constitutional law and the province of administrative function ought to leave no room for misconception; and it is possible to name some roughly definite criteria upon which such a view can be built. Public administration is detailed and systematic execution of public law. Every particular application of general law is an act of administration. The assessment and raising of taxes, for instance, the hanging of a criminal, the transportation and delivery of the mails, the equipment and recruiting of the army and navy, *etc.*, are all obviously acts of administration; but the general laws which direct these things to be done are as obviously outside of and above administration. The broad plans of governmental action are not administrative; the detailed execution of such plans is administrative. Constitutions, therefore, properly concern themselves only with those instrumentalities of government which are to control general law. Our federal constitution observes this principle in saying nothing of even the greatest of the purely executive offices, and speaking only of that President of the Union who was to share the legislative and policy-making functions of government, only of those judges of highest jurisdiction who were to interpret and guard its principles, and not of those who were merely to give utterance to them.

This is not quite the distinction between Will and answering Deed, because the administrator should have and does have a will of his own in the choice of means for accomplishing his work. He is not and ought not to be a mere passive instrument. The distinction is between general plans and special means.

There is, indeed, one point at which administrative studies trench on constitutional ground—or at least upon what seems constitutional ground. The study of administration, philosophically viewed, is closely connected with the study of the proper distribution of constitutional authority. To be efficient it must discover the simplest arrangements by which responsibility can be unmistakably fixed upon officials; the best way of dividing authority without hampering it, and responsibility without obscuring it. And this question of the distribution of authority, when taken into the sphere of the higher, the originating functions of government, is obviously a central constitutional question. If administration study can discover the best principles upon which to base such distribution, it will have done constitutional study an invaluable service. Montesquieu did not, I am convinced, say the last word on this head.

To discover the best principle for the distribution of authority is of greater importance, possibly, under a democratic system, where officials serve many masters, than under others where they serve but a few. All sovereigns are suspicious of their servants, and the sovereign people is no exception to the rule; but how is its suspicion to be allayed by *knowledge*? If that suspicion could but be clarified into wise vigilance, it would be altogether salutary; if that vigilance could be aided by the unmistakable placing of responsibility, it would be altogether beneficent. Suspicion in itself is never healthful either in the private or in the public mind. *Trust is strength* in all relations of life; and, as it is the office of the constitutional reformer to create conditions of trustfulness, so it is the office of the administrative organizer to fit administration with conditions of clearcut responsibility which shall insure trustworthiness.

And let me say that large powers and unhampered discretion seem to me the indispensable conditions of responsibility. Public attention must be easily directed, in each case of good or bad administration, to just the man deserving of praise or blame. There is no danger in power, if only it be not irresponsible. If it be divided, dealt out in shares to many, it is obscured; and if it be obscured, it is made irresponsible. But if it be centered in heads of the service and in heads of branches of the service, it is easily watched and brought to book. If to keep his office a man must achieve open and honest success, and if at the same time he feels himself intrusted with large freedom of discretion, the greater his power the less likely is he to abuse it, the more is he nerved and sobered and elevated by it. The less his power, the more safely obscure and unnoticed does he feel his position to be, and the more readily does he relapse into remissness.

11

Just here we manifestly emerge upon the field of that still larger question—the proper relations between public opinion and administration.

To whom is official trustworthiness to be disclosed, and by whom is it to be rewarded? Is the official to look to the public for his meed of praise and his push of promotion, or only to his superior in office? Are the people to be called in to settle administrative discipline as they are called in to settle constitutional principles? These questions evidently find their root in what is undoubtedly the fundamental problem of this whole study. That problem is: What part shall public opinion take in the conduct of administration?

The right answer seems to be, that public opinion shall play the part of authoritative critic.

But the *method* by which its authority shall be made to tell? Our peculiar American difficulty in organizing administration is not the danger of losing liberty, but the danger of not being able or willing to separate its essentials from its accidents. Our success is made doubtful by that besetting error of ours, the error of trying to do too much by vote. Self-government does not consist in having a hand in everything, any more than housekeeping consists necessarily in cooking dinner with one's own hands. The cook must be trusted with a large discretion as to the management of the fires and the ovens.

In those countries in which public opinion has yet to be instructed in its privileges, yet to be accustomed to having its own way, this question as to the province of public opinion is much more readily soluble than in this country, where public opinion is wide awake and quite intent upon having its own way anyhow. It is pathetic to see a whole book written by a German professor of political science for the purpose of saying to his countrymen, "Please try to have an opinion about national affairs"; but a public which is so modest may at least be expected to be very docile and acquiescent in learning what things it has *not* a right to think and speak about imperatively. It may be sluggish, but it will not be meddlesome. It will submit to be instructed before it tries to instruct. Its political education will come before its political activity. In trying to instruct our own public opinion, we are dealing with a pupil apt to think itself quite sufficiently instructed beforehand.

The problem is to make public opinion efficient without suffering it to be meddlesome. Directly exercised, in the oversight of the daily details and in the choice of the daily means of government, public criticism is of course a clumsy nuisance, a rustic handling delicate machinery. But as superintending the greater forces of formative policy alike in politics and administration, public criticism is altogether safe and beneficent, altogether indispensable. Let administrative study find the best means for giving public criticism this control and for shutting it out from all other interference.

But is the whole duty of administrative study done when it has taught the people what sort of administration to desire and demand, and how to get what they demand? Ought it not to go on to drill candidates for the public service?

There is an admirable movement towards universal political education now afoot in this country. The time will soon come when no college of respectability can afford to do without a well-filled chair of political science. But the education thus imparted will go but a certain length. It will multiply the number of intelligent critics of government, but it will create no competent body of administrators. It will prepare the way for the development of a sure-footed understanding of the general principles of government, but it will not necessarily foster skill in conducting government. It is an education which will equip legislators, perhaps, but not executive officials. If we are to improve public opinion, which is the motive power of government, we must prepare better officials as the *apparatus* of government. If we are to put in new boilers and to mend the fires which drive our governmental machinery, we must not leave the old wheels and joints and valves and bands to creak and buzz and clatter on as best they may at bidding of the new force. We must put in new running parts wherever there is the least lack of strength or adjustment. It will be necessary to organize democracy by sending up to the competitive examinations for the civil service men definitely prepared for standing liberal tests as to technical knowledge. A technically schooled civil service will presently have become indispensable.

I know that a corps of civil servants prepared by a special schooling and drilled, after appointment, into a perfected organization, with appropriate hierarchy and characteristic discipline, seems to a great many very thoughtful persons to contain elements which might combine to make an offensive official class—a distinct, semi-corporate body with sympathies divorced from those of a progressive, free-spirited people, and with hearts narrowed to the meanness of a bigoted officialism. Certainly such a class would be altogether hateful and harmful in the United States. Any measures calculated to produce it would for us be measures of reaction and of folly.

But to fear the creation of a domineering, illiberal officialism as a result of the studies I am here proposing is to miss altogether the principle upon which I wish most to insist. That principle is, that administration in the United States must be at all points sensitive to public opinion. A body of thoroughly trained officials serving during good behavior we must have in any case: that is a plain business necessity. But the apprehension that such a body will be anything un-American clears away the moment it is asked, What is to constitute good behavior? For that question obviously carries its own answer on its face. Steady, hearty allegiance to the policy of the government they serve will constitute good behavior. That *policy* will have no taint of officialism about it. It will not be the creation of permanent officials, but of statesmen whose responsibility to public opinion will be direct and inevitable. Bureaucracy can exist only where the whole service of the state is removed from the common political life of the people, its chiefs as well as its rank and file. Its motives, its objects, its policy, its standards, must be bureaucratic. It would be difficult to point out any examples of impudent exclusiveness and arbitrariness on the part of officials doing service under a chief of department who really served the people, as all our chiefs of departments must be made to do. It would be easy, on the other hand, to adduce other instances like that of the influence of Stein in Prussia, where the leadership of one statesman imbued with true public spirit transformed arrogant and perfunctory bureaux into public-spirited instruments of just government.

The ideal for us is a civil service cultured and self-sufficient enough to act with sense and vigor, and yet so intimately connected with the popular thought, by means of elections and constant public counsel, as to find arbitrariness or class spirit quite out of the question.

III

Having thus viewed in some sort the subject-matter and the objects of this study of administration, what are we to conclude as to the methods best suited to it—the points of view most advantageous for it?

Government is so near us, so much a thing of our daily familiar handling, that we can with difficulty see the need of any philosophical study of it, or the exact point of such study, should it be undertaken. We have been on our feet too long to study now the art of walking. We are a practical people, made so apt, so adept in self-government by centuries of experimental drill that we are scarcely any longer capable of perceiving the awkwardness of the particular system we may be using, just because it is so easy for us to use any system. We do not study the art of governing: we govern. But mere unschooled genius for affairs will not save us from sad blunders in administration. Though democrats by long inheritance and repeated choice, we are still rather crude democrats. Old as democracy is, its organization on a basis of modern ideas and conditions is still an unaccomplished work. The democratic state has yet to be equipped for carrying those enormous burdens of administration which the needs of this industrial and trading age are so fast accumulating. Without comparative studies in government we cannot rid ourselves of the misconception that administration stands upon an essentially different basis in a democratic state from that on which it stands in a non-democratic state.

After such study we could grant democracy the sufficient honor of ultimately determining by debate all essential questions affecting the public weal, of basing all structures of policy upon the major will; but we would have found but one rule of good administration for all governments alike. So far as administrative functions are concerned, all governments have a strong structural likeness; more than that, if they are to be uniformly useful and efficient; they *must* have a strong structural likeness. A free man has the same bodily organs, the same executive parts, as the slave, however different may be his motives, his services, his energies. Monarchies and democracies, radically different as they are in other respects, have in reality much the same business to look to.

It is abundantly safe nowadays to insist upon this actual likeness of all governments, because these are days when abuses of power are easily exposed and arrested, in countries like our own, by a bold, alert, inquisitive, detective public thought and a sturdy popular self-dependence such as never existed before. We are slow to appreciate this; but it is easy to appreciate it. Try to imagine personal government in the United States. It is like trying to imagine a national worship of Zeus. Our imaginations are too modern for the feat.

But, besides being safe, it is necessary to see that for all governments alike the legitimate ends of administration are the same, in order not to be frightened at the idea of looking into foreign systems of administration for instruction and suggestion; in order to get rid of the apprehension that we might perchance blindly borrow something incompatible with our principles. That man is blindly astray who denounces attempts to transplant foreign systems into this country. It is impossible: they simply would not grow here. But why should we not use such parts of foreign contrivances as we want, if they be in any way serviceable? We are in no danger of using them in a foreign way. We borrowed rice, but we do not eat it with chopsticks. We borrowed our whole political language from England, but we leave the words "king" and "lords" out of it. What did we ever originate, except the action of the federal government upon individuals and some of the functions of the federal supreme court?

We can borrow the science of administration with safety and profit if only we read all fundamental differences of condition into its essential tenets. We have only to filter it through our constitutions, only to put it over a slow fire of criticism and distil away its foreign gases.

I know that there is a sneaking fear in some conscientiously patriotic minds that studies of European systems might signalize some foreign methods as better than some American methods; and the fear is easily to be understood. But it would scarcely be avowed in just any company.

It is the more necessary to insist upon thus putting away all prejudices against looking anywhere in the world but at home for suggestions in this study, because nowhere else in the whole field of politics, it would seem, can we make use of the historical, comparative method more safely than in this province of administration. Perhaps the more novel the forms we study the better. We shall the sooner learn the peculiarities of our own methods. We can never learn either our own weaknesses or our own virtues by comparing ourselves with ourselves. We are too used to the appearance and procedure of our own system to see its true significance. Perhaps even the English system is too much like our own to be used to the most profit in illustration. It is best on the whole to get entirely away from our own atmosphere and to be most careful in examining such systems as those of France and Germany. Seeing our own institutions through such *media,* we see ourselves as foreigners might see us were they to look at us without preconceptions. Of ourselves, so long as we know only ourselves, we know nothing.

Let it be noted that it is the distinction, already drawn, between administration and politics which makes the comparative method so safe in the field of administration. When we study the administrative systems of France and Germany, knowing that we are not in search of *political* principles, we need not care a peppercorn for the constitutional or political reasons which Frenchmen or Germans give for their practices when explaining them to us. If I see a murderous fellow sharpening a knife cleverly, I can borrow his way of sharpening the knife without borrowing his probable intention to commit murder with it; and so, if I see a monarchist dyed in the wool managing a public bureau well, I can learn his business methods without changing one of my republican spots. He may serve his king; I will continue to serve the people; but I should like to serve my sovereign as well as he serves his. By keeping this distinction in view—that is, by studying administration as a means of putting our own politics into convenient practice, as a means of making what is democratically politic towards all administratively possible towards each—we are on perfectly safe ground, and can learn without error what foreign systems have to teach us. We thus devise an adjusting weight for our comparative method of study. We can thus scrutinize the anatomy of foreign governments without fear of getting any of their diseases into our veins; dissect alien systems without apprehension of blood-poisoning.

Our own politics must be the touchstone for all theories. The principles on which to base a science of administration for America must be principles which have democratic policy very much at heart. And, to suit American habit, all general theories must, as theories, keep modestly in the background, not in open argument only, but even in our own minds—lest opinions satisfactory only to the standards of the library should be dogmatically used, as if they must be quite as satisfactory to the standards of practical politics as well. Doctrinaire devices must be postponed to tested practices. Arrangements not only sanctioned by conclusive experience elsewhere but also congenial to American habit must be preferred without hesitation to theoretical perfection. In a word, steady, practical statesmanship must come first, closet doctrine second. The cosmopolitan what-to-do must always be commanded by the American how-to-do-it.

Our duty is, to supply the best possible life to a *federal* organization, to systems within systems; to make town, city, county, state, and federal governments live with a like strength and an equally assured healthfulness, keeping each unquestionably its own master and yet making all interdependent and co-operative, combining independence with mutual helpfulness. The task is great and important enough to attract the best minds.

This interlacing of local self-government with federal self-government is quite a modern conception. It is not like the arrangements of imperial federation in Germany. There local government is not yet, fully, local *self*-government. The bureaucrat is everywhere busy. His efficiency springs out of *esprit de corps,* out of care to make ingratiating obeisance to the authority of a superior, or, at best, out of the soil of a sensitive conscience. He serves, not the public, but an irresponsible minister. The question for us is, how shall our series of governments within governments be so administered that it shall always be to the interest of the public officer to serve, not his superior alone but the community also, with the best efforts of his talents and the soberest service of his conscience? How shall such service be made to his commonest interest by contributing abundantly to his sustenance, to his dearest interest by furthering his ambition, and to his highest interest by advancing his honor and establishing his character? And how shall this be done alike for the local part and for the national whole?

If we solve this problem we shall again pilot the world. There is a tendency —is there not?—a tendency as yet dim, but already steadily impulsive and clearly destined to prevail, towards, first the confederation of parts of empires like the British, and finally of great states themselves. Instead of centralization of power, there is to be wide union with tolerated divisions of prerogative. This is a tendency towards the American type—of governments joined with governments for the pursuit of common purposes, in honorary equality and honorable subordination. Like principles of civil liberty are everywhere fostering like methods of government; and if comparative studies of the ways and means of government should enable us to offer suggestions which will practicably combine openness and vigor in the administration of such governments with ready docility to all serious, well-sustained public criticism, they will have approved themselves worthy to be ranked among the highest and most fruitful of the great departments of political study. That they will issue in such suggestions I confidently hope.

PART TWO

VIEWS OF WELL-TRAVELED PRACTITIONERS

Woodrow Wilson's classic essay marked the beginning of concern with management in public organizations in the United States. Since that time, the study of public administration has alternated between the competing and sometimes conflicting, sometimes overlapping, approaches of political science and general administration. Those who favor the general-administration approach have tended to operate as though there was nothing particularly unique about public management. Thus, you may ask: Is there any reason to pursue the subject of public management? Is there anything we can tell students of public management about their roles that would be particularly useful? The first place to turn for answers to these questions is to people who have actually been involved in public and private management and have written or spoken thoughtfully about the similarities and differences. The purpose of our doing so is to make a case, on both experiential and normative grounds, for the idea that the development and acquisition of differentiated knowledge is a useful endeavor—indeed, that it may be critical to improved public management.

Actual management in business and government, like the study of administration by political scientists and generalists, is frequently portrayed as two cultures—as C. P. Snow portrays British humanists and scientists in the postwar era. These cultures are increasingly polarized by "a gulf of mutual incomprehension—sometimes hostility and dislike, but most of all lack of understanding" (Snow, 1962, p. 4). For example, Herman L. Weiss, former vice chairman of the board and executive officer of General Electric and chairman of the President's Commission on Personnel Interchange, describes the business and government sectors as "beset with misunderstandings about each other. Too often this leads to outright conflicts that greatly reduce the nation's capacity for doing what must be done. At a time when harmony is all-important, discord impedes progress."

It is apparent that business and government increasingly must act as partners to deal with the monumental problems that confront contemporary society—problems that range from energy scarcity to inflation, to sluggish productivity, to the human condition. Such cooperation is not a simple matter. It involves more than changing the values and attitudes of individual managers. It involves the development of managerial knowledge, skills, and tools; it entails an enhanced sensitivity to the value systems implicit in different institutions, groups, and individuals so that managers can successfully apply their knowledge, skills, and tools in recognition of the interests affected; and it involves the realization among managers that, at some level, cooperation and negotiation may be impossible and conflict insoluble, because the goals of some institutions, groups, and individuals are directly opposed to the goals of the government agencies they manage.

Although the characterization of business and government as two cultures may be too extreme, *business and government are different*. And, apparently the differences are great. For example, Michael Blumenthal describes his movement from business to government as involving "culture shock," and Donald Rumsfeld questions whether the skills learned in one sector are readily transferable to the other. What, then, are the important differences between management in business and in government? Are the differences more important than the similarities? Is anything that is learned in one sector really transferable to the other? And, most important, what do the views of practitioners who have traveled between the two sectors indicate about the special nature of public management?

This section examines these and other questions. Two political executives reflect on the differences and similarities in public and private management at the highest levels. W. Michael Blumenthal is a former chairman and chief executive officer of the Bendix Corporation who became Secretary

of the Treasury in the Carter administration. Donald Rumsfeld spent fifteen years in the government service, including such high-level political posts as the White House Chief of Staff and Secretary of Defense, before becoming president and chief executive officer of the G. D. Searle Company, a pharmaceutical firm.

In addition to these political executives, Herman Weiss presents the reflections of five career managers from business and government on their year-long experience in the President's Executive Interchange Program: Percy E. Baynes of NASA spent a year at North American Rockwell; James S. Dimling from Marathon Oil worked at the Department of Health, Education and Welfare; Francis X. Fee, a supervising auditor at the General Accounting Office, worked in corporate planning at AT&T for a year; David A. Lehman of IBM worked with the Department of Transportation; and David Sternlight from Litton Industries' economic planning office worked in the office of policy development at the Department of Commerce.

The experiences of these managers indicate that, contrary to popular views, the differences in management in business and government are less a function of ideological differences in the two sectors than of their external and internal operating environments. The most prominent feature of the government environment that distinguishes it from that of business is its high salience for the public and its scrutiny by the press and other media. What public managers espouse and do is of great interest to the public, because it can affect large segments of society, including politically important groups.

This "fishbowl" environment presents both opportunities and problems for the public manager. Rumsfeld describes press attention as an important communication device for reaching the thousands of public officials and employees within the manager's policy domain and informing them about policies or decisions by top department heads—a device not normally available to their business counterparts. But, as Blumenthal points out, public scrutiny is a mixed blessing. On one hand, it facilitates rapid communication to large and far-flung audiences. On the other hand, it discourages communication about sensitive policy matters, including policy failures, because the media tend to be critical and often unforgiving. Not only do the media not forget shortcomings in the execution of public management; they continually search for changes in the public manager's policy pronouncements and label them inconsistencies, weaknesses, or instabilities in policy. In contrast, in business such changes would be viewed as adaptive policy responses to changing environmental conditions. Consequently, Blumenthal concludes that a public manager must be more circumspect in his public statements than must a business counterpart and will benefit from leaving sufficient leeway in public statements for an unobvious policy change.

In this fishbowl environment, appearances are as important as reality. Thus, the government executive must "manage" his or her public image. As Blumenthal notes:

> . . . it [your public image] matters in terms of your relationships with others, in Washington and with your staff, which derives its power from the power and influence you have, in terms of the media that write about these things and even in terms of the President's staff. For the White House staff quite naturally is also influenced by what they perceive your relationship with the President to be.

Rumsfeld reinforces Blumenthal's view and points to the need for public managers to develop a "star quality" that gives mystique to their image with the media. Boldness, innovation, and "getting things started in the right direction" are more important than getting results, because results are difficult to gauge and seldom make the news. Interestingly, both men note that high-level business executives seldom need be concerned with their public image, because they are rarely the focus of media attention.

A second feature of the public manager's environment that distinguishes it from the business counterpart is relations with legislative bodies. The government executive's relations with the Congress or other legislatures are not at all like those between the corporate executive and the board of directors. For one thing, the latter's objectives are more in concert: The private manager and the board share a common interest in profits, dividends, and growth. In contrast, the public manager faces a legislature that generally is much larger than his or her agency, has widely diverse interests, and always has some members who will directly oppose one's policies, political party, person, or all of these.

Another important difference in this vein lies in the tenure and substantive knowledge of legislators as compared to corporate directors. Blumenthal notes that one-half of the members of the House of Representatives serve four years or less, and their service on congressional committees often bears no relationship to their knowledge and experience. Thus, most lack a ready understanding of the substantive policy issues in the committees on which they serve, and many do not care about the issues. In contrast, corporate directors are specifically chosen for their knowledge and experience, reviewed for their performance, and have no a priori limit on their tenure in office.

Still another difference along these lines relates to the fishbowl environment of the whole public sector. Publicity is important to elected officials; they often use their public association with department and agency managers to gain publicity. Thus, legislators may publicly oppose or criticize a manager's policies, while privately supporting them. There simply is no equivalent in corporate boardrooms to this public display.

The decision-making process is a third feature that distinguishes the environment of the public manager. All of our political executives and career managers in this section agree that the decision-making processes in government and business are different. The scope of considerations in government decision making is broader, extending beyond the possible effects of the decision for the agency to effects on major groups and segments of society. This complexity in scope and decision criteria led one career manager to conclude that each decision seems to require a "unique process." Control over policy levers is shared in government; therefore, no one decision maker can control the decision process or outcome. Moreover, in government there are few limits on who can get involved in the decision-making process, who can work on it, or who can speak about it.

Government decision making is slower because of the need for extensive consultation and consensus building. Although its practitioners see more tradeoffs, compromises, and political influence at work in government than in private decision making, they also point out that negotiation and bargaining are more difficult in government because of the large number of actors and interests involved. Moreover, Blu-

menthal points out that, even when negotiations in the public sector are successful, they may be treated as defeat by the media if the compromise attained is less than that sought in the official bargaining position—a tendency that undermines the very process of negotiation. All in all, government decision making is described by its practitioners as circuitous, tortuous, and frustrating, but also as amazingly successful in amalgamating many different points of view.

The practitioners see important differences in the external environments and decision-making processes of business and government, but they see some similarities in the internal management of the two bureaucracies. However, both Blumenthal and Rumsfeld note an important difference —the successful internal management of a department is a relatively secondary part of the political executive's job, whereas in business it is nearly the whole of the chief executive's job. Despite this difference in emphasis, Rumsfeld points out that many similarities between the public and private manager's jobs stem from size considerations. All large, complex bureaucracies demand a careful choice of top managers, intricate planning and budgeting, establishing priorities and communicating them, delegating tasks and relying on subordinates, and reaching down into the organization to discover how things are really functioning.

Other practitioners suggest that the similarity ends at this task-description level. Task execution involves major differences. A government executive has influence over the choice of only a few positions—the dozen or so managers at the very top. And even the choice of these managers is only partly under the control of the top executive, constrained as it is by civil service regulations, security requirements, and, possibly, confirmation by Congress. Similarly, the intellectual task of planning may be more difficult in government than in business. The public manager has less control over his or her own time and, as a result, generally has less time to think, analyze, or plan.

The task of setting priorities presents a similar problem. Public managers frequently must jump from issue to issue, decision to decision, policy to policy in response to uncontrollable pressures. The same issues, decisions, or policies rarely recur within a single manager's tenure—especially if the manager is a political executive. Thus, there is often no underlying thread of previous policy in the manager's experience that can provide a guide to which current decision situations should be given priority.

The public manager's ability to delegate tasks and rely on subordinates is also more complex in government. Blumenthal notes that government bureaus are inverted pyramids from the standpoint of the amount of work performed, with the heaviest burdens falling upon the few people at the top of the hierarchy rather than on the mass of career employees. He lays the blame for this condition not on the individual employees, but on the civil service system. Under this system it is difficult to motivate career employees by means of rewards and punishments based on performance, to advance highly capable young people rapidly up the career ladder, or to single out exceptional individuals to groom for higher-level positions.

On detailed examination, then, both the internal and the external features of management exhibit more differences than similarities between business and government. But what about the managers themselves? Are their capabilities, motivations, and behaviors different? Both career managers and political executives agree that public managers at the top are as dedicated, hardworking, intelligent, and capable as their counterparts in business. In fact, top executives in the public sector probably work harder than their business counterparts, because, as discussed above, their ability to delegate tasks is considerably less.

The motivation of public managers must also be different, because their salaries are often considerably below those of their business counterparts. Most public managers are motivated by the importance of the jobs they hold, the substantive issues they face, and the sheer thrill of participating at a center of power. As Blumenthal notes, being the sixty-fourth Secretary of the Treasury, a lineage beginning with Alexander Hamilton, brings tremendous personal satisfaction. In fact, all of the executives and career managers point to great personal satisfaction from having faced issues that they would never experience in business, from learning how things really work at the centers of the nation's power, and from living intensely, meeting new people, and working on interesting and important problems.

On balance, although the executives and managers feel that the task of management is more difficult in government, they relish the experiences they had and would do it all over again if given the opportunity.

REFERENCE

Snow, C. P. *The two cultures and the scientific revolution*. New York: Cambridge University Press, 1962.

2 | Candid Reflections of a Businessman in Washington

W. Michael Blumenthal

One very important thing you have to learn in Washington is the difference between appearance and reality. At Bendix, it was the reality of the situation that in the end determined whether we succeeded or not. In the crudest sense, this meant the bottom line. You can dress up profits only for so long—if you're not successful, it's going to be clear. In government there is no bottom line, and that is why you can be successful if you appear to be successful— though, of course, appearance is not the only ingredient of success.

To give you an example of how appearance and reality interact, and how that leads to odd results, let's take the case of the $50 tax rebate early in 1977. There was a lot of speculation about whether the President, having originally proposed the rebate, would withdraw it or go through with it. That particular event and my role in it taught me a lot of things very early. Whereas privately I was one of the leaders, if not the leader, seeking to persuade the President to kill the $50 rebate, I felt that I had to publicly defend it and argue in favor of it. After all, I was a member of his team, and until he had made up his mind what he wanted to do and it was still out there, I would support it. That led to the point where on the very day on which he decided to withdraw the rebate, I had a meeting with him in the morning, together with the Vice President, Stu Eizenstat, Bert Lance, Charlie Schultze, Jody Powell, and Ham Jordan, at which I was one of those arguing in favor of dropping the rebate. From that meeting I went straight to the National Press Club, where I defended the rebate, knowing that the President would make a decision and hoping that he would decide to kill it, as I had urged. When, that evening, he did kill it, the newspapers reported that he had pulled the rug out from under me, and many of them implied that I had no influence, that I didn't know what I was talking about.

That taught me, among other things, that appearance is as important as

Reprinted from *Fortune* Magazine, January 29, 1979, by special permission. Copyright © 1979 by Time Inc.

reality. In a business setting that distinction would not even have arisen, because newspapers would not have been interested in it. But here, since your power is based on what people think you have in the way of influence, the appearance is very important. There are instances where people appear to have influence when they have none, and where people appear not to have influence when in fact they have a lot. I suppose every Administration has people whose strongest gift is that of self-promotion.

Another example of how significant it is how you appear to the press—and how different that is in government as compared to in a corporation—has to do with the risk of changing your mind. A businessman is entitled and expected to change his mind, and there's no particular opprobrium attached to that at all. You get new facts, conditions change, the markets change, industries change, you get a new contract or you lose one, you talk to more people. You say, all right, let's abort it. Let's slow it down, or let's do something else. What counts in the end is how you come out, not whether you've changed your mind or not.

In the government, if you change your mind, you're accused of inconsistency. That's one reason there's a lot of double-talk in Washington. So I found that politicians and Secretaries of the Treasury have to go to great lengths to avoid appearing to have changed their minds, or to rationalize the fact that they are changing their minds, or to leave enough leeway in their statements so that the press never knows that they're changing their minds. Otherwise they get a finger pointed at them.

An example of this kind of thing is the changed attitude of the Administration toward capital-gains taxation. In trying to develop a rational proposal for Congress, we originally did not include a capital-gains tax provision, because we did not think it made as much sense as other types of cuts. In the light of the increased emphasis on stimulating investment and productivity, and with the statistics of a year and a half showing declining productivity, a falling stock market, and declining investment, some of us came around to the view that some revision in the capital-gains tax was O.K. Yet supporting it opened us up to the accusation of being inconsistent—why didn't we do it earlier? You learn in this job that everything you say is weighed and stored and may be dragged out and used against you, which is not what happens in business to anywhere near this extent. But of course you can't be completely consistent.

Not only is what you say used against you—it is also distorted, and you are quoted as saying something you did not say. So what you learn is that you have to express yourself very carefully, and that you have to build defenses against being misquoted and being misunderstood. Take the example of the dollar. I never said that I wanted the dollar to decline, yet I was quoted as saying that. What I said was that we favored flexible exchange rates as agreed to in the IMF, and that this means that there will be ups and downs, that we weren't pegging the rate—that's the way the system operates. But I learned that it was a bad thing to say it this way, even though it was the policy all IMF governments had agreed to follow. Referring to the possibility of fluctuation—down as well as up—opened me up to being quoted as wanting this to happen, though that's not what I said or wanted.

When you come into the job, you learn, often by mistakes, that there are

23

code words you must avoid, and others you can use to state a certain proposition. You don't speculate about hypothetical alternatives when you're in this job, and you don't allow newsmen to draw you into choices between two unacceptable alternatives. You learn that by experience. Why? Because what you say suddenly takes on wide significance that it didn't have before. Suddenly, when I say I think interest rates will rise, or I think the stock market will rise or fall, that's in every newspaper. Your words suddenly become important, and nobody is more surprised than you are, because you know you don't know that much more than you did before.

You have to be aware that the media tend to look for mistakes, because mistakes are more interesting than normal progress. They're more newsworthy. In a corporation, mistakes are of no great interest unless they lead to a major loss of profit. Mistakes by a Cabinet member are always newsworthy, so you learn to be very careful about what you reveal. You learn not to state things boldly, in a way that can be misrepresented.

Early on after I joined this Administration, I was asked what rate of unemployment I thought was acceptable, and I said zero, and went on to explain that while I recognized that this clearly was not obtainable, I felt that any level of unemployment, meaning that anybody who wants to work can't get work, is not satisfactory. The newspapers reported that as a sign of my inexperience and foolishness, because, obviously, had I been more experienced, more sophisticated, I would have known that it's impossible to have zero unemployment and I would not have been so careless in stating a goal that's clearly unobtainable.

One of the important Washington arts is using public statements to shape, influence, and enunciate policies. This, clearly, is something that is unfamiliar to the business executive. You must not be too direct about it. You do it in the topics that you choose, the emphasis you put on them, and the way in which you state them: early emphasis on the need to get the deficit down, on the fundamentals rather than wage and price controls, talking about the need to control inflation when others are talking about spending more for special-interest groups. In the fight to make inflation public enemy No. 1—to have that clearly accepted throughout the government and by the country—the role that the Secretary of the Treasury can play through public statements is something you learn by experience.

You also learn that when it comes to having and exercising influence, appearance matters a great deal. If you see the President every day, but nobody knows that you see him, your ability to get things done suffers as against if you see him once every three weeks but the fact that you do becomes known. Seeing him "on the record" is, in the Washington scene, a more important thing than seeing him "off the record." It is important to give the appearance as well as the reality of influence and power to the media. It is important because other bureaucrats read it and say, ah, he has been with the President. After all, a lot of people vie for the President's time, so it matters in terms of your relationships with others in Washington and with your staff, which derives its power from the power and influence you have, in terms of the media that write about these things, and even in terms of the President's staff. For the White House staff quite naturally is also influenced by what they perceive your relationship with the President to be.

When there is a public announcement of a program, it's a question not only of whether the President took your advice or not, but also of whether you were the first or the second to think of it, and who announced it to the public. For appearance and reality again become intertwined.

Say I think of something and I convince the President, and Cabinet member X or adviser Y announces it and somehow others on his staff let it be known that he's the one who had a lot to do with it. It will be presented to the public as being Cabinet member X's or adviser Y's program, and the inference will be that I and others had nothing to do with it. That diminishes your power and your stature.

There is a great deal of striving for exposure in the media because the right kind of exposure increases your influence. The people who come to Washington to work at the top level of government do so because they want to influence policy. On the whole, if you go to work in a corporation, it's not to influence policy, but to be successful in business terms.

Also, people who go into government at that level are more ego-oriented. Public service at the top tends to attract people with big egos. If you stacked the egos in Washington one on top of the other, the Empire State Building would be a very small building indeed by comparison. That's not true to the same extent in even the large corporations. I'm not saying that ego is not important, but even the large corporations, General Motors, General Electric, or Bendix, don't first and foremost attract people with an ego problem, the way the government does. Influencing policy can serve as an outlet for ego, and the way many do that is through public exposure.

Besides devising and influencing policy and helping to steer it through Congress, the Secretary of the Treasury bears responsibility for administering a bureaucracy of some 120,000 people, encompassing not only the Treasury staff as such, but also such important agencies as the Internal Revenue Service, the Secret Service, the Customs Service, the Mint, and the Office of the Comptroller of the Currency. Blumenthal talked about why trying to manage a large federal bureaucracy bears little resemblance to running a large corporation—and why the effort is often so frustrating.

In the first place, you find that the head of a government department or agency is not like the chief executive of a large corporation who has control over the personnel system, who can change it, can instill a certain spirit, can hire and fire. In government that kind of control does not exist.

A department like the Treasury is a conglomeration of different activities, operating under set laws about hiring and firing and the seniority system and Civil Service employment rights. So the top man coming in has very few tools with which to influence who's hired, who's fired, and who's moved where, except for the very top. So, even though I'm technically the chief executive of the Treasury, I have little real power, effective power, to influence how the thing functions.

Moreover, as in any organization, you have to decide where to put your energies. You learn very quickly that you do not go down in history as a good or a bad Secretary in terms of how well you ran the place, whether you're a good administrator or not. You're perceived to be a good Secretary in terms of whether the policies for which you are responsible are adjudged successful or not: what happens to the economy, to the budget, to inflation, and to the dollar, how well you run debt financing and international economic relations, and what the bankers and the financial community think of you. Those are the things that determine whether you are a successful Secretary.

But that's not true in a company. In a company, it's how well you run the place. The fact that Bendix under my tenure was selected as one of the five best-managed companies in the U.S. meant something to my reputation and that of my company. That's worth something on the bottom line. It wouldn't mean much if people said you run the Treasury better than anybody ever ran it. Nobody will remember that if there are currency troubles or if inflation accelerates.

Moreover, most of the people who work for you are not selected because they have administrative ability. They are selected because they have substantive knowledge in particular areas, and they get their jollies, their kicks, out of trying to have influence in those areas, not trying to become the best administrators of their particular bureaus.

Out of 120,000 people in the Treasury, I was able to select twenty-five, maybe. The other 119,975 are outside my control. And not only are they outside my control in terms of hiring or firing—they're also virtually outside my control in terms of transferring.

So it's hard to talk about running something. If you wish to make substantive changes, policy changes, and the department employees don't like what you're doing, they have ways of frustrating you, or stopping you, that do not exist in private industry. The main method they have is the Congress. If I say I want to shut down a particular unit or transfer the function of one area to another, there are ways of going to the Congress, and in fact using friends in the Congress to block the move.

They can also use the press to try to stop you. If I in Bendix wished to transfer a division from Ann Arbor to Detroit because I figured out that we could save money that way, as long as I do it decently and carefully it's of no lasting interest to the press. The press can't stop me. They may write about it in the local paper, but that's about it. Here, the very fact that I'm making the change may be widely reported and criticized, and people in Congress who want to find something to criticize me for, and those of the opposite party, will often use it to try to stop the change, stop it for the sake of stopping it.

So each time you have an administrative decision to make, which increases efficiency or which starts a new policy, you have to ask yourself, is that decision more important than the decision on interest rates, the decision on the dollar, the decision on the budget? Is it worthwhile to get adverse publicity in the newspapers, or get into a fight with Congressman X, over that issue, or should I not keep my good will so that I can use my credit with those people on the big things? As a result, a Secretary often tends to ignore administrative things because it is not worth his time, it's not where he should put his emphasis. That doesn't mean you neglect administrative matters, but it does mean that you do far, far less than you might wish, and that your priorities are far different than in business.

I remember asking a former Secretary of the Treasury years ago, when I never dreamed that I would be in his job: Why don't you do something about the U.S. Customs Service? Why don't you do something about what I saw as the excessive number of customs agents going through bags, on the grounds that they're unlikely to catch much that way? If you want to catch the people who smuggle in drugs or dangerous weapons, you have to do it a different way, perhaps with spot checks and not by going through people's individual bags. And he shrugged his shoulders and said, I have no time for that. And I thought to myself, if I ever were in a position of authority, I really would want to do something about that, because as a citizen coming through the U.S. Customs, I always resented that kind of thing, comparing it to Europe.

Now that I'm the Secretary, I realize what he meant, and I haven't done anything about it, because I've spent my time working with the President and my Cabinet colleagues on things that are more important, like economic policy.

That then leads you to the old question of motivation. In private industry you have many ways of motivating people. I can say to a young person coming up the ladder, as I did, you're doing a hell of a job, and though you're only twenty-seven years old, you've demonstrated that you have the maturity and the ability of a thirty-five-year-old, you have the wisdom of a forty-year-old, and I see in you the potential to be the chairman of this company some time, even though you're only twenty-seven, so I'm going to move you around very quickly. I'm going to raise your pay to keep you in the company. I'm going to reward you at the end of the year with a bonus if you do a certain job. You could earn a big bonus. And I can set up a system in the company to pick out the bright young people to do that with, and really develop quality in the company.

That's impossible in the government, because if I do it with one, all the other twenty-seven-year-olds say, what about me? If you say well, you're not as good, you may quite possibly be sued. So it just cannot be done. You have almost no control over selection. Hiring goes off a list. And to go outside that system involves more bureaucratic footwork than it is worth.

There's also the problem of retirement. Under the Civil Service, you don't have to retire until you're seventy. And since it is virtually impossible to prove that a person doesn't perform anymore, some people just stay around and do little or nothing. So you see more and more people, a great many more than you really need, and there's no practical way of retiring them.

So in fact, one leaves them there. The result is that a government bureaucracy, in terms of a structure, is the opposite in many ways from a private bureaucracy. A government bureaucracy, in terms of work load, is an inverted pyramid. The amount of work varies with how far up you are—the people at the top do most of the work and have most of the pressure and cannot delegate.

That isn't the way a private bureaucracy is. In business, you work hard at the top, but you can delegate. If I'm a good executive, I can go and play tennis on the weekend because I've picked a lot of good people. And they in turn have developed good staff, and everyone is motivated to pitch in. In the government, if you try to do that, you'll be known as someone who plays tennis, so he can't be very dedicated. So you can't delegate.

In other words, the popular perception of government bureaucracy as being more inefficient than private bureaucracies is true, except at the senior levels. At the level GS-15 to 18, you have officials who are very dedicated, who work as hard as their counterparts in private business, or harder. They work extremely hard for relatively low pay and produce extremely well. But they're also the victims of this inverted pyramid.

There are, of course, others at lower levels who are equally dedicated, but what I'm saying is that the rank and file, because of the way the system is organized, tend to be less efficient and slower and more bureaucratic. I'm not saying that they couldn't be led, if we had the possibility to lead them, if we had the possibility to motivate them, if we had the possibility to hire and fire them, to move them around, they would function just as well as anybody else. There's nothing inherent in a bureaucrat that makes him less efficient. It's the way the system is structured. So I'm not indicting the people; I'm indicting the system. It's an important distinction.

One thing to realize is that the tests of efficiency and cost-effectiveness, which are the basic standards of business, are in government not the only—and frequently not even major—criteria. For example, to a politician the most efficient way of controlling the cost of government is to put ceilings on the number of people you can employ. But in the Treasury, which collects money rather than spends it, this doesn't really make sense. If you can have another 1,000 people in the IRS, you can make more money for the government. Yet, to those in government and in the Congress the appearance of having controlled the number of people may be worth more than the reality of how much money you've actually collected in the end. Or you may have to maintain government jobs in a particular locale, which may be very inefficient, because a member of Congress from that area wants that bit of extra service and can make life difficult for you on a totally different issue. That kind of interplay, of accepting inefficiency in one area to achieve certain goals in another area, is foreign to a businessman.

If all that sounds too discouraging, let me add that there are some hopeful notes. For one thing, President Carter has a real interest in management. He has fought successfully for Civil Service reform, which will now give us new and better ways to attract good young people and to train and motivate them better. At the Treasury Department, we've even begun to initiate a small incentive-pay program in the office of the Secretary, and the staff is eager to make it work.

Along with his other trials and tasks, a Secretary of the Treasury has to deal with Congress. Superficially, the role of the overseeing committees of House and Senate might seem to be akin to that of a company's board of directors. But, for reasons that Blumenthal explained, it doesn't work out that way.

In business, the directors and the shareholders essentially have a common interest. They share the interests of the top management, which are to have an organization that grows, that is increasingly profitable, that is respected, and that pays well in profits and dividends.

The Congress's interests are much more diverse. When I am called to testify before the Congress, I am called by people who do not necessarily have the same interests that I do. In fact, many of them have quite divergent interests, being from the opposition or holding different political views. A big part for them is to find out what I do wrong, not to emphasize what I do right.

Secondly, even those who are not in the opposite party have a personal interest, because politicians are individual entrepreneurs. When they call me to appear, they often use my presence to get on television. But when they have a love feast with a Cabinet member, it's not as easy to get on television as when they shake their finger at you.

So the difference between appearance and reality again becomes important. They may shake their finger at you, but tell you privately that you're doing the right thing—carry on, but you know what I have to do. They assume that you understand it, that you're laughing at it, and that you're prepared to play that game. So time and again, they will castigate you in front of the press, but put their arm around you privately.

Another problem is the very rapid turnover in the Congress. Half the members of the House have served four years or less. About forty members of the Senate have been elected since 1975. The process of education is constantly going on, and learning about the highly technical areas that we have to deal with takes time.

Quite a few of the people who are elected have neither the background nor the long-term interest to learn about it. Some of them get assigned to these committees by accident. To be sure, a number have a sincere interest in the substance, but that is a relatively limited group.

Moreover, members of Congress represent very different interest groups, which is not true of shareholders. On the House Ways and Means Committee, for example, Charlie Rangel represents the people in Harlem, watching what I do on tax policy from the point of view of what is good for the poor and lower-income people and the most discriminated-against group in the society, the young blacks. He's concerned about an area where the rate of unemployment for young people is 30 percent. That's entirely different than Joe Waggonner on the committee; he is from down in Louisiana, representing people who are in the oil business.

So therefore you are not dealing with a monolithic group. They have certain things in common, getting on television being one of them, but they have very different backgrounds and represent very different constituent interests. By definition, you cannot please all of them. And whatever policy you follow, you are certain to be attacked and criticized, which is not true in the private sector. So what you learn is that there is no way to please your constituents in this job the way you can please your constituents in the private sector. You have to learn to live with that situation and survive within it.

Possibly the most difficult adjustment a business executive who moves into a top job in Washington has to make is learning to live with a far more complex decision-making process, in which just about everyone wants to have his say, and which he can influence but not control.

The big difference in the development and administration of a policy is that in a company you can clearly define who's involved. If I have to decide what the policy of the Bendix Corporation should be toward doing business with, say, Japan, I can pick three or four executives, assign them responsibilities for taking preliminary trips, for staffing out optional courses of action. I can get one or more lawyers and financial people involved, get a proposal written, restrict it to a certain group of people, take it to my board if it's a board matter, propose a policy, get it approved, and then control who will implement it.

In the government no one has the power to decide that this is the policy he wants to develop, these are the people who are going to develop it, this is how it's going to be decided, and these are the folks who are going to administer it. No one, not even the President, has that kind of power.

Take the same example, the framing of a U.S. economic policy toward Japan. If the President said to me, you develop one, Mike, the moment that becomes known there are innumerable interest groups that begin to play a role. The House Ways and Means Committee, the Senate Finance Committee, and every member on them and every staff member has an opinion and seeks to exert influence. Also the Foreign Relations Committee, the oversight committees, and then the interest groups, business, the unions, the State Department, Commerce Department, OMB, Council of Economic Advisers, and not only the top people, but all their staff people, not to speak of the President's staff and the entire press.

So it's assigned to me, but I can't limit who gets in on the act. Everyone gets a piece of the action. I'm constantly amazed when I have the lead responsibility to find two people talking to each other and negotiating something—when I haven't assigned them any responsibility. They're not in the loop. But everybody wants to be in the loop.

Therefore, to control the development of a policy, to shape out of that cacophony of divergent interests and dissonant voices an approach that eventually leads to a consensus and can be administered in a coherent fashion is an entirely different task in the government than it is for the chief executive of a company. There you can control the process and tell group executive A, you're not involved, stay out of it. And he will, and he must. In government, that's simply unworkable. So you have to learn to become one of a large number of players in a floating crap game, rather than the leader of a well-organized casino that you're in charge of. I should emphasize that this is not a complaint—that the diversity of interests seeking to affect policy is the nature and essence of democratic government.

One of the reasons so many businessmen fail in the government or get frustrated and quit is that they cannot take this system. They say, I'm just sick and tired of everybody and his cousin getting in on it. You can't keep anything secret, private—anything.

If I decide within the Treasury that there are good reasons why I want only three or four people in on something, I have the most terrible problems to keep it that way, because everybody feels that he or she has a legitimate piece of the action and must be involved. If I decide I want to do something on the dollar and I don't want a particular person involved, I have nothing but trouble with him. He spends all his time picking at the sides, trying to find out what the thing means. It's very difficult. He gets his jollies out of being involved. If I exclude him, I'm insulting him. I can't reward him with higher pay. He is part of a system where he's used to fighting his way into things.

Let's say we have at Bendix a certain policy and I think it makes no sense, although it's been done that way ever since Mr. Bendix organized the company more than half a century ago. I can get a small group of people together and do all the studies, talk to my bankers, make a decision, and at the right point bring everybody in on it.

Here, the moment I try to do that, everybody wants to get in the act, everybody has an opinion, and I start hearing from Congress before I've even made a decision. And you might as well not fight against it. To move within that process and still come out with the right decision is the essential difference between what you do as a senior executive in the government and what you do in business.

Another part of the problem is how to come through this process, accomplish something positive, and yet avoid appearances that undermine your real influence and effectiveness. For example, let's go back to the tax bill and what I learned from it. If I take the position that the lowest maximum tax rate I will accept on capital gains is 35 percent, because I know we will come out at 28, but in order to come out at 28 I have to argue for 35, that's a perfectly logical approach in business. Nobody will point the finger at you for arguing vigorously in public for 35. If you then come out at 28, you've driven a hard bargain. In the government, if a member of the Cabinet does that, the newspapers will write that he failed. He asked for 35 and he didn't get it. Therefore he's a weak Secretary.

In the shaping of the tax bill, I played the role of being truly the man in the center, negotiating with some people in the Administration to move them this way, negotiating with the Congress to move them that way, having limited control over the process because lots of people were involved, lots of pressure groups. I was trying to come out in the middle. Positions we took weren't necessarily the final ones—they were negotiating positions. Naturally, every position I took was reported in the newspapers, and score was kept of whether we came out there or not. If we didn't, some people would say I didn't really succeed.

Now, I hope people realize that I had a relatively constructive role in all of this. I hope. Some of them don't understand, but most of them do. So what you do vis-à-vis the newspapers, through what you imply, and through what you say and don't say, becomes a very important part of the equation.

With the next tax bill, I will be able to maneuver better than with the first one because I've been through it once now. I know what happens the last night. I've seen it myself now. I know what happens in the weeks before. I know how you mobilize the press. You've got to learn all that.

For all the differences between the corporate world and Washington, Blumenthal found, some of the basic principles of good management are valid in both.

All of this having been said, it's still true that some of the basic rules that I learned and applied successfully in business and hope to apply again when I return to business, are equally important in government, except they are not the only things that are required for success. Business is simple to succeed in if you follow a few simple rules. Government is harder. In both, the choice of people for the top jobs is extremely important. The more time you can take to pick top-quality people, the better off you will be.

I have my share of shortcomings as an executive, but one of my strengths has always been that I recognize a good person. The Treasury is effective today, and I feel I am increasingly effective within the government because I chose very good people. I took more time to put that group of people together than most others did, and in the end, I think, person for person I wound up with a more competent group of people. That pays off in the government, just as in business. The problem is that in government it isn't enough—not by a long shot.

The second thing is delegation of authority. You've got to learn to delegate to your executives, and you've got to back them and trust them. A good executive knows how to pick good people and then is not afraid to delegate to them, not afraid to back them, and not afraid to give them credit—it's harder to do in Washington, but it's just as important as it is in business.

Thirdly, it pays to know your facts. In business, as well as in government, the more you are the kind of person who is interested, willing, and capable of knowing the substance of an issue, the better off you'll be.

Finally, be honest, even though temptation to play games in the government is much greater.

If you stick to those principles, eventually—at least that's my feeling—you'll do all right in the government. The problem is that just being honest, knowing your facts, delegating, backing, and giving credit, and knowing how to pick good people is not enough.

When you make a mistake in picking people, you can't get rid of them, as you can in the business world. When you give credit, you may find that you're hurting yourself, if you are not also identified with the success. Knowing your brief isn't enough if someone else doesn't know the brief as well, but is skilled at presenting himself as if he knew the brief better. And sometimes people who are not honest can for a while get further than those who are, although their staying power tends to be limited. So the principles for a top manager are the same, but they do not lead to success as surely in government as they do in business.

In both business and government, it is very important to know how to select the critical issues, to let the others go, and to make time to think. In government, that's very, very difficult because of the ceremonial pressures on you. The only way to do it is to hold rigidly to a certain schedule, and to take regular vacations. I will not start before seven-thirty in the morning and I rarely go past seven-thirty in the evening. I do not accept more than one or two social engagements a week, at most. I reserve Sundays strictly for myself, and I take at least four short vacations a year. It's during the evenings, on Sundays, and on those vacations that I reflect on things.

Frustrating and grueling as life at the top in Washington can be, it also holds satisfactions and challenges that are not often matched in corporate life. Blumenthal has no hesitation about recommending the experience to other American business executives.

What do you get out of being in government? If you believe in a participatory democracy in which you have a right to criticize, a duty to criticize, and you feel that you can have an impact on what happens, what greater thrill is there than to be at the center, where the decisions are made, and having criticized, to try to do better? From now on, whenever my business friends speak of those fools in Washington, I can say to them, well, you go there and do better.

So I get out of it the satisfaction, the thrill of participating at the center of the decision-making process and helping to make the kind of system of government work that I believe to be the best. I get the personal satisfaction of having been selected to be one of those with the opportunity to play that role. I get the personal satisfaction of being the sixty-fourth Secretary of the Treasury, beginning with Alexander Hamilton, here in my adopted country. [Blumenthal was born in Germany.]

I get the chance to show that I can do as good a job as most and better than many in representing within the government the kind of balanced economic and financial viewpoint that a Treasury Secretary should bring to the job.

I live intensely. I meet a lot of interesting people. I am exposed to a fascinating set of problems, many of which I can't solve but I learn a lot about. I have tasks that are greater than I am, which is the measure of a good job. If you feel your potential is greater than your job, you get dissatisfied. To have a job where your potential is clearly not as great as the job and never can be, that's a very satisfying thing.

And you learn things you otherwise wouldn't learn. I enjoy knowing what the presidency really is. I really know what a President does, and I get an insight into what happens in the Soviet Union, what happens in Iran, and what the oil politics really are, and much more.

To be sure, there are frustrations. When you think you are moving things in the right direction, for example, and then you find that someone who really doesn't understand has totally subverted, totally undone it. Or he gets into the act and is just gumming it up. Or when you see silly things in the paper about yourself, when you read lies, when you read distortions, accusations, accusing you of stupidity, banality, you say why am I doing this, why? And you're very frustrated that you can't deal with it, that the cards are stacked against you.

Moreover, you sacrifice something in terms of peace and quiet, in terms of privacy. The loss of privacy is a tremendous thing. I can't go anywhere without being recognized and people staring, and I hate that. Yet I know that within a few months of leaving this job, my face won't be in the newspaper anymore, so nobody will know who I am. I look forward to that.

I will be free. I won't have to worry about where I go to shop, what car I drive, whom I'm seen with. I won't have to work hard if I don't want to, although I probably will. And in terms of doing interesting things, having had this experience as Secretary of the Treasury should provide opportunities to find other challenges.

My advice to businessmen about going into government is: If you want the thrill of serving your country in a really tough job, don't pass it up. You should recognize that you lose your anonymity for a while, you lose your freedom in many ways, you work harder than you ever did before, the level of frustrations will rise inordinately, and you'll take great risks of being portrayed as something that you're not. But it's worth doing.

33

3 | A Politician-Turned-Executive Surveys Both Worlds

Donald Rumsfeld

After the 1976 election, having been in government that many years, I didn't want to make a decision right away. While sorting out what I would do next, I lectured at Princeton's Woodrow Wilson School of Public and International Affairs and Northwestern's Graduate School of Management. It wasn't too long before I pretty well figured out that I wanted to be in business. I've never had an opportunity to develop any great appetite for having money. I finished government with very modest savings, but I was happy. All of the business opportunities presented to me were so much better paid than I was accustomed to in government that salary certainly wasn't the deciding factor. My desire was to be fully engaged, not just peripherally involved. I didn't want to be associated with a company in a non-central position.

In any event, the Searle family, having decided to bring in outside management, offered me this job. In April, 1977, I decided to do it, starting in June. I spent the intervening period talking to people, accumulating different perspectives on what was working well and what might need attention. I established task forces with a mix of directors, employees, and outsiders on each, concentrating on five areas: financing, government compliance, scientific research, corporate costs, and an examination of Searle's various businesses throughout the world.

We weren't trying to reinvent the wheel. Searle was and is a good company, but it was a small pharmaceutical house, which had grown into one that diversified and expanded throughout the world. With the help of the task forces, we came to some conclusions about what needed to be done. We decided to divest twenty of our marginal businesses. We also agreed that it would be helpful to have an outside board of directors. We reviewed our Puerto Rican portfolio and repatriated a considerable sum of money. We decided to move to a less centralized organization and reduced the corporate headquarters staff from 850 to under 350.

Reprinted from *Fortune* Magazine, September 10, 1979, by special permission, Copyright © 1979 by Time, Inc.

It also became clear that Searle's research had been fairly dry for a number of years. The product line was aging. So we decided to bring in a new senior vice president for research and development: Dr. Daniel Azarnoff, a highly respected medical doctor and scientist. At the same time, we began to develop a licensing and acquisition activity focused on supplementing our remaining businesses.

What we did, essentially, was to tidy up some of the pieces that didn't seem to be suitable platforms for growth. I enjoy working with talented people, learning from them, and arranging them in a way that they can be more productive. This wasn't a pat situation that one could just preside over. It was a company that was going down for eight quarters in a row. We now have five consecutive quarters going up, and there is no doubt that things are improving.

There are always risks, but I am used to risks. I ran for Congress right here in the Thirteenth District of Illinois when I was twenty-nine years old and there weren't many people around who thought I had much of a chance to win. It seems like an incredible decision now. But it proved right.

Rumsfeld regards his government experience as useful training for his present c.e.o.'s job, but he cites many differences in the way politicians and business executives function.

My observation has been that many public officials are constantly trying to create the impression that they are omniscient and omnipresent—they know everything and do everything. In business, it's clearly possible to say: "I delegate"—and then not even try to answer every letter yourself or meet with every person. In business, you get a chance to think more, to read more, to be more reflective, to plan more. My whole being says there's an awful lot I don't know, and therefore I rely on the knowledge and experience of others. This has been true in each post I've held. But politicians do not tend to get up in the morning and announce to the world that there's an awful lot they don't know. Therefore, the time demands on a government leader are usually much greater than on a business leader. It's part of the charade of seeming to be doing everything yourself.

In business, on the other hand, you're pretty much judged by results. I don't think the American people judge government officials this way. However, they do expect their President to plant some standards out there and to at least get started in the right direction. In business, you don't get a lot of points for just starting in the right direction.

One of the most incisive observations I think Mr. Blumenthal made in his interview with *Fortune* was the difference between appearance and reality. He felt that in government appearance was everything, whereas in business, reality was everything. One of the tasks of a manager in either arena, it seems to me, is to try to see that the perception is as close to the reality as possible. But this is much more difficult in government.

There, the managers may not *know* what the right course is, even after many years. So they tend to look only to effort. In government, too often you're measured by how much you seem to care, how hard you seem to try—things that do not necessarily improve the human condition. But if you begin with the assumption that the government is there to serve the American

35

people in specific ways, then the measurement realistically should be: How does all this affect the people for good or ill?

Look at the problem President Carter is facing right now—the disbelief, the cynicism about government, the feeling that promises have not been kept, that many high hopes have not been fulfilled. This isn't just a problem of Mr. Carter's. It seems to me that it's a problem of government. The fact is, it's a lot easier for a President to get into something and end up with a few days of good public reaction than it is to follow through, to pursue policies to a point where they have a beneficial effect on human lives.

Business is also more forgiving of mistakes. In government, you are operating in a goldfish bowl. You change your mind or make a blunder, as human beings do, and it's on the front page of every newspaper. It seems to make people in government less willing to correct their mistakes. This is in contrast to the way things happen in a boardroom. There it is expected that one will alter direction as new information becomes available.

Another big difference: the star quality that gives to many politicians a mystique. You tend to have—or seek—this mystique in government. But my impression is that in business you don't need to wear a grenade on your belt, or a black patch over one eye, so much as you need to be right and achieve results.

There's another important distinction. The goal in government is generally accepted as a worthy one—a legitimate human endeavor. That's not to say all people engaged in government are viewed as legitimate. But the *purpose* of government is. On the other hand, there are many people in the world who simply don't consider business a worthy activity. They characterize profits as evil and business as an essentially selfish activity. They don't appreciate that society is damaged when enterprise is stifled.

Rumsfeld also sees many similarities between the requirements of a good executive in government and business.

Many of the similarities stem from size, and there are certain things unique to big organizations. They require a variety of competencies, along with intricate planning and budgeting. However, planning in business is more analytical and thoughtful than in government. You are in a less reactive mode. For example, if it evolves in the Pentagon that a weapons system doesn't work, it may have international implications, it becomes a congressional problem, an OMB problem, as well as one having national-security implications. Suddenly, you have a multiplicity of public pressures that wouldn't show up in a boardroom. In business the first task would be to work out the problem. In government, a great deal of time is taken up dealing with these pressures.

When I came to Searle, the company was suffering from the digestive problems of a small company that had rapidly become a large multinational corporation operating in a difficult competitive and regulatory environment. The organization's skills, systems, and procedures had not evolved at the same pace at which its business had grown. There also were difficulties with the Food and Drug Administration, particularly about two of our prescription drugs: Aldactone and Aldactazide, which are used to treat hypertension. I was told that Searle wanted a president who had experience with large complex international organizations and was accustomed to operating under difficult conditions.

In any large organization, there is always the need to reach down and know how things are really functioning. You need to know you're getting the truth, hearing the bad news as well as the good. In government there is such intense press coverage that things tend to get aired more extensively and earlier. As a matter of fact, in the kind of government positions I was in at the White House and Defense Department there was such a flood of information it was like drinking out of a fire hose. That is not true in business. Even so, it's possible to get the necessary information in a business setting. I make it a point periodically to have lunch with salesmen, lab technicians, and others on the lower levels at Searle.

Another similarity between government and business is the need to establish priorities—to make sure you're spending your time on what's important. It is useful to ask whether you are working off your "in" basket or whether the organization is working off your "out" basket. If it's the former, you may be reacting rather than leading the organization toward agreed-upon priorities. I've always been an avid memo writer. At NATO they called them "yellow perils" (written on yellow paper), in the Pentagon, "Rumsfeld's snowflakes" (white paper).

We know that in government even a President can't will something to happen. He governs by consent. In business, although it is more responsive than government, things don't just happen by command, either. It is helpful if employees understand what the direction is and why. To a great extent success will depend on *their* execution.

In business, however, there's a communication tool that's missing—the press. Take the Pentagon: roughly two million men and women in uniform, at least another million each in civilian employment, the Reserves, and contract work. You can communicate with five million people a lot easier through the media than you can through an internal information system. Call a press conference and you can reach most everybody instantaneously. That tool is not available in business.

Rumsfeld believes that it was a much more difficult transition going from Congress to the executive branch than it was going from the Pentagon to Searle.

As a Congressman, your power is very limited, in the sense that you're one of 435—although certainly some are more influential than others in achieving legislative goals. In the legislative branch it is frequently possible to inhibit, delay, or stop something from happening. But a legislator has very little ability to make something happen. Unlike the way it was in the days of Sam Rayburn, the House of Representatives has a horizontal leadership structure. Business organizations are built like a pyramid.

In the case of the executive branch, there is a tendency to attribute great power to the White House staff. I think that's somewhat of a myth. The truth of the matter is, it's the President's power and policies that are being implemented, for good or ill. If it's the President's desire to be isolated, he will be. Nobody in the executive branch wants to crack the President.

When President Carter came to the White House, he established an organization that seemed to be a reaction to the Nixon Administration rather than establishing a structure that would work. In effect, he said he wanted a strong Cabinet government. He did not want a White House chief of staff, he wanted openness, he wanted people to say what they thought. Now he has a record that is not meeting with very much approval. Apparently he has now concluded that his management approach was wrong. However, instead of simply changing his approach, he has seemed to be punishing the people who had followed his instructions. Well, if it doesn't work out, don't blame Hamilton Jordan. Blame the President. If it does work out, don't credit Hamilton Jordan. Credit the President.

There's no way the President can micro-manage the federal government. Walking away, that's the key job in business, too. In a diversified, worldwide corporation, which has a multiplicity of interactions with customers, competitors, and governments, the single most important task of the chief executive is to select the right people. I've seen terrible organization charts in both government and business that were made to work well by good people. I've seen beautifully charted organizations that didn't work very well because they had the wrong people.

The decision-making process in government has long been reputed to be far more cumbersome than in business. Rumsfeld defines some of the problem-solving differences.

It has become almost a cliché for people to say: "Oh, government, it's so frustrating." There's no question that the President has the power. The Cabinet officer doesn't. The White House staff doesn't. If someone finds that frustrating, then he shouldn't do it.

Presidents themselves are often frustrated. A President gets into the Oval Office and starts reaching around for the levers of economic power, and he finds he doesn't have them all. Congress has some. So has the Federal Reserve Board. So have business, labor, consumers. There's no one lever with which he can make the economy zig or zag at his whim.

Did I find it frustrating as the White House chief of staff? Toughest job I ever had, but ... If you find it unpleasant to cope with a complex problem that is simultaneously the business of four or five Cabinet departments, several public-interest groups, and the Congress, and one that the President will finally decide, then it's frustrating. On the other hand, if you find that kind of situation a challenge, then it's stimulating, particularly when you see progress made. I found it tough, challenging, exhausting, but not frustrating.

In the decision-making process for G. D. Searle, my natural instinct is to consult the key managers and others whose advice is needed and who will help execute the decisions. As a Cabinet officer, naturally, you have many consulting layers. You learn to think what's best from the President's standpoint, taking into account not only your own department, but three or four other departments, the public, and Congress. You learn to think three-dimensionally. When you finally put to the President a set of options, you try to show how your recommendation fits or fails to fit with the other perspectives, how it impinges on other decisions, and then you argue your case. Now, I don't find that unduly burdensome or frustrating. It's just more complex and much more time consuming.

You might ask, do you get so bureaucratized that you forget how to operate any other way? No. It's a lot easier to decompress and not have to deal with a layer or two than it is to add one or two. But it's not clear to me that skills are readily transferrable between business and government. I've heard executives who have been successful in the private sector say: "I want to get into government." But there's no particular reason why a successful business-man should be successful in government—or the reverse.

In private industry, Rumsfeld sees firsthand the pervasiveness of government involvement in business.

When I get up in the morning as a businessman, I think a lot more about government than I do about our competition, because government is that much involved—whether it's HEW, IRS, SEC, FTC, FDA. I always understood the problem intellectually, but the specific inefficiencies that result from the government injecting itself into practically every aspect of our business—this is something one can feel only by being here.

Some years back, the thought was that government acted like an umpire, calling the balls and strikes. Today, it's a participant in practically everything we do—and at a cost far greater than the benefit. It's no accident that U.S. productivity growth ranks so low, that our balance of trade is suffering, that the number of patents issued to Americans is decreasing. It's because of the weight of government—the layering upon layering of regulation and intervention. There has to be a reversal of this. If I were back in government I would pursue deregulation much more persuasively now that I've been the head of a large corporation.

Businessmen are often credited with being much more innovative and free-wheeling than government officials. Rumsfeld describes the dangers he sees in being either excessively innovative or excessively zealous in maintaining the status quo and strict management control.

When I took over at Searle, I was asked to be chief executive officer and to run the company in a manner that would be profitable, professional, and consistent with the long-term interests of the shareholders, employees, customers, and the society in which we function. I was not asked to be either innovative or not innovative. I was asked to get results.

In Washington I saw people come tripping over their shoelaces into the President's office and say: "Look here, I have a brand-new idea—it is bold, new, and innovative," as though that was automatically good. An idea that is bold, new, and innovative can also be wasteful, harmful, and unwise. Innovation became a way of life in the Sixties during the Great Society. If someone came up with an idea that had never been tried before, it was—by definition —good. If it was also big and expensive, it was, by definition, even better. Utter nonsense. Things can be small and good. Things can be tried and tested and at the same time be constructive, powerful, effective, and helpful to society.

Of course, a stream of competitive ideas and views keeps converging on a manager, whether he's in government or business. As a result, a manager can get too fully engaged. It's important for him to stay loose enough, separated enough from the flow of details, so he can see trends and modify and improve the situation. That's terribly important.

I was a flight instructor in the Navy. The first thing a fledgling pilot usually does, when he climbs into a plane, is to grab hold of the stick and squeeze it so hard that he gets a sore arm. With a grip that tight, every movement is jerky. When government officials get into a tight situation, they have a tendency to do the same thing. They get jerky, overcontrol, micro-manage. A White House chief of staff who tells a Cabinet officer which secretary to hire is overcontrolling.

There has been speculation that Rumsfeld will soon reimmerse himself in politics, perhaps running in 1980 for the Illinois Senate seat to be vacated by Adlai Stevenson. While he dismisses this possibility, he is open-minded about the possibility of his eventual return to government.

The quick answer to that question is yes. I expect that at some point the odds favor my being involved in government again. One, I enjoyed it. Two, I think I did a good job. Three, I'm interested in our country and the world. Now does that mean I'm thinking about it? No. Does that mean I have an idea of how it might occur? No, not any. Does it mean I have the remotest idea when? No, I don't.

It is inevitable that the press continue to speculate about my running for some public office. That's one of the reasons why I signed a five-year contract with Searle in 1977. I don't feel that I needed a contract. I wanted the contract to signify the degree of commitment on my part.

You know, it took my wife and me five years to pay off the money I borrowed to run for Congress in 1962. Living on a government salary was a strain. But the fact that I was making a fraction of what I could have been making in the private sector has never burdened our family. Finding out that life isn't easy is not a bad thing for children growing up. But at forty-seven, as I am now, I would rather have movers move me than do the U-Haul bit. I did the U-Haul bit every time before I came to Searle.

4 | Why Business and Government Exchange Executives

Herman L. Weiss

Not since World War II has it been so apparent that the federal government and private business must act as full-time partners to deal with the monumental problems that confront contemporary society. Yet the public and the private sectors are beset with misunderstandings about each other. Too often this leads to outright conflicts that greatly reduce the nation's capacity for doing what must be done. At a time when harmony is all-important, discord impedes progress.

The problem is a people problem stemming from the fact that those in government and those in business approach their tasks in different ways, though not so differently as is generally suspected.

To solve this problem and to satisfy all the nation's yearnings—for equal opportunity and preservation of the natural environment, for such enormous projects as Apollo and the development of effective energy and transportation programs—the country must foster sympathetic understanding among those who make the crucial decisions in both the public and the private sectors. The United States needs a new host of hybrid leaders, men and women who have firsthand experience in solving the problems and melding the methods of both government and business.

Leaders in industry ought to have sufficient background to serve on government advisory boards or to hold high appointive positions up to cabinet rank; those in government should understand how to work with companies, large and small, in the execution of large projects and in the management of social and environmental problems.

Unfortunately, among the thousands of leaders in business and government, only a very few fully appreciate the problems of both sectors or the ways they function.

The President's Executive Interchange Program was formed to build up a cadre of such leaders. (This program is the chief activity of the President's Commission on Personnel Interchange.) The program chooses rising executives of exceptional ability and promise from each sector and exposes them to the ways in which the opposite sector works and thinks. During an interchange period of one or two years, each participating manager holds down a full-time job of considerable importance in a host company or government agency. Under its charter, the commission can arrange for the interchange of other kinds of people—of scientists or inventors, for example, or public relations experts—but its lean resources have led it to concentrate exclusively on the interchange of executives as its priority program. At present, 45 executives from the private sector are at work in critical managerial jobs in various agencies of the federal government. Meanwhile, 35 from government are busy in similarly critical positions in private companies. In the next group, coming on board late this summer, we expect that the numbers will be somewhat greater, with more than 50 people from each sector participating. The reader might look at the details on the program presented in the ruled insert on page 43. As explained there, participation has increased substantially since the first year.

How successful is the interchange program? One way—I think the most valid way—to evaluate the success of the program is to listen to individual participants' reactions. Thus, the bulk of this article consists of an informal colloquium in which five former participants speak for themselves, exchanging ideas and opinions about their participation in the program. These five executives were picked because they are highly articulate men; also, they happened to be available for the symposium. They are:

Percy E. Baynes
National Aeronautics and Space Administration

James S. Dimling
Marathon Oil Company

Francis X. Fee
General Accounting Office

David A. Lehman
International Business Machines Corporation

David Sternlight
Atlantic Richfield Company

THE COLLOQUIUM

The moderator of the colloquium was George A. W. Boehm, formerly a *Fortune* editor and now a free-lance writer. He structured his questioning loosely, and the participants spoke freely. To preserve the flavor of the conference, we present the whole symposium here in question-and-answer form.

Question First, what about the two stereotypes? People talk about the sheep and the wolves—the government executive who goes strictly by the book and is concerned, above all, about personal security, and the business executive who is a ruthless go-getter, hungry for success. Does your personal

Facts about the program

The President's Commission on Personnel Interchange was authorized in a law signed by Lyndon B. Johnson on January 19, 1969, his last full day as president. The first group of participants was chosen a little more than a year later, and they began their new duties in late summer 1970. (Tours generally begin in August or September, although there have been exceptions.)

Most of the candidates are young and rapidly advancing executives. They have all been sponsored by government officers of cabinet rank or by top managers of their companies. While participants from the private sector have been the more plentiful in former years, the balance between public and private is nearly even, as the figures show below.

These young executives are generally between the ages of 30 and 40 and have been earning $25,000 or more annually in base pay. Program salaries are negotiated between host organization and candidate, but generally the candidate receives a modest raise in pay as compensation for such expenses as moving or maintaining two homes.

Last year, for example, the average executive transferring from government to business and industry was paid $29,200, whereas his government salary was $26,000. Those switching from industry to government got roughly the same advance, from an average of $27,500 to $30,700. Almost all those entering government were assigned to Civil Service Grade 15, while those coming from government had usually achieved Grade 14 or 15. Most, if not all, fringe benefits have usually been continued by the sponsor.

The commission's initial function is to act as a sort of marriage broker, arranging interviews between candidates and host agencies or companies that have indicated a willingness to furnish an appropriate job. Candidates receive an orientation to the purposes of the program at five-day conferences conducted by the Brookings Institution, which holds separate meetings for people from the private and the public sectors. Various speakers describe central issues and the differences between working for government and working for a private company.

Once final selections have been made and the participants established in their exchange jobs, an effort is made to integrate them into their new communities. The participants have frequent opportunities to engage in orientation sessions, short trips, briefings, and meetings with such key figures as congressmen and their aides and men in the top management of companies. As explained in the conclusion of the article, this facet of the program is being expanded so that the year spent in the opposite sector will be as enriching as possible.

Near the end of their tour of duty, participants from both sectors go on retreat to discuss their experiences and to suggest changes for the program. Many of them have a feeling of kinship for each other. The commission intends to create a mechanism by which former participants can get together for a few days periodically.

The President's Commission on Personnel Interchange is operated by a small professional staff headed by Executive Director Jay I. Leanse.

Participants	1970–71	1971–72	1972–73	1973–74
From government	11	8	15	35
From the private sector	19	24	57	45

experience in the exchange program bear out the truth of this contrast? Are motivations and behavior really so different?

Francis Fee: Perhaps I'm not the best person to answer that question, because I went from government, which is the largest employer in the country, to AT&T, which is the second largest. But really the two are very much alike. AT&T may even be a more bureaucratic organization than the government in some ways. People in the private sector are concerned about whether or not they have a window or a rug. I don't think people in government worry about such things.

I think you have basically the same types of people in both sectors, doing the same kinds of projects. On the other hand, there are some differences in motivation between industry and government. A government worker feels a bit more secure and has a tendency to become a little more lax in his job. In some agencies I have been with, he at least knows when his next promotion is going to come.

But there are a lot more highly motivated individuals in government than most people think, although the motivations are somewhat different from those in business. For one thing, industry pays better; hence the financial incentive is stronger in business.

Percy Baynes: I also went from government to industry, and the ways I spent my days in government and business were similar. I went to the aerospace industry, and they spend very little money on the physical plant. There is no question of rugs as a status symbol. The supervisor or the manager works in an open space, along with the workers.

I disagree with Mr. Fee that higher pay in industry may be a major incentive. What really motivated the engineers I worked with was the challenge before them—particularly, working on the space shuttle program. The shuttle actually presented management with more of a challenge than Apollo did. We were faced with the firm decision to go with the space shuttle, and our problem was to design and build the orbiter for the space shuttle, not so much to advance the state of the art.

Question: Now let's hear from someone who went from industry to government.

James Dimling: I did. And I found a surprising number of intelligent, hardworking, dedicated individuals at the managerial level of government. Although government salaries are competitive with those of industry up to a pretty high level, they are not competitive near the top. And that means that the individual in government must have motivations other than his pay.

David Lehman: The biggest change the program made in my attitude—I joined the Department of Transportation from IBM—was the recognition of the quality of the people I worked with. I was very impressed with their intellectual ability and with the harddriving nature of many people in the super grades. I gained a great deal of respect for these people and confidence in their ability to manage their agency, and I guess I had not held that viewpoint before. I used to feel that the ordinary bureaucrat was below average in capability.

That was not the case. The super grades were largely filled with people who had grown up in the agency. They were dedicated, they worked very hard, and I think I worked harder there than I ever did at IBM, every single day and weekend from October first to April first, with Christmas Eve and Christmas Day off. I got so involved, in fact, that I didn't do some of the social things I was looking forward to when I went to Washington. But we made some lifelong friends in government and also in some of the embassies. And you can never attach a value to such personal gains; you simply have to put them down as an incredible plus.

Question: Is the decision-making process greatly different in the public and the private sectors?

James Dimling: I found it so. The government process is much more circuitous. There are more tradeoffs to be examined, more compromises to be made. Political influences are prominent in decision making within government, but they aren't really an important factor in industry.

I found, at times, a reluctance to make some of the tough, day-to-day decisions. Some people tended to retreat to long-range planning as a kind of security blanket. In industry, I'd say, there is more of an involvement in day-to-day operating decisions at the expense of long-range planning.

I think this cautiousness is a substantial failing. This kind of uncertainty and delay often seems worse at the appointive level than in the civil service ranks. When there is a change in administration or a blowup such as Watergate, policy-making posts sometimes remain unfilled for several months.

I have never come in contact with such discontinuities in industry. Positions of that stature, and of that authority and responsibility, are filled immediately. There is a management succession that is constantly ready to move, and one can usually identify the likely successors for a particular position.

Question: This is an interesting point. Did any of you gentlemen see ways of strengthening the continuity in policy and decision making while you were in the program?

David Sternlight: Yes, I did, especially during a special trip to London, where my group was shown some of the workings of the British government. It was quite an interesting comparison. Under the British system, when the party in power changes, the only personnel changes are in a very, very small number of new key ministers. This is one basic reason why the change is not nearly so drastic as it is in the United States. Professionals in the British civil service include people at much higher levels of responsibility. There is a minimum of turnover at high policy-making levels.

These more or less permanently established civil servants have a kind of responsibility seldom found in our own civil service. Their responsibility is to analyze the kinds of policy that may interest the government in power, describe the consequences of policy alternatives, and then let the cabinet ministers make the decisions.

These top British civil servants are highly skilled, and yet they seem to be apolitical. Because they stand apart from the actual making of decisions, they are not regarded as a threat by any of the different political parties.

I am not sure we want to adopt the British system in toto. But I do think we should consider modifying our own system to raise the level of what are generally considered career positions and to establish career management of a serious kind for people above what is now the Grade 18 level. Right now, the civil service prepares a lot of data and statistical reports on the upper level of the federal government. It does not, however, have a really effective program for managing the careers of its top people.

Percy Baynes: I agree, and I'd like to reinforce that one point. If the concept of the bureau chief were really in force in the United States, I think it would provide the type of continuity we are looking for. But the bureau chief is really not a civil service type; he is more like a cabinet secretary and therefore vulnerable to change. He would be more secure if his position were upgraded to something that resembles the upper ranks in the British model.

Question: Mr. Sternlight, you switched to a different company after you finished your tour with the government. Do you have further comparisons to make?

David Sternlight: Yes. First of all, the criteria for a correct decision are usually, though not always much more straightforward and obvious in industry, and so are the criteria by which others evaluate decisions. This holds for both companies I worked for and, I suspect, for the vast majority of other companies too.

In government, it isn't just that public opinion is hanging over your head. Most decisions there are very, very complicated in terms of whom they affect —what groups in the country, for instance—and the ways those people are affected. And so you have to trade off many more factors to arrive at what might be considered a correct decision.

Question: Would you give us a concrete example?

David Sternlight: Well, there are a number of short-term policies that the government might apply to deal with gasoline shortages. One is rationing; another is taxation; a third is to allow the free-market price to rise until it discourages demand. Now, each one affects different income groups differently. Rationing, for example, guarantees people with low incomes as much gasoline as anyone else. On the other hand, a high free-market price or much higher taxation would give the affluent an advantage. Then you have to take into account the inflationary impact of much higher gasoline prices. And so on.

The decision gets so complicated that in the end you are sure of only one thing: that there is no right decision, but there is probably a decision that will seem to be best on many different grounds. So you settle for the best of a series of alternatives, none of which is really close to ideal. Each decision seems to require a slightly different process, almost a unique process in many cases.

Question: That would also apply for broad policy issues?

David Sternlight: Very much so. That's one reason why government policy making is quite different from that in industry. I noticed that the people in government tend to live more from issue to issue. They tend to go from subject to subject, and once a given subject is dealt with, it tends to disappear —to go to an operational level or to vanish completely—at least, until the next time that issue comes up.

When I was in the Department of Commerce, one of the first things that commanded attention was the question of U.S.–U.S.S.R. relations and East-West trade. Then we moved on to questions of employment, then to improving the productivity of American industry, then to how we could capitalize on the advantage of U.S. technology in international trade, then to currency revaluation as a solution to our trade deficit.

Question: Could you compare that with your industrial experience? Is there much tendency in business to jump from problem to problem in rapid succession?

David Sternlight: No, the procedure seems much more stable. Instead of being continually shifted from one compartment to another for successive reevaluations, the task of structuring a problem and its solution seems to follow an underlying thread of policy. This can be done because of the much narrower effect a decision has on a particular corporation, even on the largest and most diversified one. The same issues in different forms keep coming up over and over again. After a while, you build a base of experience and expertise that allows you to deal with each issue in the context of everything that's gone on before.

Another reason for this big difference is that the government's policy-making shops respond drastically to a change in top management, such as a new cabinet secretary. Then basic issues are commonly rediscovered and thought out all over again. The bureaucracy—that is, the civil service—provides a kind of continuity, but it's not the strong sort of continuity you find in industry.

Even though industrial companies may change their leadership from time to time and even make some major shifts in policy direction, I have never observed the kind of inefficiency and inertia that often follows an upheaval at the top of a government agency. When this kind of confusion does occur in a company, it can be the sign of an impending inability to operate at all.

David Lehman: I'd like to add something here. Basically, I found that I probably had more responsibility in government than I did at IBM; government problems affect the entire nation, and some of the things I was working on will affect the world transportation system, so I was very much impressed by the scope and complexity of the problem. On the other hand, I feel that I had more flexibility at IBM—I could react quicker.

But, looking back at my government experience, I now realize that some extremely complex things *did* get done, despite the handicap of inflexibility. What impresses me so much about the government is the fact that the people there have to amalgamate a number of diverse points of view and that they actually succeed in doing so. This is really the essence of the difficulty of government: to take into account the problems that the air carriers face, the traveling public, the business community, the manufacturers, and so on. In business the problems are so much cleaner, more definable.

Question: Do the government men with industry experience share this view?

Percy Baynes: Speaking for myself, the answer is basically *yes*. The decision-making process is essentially the same in the public and the private sectors, but the turnaround is much faster in industry. An industrial line manager has more responsibility to make decisions on resource allocation or whatever, whereas a government manager is required to get various approvals.

Francis Fee: May I add to what Mr. Baynes has said? I also found that the turnaround time is very quick in industry as compared with government. In industry, unless a decision is made, a chance to make a profit may be lost irrevocably. In government, the reason that people are a little reluctant to make a decision that quickly, and the reason for having such a long chain of command before somebody finally does come to a decision, is that public opinion is hanging over your head all the time. The government worker is very much aware of what the public will think if he chooses the wrong course, and of how many people it may affect. Sometimes his social conscience overrides any thoughts he may have of what a decision will do to advance or retard his career—especially in the short run.

Nonetheless, because of my New York experience, I realized that our bunch in Washington takes an inordinately long time in putting out a finished product—in our case, a report to Congress.

There are ways to speed up that process, by deviating from the traditional approach of accountants. Mostly, it's a matter of bringing in different disciplines to help. The GAO is basically a group of accountants and business administration people. Several years ago we started to get different kinds of people to help us evaluate federal programs—mathematicians, engineers, statisticians, and experts in electronics and computers, among others.

While I was in New York, I had a chance to work with an extremely diverse group of people, and it convinced me that the GAO can make still better use of other talents and equipment.

Question: From the viewpoint of your own careers and your sponsoring organizations, did your participation in the program come at the right time, or too soon, or too late?

David Lehman: For me it was just the right time. I had had ten years at IBM. I was brought into the Department of Transportation, and while I did not have specific experience in civil aviation and other transportation matters,

I had had a great deal of experience working on unstructured problems. It was possible for me to spend a year away without injuring either myself or IBM, I felt I had a great deal to contribute, I was open to all suggestions, and I didn't have any particular ax to grind. For me the experience came at an opportune moment.

When I returned to IBM, my new experience had a very beneficial effect on my advancement. IBM has not capitalized directly on my knowledge of transportation, but my experience in Washington has drawn me to the attention of top management. I'm sure it has accelerated my career.

Percy Baynes: I also entered the program at the right stage. I went to Rockwell in 1972, just when that company had received the authority to design and build the orbiter for the space shuttle program. So, while NASA, my own agency, was phasing out Apollo, I got in on the ground floor of the next very big space project. But, beyond that, the experience broadened my image of the kinds of things I can accomplish personally. It broadened other people's views of me.

Question: You five men and almost all other executives in the exchange program have spent just about one year away from your regular jobs. Do you think that one year is enough?

Francis Fee: At the beginning I spent some down time because I had to orient myself and acclimatize myself to a new environment. I don't think you get going at full steam until the fourth to sixth month on the new job. I would have liked to have my one-year stretch extended to fifteen or eighteen months.

David Lehman: I'll have to disagree with Mr. Fee. My job was terribly exciting for the entire thirteen months, and there was a tremendous temptation to stay longer. I think some are tempted to stay for good. But I come from the business world, which moves fast. A man should not stay too long in his government post—he should come back after a year, or he may be forgotten. I would like to return to government service again some time later, but for the first time, one year was enough.

Percy Baynes: The same applies to government men. If they stay away for longer than a year, they are likely to be forgotten.

Francis Fee: One thing is sure—you need time to get back inside your old organization. I might like to try the switch again, but not for another three or four or five years. And then perhaps in a different industry, or at a different level of authority.

David Sternlight: For myself, I found that I entered the program at exactly the right stage of my career. Five years earlier, I was still trying to make some major contributions to my company, to establish my position. Five years later, I think, I would have been at a point in my career when it would have been too late to go, and possibly inappropriate.

Question: Gentlemen, have your attitudes toward the opposite sectors changed drastically because of your program experience?

David Sternlight: My comment is a little different from the conventional wisdom on that subject. Prior to the program, my contact with government people had been on a technical level. Those I had dealt with had been in charge of very large-scale technical projects—fleets of ships, cancer research programs, that sort of thing. I had an unrealistically high set of expectations about government people. I thought they were all superb.

Then, when I went into government for a year, I came into contact with a cross section of government people—not just the top scientists and technologists. I now have the view that government people are, well, like everybody else. Some are simply outstanding, while others perform fairly routine functions. On the whole, I guess, they vary just as widely as do the people in any good industrial company.

David Lehman: My attitude changed also, but in a different way. There are two ideas I would like to offer. First, in business, you tend to view a problem from a single perspective—that of your company or industry. I feel that my government experience has expanded my intellectual resources—and heightened my awareness of the multidimensional aspects of each problem so that I think it out far more keenly than before and try to be more astute about weighing the factors that bear on it. I have seen how necessary it is to look at a spectrum of attitudes before creating government policy.

Second, I discovered that government has something to learn from industry about human resources. There are a lot of people in government whose talents are not being used nearly as effectively as they would be in industry. This is partly because factors such as time, human resources, and personalities are seldom taken into account in organizational changes in government. Government agencies could revitalize themselves if they were able to change their structures more rapidly and flexibly. Then their people would find themselves in stimulating new environments, not entrenched in old situations.

Question: How do our gentlemen from government feel about that?

Francis Fee: I did go from government to industry, and my opinion of the government worker did not change as a result of the move. I may be a bit biased, but I had—and still have—a fairly high opinion of government people, with whom I had worked for nine years before I entered the program. I don't think I met any group of people in industry who were markedly superior to government employees.

For the benefit of participants moving in the opposite direction—that is, coming into GAO from industry—there was an orientation program, primarily to give them an idea of how the government works. At the end of orientation week, they seemed to have a general impression that the government is quite messed up—nothing but a bunch of bureaucrats sitting in Washington and accomplishing very little.

When we met with them all again at the end of the year, I tried to find out whether this impression of government and government people had changed.

It had. There are an awful lot of capable people in government—a fact that many of the participants in the program grew to realize.

Question: Would any of you gentlemen from industry care to comment on the point Mr. Fee has just made?

James Dimling: This may be an oversimplification, but I was encouraged by what I found out about the bureaucracy and discouraged by what I learned about Congress. The administrative branch of government deals with problems of tremendous scope and complexity, and I was greatly impressed by the dedication and motivation of the people trying to solve these problems. Comparatively speaking, Congress is inadequately staffed. It does not even have the supporting services to address its problems.

David Sternlight: My experience is similar to Jim Dimling's. I thought the contacts with Congress were probably the weakest part of the program. True, we had some fair, off-the-record meetings, but they were not structured to lead to more extensive and detailed contacts with either congressmen or their staffs.

On the other hand, I got to meet many of the people in the cabinet department in which I was working and many people from other agencies when I served on interagency groups. As a result, I feel I have a good insight into the executive branch, its mechanisms, and its people. And I feel very secure about that part of our government.

Question: To what extent has the program tempted you to change from government to industry or vice versa?

David Lehman: After returning to the company, I was offered an appointive position in government, but the offer came prematurely in my career. In time, however, I would be very interested in taking on a certain task-oriented assignment and in being on an appointive commission, perhaps for an indefinite period.

James Dimling: I feel the same way—several of us may avail ourselves of opportunities to return to government in a different kind of position, dealing with whatever problems are vital at the time. But one thing I learned is how much would be involved if I were to make a permanent switch. People do realize this, and I think that restrains them from making any fast decisions.

Percy Baynes: While we're on the subject, let's not forget the element of loyalty. The government nominated me after 15 years of service—I felt somehow obligated to return to NASA. Otherwise, I would not be helping to achieve one of the chief purposes of the program, which is to bring back to government some of the knowledge gained in industry.

Question: What has it been like to return to your old organization? Any peculiar problems or new opportunities? What were the specific benefits you brought back?

Percy Baynes: One of the things I learned is that the government can work more smoothly with industry if it starts identifying and clearly stating its needs early in the procurement process. I have seen industry waste time and money mobilizing for a job that has not been clearly defined at the start.

Another helpful change would be to standardize the ways in which government approaches industry. Many industries look on government people as paper pushers who are more concerned about filling out the right forms than about doing high-quality work. This misunderstanding would largely disappear if the government were to coordinate its ways of making contacts. And if several agencies are involved with one particular company, they should get together and deal with the company through one man or through a small group of men.

Francis Fee: During my year at AT&T I did much the same thing that the GAO does for the government. The GAO studies issues. I learned how to carry out this kind of audit better. As I indicated earlier, I learned the value of an audit team made up of men from a great many disciplines.

Another thing: it takes a lot of time to get things done in government because of this circuitous decision-making process. Maybe, also, we spend too much time justifying our work. We feel we have to be extremely certain that what we report is fact and that it is fully supported, and I think we tend to gather a great deal more supporting data than we actually need. One of the things we did at AT&T was to gather just enough facts to support a point and then go ahead and make the point.

Question: Did any of you encounter any conflicts of interest?

David Sternlight: I came from a company that is one of the country's major shipbuilders, among other things, and I went into the Department of Commerce, which includes the Maritime Administration. My background was no secret, but I leaned over backward to avoid conflicts of interest. I disqualified myself from any involvement in maritime policy issues that might have had any impact on the company I came from. If I had not done so myself, I am sure that others would have insisted on it.

David Lehman: The same here. When I first planned to spend a year in Washington, all the prospective job offerings were carefully scrutinized by our chief legal counsel at IBM. I was interested in a Department of Transportation job, and he OK'd that because the possibility of a conflict of interest would be practically zero. As a result of careful checking beforehand, neither I nor the company nor the agency had any worries on this score.

David Sternlight: I think this point can be carried beyond reason. Let's not lose sight of mutual interests and common interests—they're why the program exists. We live in a society where the worst relationship between the government and any other sector would be the kind in which the government slips something under the door and the recipient slips something back over the transom. Open exchange lessens the chance of such nonsense. I would like to see similar programs involving the academic community and other sectors of society. We need that kind of interchange. We need it badly.

TOWARD A LASTING ALLIANCE

In his last comment, Mr. Sternlight stated the essential motive of the program and the reason for its success to date. Ignorance leads to fear, fear breeds mistrust, and mistrust leads to conflict. The aim of our commission is to break this disruptive chain and to enhance harmony among various groups in the nation. It is still trying to improve the program toward that end:

- For one thing, the commission has greatly improved the balance between those coming from government and those going to government. Until this year, the participants moved mainly in one direction: a large majority of them came from the private sector. (See the ruled insert.) The commission searched for the reason and concluded that top management in most companies fundamentally mistrusts the capability of government workers. Industry is reluctant to pay $25,000 or more to a man who it thinks may not perform at company standards. It has taken a lot of time and personal persuasion, but a large number of company executives are now convinced that exchange participants from government are men of top quality who are likely to pay their own way. From now on, let's hope the exchanges will be roughly equal; they were nearly so this year.

- The commission is opening the program to a few older men from industry, aged 45 to 50, whose selection for a tour in Washington will be in effect final preparation for a step up that could be to a vice presidency or some other position of top responsibility. Hopefully, these will be men who will eventually represent their companies in their most important dealings with government.

- The basic job selection procedure has also been improved. Instead of trying to match a man to a particular job, as in the beginning, the commission now arranges for about three times as many job offerings as there are candidates. This arrangement enables a man to shop around and find exactly the kind of work that suits him best. Usually he is afforded an opportunity for four to five in-depth interviews before making up his mind. Even at the present time, a candidate can change assignments in midstream if that is desirable.

  Despite our success in matching men with jobs in the opposite sector, almost all of them retain strong loyalty toward their old organizations. During the first three years of the program, only three men from industry remained with government, while the same number from government stayed in industry. This rate of turnover seems to me to be surprisingly small, all factors considered.

- Participants coming to government from industry have little trouble getting to know each other, for most of them are concentrated in Washington. They are often invited to meet with cabinet officers, congressmen, and top executives in agencies other than their own, for example, and social gatherings are planned to include their wives.

53

Those in the private sector, however, are spread out all over the country. The commission is now trying to create the same kind of helpful atmosphere for some of the government executives who are working in the private sector as the industry executives enjoy in Washington. The government executives have been concentrated in five areas (Chicago, Detroit, Los Angeles, New York, and San Francisco); they visit other companies in their area and attend briefings with chief executives. They also confer with other executive participants; like their counterparts in Washington, they are invited to social functions involving their families.

These are some of the ways by which the President's Commission on Personnel Interchange is trying to build new bridges that will establish and maintain a lasting alliance between the future leaders of U.S. government and business. The program itself is surely a unique experience for talented and ambitious individuals approaching the peaks of their careers. There is every reason to believe, however, that their experiences will benefit the entire nation, perhaps in ways that no one can yet fully appreciate.

PART THREE

IS PUBLIC MANAGEMENT SIMILAR TO OR DIFFERENT FROM PRIVATE MANAGEMENT?

art Three presents the views of academics and researchers on the question of whether public and private management are similar or different. We do not try to weigh the evidence presented for or against the proposition that there are more similarities than differences. Empirically based comparative analysis of points where public and private management converge or diverge is sparse. What we attempt to show, therefore, is that those who advocate that public and private management are similar and their counterparts who argue that they are different approach the issue from vastly different perspectives or biases. We identify the different perspectives from which various analysts have viewed the question and from which it might be viewed by other analysts. To a lesser extent, we show how each analyst's perspectives influence his or her conclusions.

Before examining these perspectives, it is useful to summarize each analyst's conclusions. Michael A. Murray, whose experience includes teaching at the Graduate School of Management at Northwestern University, conducts a dialectic examina-

tion of the specific points of similarity and difference extant in the published literature in the field. He concludes that public and private management are not inherently different. Whatever differences exist, he contends, tend to be formalisms and superficialities rather than actual differences in substance, procedure, or methods.

Graham T. Allison is Dean of the Kennedy School of Government at Harvard University. He examines the testimony and case experiences of managers who have operated in both sectors and discusses the general literature in the field. He concludes "that public and private management are at least as different as they are similar, and that the differences are more important than the similarities."

Hal G. Rainey, Robert W. Backoff, and Charles H. Levine are faculty members of schools of public administration. They systematically examine propositions about the differences between public and private organizations in light of the available empirical research. And they conclude that the body of existing knowledge simply does not provide clear, concise answers to support or rebut the propositions. We present their article here so that you may weigh the evidence that supports or rebuts the arguments of Murray and Allison.

Our view is that there are similarities between public and private management. But there also are differences, and these differences are sufficiently clear and important to warrant the consideration of public management as a special professional field and object of study. Our basis for this conclusion in the current readings will become clear after we consider the perspectives from which the question: "Are public and private management basically similar or different?" is viewed.

In the accompanying table, we present some of the perspectives that characterize the works of analysts who compare public and private management. The common orientations of each side in the debate are reflected in their answers to four questions that are implicitly or explicitly addressed in the comparisons they draw. The researchers who conclude that public and private management are alike, of whom Murray is representative, provide essentially similar responses to the four questions. Analysts who, like Allison, arrive at the conclusion that public and private management are different also tend to answer the

Perspectives of Analysts Who Assess Similarities and Differences Between Public and Private Management

Issues raised in drawing comparisons	Perspectives of analysts (e.g., Murray) who conclude that public and private management are more similar than different	Perspectives of analysts (e.g., Allison) who conclude that public and private management are more different than similar
What is an organization's proper role toward its external environment?	To achieve *instrumental* goals	To achieve *social* goals
Can similarities and differences in the management of organizations be understood by looking at the parts or the whole of management?	The similarities and differences can be understood by comparing parts.	The similarities and differences can only be understood by comparing the whole.
Are all similarities and differences of equal importance?	Similarities and differences are weighted equally.	Some similarities and differences are more important than other similarities and differences.
Should proof of the existence of similarities and differences between organizations be based on case experiences or on dominant patterns within the entire population of organizations?	Case experiences	Dominant patterns

questions in uniform, but correspondingly opposite, ways from Murray and others.

The first issue over which those who compare public and private management diverge is how each perceives the role of the organization vis-à-vis its external environment. Instrumentally oriented analysts tend to perceive the social role of all organized activity as efficient production—whatever the context. However, the appropriate context most often is that of business organizations, where the products are divisible goods and where individuals can vote for various goods with their pocketbooks. In contrast, the analysts who argue that public management is different perceive the role of an organization as the provision of social goods to various constituencies who can vote only in a general way for more or less production. Often, these goods, e.g., education and defense, are indivisible in the sense that they must be provided to everyone, and recipients cannot be chosen on the basis of ability to pay. In this context (usually government), efficient production is important, but the equitable provision of services is a supravalue. In fact, a fundamental distinction between the instrumental and the social orientations is that only the latter perspective incorporates the pursuit of social equity as an organizational goal.

Thus, the instrumental analyst is likely to insist that the performance of public and private organizations be judged on the same criteria of efficiency. When pushed, however, the instrumental analyst admits that the major fruits of efficiency—profits—are not the sole or main reason for the existence of private business, much less government. According to Murray, other advantageous business activities include "products, services, employment, and all the 'hidden hand' effects of community and social contribution."

The perspectives of those comparing public and private organizations also differ on the use of partial or holistic analytic approaches. Partial approaches tend to look at the specific details of public and private management—to break down the overall question of differences into subquestions about differences in contexts, ends, means, procedures, and methods. For example, Murray deals in the following way with the differences and similarities between public and private planning:

> Planning is an activity common to both the public and private sectors.... There are two ways to view planning.... In terms of process, planning means lateral consultation, sharing of information, discussion of short- and long-range objectives.... Planning as a means of control refers to a system of gathering information and marshalling available resources in a sequential priority framework in order to maximize agreed-upon objectives.
> ... The question ... is whether one mode is used more in business or in public.... Distinctions blur when applied to actual situations.... the vital circumstances surrounding any planning effort are intangible, ad hoc, and uncertain. In both the public sector and the private sector this is evidenced by the first impulse of planners to "get more, or better, data." ... It is true that planners seem more common in government circles than in private firms. But this may be simply a matter of labels, i.e., calling the corporate finance officer financial analyst instead of resident planner, or calling the city planner by that title instead of research associate. In either area planning is at best a secondary function, and the point is that in actual situations the process of planning appears to be the same.

Murray's analysis thus omits consideration of the critical contextual and substantive differences between public and private planning activities. For example, economic planning occurs in both sectors, but national economic planning is substantively different from business economic planning, although identical economic models may be used. The difference stems from the fact that government planners can manipulate and control, in varying degrees, public policy represented by the independent variables in the model to affect national economic goals, whereas corporate planners can only consider the effects of such manipulations for their sector of the economy. Presidential administrations are made or broken on the basis of the effects of their economic policies, whereas corporate regimes may only be called to task for making poor forecasts of market conditions.

In theory, the answers to partialled questions of similarities and differences can be based on empirical quantitative research. As a consequence, the partial analyst's approach has gained considerable credibility because of its "scientific" character. But it tends to be inconclusive nonetheless; the results of piecemeal examinations frequently conflict, and they are often at variance with the results obtained from holistic views of public and private management. Finally, partial analysts tend to couch their normative conclusions in descriptive terms. For example, the bases for Murray's conclusion that there are no "inherent" differences between public and private management are carefully selected illustrations, which suggest that the similarities are many and clear-cut and the distinctions increasingly blurred—matters of degree or more sentiment than fact.

In contrast, a holistic approach argues that the management of organizations cannot be adequately understood by looking only at the parts, because the whole is greater than the sum of the parts. In particular, different organizational contexts dictate different means and ends, which, while they may be similar in particular details, are vastly different when viewed in toto. For example, the public's attitude toward government, which swings from the slightly negative to the highly negative, is a crucial contextual factor affecting government management. It creates demands and constraints on public managers unlike those found in the private sector. Public attitudes seriously affect the public manager's self-image, motivation, ability to generate external support, to recruit, promote, and retain qualified personnel, and to carry out programmatic missions effectively.

A third perspective on the similarities and differences between public and private management involves the weighting of similarities and differences. The central question is not whether similarities and differences exist, or whether they number about the same, but: Are the similarities more important than the differences?

Both Murray and Allison identify certain general management functions that are similar in the public and private sector. Both analysts further agree that these functions—planning, organizing, staffing, directing, coordinating, reporting, and budgeting (or some similar classification)—bear identical labels but take on different meanings in public and private settings. But here Murray and Allison part company. For Allison, these different meanings are critical differences that outweigh the similarities. As evidence for his view, Allison cites the testimony of general managers in both business and government: "All judge public management different from private management—and harder!" Moreover, he reviews in detail several orthogonal lists of dimensions that illustrate "critical" differences. For one of the simplest dimensions, time perspective, he notes the following:

> Government managers tend to have relatively short time horizons dictated by political necessities and the political calendar, while private managers appear to take a longer time perspective oriented toward market developments, technological innovation and investment, and organization building [from John T. Dunlop's "impressionistic" comparison of business and government management].

> The private chief begins by looking forward a decade, or thereabouts, his likely span barring extraordinary troubles. The first-term President looks forward four years at most, with the fourth (and now even the third) year dominated by campaigning for re-election [from Neustadt's analysis of differences between corporate executive officers of major corporations and American presidents].

To Allison and others who are seeking to identify critical differences, these features are perceived as having a considerable impact on the overall character of management in the public sector. In contrast, when Murray considers his own list of differences between public and private management, he uniformly concludes that the differences are more a matter of appearance than reality, perception than fact, degree than real substance. To Murray and others of whom his perspective is representative, these differences are unimportant or increasingly blurred.

Another issue affecting conclusions about the similarities and differences between public and private management is whether the perspective reflects an analysis of the whole population or of specific cases. A case analyst finds cases or samples that illustrate a particular point of view. To the analyst concerned about generalization, the question more appropriately is whether these cases or samples are representative of the whole population and the distribution of organizations in the population.

John Dunlop (as cited by Allison) argues that "the real world of management is composed of distributions, rather than single undifferentiated forms, and there is an increasing variety of hybrids." Thus, organizations can rarely be separated into two homogeneous piles—one public and one private. For each major dimension of organization, specific entities can be located on a spectrum, and on many dimensions, organizations classified as predominantly public may overlap those classified as predominantly private. A failure to recognize this distributional quality has led some case analysts, such as Murray, to move from an instance of management similarity between two organizations, one public and one private, to general propositions about management similarities between public and private institutions.

As noted by Rainey, Backoff, and Levine, the current body of research on organizations does not contain the penetrating comparisons, within or across business and government organizations, that would confirm or disconfirm such general propositions. The two disciplines that have dominated organization research—organization behavior and political science—have contributed to this state of affairs. Organizational analysts have tended to approach the study of public and private management by focusing on parts, processes, and samples, whereas political analysts have tended to focus on wholes, outcomes, and distributions. It is hardly surprising that the current body of research provides little conclusive evidence for or against basic similarities and differences within public and private management, much less between these two broad categories.

5 | Comparing Public and Private Management: An Exploratory Essay

Michael A. Murray

Historically in America two different institutional approaches to management science have developed: one in the private sector and one in the public sector. This dual development, however, has not gone unchallenged. For perhaps two generations scholars and practitioners have realized that management can be viewed as a generic process, with universal implications and with application in any institutional setting—whether a private firm or a public agency. More recently, on the assumption that public and private management have much to share, a new body of literature has developed around the idea of general management. Especially significant, entire new management schools are being founded on the generic model. The historic "separate but equal" doctrine is being challenged by a nascent integrationist movement.

Like the movement in the race area, however, the integrationist policy is not progressing with "due speed." There are many reasons for this. One is the traditional mistrust or misunderstanding between the public and private practitioner. Another is the perceived threat which the merger poses to free-standing schools of business and to schools of public administration. A more significant reason perhaps, is the lack of development of the concept that public and private management have points in common. If one examines the literature, or pages through the brochures of the new schools of management, there is little specific comparative analysis that is discussion of points where public and private management converge or diverge.

The important question then is what are the areas of comparison; and what specifically are the similarities and differences? In short, are public and private management comparable?

· · · ·

I. SUBSTANTIVE ISSUES: INHERENT CONFLICT OR NATURAL CONGRUENCE?

■ 5 ■
Michael A. Murray

The key substantive issue is whether there is an inherent conflict between the rational, private management model with its criteria of economic efficiency and the political public management model with its criteria of consensus and compromise. Obviously these are idealized types and this perhaps is the first and most important point to be made.

Fact vs. Value: The Context of Decision Making

Although conventional taxonomy divides society into two sectors, public and private, the actual similarities between a business firm and a government organization are increasingly apparent. In any complex organization, "defining purposes and objectives, planning, organizing, selecting managers, managing and motivating people, controlling and measuring results, and using a variety of analytical, problem solving and managerial techniques ... are essential."[1] The point is that these elements are relevant in any complex organization and are common aspects of a universal or generic management process, whether in the private or the public sector.

But are they the same? That is, are similar activities comparable even though the institutional setting differs? In his famous discussion of fact and value, Herbert Simon argued no. Simon argued that the means of administration (the facts) are quite different from the ends (the values). To ignore this central difference, he said, is to ignore the importance of the end or value as the major independent variable. The inference is that the values of the public sector, aimed at consensus, are different than the values of the private sector, aimed at profits. Hence, it is a misrepresentation to say that the value, or the context of the decision, is not important. What is important in the managerial relationship is not the tool, the means, but the context of the decision, the ends. If the context is different, then the values are different, and thus the application and function of the tool is different. In brief, Simon argued that the *process* of management has a value component itself and that fact cannot be separated from value.[2]

Many public administrators cite this argument as evidence of the chasm separating public administration and business administration. But as Norton Long has pointed out, Simon's distinction between fact and value has one fatal flaw. "It does not accord with the facts of administrative life."[3] Though the quest for scientific distinctions has a psychological appeal, it runs the risk of becoming ivory tower escapism.[4] The same can be said of Simon's implication that business and government administration are different. Built on the sandy base of logical positivism, Simon's argument derives from formal distinctions and ignores the *informal* mix between public and private activities. There is another problem with Simon's argument. Even if we accept his distinction between fact and value, the question remains: are the ends of government and business different?

Profits vs. Politics

To ask whether the values of the private sector differ from the objectives of the public sector is to ask a large question and a normative question; a question surrounded by a great deal of controversy. The issues will not be resolved

PART THREE
IS PUBLIC
MANAGEMENT
SIMILAR TO OR
DIFFERENT FROM
PRIVATE
MANAGEMENT?

in this paper, but the question remains: Are the differences real or superficial?

To begin, the notion that profits are the sole or main reason for the existence of private business is itself misleading. First of all, profits are an essential requirement for existence; but the focus on profits as the single objective distorts or minimizes other advantageous business activities such as products, services, employment, and all of the "hidden hand" effects of community and social contribution. A second point is that, while profits are a handy measure, benefits and costs do not always lend themselves to a monetary judgment of effectiveness.[5]

On the other hand, to say that profits are never the objective of public sector activities is equally misleading. Government projects are notoriously subject to cost-benefit analysis, and efficiency in government is a by-word of bureaucrats. Once stereotypes are discarded, similarities emerge.

To carry the argument further, however, a distinction made is that the criteria of political decisions are based on objectives of compromise, consensus, and democratic participation, and that these are quite different from the private sector objectives of efficiency, rationality, and profit or product maximization. But this also is an idealized type. As Theodore Levitt argues, "The culture of private bureaucracies is ... basically the same as that of public bureaucracies...."[6] That is, the desire for personal power and security is the same; responsiveness to outside pressures is the same. In short, once general priorities are established, private and public bureaucracies operate about the same.

Are the Objectives Measurable?

Beyond the abstract question of whether rational man differs from political man, the issue is whether objectives in the public and private areas are capable of comparison. The problem arises because objectives in the private sector often can be reduced to clear, concise, and quantifiable statements. Many public organizations must deal in social intangibles such as the right to privacy, increased political participation, or improving quality of life. Those are difficult to articulate in any clear specific way.

One example of this is the notion of divisible and indivisible services. In the private area goods and services can be purchased on an individual basis. Hence they can be defined and delivered in specific tangible ways. In the public sector many services such as clean air, decent housing, and adequate education are indivisible in the sense that these are communal services which increasingly have to be "purchased" jointly. Hence the problem of individual values has to be stated in the general terms of social choice. Such a conceptualization can only be stated in generalizations.[7]

Which One Is Better: The Normative Issue

Another normative argument is that the modern technologies of business administration are somehow superior to the less systematic and structured tools of the public sector. Indeed the popular disdain toward the public sector is reflected in choice of terms. For example, we often use the term management when referring to private business, but substitute the term administration when talking of public organizations. In part this reflects the acceptance of the private enterprise ethic in our social labels. In part it reflects the less attractive position of the public service in a country where for the past century industrialization was the most exciting thing happening. Recently some of this has changed.

Perhaps because of the Depression, but certainly dating from that point, the myth of the well-managed firm has been challenged. The legend of private efficiency lives in company brochures but is seldom realized in the lives of millions of Americans who fight the daily battle with insurance agencies or auto mechanics or TV repairmen. As early as 1945 the dean of public administration, Paul Appleby, argued that the alleged superiority of business represented a gross over-generalization which did not withstand close analysis.[8] Today we can ask the same kinds of comparative questions as 30 years ago. Is business less corrupt than government? Are public administrators less moral than business executives? Is fiscal management better in the aerospace industry than it is in Health, Education, and Welfare? The point is that what we find overall are more similarities than differences; a blending and mix between public and private. Neither sector has a corner on the morals market.

Government Attitudes vs. Business Attitudes

In the end many of these normative issues are related to questions of attitude. This is a central point in the comparative literature: "that the dissimilarity between government and all other forms of social action is greater than any similarity among those other forms themselves," and that the major difference is one of attitude.[9]

Today we are beginning to question even this attitudinal difference. For example, is it true that former businessmen cannot adjust to the chaotic world of government? The fact is that some can and some cannot, but generalizations do not hold. Likewise, it is inaccurate to say that all public officials are non-materialistic do-gooders who disdain the profit motive. These are obviously stereotypes which do not fit the facts. In short, in a democracy there is a great deal of consensus on values and norms; and attitudes between businessmen and career bureaucrats are not necessarily contradictory. More and more old stereotypes are being challenged. Nonetheless, these attitudinal, normative issues are difficult to resolve. Hence, we turn to more specific criteria for comparison.

II. PROCEDURAL ISSUES: IS MANAGEMENT A UNIVERSAL PROCESS?

In a procedural context, management might be defined as any activity or behavior concerned mainly with the means for carrying out prescribed ends. Although the ends of the business sector and government agencies might be different, often the means of achieving these ends are quite similar. These common procedural elements or aspects permit academics and practitioners to view management as a universal process.

But is it? We know from Part I that there are important distinctions between public and private values and objectives. Do these substantive differences affect procedural matters as well? Or are we so conditioned to examining the boundaries of things that we miss the thing itself?

63

PART THREE
IS PUBLIC
MANAGEMENT
SIMILAR TO OR
DIFFERENT FROM
PRIVATE
MANAGEMENT?

The Accountability Factor: The Goldfish Bowl vs. The Closed Board Room

Almost 50 years ago John Dewey said that the line between public and private "is to be drawn on the basis of the extent and scope of the consequences of acts which are so important as to need control...."[10] Consequences which affect only those directly involved in the transaction are private. Consequences which affect others beyond those immediately concerned are public, and need to be regulated.

In this concept of consequence and regulation we find the germ of the procedural difference between public and private management. What Dewey is saying, and what others have said before and after, is that the key distinction between the public and private sectors is the accountability factor, the degree to which the institution is responsible to others for its actions.

The argument is that the business sector operates in relative, although not complete, autonomy and perhaps secrecy; free of the checks and balances of the public arena. The public sector, on the other hand, is subject to the pressure of the press and to public scrutiny, it operates in a "goldfish bowl."

For example, government's susceptibility to public criticism is sometimes carried to extremes, and at the very least complicates public management and brings into play organizational forms and methods of accountability which explain many of the differences between public and private administration. An example of this is the public corporation. In creating such corporations, government intended to establish businesslike agencies that would permit government institutions to provide services in a modern businesslike manner. But because of the political environment in which public agencies function, guidelines and measures were introduced, aimed mainly at establishing fiscal accountability, which undercut the principal advantages of the corporation device.

This is the point repeated in the literature, that government administration differs from all other administrative work because it is subject to public scrutiny and outcry. Every change in government has to be thought about in terms of the possible public agitation resulting from it.[11]

But in the past quarter century conditions have changed. As Daniel Bell argues, in the postindustrial society every organization is politicized, including the private firm. A specific change is increase in public regulation of the so-called "private firm." The regulation of air and water pollution is only one example; automobile safety and airline schedules are others. In an age of communal pressure and political mobilization even private firms are not dispensed from public scrutiny. The line between public and private has blurred, and today the businessman faces as much public as the public official. Consider the fact that bureaucrats often operate in relative privacy while businessmen squirm under the glare of the public eye.

Evaluation Techniques: Social Good and Fiscal Control

A second comparison concerns the application of evaluation techniques. Simplified, the argument is as follows. In the private sector it is quite easy to go to the bottom line and determine whether the firm or organization is measuring up to its organizational goal. This can be translated very easily in terms of profits and losses.

In the public sector, even though modern, businesslike fiscal control techniques are utilized, they are less easily transferable to public "social good" questions. A good example of this might be the popular pressure to apply cost-benefit analysis to War on Poverty programs. As proponents of the community action program argued, some of the objectives of the War on Poverty were to reverse apathy and powerlessness, the chief characteristics of the poor. This meant designing political mobilization activities to counter-condition long-range and inbred psychological attitudes of shiftlessness and withdrawal; to generate feelings of pride and involvement. Such psychological or intrapsychic reflections of economic disparity are often difficult, if not impossible, to measure in terms of traditional or even modern businesslike techniques. Recall the debate of a few years ago when OEO officials complained that *economic* cost-accounting tools were irrelevant to measuring the long-range *political* goals of the poverty program.

This "bottom line" distinction has other implications. It also means, for example, that government and public agencies do not have that measure of achievement which the business sector enjoys. Without clear standards of government performance often public administration results in sloppy or irrational activities. Things slide along often to the detriment of accountability. The point is that it is very difficult in the public sector to clarify objectives and then to apply the sophisticated, precise tools of profit and loss to measure performance.

A final point, however, is that it is difficult to measure quality in both sectors and that the attempt to apply fiscal control simply represents a first step in developing science in either sector.

Criteria of Decision Making: Rational Man vs. Political Man

Although decision making is the basic operation of management, it has been argued that this operation varies in the public and private sectors. For example, even though the *formal steps* in decision making are technically the same (definition of problem, outlining options, crystallizing preferred response, allocating resources, etc.), the *criteria* of decision making are different. That is, the logic, or mode of thinking, the movement from point to point, is different. In a word, it is often argued that the technology of decision making varies from private to public areas.

An understanding of the term technology is important here. As used in this paper, the term technology means "not simply a 'machine', but a systematic, disciplined approach to objectives, using a calculus of precision and measurement and a concept of system that are quite at variance with traditional and . . . intuitive modes."[12] The difference may be one of degree but the reality is that the systems approach has triumphed in the private sector while it is viewed with some distrust in the public sector.

There are several reasons for this. One is the fact that a technological conception of a problem limits the focus to those factors that can be expressed quantitatively and which fit certain models.[13] This encroachment of economics into intrinsically political processes is inherently contradictory. The emphasis, automatically, is on neatness and order versus social disorder; technical precision versus confusion and conflict; gestalt theories instead of ad hoc piecemeal fragmentation; efficient management versus "bumbling bureaucracy."[14] In short, the distinction is between a process of management

PART THREE
IS PUBLIC
MANAGEMENT
SIMILAR TO OR
DIFFERENT FROM
PRIVATE
MANAGEMENT?

based on criteria of economy, efficiency, and rational results, versus a process of decision making based on ideas of consensus, the broadest social good, and "muddling through."

Another reason why "technology" has been resisted in the public sector is the assumption that governmental problems are basically social in nature. Although many of society's pressing problems have been generated or aggravated by technological change and development (e.g., transportation problems, housing design), the technical solution is not automatically transferable. Referring to a range of social ills, Ida Hoos analogized that "calling upon an engineer to cure them is much like asking an economist to treat a heart ailment because the patient became ill over money matters."[15]

The counterpart is that whether or not technology, and particularly systems analysis, is appropriate to public decisions, it is in fact being applied. Some would say that Bertram Gross' fears about a new breed of technipols have been realized. In this sense, government has accepted business as its model and economics as its decision-making means. Hence, the theoretical differences in modes of public and private criteria may well be moot at this point.

Personnel Systems

In reflecting on comparisons between business and government, Paul H. Appleby argued:

> It is exceedingly difficult clearly to identify the factors which make government different from other activity in society. Yet this difference is a fact and I believe it to be so big a difference that the dissimilarity between government and all other forms of social action is greater than any dissimilarity among those other forms themselves. Without a willingness to recognize this fact, no one can even begin to discuss public affairs to any good profit or serious purpose.[16]

The single most determinative factor that Appleby identified was personnel. One aspect of this difference has to do with recruiting patterns; a second element has to do with socializing processes.

In the private sector candidates theoretically are recruited through formal credentialing systems. In the public sector, recruitment, especially for top-level positions, is often informal, ad hoc, and on a personal (who do you know) basis. At least this is the accepted notion. Realistically, it is difficult to say whether there is more or less nepotism in business than in government. Are appointments in government more or less a function of pull and privilege than in the business world? Obviously, it would be hard to prove the argument one way or the other.

With regard to differences in socialization, a number of points can be made. On the one hand, some observers view background as the critical variable. For example, some businessmen do poorly in government. They come into government service with strong personalities and are unable to adjust to situations which they cannot control. There is a contradiction between the businessman's attitude and government needs. The businessman sees his role as executive, as decision maker. Yet the reasons for bringing him into government may have been simply to coopt his support, to win legitimacy for policies made, or to seek his prestige in order to maintain national unity. These are political as opposed to business reasons.

On the other hand, businessmen have traditionally succeeded in government executive positions indicating that their skills are transferable. This is likely to continue especially given the current disaffection with the politician image. In fact, businessmen may, because of their supposed neutrality, be in even greater demand. The operational question is the reverse of this: whether ex-government people can shift into the private sector. On this score, there is some evidence that former administration officials are prime candidates for top corporate positions and that public experience is not an undesirable reference.

Planning

Planning is an activity common to both the public and private sectors. Although the term refers generally to the process of uniting ideas with action, it needs to be analyzed in its specific institutional setting.

There are two ways to view planning: as a process of decision making or as a means of control. In terms of process, planning means lateral consultation, sharing of information, discussion of short- and long-range objectives. It implies a participatory process in order to come up with mutually satisfactory goals.

Planning as a means of control refers to a system of gathering information and marshalling available resources in a sequential priority framework in order to maximize agreed-upon objectives.

The advantages and disadvantages of each approach have been discussed elsewhere.[17] The question for this article is whether one mode is used more in business or in public. As in many of the areas discussed, distinctions blur when applied to actual situations. Consider the fact that the vital circumstances surrounding any planning effort are intangible, ad hoc, and uncertain. In both the public sector and the private sector this is evidenced by the first impulse of planners, to "get more, or better, data." Planning is an eclectic science with no distinct theoretical base. As such it is hardly a precise science. It is true that planners seem more common in government circles than in private firms. But this may be simply a matter of labels, i.e., calling the corporate finance officer financial analyst instead of resident planner, or calling the city planner by that title instead of research associate. In either area planning is at best a secondary function, and the point is that in actual situations the process of planning appears to be the same.

The Efficiency Question

Too much has been written on the subject of government waste and business efficiency for this article to dispel any widespread notions. But a few comments are in order.

If one accepts the notion that the business of government is politics (the allocation of authority for a society) and that the goal is not efficiency by resolution of conflict, then it is impossible to say that government is less efficient than business.

There are three important points to be made. First, in terms of efficiency it is difficult to compare the two areas. It is the old apples and oranges problem. Is the Supreme Court less efficient in protecting the first amendment than General Motors is in producing cars? Is Boeing Aircraft more efficient in what

PART THREE
IS PUBLIC
MANAGEMENT
SIMILAR TO OR
DIFFERENT FROM
PRIVATE
MANAGEMENT?

it does than TVA is in producing electricity? To go even further, it is difficult to make comparisons within a particular area, public or private. For example, in the so-called private sector, is the *New York Times* more or less efficient in producing news than the Chicago Bears organization is in producing entertainment? The point is obvious: If this quantity efficiency cannot easily be measured within one supposedly similar area, then how are comparisons to be made between different areas?

There is a second point. In government what appears to be inefficiency is sometimes essential to the public purpose of the agency. For example, millions of dollars spent every year on public scrutiny of government activities operates in the public interest, and the net effect is to make the agency more efficient in terms of its central purpose which is political responsiveness.

The third point is that in terms of efficiency the private sector is not without criticism; business has its share of horror stories. The facts emerging from the aerospace industry belie the notion of rational, efficient operations in private industry. Efficiency and waste it seems are more a matter of case-by-case analysis than across-the-board generalizations.

Theoretically similar principles of hierarchic control, comprehensive coordination, the rule of merit, and line of authority apply in both the public and private sectors. A word on each of these is in order.

With regard to the principle of hierarchic control, the theory of the scalar process, or the application of superior-subordinate relationship is honored in every formal organizational chart but seldom in fact. This applies to the private sector myth of "chairman of the board" and to the ceremonial role of the "agency director" in public affairs. In either case the head is often a ceremonial figure with political as opposed to operational duties.

Coordination, a second principle, means the rational allocation of resources to meet needs and depends on two factors: (1) definition of need, and (2) availability of resources. Coordination is, however, a similar process in any operation since it relates to maximization of agency goals.

The rule of merit is protected by informal systems, as well as by formal codes and contracts in both the public and private sectors, but it is violated with equal impunity in either area. The temporary assignment in the civil service has as its counterpart the position of management consultant in private industry.

Another principle is that authority should be commensurate with responsibility. This is the cardinal rule of management and a central objective of public and private practitioners. The fact that it remains a central objective underscores its absence in either area.

Conclusion

1. Substantive Issues: More Blurring Than Bifurcation

The large issue, the central question, is whether public and private management are inherently different. Based on this exploratory survey of the issues, the answer is a cautious no, not at this time. In Daniel Bell's postindustrial society, characterized by a diffusion of goods, there may be a growth of public

Peak; or divide in two

decision making which so overwhelms the free market as to radically alter the society. As yet this has not happened. The situation that seems to be evolving is a mixture of public-private, government-market decision making with a blurring of the lines rather than a distinct bifurcation of responsibilities. This is reflected in the analysis of the substantive areas like objective setting and evaluation techniques. Few lasting differences were found. For example, the central issue of different value systems seems to be more a difference of degree and emphasis than of substance. Politics conditions judgment in both areas; private decisions transcend immediate application in either sector. Boundaries between public and private activity seem to be blurring. At any rate, in areas such as attitudes and values it will require a good deal more behavioral research to establish the fact of difference as opposed to the sentiment of difference.

2. Procedural Issues: Distinctions Not Differences

As Justice Holmes once remarked to a lawyer making a fine legal point: That's a distinction, but not a difference. The same dictum applies to the survey of procedural areas. For example, in the area of ethics it is true that the public sector conduct is characterized by clear, formal, even legal guidelines (the Constitution, conflict of interest laws, etc.). It is also true that these laws are honored as much in the breach as in the fact. In the private sector, although pressures and constraints may be informal, studies have shown that private executives are extremely sensitive to the appearance of ethical behavior. Some argue that this has led to a conformist type mentality in the private sector. At any rate, ethical questions seem to be reemerging as legitimate issues in either sector and where differences exist they are formal and superficial, i.e., legalistic in nature. In actual practice this difference dissipates.

3. Apples and Oranges

A third conclusion has to do with the "apples and oranges" syndrome of comparing unlike objects. On the question of efficiency, for example, it is impossible to match political efficiency with economic efficiency. One must judge one agency's political efficiency with another agency's political efficiency, and so on. It is unfair and illogical to use the efficiency criterion alone and apply it to the public and private sectors.

4. Myths and Sentiments

A fourth conclusion is that some of our most cherished and popular myths do not hold up under cold analysis. For example, is private management superior to public administration in terms of waste management? Not by aerospace industry standards. Is the public sector run more openly and democratically? Not if public sentiment and recent criminal cases against officials is any measure. The view of "big bureaucracy" as a mismanaged monolith is as unrealistic as the view of business as a social rip off. The law of variations tells us that the situation differs as management practice varies—from case to case.

5. The Primacy of Method

The essential issue it seems is not what procedural or substantive distinctions or differences exist, but what *management tools* are applied to problem

69

PART THREE
IS PUBLIC
MANAGEMENT
SIMILAR TO OR
DIFFERENT FROM
PRIVATE
MANAGEMENT?

solving, whether in the public or the private sector. The choice of tools and models is the critical intervening variable between the definition of the problem and the crystallization of a policy. With regard to public-private activities it is clear that what may be acceptable in the private sector in the technical sense may be completely unsatisfactory in the public area where social questions cannot be subordinated to technical approaches.

The issue, of course, is only part of a larger question facing a society enamored of systems approaches, and empirical models and quick technological solutions. As suggested above, it may be too late to raise the issue; the public sector already relies on modern technical solutions to a great degree. Ida Hoos has noted:

> The main myths in the business world that most needed exploration and explosion have become doxology in government circles, with critical inquiry tantamount to heresy. Indeed, he who has the temerity to raise questions runs the risk of being considered not only anachronistically and iconoclastically unscientific but probably a bit subversive and un-American as well.[18]

At the risk of being unpatriotic, it is this reckless application of cheap, visible, quantitative solutions to social problems which poses the greatest threat to problem solving and ultimately to harmonious interface between the public and private sectors. As Robert Merton has said:

> The technician sees the nation quite differently from the political man: to the technician, the nation is nothing more than another sphere in which to apply the instruments he has developed. To him, the state is not the expression of the will of the people nor a divine creation nor a creature of class conflict. It is an enterprise providing services that must be made to function *efficiently*.[19]

Or as others have said: data does not automatically solve problems; human beings, with the help of data, are capable of problem solving.

Rather than conceptualizing management in the public sector as an extension of private sector practices and values, this article points toward an increasing convergence in management processes in the public and private sectors. Traditional barriers and distinctive patterns in decision making and goal definition are breaking down. While prevailing ideal-type models stress the uniqueness of public organizations as opposed to private organizations, this article argues that in the post industrial society, which is emerging in the U.S., the old distinctions are no longer operational. Both in the handling of substantive issues and procedural matters, actual management practices point to a blurring of public and private sectors rather than to a bifurcation. Public and private management procedures, operations, and goals cannot be viewed as separate processes.

NOTES

[1]Fredric H. Genck, "Public Management in America," *AACSB Bulletin,* Vol. 9, No. 3 (April 1973), p. 6.

[2]Herbert A. Simon, *Administrative Behavior* (New York: Macmillan, 1949).

[3]Norton Long, "Public Policy and Administration: The Goals of Rationality and Responsibility," *Public Administration Review,* Vol. 14, No. 1 (Winter 1954), p. 22.

[4]Ibid.

[5]Genck, op. cit., p. 7.

[6]Theodore Levitt, *The Third Sector* (New York: Amacom, 1973), pp. 28–29.

[7]See *The Future of the American Government*, Daniel Pearlman (ed.) (Boston: Houghton Mifflin, 1968), especially foreword by Daniel Bell.

[8]Paul H. Appleby, *Big Democracy* (New York: Knopf, 1945), pp. 50–51.

[9]Ibid., p. 1.

[10]John Dewey, *The Public and Its Problems* (New York, 1927), p. 15.

[11]Appleby, op. cit.

[12]Daniel Bell, "Trajectory of an Idea," in *Toward the Year 2000*, Daniel Bell (ed.) (Boston: Houghton Mifflin, 1968), p. 5.

[13]Ida R. Hoos, *Systems Analysis in Public Policy: A Critique* (Berkeley: University of California Press, 1972), p. 26.

[14]Ibid., p. 89.

[15]Ibid., p. 24.

[16]Appleby, op. cit., p. 1.

[17]Aaron Wildavsky, *The Politics of the Budgetary Process* (Boston: Little, Brown, 1964), especially chap. 5.

[18]Hoos, op. cit., p. 196.

[19]Quoted in Frank Trippet, "The Shape of Things as They Really Are," *Intellectual Digest* (December 1972), p. 28.

6

Public and Private Management: Are They Fundamentally Alike in All Unimportant Respects?

Graham T. Allison, Jr.

My subtitle puts Wallace Sayre's oft-quoted "law" as a question. Sayre had spent some years in Ithaca helping plan Cornell's new School of Business and Public Administration. He left for Columbia with this aphorism: Public and private management are fundamentally alike in all unimportant respects.

Sayre based his conclusion on years of personal observation of governments, a keen ear for what his colleagues at Cornell (and earlier at OPA) said about business, and a careful review of the literature and data comparing public and private management. Of the latter there was virtually none. Hence, Sayre's provocative "law" was actually an open invitation to research.

Unfortunately, in the 50 years since Sayre's pronouncement, the data base for systematic comparison of public and private management has improved little. Consequently, when Scotty Campbell called six weeks ago to inform me that I would make some remarks at this conference, we agreed that I would, in effect, take up Sayre's invitation to *speculate* about similarities and differences among public and private management in ways that suggest significant opportunities for systematic investigation.

To reiterate: This paper is not a report of a major research project or systematic study. Rather, it is a response to a request for a brief summary of reflections of a dean of a school of government who now spends his time doing a form of public management—managing what Jim March has labeled an "organized anarchy"—rather than thinking, much less writing.[1] Moreover, the speculation here will appear to reflect a characteristic Harvard presumption that Cambridge either is the world, or is an adequate sample of the world. I say "appear" since as a North Carolinean, I am self-conscious about

This article was presented as part of the Public Management Research Conference, Brookings Institution, Washington, D.C., November 1979.

this parochialism. Nevertheless, I have concluded that the purposes of this conference may be better served by providing a deliberately parochial perspective on these issues—and thereby presenting a clear target for others to shoot at. Finally, I must acknowledge that this paper plagiarizes freely from a continuing discussion among my colleagues at Harvard about the development of the field of public management, especially from Joe Bower, Hale Champion, Gordon Chase, Charles Christenson, Richard Darman, John Dunlop, Phil Heymann, Larry Lynn, Mark Moore, Dick Neustadt, Roger Porter, and Don Price. Since my colleagues have not had the benefit of commenting on this presentation, I suspect I have some points wrong, or out of context, or without appropriate subtlety or amendment. Thus, I assume full liability for the words that follow.

This paper is organized as follows:

- Section 1 frames the issue: What is public management?

- Section 2 focuses on similarities: How are public and private management basically alike?

- Section 3 concentrates on differences: How do public and private management differ?

- Section 4 poses the question more operationally: How are the jobs and responsibilities of two specific managers, one public and one private, alike and different?

- Section 5 attempts to derive from this discussion suggestions about promising research directions and then outlines one research agenda and strategy for developing knowledge of and instruction about public management.

SECTION 1: FRAMING THE ISSUE
WHAT IS PUBLIC MANAGEMENT?

What is the meaning of the term "management" as it appears in Office of *Management* and Budget, or Office of Personnel *Management?* Is "management" different from, broader or narrower than "administration"? Should we distinguish between management, leadership, entrepreneurship, administration, policy making, and implementation?

Who are "public managers"? Mayors, governors, and presidents? City managers, secretaries, and commissioners? Bureau chiefs? Office directors? Legislators? Judges?

Recent studies of OPM and OMB shed some light on these questions. OPM's major study of the "Current Status of Public Management Research" completed in May 1978 by Selma Mushkin of Georgetown's Public Service Laboratory starts with this question. The Mushkin report notes the definition of "public management" employed by the Interagency Study Committee on Policy Management Assistance in its 1975 report to OMB. That study identified the following core elements:

1. *Policy management:* The identification of needs, analysis of options, selection of programs, and allocation of resources on a jurisdiction-wide basis.

PART THREE
IS PUBLIC
MANAGEMENT
SIMILAR TO OR
DIFFERENT FROM
PRIVATE
MANAGEMENT?

2. *Resource management:* The establishment of basic administrative support systems, such as budgeting, financial management, procurement and supply, and personnel management.

3. *Program management:* The implementation of policy or daily operation of agencies carrying out policy along functional lines (education, law enforcement, etc.).[2]

The Mushkin report rejects this definition in favor of an "alternative list of public management elements." These elements are:

- Personnel Management (other than work force planning and collective bargaining and labor management relations)
- Work Force Planning
- Collective Bargaining and Labor Management Relations
- Productivity and Performance Measurement
- Organization/Reorganization
- Financial Management (including the management of intergovernmental relations)
- Evaluation Research, and Program and Management Audit.[3]

Such terminological tangles seriously hamper the development of public management as a field of knowledge. In our efforts to discuss public management curriculum at Harvard, I have been struck by how differently people use these terms, how strongly many individuals feel about some distinction they believe is marked by a difference between one word and another, and consequently, how large a barrier terminology is to convergent discussion. These verbal obstacles virtually prohibit conversation that is both brief and constructive among individuals who have not developed a common language or a mutual understanding of each others' use of terms. (What this point may imply for this conference, I leave to the reader.)

This terminological thicket reflects a more fundamental conceptual confusion. There exists no overarching framework that orders the domain. In an effort to get a grip on the phenomena—the buzzing, blooming confusion of people in jobs performing tasks that produce results—both practitioners and observers have strained to find distinctions that facilitate their work. The attempts in the early decades of this century to draw a sharp line between "policy" and "administration," like more recent efforts to mark a similar divide between "policy making" and "implementation," reflect a common search for a simplification that allows one to put the value-laden issues of politics to one side (who gets what, when, and how), and focus on the more limited issue of how to perform tasks more efficiently.[4] But can anyone really deny that the "how" substantially affects the "who," the "what," and the "when"? The basic categories now prevalent in discussions of public management—strategy, personnel management, financial management, and control—are mostly derived from a business context in which executives manage hierarchies. The fit of these concepts to the problems that confront public managers is not clear.

Finally, there exist no ready data on what public managers do. Instead, the academic literature, such as it is, mostly consists of speculation tied to bits and pieces of evidence about the tail or the trunk or other manifestation of the proverbial elephant.[5] In contrast to the literally thousands of cases describing problems faced by private managers and their practice in solving these problems, case research from the perspective of a public manager is just beginning.[6] ... But the paucity of data on the phenomena inhibits systematic empirical research on similarities and differences between public and private management, leaving the field to a mixture of reflection on personal experience and speculation.

For the purpose of this presentation, I will follow Webster and use the term management to mean the organization and direction of resources to achieve a desired result. I will focus on *general managers,* that is, individuals charged with managing a whole organization or multifunctional subunit. I will be interested in the general manager's full responsibilities, both *inside* his organization in integrating the diverse contributions of specialized subunits of the organization to achieve results, and *outside* his organization in relating his organization and its product to external constituencies. I will begin with the simplifying assumption that managers of traditional government organizations are public managers, and managers of traditional private businesses, private managers. Lest the discussion fall victim to the fallacy of misplaced abstraction, I will take the Director of EPA and the Chief Executive Officer of American Motors as, respectively, public and private managers. Thus, our central question can be put concretely: In what ways are the jobs and responsibilities of Doug Costle as Director of EPA similar to and different from those of Roy Chapin as Chief Executive Officer of American Motors?

SECTION 2: SIMILARITIES:
HOW ARE PUBLIC AND PRIVATE MANAGEMENT ALIKE?

At one level of abstraction, it is possible to identify a set of general management functions. The most famous such list appeared in Gulick and Urwick's classic *Papers in the Science of Administration.*[7] Gulick summarized the work of the chief executive in the acronym POSDCORB. The letters stand for:

- Planning
- Organizing
- Staffing
- Directing
- Coordinating
- Reporting
- Budgeting

With various additions, amendments, and refinements, similar lists of general management functions can be found through the management literature from Barnard to Drucker.[8]

I shall resist here my natural academic instinct to join the intramural debate among proponents of various lists and distinctions. Instead, I simply offer one composite list (see Table 6-1) that attempts to incorporate the major functions that have been identified for general managers, whether public or private.

These common functions of management are not isolated and discrete, but rather integral components separated here for purposes of analysis. The character and relative significance of the various functions differ from one time to another in the history of any organization, and between one organization and another. But whether in a public or private setting, the challenge for the general manager is to integrate all these elements so as to achieve results.

SECTION 3: DIFFERENCES: HOW ARE PUBLIC AND PRIVATE MANAGEMENT DIFFERENT?

While there is a level of generality at which management is management, whether public or private, functions that bear identical labels take on rather different meaning in public and private settings. As Larry Lynn has pointed

out, one powerful piece of evidence in the debate between those who emphasize "similarities" and those who underline "differences" is the nearly unani-
mous conclusion of individuals who have been general managers in both
business and government. Consider the reflections of George Shultz (former
Director of OMB, Secretary of Labor, Secretary of the Treasury; now President of Bechtel), Donald Rumsfeld (former congressman, Director of OEO,
Director of the Cost of Living Council, White House Chief of Staff, and
Secretary of Defense; now President of GD Searle and Company), Michael
Blumenthal (former Chairman and Chief Executive Officer of Bendix, Secretary of the Treasury, and now Vice Chairman of Burrows), Roy Ash (former
President of Litton Industries, Director of OMB; now President of Addresso-
graph), Lyman Hamilton (former Budget Officer in BOB, High Commissioner
of Okinawa, Division Chief in the World Bank and President of ITT), and
George Romney (former President of American Motors, Governor of Michigan and Secretary of Housing and Urban Development).[9] All judge public
management different from private management—and harder!

Three Orthogonal Lists of Differences

My review of these recollections, as well as the thoughts of academics, has
identified three interesting, orthogonal lists that summarize the current state
of the field: one by John Dunlop; one major *Public Administration Review*
survey of the literature comparing public and private organizations by Hal
Rainey, Robert Backoff, and Charles Levine; and one by Richard E. Neustadt
prepared for the National Academy of Public Administration's Panel on Presidential Management.

John T. Dunlop's "impressionistic comparison of government management
and private business" yields the following contrasts.[10]

1. *Time perspective:* Government managers tend to have relatively short
   time horizons dictated by political necessities and the political calendar,
   while private managers appear to take a longer time perspective oriented toward market developments, technological innovation and investment, and organization building.

2. *Duration:* The length of service of politically appointed top government managers is relatively short, averaging no more than 18 months
   recently for assistant secretaries, while private managers have a longer
   tenure both in the same position and in the same enterprise. A recognized element of private business management is the responsibility to
   train a successor or several possible candidates while the concept is
   largely alien to public management since fostering a successor is perceived to be dangerous.

3. *Measurement of performance:* There is little if any agreement on the
   standards and measurement of performance to appraise a government
   manager, while various tests of performance—financial return, market
   share, performance measures for executive compensation—are well
   established in private business and often made explicit for a particular
   managerial position during a specific period ahead.

4. *Personnel constraints:* In government there are two layers of managerial officials that are at times hostile to one another: the civil service (or

PART THREE
IS PUBLIC
MANAGEMENT
SIMILAR TO OR
DIFFERENT FROM
PRIVATE
MANAGEMENT?

now the executive system) and the political appointees. Unionization of government employees exists among relatively high-level personnel in the hierarchy and includes a number of supervisory personnel. Civil service, union contract provisions, and other regulations complicate the recruitment, hiring, transfer, and layoff or discharge of personnel to achieve managerial objectives or preferences. By comparison, private business managements have considerably greater latitude, even under collective bargaining, in the management of subordinates. They have much more authority to direct the employees of their organization. Government personnel policy and administration are more under the control of staff (including civil service staff outside an agency) compared to the private sector in which personnel are much more subject to line responsibility.

5. *Equity and efficiency:* In governmental management great emphasis tends to be placed on providing equity among different constituencies, while in private business management relatively greater stress is placed upon efficiency and competitive performance.

6. *Public processes versus private processes:* Governmental management tends to be exposed to public scrutiny and to be more open, while private business management is more private and its processes more internal and less exposed to public review.

7. *Role of press and media:* Governmental management must contend regularly with the press and media; its decisions are often anticipated by the press. Private decisions are less often reported in the press, and the press has a much smaller impact on the substance and timing of decisions.

8. *Persuasion and direction:* In government, managers often seek to mediate decisions in response to a wide variety of pressures and must often put together a coalition of inside and outside groups to survive. By contrast, private management proceeds much more by direction or the issuance of orders to subordinates by superior managers with little risk of contradiction. Governmental managers tend to regard themselves as responsive to many superiors while private managers look more to one higher authority.

9. *Legislative and judicial impact:* Governmental managers are often subject to close scrutiny by legislative oversight groups or even judicial orders in ways that are quite uncommon in private business management. Such scrutiny often materially constrains executive and administrative freedom to act.

10. *Bottom line:* Governmental managers rarely have a clear bottom line, while that of a private business manager is profit, market performance, and survival.

Second, the *Public Administration Review's* major review article comparing public and private organizations, by Rainey, Backoff, and Levine, attempts to summarize the major points of consensus in the literature on similarities and differences among public and private organizations.[11] [Their summary is presented in Table 7-1 on pages 96–97.]

Third, Richard E. Neustadt, in a fashion close to Dunlop's, notes six major differences between Presidents of the United States and Chief Executive Officers of major corporations.[12]

1. *Time horizon:* The private chief begins by looking forward a decade, or thereabouts, his likely span barring extraordinary troubles. The first-term President looks forward four years at most, with the fourth (and now even the third) year dominated by campaigning for reelection. (What second-termers look toward we scarcely know, having seen but one such term completed in the past quarter century.)

2. *Authority* over the enterprise. Subject to concurrence from the Board of Directors which appointed and can fire him, the private executive sets organization goals, shifts structures, procedure, and personnel to suit, monitors results, reviews key operational decisions, deals with key outsiders, and brings along his Board. Save for the deep but narrow sphere of military movements, a President's authority in these respects is shared with well-placed members of Congress (or their staffs); case by case, they may have more explicit authority than he does (contrast authorizations and appropriations with the "take-care" clause). As for "bringing along the Board," neither the Congressmen with whom he shares power or the primary and general electorates which "hired" him have either a Board's duties or a broad view of the enterprise precisely matching his.

3. *Career system:* The model corporation is a true career system, something like the Forest Service after initial entry. In normal times the chief himself is chosen from within, or he is chosen from another firm in the same industry. He draws department heads et al. from among those with whom he's worked, or whom he knows in comparable companies. He and his principal associates will be familiar with each other's roles—indeed he probably has had a number of them—and also usually with one another's operating styles, personalities, idiosyncrasies. Contrast the President who rarely has had much experience "downtown," probably knows little of most roles there (much of what he knows will turn out wrong), and less of most associates whom he appoints there, willy nilly, to fill places by Inauguration Day. Nor are they likely to know one another well, coming as they do from "everywhere" and headed as most are toward oblivion.

4. *Media relations:* The private executive represents his firm and speaks for it publicly in exceptional circumstances; he and his associates judge the exceptions. Those aside, he neither sees the press nor gives its members access to internal operations, least of all in his own office, save to make a point deliberately for public-relations purposes. The President, by contrast, is routinely on display, continuously dealing with the White House press and with the wider circle of political reporters, commentators, columnists. He needs them in his business, day by day, nothing exceptional about it, and they need him in theirs: the TV network news programs lead off with him some nights each week. They and the President are as mutually dependent as he and Congressmen (or more so). Comparatively speaking, these relations overshadow most administrative ones much of the time for him.

PART THREE
IS PUBLIC
MANAGEMENT
SIMILAR TO OR
DIFFERENT FROM
PRIVATE
MANAGEMENT?

5. *Performance measurement:* The private executive expects to be judged, and in turn to judge subordinates, by profitability, however the firm measures it (a major strategic choice). In practice, his Board may use more subjective measures; so may he, but at risk to morale and good order. The relative virtue of profit, of "the bottom line" is its legitimacy, its general acceptance in the business world by all concerned. Never mind its technical utility in given cases, its apparent "objectivity," hence "fairness," has enormous social usefulness: a myth that all can live by. For a President there is no counterpart (except *in extremis* the "smoking gun" to justify impeachment). The general public seems to judge a President, at least in part, by what its members think is happening to them, in their own lives; Congressmen, officials, interest groups appear to judge by what they guess, at given times, he can do for or to their causes. Members of the press interpret both of these and spread a simplified criterion affecting both, the legislative box-score, a standard of the press's own devising. The White House denigrates them all except when it does well.

6. *Implementation:* The corporate chief, supposedly, does more than choose a strategy and set a course of policy; he also is supposed to oversee what happens after, how in fact intentions turn into results, or if they don't to take corrective action, monitoring through his information system, acting, and if need be, through his personnel system. A President, by contrast, while himself responsible for budgetary proposals, too, in many spheres of policy, appears ill-placed and ill-equipped, to monitor what agencies of states, of cities, corporations, unions, foreign governments are up to or to change personnel in charge. Yet these are very often the executants of "his" programs. Apart from defense and diplomacy the federal government does two things in the main: It issues and applies regulations and it awards grants in aid. Where these are discretionary, choice usually is vested by statute in a Senate-confirmed official well outside the White House. Monitoring is his function, not the President's except at second-hand. And final action is the function of the subjects of the rules and funds; they mostly are not federal personnel at all. In defense, the arsenals and shipyards are gone; weaponry comes from the private sector. In foreign affairs it is the *other* governments whose actions we would influence. From implementors like these a President is far removed most of the time. He intervenes, if at all, on a crash basis, not through organizational incentives.

Underlying these lists' sharpest distinctions between public and private management is a fundamental *constitutional difference.* In business, the functions of general management are centralized in a single individual: the Chief Executive Officer. The goal is authority commensurate with responsibility. In contrast, in the U.S. government, the functions of general management are constitutionally spread among competing institutions: the executive, two houses of Congress, and the courts. The constitutional goal was "not to promote efficiency but to preclude the exercise of arbitrary power," as Justice Brandeis observed. Indeed, as *The Federalist Papers* make starkly clear, the aim was to create incentives to compete: "The great security against a gradual concentration of the several powers in the same branch, consists in giving those who administer each branch the constitutional means and personal motives to resist encroachment of the others. Ambition must be made to counteract ambition."[13] Thus, the general management functions concentrated in the CEO of a private business are, by constitutional design, spread in the public sector among a number of competing institutions and thus shared by a number of individuals whose ambitions are set against one another. For most areas of public policy today, these individuals include at the federal level the chief elected official, the chief appointed executive, the chief career official, and several congressional chieftains. Since most public services are actually delivered by state and local governments, with independent sources of authority, this means a further array of individuals at these levels.

SECTION 4: AN OPERATIONAL PERSPECTIVE: HOW ARE THE JOBS AND RESPONSIBILITIES OF DOUG COSTLE, DIRECTOR OF EPA, AND ROY CHAPIN, CEO OF AMERICAN MOTORS, SIMILAR AND DIFFERENT?

If organizations could be separated neatly into two homogeneous piles, one public and one private, the task of identifying similarities and differences between managers of these enterprises would be relatively easy. In fact, as Dunlop has pointed out, "the real world of management is composed of distributions, rather than single undifferentiated forms, and there is an increasing variety of hybrids." Thus for each major attribute of organizations, specific entities can be located on a spectrum. On most dimensions, organizations classified as "predominantly public" and those "predominantly private" overlap.[14] Private business organizations vary enormously among themselves in size, in management structure and philosophy, and in the constraints under which they operate. For example, forms of ownership and types of managerial control may be somewhat unrelated. Compare a family-held enterprise, for instance, with a public utility and a decentralized conglomerate, a Bechtel with ATT and Textron. Similarly, there are vast differences in management of governmental organizations. Compare the Government Printing Office or TVA or the Police Department of a small town with the Department of Energy or the Department of Health and Human Services. These distributions and varieties should encourage penetrating comparisons within both business and governmental organizations, as well as contrasts and comparisons across these broad categories, a point to which we shall return in considering directions for research.

Absent a major research effort, it may nonetheless be worthwhile to examine the jobs and responsibilities of two specific managers, neither polar extremes, but one clearly public, the other private. For this purpose, and primarily because of the availability of cases that describe the problems and opportunities each confronted, consider Doug Costle, Administrator of EPA, and Roy Chapin, CEO of American Motors.[15]

Doug Costle, Administrator of EPA, January 1977

The mission of EPA is prescribed by laws creating the agency and authorizing its major programs. That mission is "to control and abate pollution in the

PART THREE
IS PUBLIC
MANAGEMENT
SIMILAR TO OR
DIFFERENT FROM
PRIVATE
MANAGEMENT?

areas of air, water, solid wastes, noise, radiation, and toxic substances. EPA's mandate is to mount an integrated, coordinated attack on environmental pollution in cooperation with state and local governments."[16]

EPA's organizational structure follows from its legislative mandates to control particular pollutants in specific environments: air and water, solid wastes, noise, radiation, pesticides, and chemicals. As the new Administrator, Costle inherited the Ford Administration's proposed budget for EPA of $802 million for federal 1978 with a ceiling of 9,698 agency positions.

The setting into which Costle stepped is difficult to summarize briefly. As Costle characterized it:

- "Outside there is a confusion on the part of the public in terms of what this agency is all about: what it is doing, where it is going."

- "The most serious constraint on EPA is the inherent complexity in the state of our knowledge, which is constantly changing."

- "Too often, acting under extreme deadlines mandated by Congress, EPA has announced regulations, only to find out that they knew very little about the problem. The central problem is the inherent complexity of the job that the agency has been asked to do and the fact that what it is asked to do changes from day to day."

- "There are very difficult internal management issues not amenable to a quick solution: the skills mix problem within the agency; a research program with laboratory facilities scattered all over the country and cemented in place, largely by political alliances on the Hill that would frustrate efforts to pull together a coherent research program."

- "In terms of EPA's original mandate in the bulk pollutants we may be hitting the asymptotic part of the curve in terms of incremental clean-up costs. You have clearly conflicting national goals: energy and environment, for example."

Costle judged his six major tasks at the outset to be:

- Assembling a top management team (six assistant administrators and some 25 office heads);

- Addressing EPA's legislative agenda (EPA's basic legislative charter—the Clean Air Act and the Clean Water Act—were being rewritten as he took office; the pesticides program was up for reauthorization also in 1977);

- Establishing EPA's role in the Carter administration (aware that the administration would face hard tradeoffs between the environment and energy, energy regulations and the economy, EPA regulations of toxic substances and the regulations of FDA, CSPS, and OSHA. Costle identified the need to build relations with the other key players and to enhance EPA's standing);

- Building ties to constituent groups (both because of their role in legislating the agency's mandate and in successful implementation of EPA's programs);

- Making specific policy decisions (for example, whether to grant or deny a permit for the Seabrook Nuclear Generating Plant cooling system. Or how the Toxic Substance Control Act, enacted in October 1976, would be implemented: This act gave EPA new responsibilities for regulating the manufacture, distribution, and use of chemical substances so as to prevent unreasonable risks to health and the environment. Whether EPA would require chemical manufacturers to provide some minimum information on various substances, or require much stricter reporting requirements for the 1,000 chemical substances already known to be hazardous, or require companies to report all chemicals, and on what timetable, had to be decided and the regulations issued);

- Rationalizing the internal organization of the agency (EPA's extreme decentralization to the regions and its limited technical expertise).

No easy job.

Roy Chapin and American Motors, January 1977

In January 1967, in an atmosphere of crisis, Roy Chapin was appointed Chairman and Chief Executive Officer of American Motors (and William Luneburg, President and Chief Operating Officer). In the four previous years, AMC unit sales had fallen 37 percent and market share from over six percent to under three percent. Dollar volume in 1967 was off 42 percent from the all-time high of 1963 and earnings showed a net loss of $76 million on sales of $656 million. Columnists began writing obituaries for AMC. *Newsweek* characterized AMC as "a flabby dispirited company, a product solid enough but styled with about as much flair as corrective shoes, and a public image that melted down to one unshakeable label: loser." Said Chapin: "We were driving with one foot on the accelerator and one foot on the brake. We didn't know where the hell we were."

Chapin announced to his stockholders at the outset that "we plan to direct ourselves most specifically to those areas of the market where we can be fully effective. We are not going to attempt to be all things to all people, but to concentrate on those areas of consumer needs we can meet better than anyone else." As he recalled: "There were problems early in 1967 which demanded immediate attention, and which accounted for much of our time for several months. Nevertheless, we began planning beyond them, establishing objectives, programs and timetables through 1972. Whatever happened in the short run, we had to prove ourselves in the marketplace in the long run."

Chapin's immediate problems were five:

- The company was virtually out of cash and an immediate supplemental bank loan of $20 million was essential.

- Car inventories—company owned and dealer owned—had reached unprecedented levels. The solution to this glut took five months and could be accomplished only by a series of plant shutdowns in January 1967.

- Sales of the Rambler American series had stagnated and inventories were accumulating: A dramatic merchandising move was concocted and implemented in February, dropping the price tag on the American to a position midway between the VW and competitive smaller U.S. compacts, by both cutting the price to dealers and trimming dealer discounts from 21 percent to 17 percent.

- Administrative and commercial expenses were judged too high and thus

PART THREE
IS PUBLIC
MANAGEMENT
SIMILAR TO OR
DIFFERENT FROM
PRIVATE
MANAGEMENT?

a vigorous cost reduction program was initiated that trimmed $15 million during the first year. Manufacturing and purchasing costs were also trimmed significantly to approach the most effective levels in the industry.

- The company's public image had deteriorated: The press was pessimistic and much of the financial community had written AMC off. To counteract this, numerous formal and informal meetings were held with bankers, investment firms, government officials, and the press.

As Chapin recalls, "with the immediate fires put out, we could put in place the pieces of a corporate growth plan—a definition of a way of life in the auto industry for American Motors. We felt that our reason for being, which would enable us not just to survive but to grow, lay in bringing a different approach to the auto market—in picking our spots and then being innovative and aggressive." The new corporate growth plan included a dramatic change in the approach to the market to establish a "youthful image" for the company (by bringing out new sporty models like the Javelin and by entering the racing field), "changing the product line from one end to the other" by 1972, acquiring Kaiser Jeep (selling the company's nontransportation assets and concentrating on specialized transportation, including Jeep, a company that had lost money in each of the preceding five years, but that Chapin believed could be turned around by substantial cost reductions and economies of scale in manufacturing, purchasing, and administration).

Chapin succeeded: for the year ending September 30, 1971, AMC earned $10.2 million on sales of $1.2 billion. Recalling the list of general management functions in Table 6-1, which similarities and differences appear salient and important?

Strategy

Both Chapin and Costle had to establish objectives and priorities and to devise operational plans. In business, "corporate strategy is the pattern of major objectives, purposes, or goals and essential policies and plans for achieving these goals, stated in such a way as to define what business the company is in or is to be in and the kind of company it is or is to be."[17] In reshaping the strategy of AMC and concentrating on particular segments of the transportation market, Chapin had to consult his Board and had to arrange financing. But the control was substantially his.

How much choice did Costle have at EPA as to the "business it is or is to be in" or the kind of agency "it is or is to be"? These major strategic choices emerged from the legislative process which mandated whether he should be in the business of controlling pesticides or toxic substances and if so on what timetable, and occasionally, even what level of particulate per million units he was required to control. The relative role of the President, other members of the Administration (including White House staff, Congressional relations, and other agency heads), the EPA Administrator, Congressional committee chairmen, and external groups in establishing the broad strategy of the agency constitutes an interesting question.

Managing Internal Components

For both Costle and Chapin, staffing was key. As Donald Rumsfeld has observed:

the single most important task of the chief executive is to select the right people. I've seen terrible organization charts in both government and business that were made to work well by good people. I've seen beautifully charted organizations that didn't work very well because they had the wrong people.[18]

The leeway of the two executives in organizing and staffing were considerably different, however. Chapin closed down plants, moved key managers, hired and fired, virtually at will. As Michael Blumenthal has written about Treasury,

> if you wish to make substantive changes, policy changes, and the Department's employees don't like what you're doing, they have ways of frustrating you or stopping you that do not exist in private industry. The main method they have is Congress. If I say I want to shut down a particular unit or transfer the function of one area to another, there are ways of going to Congress and in fact using friends in the Congress to block the move. They can also use the press to try to stop you. If I at Bendix wished to transfer a division from Ann Arbor to Detroit because I figured out that we could save money that way, as long as I could do it decently and carefully, it's of no lasting interest to the press. The press can't stop me. They may write about it in the local paper, but that's about it.[19]

For Costle, the basic structure of the agency was set by law. The labs, their location, and most of their personnel were fixed. Though he could recruit his key subordinates, again restrictions like the conflict of interest law and the prospect of a Senate confirmation fight led him to drop his first choice for the Assistant Administrator for Research and Development, since he had worked for a major chemical company. While Costle could resort to changes in the process for developing policy or regulations in order to circumvent key office directors whose views he did not share, for example, Eric Stork, the Deputy Assistant Administrator in charge of Mobile Source Air Program, such maneuvers took considerable time, provoked extensive infighting, and delayed significantly the development of Costle's program.

In the direction of personnel and management of the personnel system, Chapin exercised considerable authority. While the United Auto Workers limited his authority over workers, at the management level he assigned people and reassigned responsibility consistent with his general plan. While others may have felt that his decisions to close down particular plants or to drop a particular product were mistaken, they complied. As George Shultz has observed: "One of the first lessons I learned in moving from government to business is that in business you must be very careful when you tell someone who is working for you to do something because the probability is high that he or she will do it."[20]

Costle faced a civil service system designed to prevent spoils as much as to promote productivity. The Civil Service Commission exercised much of the responsibility for the personnel function in his agency. Civil service rules severely restricted his discretion, took long periods to exhaust, and often required complex maneuvering in a specific case to achieve any results. Equal opportunity rules and their administration provided yet another network of procedural and substantive inhibitions. In retrospect, Costle found the civil service system a much larger constraint on his actions and demand on his time than he had anticipated.

PART THREE
IS PUBLIC
MANAGEMENT
SIMILAR TO OR
DIFFERENT FROM
PRIVATE
MANAGEMENT?

In controlling performance, Chapin was able to use measures like profit and market share, to decompose those objectives to subobjectives for lower levels of the organization and to measure the performance of managers of particular models, areas, divisions. Cost accounting rules permitted him to compare plants within AMC and to compare AMC's purchases, production, and even administration with the best practice in the industry.

Managing External Constituencies

As Chief Executive Officer, Chapin had to deal only with the Board. For Costle, within the executive branch but beyond his agency lay many actors critical to the achievement of his agency's objectives: the President and the White House, Energy, Interior, the Council on Environmental Quality, OMB. Actions each could take, either independently or after a process of consultation in which they disagreed with him, could frustrate his agency's achievement of its assigned mission. Consequently, he spent considerable time building his agency's reputation and capital for interagency disputes.

Dealing with independent external organizations was a necessary and even larger part of Costle's job. Since his agency's mission, strategy, authorizations, and appropriations emerged from the process of legislation, attention to Congressional committees, and Congressmen, and Congressmen's staff, and people who affect Congressmen and Congressional staffers rose to the top of Costle's agenda. In the first year, top level EPA officials appeared over 140 times before some 60 different committees and subcommittees.

Chapin's ability to achieve AMC's objectives could also be affected by independent external organizations: competitors, government (the Clean Air Act that was passed in 1970), consumer groups (recall Ralph Nader), and even suppliers of oil. More than most private managers, Chapin had to deal with the press in attempting to change the image of AMC. Such occasions were primarily at Chapin's initiative, and around events that Chapin's public affairs office orchestrated, for example, the announcement of a new racing car. Chapin also managed a marketing effort to persuade consumers that their tastes could best be satisfied by AMC products.

Costle's work was suffused by the press: in the daily working of the organization, in the perception by key publics of the agency and thus the agency's influence with relevant parties, and even in the setting of the agenda of issues to which the agency had to respond.

For Chapin, the bottom line was profit, market share, and the long-term competitive position of AMC. For Costle, what are the equivalent performance measures? Blumenthal answers by exaggerating the difference between appearance and reality:

> At Bendix, it was the reality of the situation that in the end determined whether we succeeded or not. In the crudest sense, this meant the bottom line. You can dress up profits only for so long—if you're not successful, it's going to be clear. In government there is no bottom line, and that is why you can be successful if you appear to be successful—though, of course, appearance is not the only ingredient of success.[21]

Rumsfeld says:

> In business, you're pretty much judged by results. I don't think the American

people judge government officials this way. . . . In government, too often you're measured by how much you seem to care, how hard you seem to try—things that do not necessarily improve the human condition. . . . It's a lot easier for a President to get into something and end up with a few days of good public reaction than it is to follow through, to pursue policies to a point where they have a beneficial effect on human lives.[22]

As George Shultz says:

In government and politics, recognition and therefore incentives go to those who formulate policy and maneuver legislative compromise. By sharp contrast, the kudos and incentives in business go to the persons who can get something done. It is execution that counts. Who can get the plant built, who can bring home the sales contract, who can carry out the financing, and so on.[23]

This casual comparison of one public and one private manager suggests what could be done—if the issue of comparisons were pursued systematically, horizontally across organizations and at various levels within organizations. While much can be learned by examining the chief executive officers of organizations, still more promising should be comparisons among the much larger numbers of middle managers. If one compared, for example, a Regional Administrator of EPA and an AMC division chief, or two Comptrollers, or equivalent plant managers, some functions would appear more similar, and other differences would stand out. The major barrier to such comparisons is the lack of cases describing problems and practices of middle-level managers.[24] This should be a high priority in further research.

The differences noted in this comparison, for example, in the personnel area, have already changed with the Civil Service Reform Act of 1978 and the creation of the Senior Executive Service. Significant changes have also occurred in the automobile industry: under current circumstances, the CEO of Chrysler may seem much more like the Administrator of EPA. More precise comparison of different levels of management in both organizations, for example, accounting procedures used by Chapin to cut costs significantly as compared to equivalent procedures for judging the costs of EPA mandated pollution control devices, would be instructive.

SECTION 5: IMPLICATIONS FOR RESEARCH ON PUBLIC MANAGEMENT

The debate between the assimilators and the differentiators, like the dispute between proponents of convergence and divergence between the U.S. and the Soviet Union reminds me of the old argument about whether the glass is half full or half empty. I conclude that public and private management are at least as different as they are similar, and that the differences are more important than the similarities. From this review of the "state of the art," such as it is, I draw a number of lessons for research on public management. I will try to state them in a way that is both succinct and provocative:

- First, the demand for performance from government and efficiency in government is both real and right. The perception that government's performance lags private business performance is also correct. But the notion that there is any significant body of private management practices and

PART THREE
IS PUBLIC
MANAGEMENT
SIMILAR TO OR
DIFFERENT FROM
PRIVATE
MANAGEMENT?

skills that can be transferred directly to public management tasks in a way that produces significant improvements is wrong.

- Second, performance in many public management positions can be improved substantially, perhaps by an order of magnitude. That improvement will come not, however, from massive borrowing of specific private management skills and understandings. Instead, it will come, as it did in the history of private management, from an articulation of the general management function and a self-consciousness about the general public management point of view. The single lesson of private management most instructive to public management is the prospect of substantial improvement through recognition of and consciousness about the public management function.

Alfred Chandler's prize-winning study, *The Visible Hand: The Managerial Revolution in American Business,*[25] describes the emergence of professional management in business. Through the nineteenth century most American businesses were run by individuals who performed management functions but had no self-consciousness about their management responsibilities. With the articulation of the general management perspective and the refinement of general management practices, by the 1920s, American businesses had become competitive in the management function. Individuals capable at management and self-conscious about their management tasks—setting objectives, establishing priorities, and driving the organization to results—entered firms and industries previously run by family entrepreneurs or ordinary employees and brought about dramatic increases in product. Business schools emerged to document better and worse practice, largely through the case method, to suggest improvements, and to refine specific management instruments. Important advances were made in technique. But the great leaps forward in productivity stemmed from the articulation of the general management point of view and the self-consciousness of managers about their function. (Analogously, at a lower level, the articulation of the salesman's role and task, together with the skills and values of salesmanship made it possible for individuals with moderate talents at sales to increase their level of sales tenfold.)

The routes by which people reach general management positions in government do not assure that they will have consciousness or competence in management. As a wise observer of government managers has written,

> One of the difficult problems of schools of public affairs is to overcome the old-fashioned belief—still held by many otherwise sophisticated people—that the skills of management are simply the application of "common sense" by any intelligent and broadly educated person to the management problems which are presented to him. It is demonstrable that many intelligent and broadly educated people who are generally credited with a good deal of "common sense" make very poor managers. The skills of effective management require a good deal of uncommon sense and uncommon knowledge.[26]

I believe that the most significant aspect of the Civil Service Reform Act of 1978 is the creation of the Senior Executive Service: the explicit identification of general managers in government. The challenge now is to assist people who occupy general management positions in actually becoming general managers.

- Third, careful review of private management rules of thumb that can be adapted to public management contexts will pay off. The 80-20 rule—80 percent of the benefits of most production processes come from the first 20 percent of effort—does have wide application, for example, in EPA efforts to reduce bulk pollutants.

- Fourth, Chandler documents the proposition that the categories and criteria for identifying costs, or calculating present value, or measuring the value added to intermediate products are not "natural." They are invented: creations of intelligence harnessed to operational tasks. While there are some particular accounting categories and rules, for example, for costing intermediate products, that may be directly transferable to public sector problems, the larger lesson is that dedicated attention to specific management functions can, as in the history of business, create for public sector managers accounting categories, and rules, and measures that cannot now be imagined.[27]

- Fifth, it is possible to learn from experience. What skills, attributes, and practices do competent managers exhibit and less successful managers lack? This is an empirical question that can be investigated in a straightforward manner. As Yogi Berra noted: "You can observe a lot just by watching."

- Sixth, the effort to develop public management as a field of knowledge should start from problems faced by practicing public managers. The preferences of professors for theorizing reflects deep-seated incentives of the academy that can be overcome only by careful institutional design.

In the light of these lessons, I believe one strategy for the development of public management should include:

- *Developing a significant number of cases on public management problems and practices.* Cases should describe typical problems faced by public managers. Cases should attend not only to top-level managers but to middle and lower-level managers. The dearth of cases at this level makes this a high priority for development. Cases should examine both general functions of management and specific organizational tasks, for example, hiring and firing. Public management cases should concentrate on the job of the manager running his unit.

- *Analyzing cases to identify better and worse practice.* Scientists search for "critical experiments." Students of public management should seek to identify "critical experiences" that new public managers could live through vicariously and learn from. Because of the availability of information, academics tend to focus on failures. But teaching people what not to do is not necessarily the best way to help them learn to be *doers.* By analyzing relative successes, it will be possible to extract rules of thumb, crutches, and concepts, for example, Chase's "law": Wherever the product of a public organization has not been monitored in a way that ties performance to reward, the introduction of an effective monitoring system will yield a 50 percent improvement in that product in the short run. GAO's handbooks on evaluation techniques and summaries suggest what can be done.

89

PART THREE
IS PUBLIC
MANAGEMENT
SIMILAR TO OR
DIFFERENT FROM
PRIVATE
MANAGEMENT?

- *Promoting systematic comparative research:* management positions in a single agency over time; similar management positions among several public agencies; public management levels within a single agency; similar management functions, for example, budgeting or management information systems, among agencies; managers across public and private organizations; and even cross-nationally. The data for this comparative research would be produced by the case development effort and would complement the large-scale development of cases on private management that is ongoing.

- *Linking to the training of public managers.* Intellectual development of the field of public management should be tightly linked to the training of public managers, including individuals already in positions of significant responsibility. Successful practice will appear in government, not in the university. University-based documentation of better and worse practice, and refinement of that practice, should start from problems of managers on the line. The intellectual effort required to develop the field of public management and the resources required to support this level of effort are most likely to be assembled if research and training are vitally linked. The new Senior Executive Service presents a major opportunity to do this.

The strategy outlined here is certainly not the only strategy for research in public management. Given the needs for effective public management, I believe that a *major* research effort should be mounted and that it should pursue a number of complementary strategies. Given where we start, I see no danger of overattention to, or overinvestment in the effort required in the immediate future.

Any resemblance between my preferred strategy and that of at least one school of government is not purely coincidental.

NOTES

[1]In contrast to the management of structured hierarchies, for which the metaphor of a traditional football game in which each team attempts to amass the larger number of points is apt, an organized anarchy is better thought of as a soccer game played on a round field, ringed with goals; players enter and leave the field sporadically, and while there vigorously kick various balls of sundry sizes and shapes toward one or another of the goals, judging themselves and being judged by assorted, ambiguous scoring systems. See Michael Cohen and James March, *Leadership and Ambiguity* (McGraw-Hill, 1974).

[2]Selma J. Mushkin, Frank H. Sandifer, and Sally Familton, *Current Status of Public Management: Research Conducted by or Supported by Federal Agenices* (Washington, D.C.: Public Services Laboratory, Georgetown University, 1978), p. 10.

[3]Ibid., p. 11.

[4]Though frequently identified as the author who established the complete separation between "policy" and "administration," Woodrow Wilson has in fact been unjustly accused. "It is the object of administrative study to discover, first, what government can properly and successfully do, and, secondly, how it can do these proper things with the utmost possible efficiency ..." (Wilson, "The Study of Administration," published as an essay in 1887 and reprinted in *Political Science Quarterly*, December 1941, p. 481 [included in this volume as Chapter 1]). For another statement of the same point, see Brooks Adams, *The Theory of Social Revolutions* (Macmillan 1913), pp. 207–208.

[5]See Dwight Waldo, "Organization Theory: Revisiting the Elephant," *PAR* (November–

December 1978). Reviewing the growing volume of books and articles on organization theory, Waldo notes that "growth in the volume of the literature is not to be equated with growth in knowledge."

[6]See *Cases in Public Policy and Management* (Spring 1979) of the Intercollegiate Case Clearing House for a bibliography containing descriptions of 577 cases by 366 individuals from 79 institutions. Current casework builds on and expands earlier efforts of the Inter-University Case Program. See, for example, Harold Stein, ed. *Public Administration and Policy Development: A Case Book* (Harcourt, Brace, and World, 1952), and Edwin A. Bock and Alan K. Campbell, eds., *Case Studies in American Government* (Prentice-Hall, 1962).

[7]Luther Gulick and Al Urwick, ed., *Papers in the Science of Public Administration* (Institute of Public Administration, 1937).

[8]See, for example, Chester I. Barnard, *The Functions of the Executive* (Howard University Press, 1938), and Peter F. Drucker, *Management: Tasks, Responsibilities, Practices* (Harper and Row, 1974). Barnard's recognition of human relations added an important dimension neglected in earlier lists.

[9] See, for example, "A Businessman in a Political Jungle," *Fortune* (April 1964); "Candid Reflections of a Businessman in Washington," *Fortune* (January 29, 1979); "A Politician Turned Executive," *Fortune* (September 10, 1979); and "The Ambitions Interface," *Harvard Business Review* (November–December, 1979) for the views of Romney, Blumenthal, Rumsfeld, and Shultz, respectively. [Blumenthal and Rumsfeld are included in this volume in Chapters 2 and 3, respectively.]

[10]John T. Dunlop, "Public Management," draft of an unpublished paper and proposal, Summer 1979.

[11]Hal G. Rainey, Robert W. Backoff, and Charles N. Levine, "Comparing Public and Private Organizations," *Public Administration Review* (March–April, 1976). [Included in this volume as Chapter 7].

[12]Richard E. Neustadt, "American Presidents and Corporate Executives," a paper prepared for a meeting of the National Academy of Public Administration's Panel on Presidential Management, October 7–8, 1979.

[13]*The Federalist Papers*, No. 51. The word "department" has been translated as "branch," which was its meaning in the original papers.

[14]Failure to recognize the fact of distributions has led some observers to leap from one instance of similarity between public and private to general propositions about similarities between public and private institutions or management. See, for example, Michael Murray, "Comparing Public and Private Management: An Exploratory Essay," *Public Administration Review* (July–August, 1975). [Included in this volume as Chapter 5].

[15]These examples are taken from Bruce Scott, "American Motors Corporation" (Intercollegiate Case Clearing House #9-364-001); Charles B. Weigle with the collaboration of C. Roland Christensen, "American Motors Corporation II" (Intercollegiate Case Clearing House #6-372-350); Thomas R. Hitchner and Jacob Lew under the supervision of Philip B. Heymann and Stephen B. Hitchner, "Douglas Costle and the EPA (A)" (Kennedy School of Government Case #C94-78-216); and Jacob Lew and Stephen B. Hitchner, "Douglas Costle and the EPA (B)" (Kennedy School of Government Case #C96-78-217). For an earlier exploration of a similar comparison, see Joseph Bower, "Effective Public Management," *Harvard Business Review* (March–April, 1977).

[16]U.S. Government Manual, 1978/1979, 507.

[17]Kenneth R. Andrews, *The Concept of Corporate Strategy* (Dow Jones–Irwin, 1971), p. 28.

[18]"A Politician-Turned-Executive," *Fortune* (September 10, 1979), p. 92. [Included in this volume as Chapter 3].

[19]"Candid Reflections of a Businessman in Washington," *Fortune* (January 29, 1979), p. 39. [Included in this volume as Chapter 2].

[20]"The Abrasive Interface," *Harvard Business Review* (November–December 1979), p. 95.

[21]*Fortune* (January 29, 1979), p. 36.

[22]*Fortune* (September 10, 1979), p. 90.

[23]*Harvard Business Review* (November–December 1979), p. 95.

PART THREE
IS PUBLIC
MANAGEMENT
SIMILAR TO OR
DIFFERENT FROM
PRIVATE
MANAGEMENT?

[24]The cases developed by Boston University's Public Management Program offer a promising start in this direction.

[25]Alfred Chandler, *The Visible Hand: The Managerial Revolution in American Business* (Belknap Press of Harvard University Press, 1977).

[26]Rufus Miles, "The Search for Identity of Graduate Schools of Public Affairs." *Public Administration Review* (November 1967).

[27]Chandler, op. cit., pp. 277–79.

7 | Comparing Public and Private Organizations

Hal G. Rainey
Robert W. Backoff
Charles H. Levine

This article presents a number of propositions about differences in public and private organizations, which have implications for their management.[1] The propositions extend and refine consideration of the question which was recently addressed by Michael A. Murray (36). Murray suggests that public and private organizations are converging and facing similar constraints and challenges, and that management in all types of organizations should be viewed as a generic process. Yet our inquiry into this comparative question points to the conclusion that it is premature to discount the significance of public-private differences and their implications for management training and practice.

Numerous scholars and observers, of considerable reputation and experience, have addressed themselves to the comparative issue, and it is important that their observations be compiled and considered. Yet no systematic effort at integration has covered relatively recent contributions.[2] In making such a review, we found consensus on a number of important distinctions, which are relevant to research, training, and practice. Moreover, in addition to these specific points of agreement, there are general reasons to approach the subject of public-private comparisons carefully, and to avoid premature dismissal of its significance:

1. *Normative, prescriptive implications:* There are widely discussed concerns over whether various aspects of the convergence of the two sectors are good or bad. Solutions are proposed and arguments made concerning the appropriate roles and functions of the organizations in the two sectors. A ready example is the concern over "capture" of the regulatory agencies, and the proposal that some activities be deregulated. Generally, then, which techniques and attributes of public and private organizations should be preserved or abolished, exchanged or kept separate?

PART THREE
IS PUBLIC
MANAGEMENT
SIMILAR TO OR
DIFFERENT FROM
PRIVATE
MANAGEMENT?

2. *Implications for knowledge and understanding:* Prescriptions will be no better than our understanding of the phenomena. Deregulation proposals, for instance, will provide successful solutions only if their underlying assumptions about the effects of market competition are accurate. To the extent, then, that there is still a divergence between public and private organizations and their management, the divergence should be isolated and studied as a source of information about the workings of organizations in an increasingly complex society.

3. *Theoretical implications:* Consideration of the comparative question involves some of the basic issues in the effort to systematize knowledge about organizations and management, including the choice of units and levels of analysis and of major variables. These choices are in turn related to the effort to devise concepts, testable propositions, and models.

Analysis of similarities and differences between public and private organizations raises major difficulties of classification and definition which will not be quickly resolved. Nevertheless, an effort must be made to clarify the issue by suggesting resolutions to the classificatory problems, before proceeding to the comparisons themselves.

APPROACHES TO CLASSIFICATION AND DEFINITION

Ideally, an inquiry such as this would involve two steps: (1) A clear definition of "public" and "private" sector organizations, which would specify the essential or basic differences and draw a clear line between the two. (2) Specification of the full range of variation, which is empirically and logically related to the basic or "defining" differences. Unfortunately, success at the first step is elusive or impossible, as one can see in the efforts at delineation of the subject matter of public administration (10)(27). This difficulty complicates the issue, but as we will soon see, there are a number of authors who nevertheless get on with the second step.

The difficulty of saying precisely and thoroughly what we mean by "public" and "private" is reflected in a number of methods of handling the issue which can be observed in the literature, and which might be characterized as follows: (1) *Common sense approaches,* in which an author discusses the relationship of the sectors without explicit definitions, apparently assuming that everyone has an adequate idea of what he is talking about. Weidenbaum (58) is concerned that government-by-contract will cause some corporations to lose their "essential privateness," but never explicitly defines his meaning. (2) *Practical definitions,* in which unsubtle rules of thumb are applied, due to the need for a definition. The Bureau of Labor Statistics, for example, calculates indices in which the Postal Service and TVA are counted as private sector activities. (3) *Denotative approaches,* in which a sector is delineated by simply listing the activities or organizations which fall within its purview (17). (4) *Analytic approaches,* which attempt distinctions on the basis of defining factors or sets of factors. Economists, for example, frequently base the distinctions on the nature of the goods produced, i.e., the concept of "social" or "collective" goods.

Yet none of these approaches can succeed in drawing a clear line between the sectors (25). There are always intermediate types, and overlaps on various dimensions. The wide, varied, and continually evolving engagement of government in aspects of life in the United States formerly considered private, or still predominantly so, causes a "blurring" or convergence of the sectors which has been frequently noted (9)(10)(19). This "blurring" seems to involve two interrelated phenomena. First, there is an intermingling of governmental and nongovernmental activities, which is observable in government regulation of various activities, and in various "mixed" undertakings such as public enterprises and provision of government services by contract with private corporations. The other, related aspect is an increasing similarity of function, context, or role of the organizations in the two sectors. Gawthorp (19) argues that coping with environmental "turbulence" will be such a major concern of managers in both sectors that differences on other factors will be overshadowed. Weidenbaum (58) observes that some corporations are so dependent on government contracts that they may take on certain attributes of government agencies. Galbraith (18) argues that many firms have so much market power and influence on the public interest that it is no longer appropriate to regard them as "private." Similarly, there are discussions of the need for greater social responsibility and public accountability on the part of private corporations (37)(38)(44).

This "blurring" certainly complicates the delineation of the sectors, but the real question is how much to make of it. A distinction can be blurred and still be meaningful; a number of authors note this difficulty in clear differentiation, yet go on to cite important differences between public and private organizations (5)(9)(10)(25)(57)(58). It seems clear that one could identify large groups of organizations which represent a hard core of public and private organizations, in that they are distinct on a number of basic characteristics (and magnitudes). Even though no single organization need have all of these basic attributes, it seems reasonable to speak of "typical" government and business organizations, in the fashion of Banfield (5) and Weidenbaum (58), which share a large proportion of this cluster of attributes (3).[3]

CRITERIA OF THE SEARCH

Having addressed these problems concerning definition and classification, one can turn to a considerable literature which addresses the broader question of the full set of possible distinctions between public and private organizations and management. In compiling these references, a number of guidelines were followed. The review covered relatively visible and accessible materials (major texts, journals, and convention presentations) which were for the most part relatively recent. Except in a few cases they were explicitly comparative of public and private organizations or administrative processes in the United States. Reported below are most of the observations and propositions which were stated by several authors with enough similarity in phrasing and intent to make it seem reasonable to group them into one (see Table 7-1 for summary of propositions).

There were many problems encountered in making such a compilation, and inevitably some violence was done to the phrasing, logic, and priorities of

PART THREE
IS PUBLIC
MANAGEMENT
SIMILAR TO OR
DIFFERENT FROM
PRIVATE
MANAGEMENT?

TABLE 7-1
Summary of Literature on Differences Between Public and Private Organizations: Main Points of Consensus

The following table presents a summary of the points of consensus by stating them as propositions regarding the attributes of a public organization, relative to those of a private organization.

Topic	Proposition
I. Environmental Factors	
I. 1. Degree of market exposure (Reliance on appropriations)	I. 1.a. Less market exposure results in less incentive to cost reduction, operating efficiency, effective performance.
	I. 1.b. Less market exposure results in lower allocational efficiency (reflection of consumer preferences, proportioning supply to demand, etc.)
	I. 1.c. Less market exposure means lower availability of market indicators and information (prices, profits, etc.)
I. 2. Legal, formal constraints (courts, legislature, hierarchy)	I. 2.a. More constraints on procedures, spheres of operations (less autonomy of managers in making such choices)
	I. 2.b. Greater tendency to proliferation of formal specifications and controls.
	I. 2.c. More external sources of formal influence, and greater fragmentation of those sources.
I. 3. Political influences	I. 3.a. Greater diversity and intensity of external informal influences on decisions (bargaining, public opinion, interest group reactions)
	I. 3.b. Greater need for support of "constituencies"—client groups, sympathetic formal authorities, etc.
II. Organization-Environment Transactions	
II. 1. Coerciveness ("coercive," "monopolistic,"unavoidable nature of many government activities)	II. 1.a. More likely that participation in consumption and financing of services will be unavoidable or mandatory. (Government has unique sanctions and coercive powers.)
II. 2. Breadth of impact	II. 2.a. Broader impact, greater symbolic significance of actions of public administrators. (Wider scope of concern, such as "public interest.")
II. 3. Public scrutiny	II. 3.a Greater public scrutiny of public officials and their actions.
II. 4. Unique public expectations	II. 4.a. Greater public expectations that public officials act with more fairness, responsiveness, accountability, and honesty.
III. Internal Structures and Processes	
III. 1. Complexity of objectives, evaluation and decision criteria	III. 1.a. Greater multiplicity and diversity of objectives and criteria.

Topic	Proposition	
	III. 1.b.	Greater vagueness and intangibility of objectives and criteria.
	III. 1.c.	Greater tendency of goals to be conflicting (more "tradeoffs")
III. 2. Authority relations and the role of the administrator	III. 2.a.	Less decision-making autonomy and flexibility on the part of public administrators.
	III. 2.b.	Weaker, more fragmented authority over subordinates and lower levels. (1. Subordinates can bypass, appeal to alternative authorities. 2. Merit system constraints.)
	III. 2.c.	Greater reluctance to delegate, more levels of review, and greater use of formal regulations. (Due to difficulties in supervision and delegation, resulting from III. 1.b.)
	III. 2.d.	More political, expository role for top managers.
III. 3. Organizational performance	III. 3.a.	Greater cautiousness, rigidity. Less innovativeness.
	III. 3.b.	More frequent turnover of top leaders due to elections and political appointments results in greater disruption of implementation of plans.
III. 4. Incentives and incentive structures	III. 4.a.	Greater difficulty in devising incentives for effective and efficient performance.
	III. 4.b.	Lower valuation of pecuniary incentives by employees.
III. 5. Personal characteristics of employees	III. 5.a.	Variations in personality traits and needs, such as higher dominance and flexibility, higher need for achievement, on part of government managers.
	III. 5.b.	Lower work satisfaction and lower organizational commitment.

(III. 5.a. and III. 5.b. represent results of individual empirical studies, rather than points of agreement among authors.)

some of the authors. Nevertheless, the material that follows provides a reasonable summary of the major points of consensus in the literature.

FINDINGS

The points of consensus are grouped into several categories which are our own devices for presenting the material. We proceed from what we interpreted as environmental factors, to propositions about transactions of organi-

PART THREE
IS PUBLIC
MANAGEMENT
SIMILAR TO OR
DIFFERENT FROM
PRIVATE
MANAGEMENT?

zations with their environments, then to propositions concerning factors within organizations, including the individual in the organization. The interrelationships mentioned are those cited in the literature, although numerous other relationships among the factors and propositions could be proposed.

I. Environmental Factors

A number of the assertions by authors can be fairly characterized as involving factors which are environmental, in the sense that they are external to organizations, and are largely out of their control. Most of the relationships of these factors with internal structures and processes will be mentioned in following sections.

I.1. Market exposure

Many references cite differences between public and private organizations which are related to involvement or lack of involvement with the economic market as a source of resources, information, and constraints. As a source of revenues and resources, it is argued, the market enforces relatively automatic penalties and rewards, and thus provides incentives to cost reduction, operating efficiency, and effective performance (2)(9)(12) (29)(40)(46) (48)(52)(55)(57). On the other hand, organizations which obtain resources through an appropriations process in a political context are less subject to such influences; cost reductions might be avoided or deemphasized on a number of bases, such as political influences or a number of multiple, vague criteria of a "public interest" nature. Appropriations may be based largely on past levels, thus creating an incentive to use up previous appropriations. Drucker (16) discounts the importance of some of the other distinctions mentioned in this summary, yet stresses the tendencies to ineffectiveness on the part of organizations which acquire resources via "budget allocations" instead of market performance. It is frequently argued that managers of organizations financed by appropriations will seek organizational growth and personal aggrandizement by maximizing appropriations, and thus tend to deemphasize operating efficiency (12)(16) (40)(52). Closely related to this entire set of propositions about the influence of the market mechanism on operating efficiency and effectiveness are several proposals for improving administration of government programs by the introduction of market-type competition among programs providing services (29)(40) (48)(52).

A number of authors also stress the connection between exposure to economic markets and allocational efficiency, in the economist's sense of maximizing satisfaction by matching supply to demand, reflecting consumer preferences, etc. (9)(13)(40) (41)(47)(52). Ostrom (41), for example, argues that public organizations are subject to a number of dysfunctions, including less sensitivity to diseconomies of scale, failure to proportion supply to demand, failure to adequately account for consumer preferences, and a number of other failings. A number of authors, particularly those who might be characterized as "public choice" economists, stress the difficulties and possible allocational inefficiencies which are inherent in allocation via "social valuation" processes (6)(26)(41).

Intermingled with the foregoing ideas about operating and allocational efficiency are frequent references to the importance of the market as a source of relatively clear, quantitative demand indicators, goals, and performance measures (i.e., prices, sales, profits) (5)(9)(12) (14)(20) (33)(51). Such relatively clear information is conducive to operating efficiency and effectiveness, because it clarifies objectives and performance evaluation. It aids in achievement of allocational efficiency through clearer indications of user preferences, economies of scale, and demand for particular services.

■ 7 ■
Hal G. Rainey
Robert W. Backoff
Charles H. Levine

I. 2. Legal and formal constraints   In positing differences in public and private organizations in the United States, a number of authors focus on the impact of the formal, legal environment of government organizations, especially as it relates to their autonomy and flexibility.

It is argued that while private organizations need only obey the law and the regulations of regulatory agencies, government organizations tend to have their purposes, methods, and spheres of operation defined and constrained by law and legally authorized institutions to a much greater degree (5)(31)(33) (39)(51) (53)(61). One effect of these constraints is that public managers have less choice as to entry and withdrawal from various undertakings (5).

Others note a tendency to "legalism" (31) and "legal habit" (21) in the public sector—a proliferation of formal specifications and controls by statute, court rulings, and hierarchical superiors (8). Similarly, Dahl and Lindblom (12) attach significance to the fact that public agencies are subject to hierarchically or bureaucratically administered external controls. Several authors, in citing the fragmentation of authority in government and government organizations, see it as a result of multiple formal checks and institutions (see III. 2. below). Finally, regular popular elections and political appointments, as formal mechanisms of leader selection, are cited as a disruptive influence on internal operations in government agencies (5)(7)(56).

I. 3. Political influences   Reference to popular elections and political appointments brings up another set of observations, those concerning "political" influences on the operations of government organizations (1)(20)(21) (25)(31)(33) (52)(57) (59)(61). These propositions are interrelated with those concerning formal influences, but tend to be broader, encompassing not only the multiple formal, institutional constraints, but also the less formalized processes of influence, such as interest group demands and lobbying, and interventions by individual congressmen. These assertions range from very broad references to the more "political" character of government work (1) to somewhat more specific observations about the effects of greater diversity and intensity of influences on government decision making (56). It is argued that these multiple, diverse interests necessitate bargaining (11)(12), and make objectives and decision-making criteria more complex, due to greater concern for "public opinion" (59) and the reactions of various interests (21)(26) (31)(33). Another consequence is the requirement that agencies and their managers build support from various constituencies, interests, and authorities (34)(57)(61).

II. Organization-Environment Transactions

A number of propositions are primarily concerned with characterizing the relationship of the organization to the entities in its environment. Some of these assertions are very similar, in their implications for internal operations,

PART THREE
IS PUBLIC
MANAGEMENT
SIMILAR TO OR
DIFFERENT FROM
PRIVATE
MANAGEMENT?

to some of those already noted, but are sufficiently different in approach to be listed separately.

II. 1. Coerciveness   Sometimes the coercive, monopolistic, or "unavoidable" nature of actions by government entities is cited as a basic distinction between public and private organizations (5)(10)(30) (31)(51)(58). Individuals cannot avoid participation in the financing of most government activities, and in the consumption of many of the outputs of government. Obviously, this proposition can be related to the absence of the market mechanism, which provides for individual choice in the consumption of goods and services. The coercive nature of most government actions might be cited as a fundamental justification for constitutional checks and balances and extensive formal control mechanisms.

II. 2. Nature of policy impacts   There are a number of propositions which might be roughly categorized as references to the greater influence or impact of public sector decisions: Appleby (1) sees government as distinct due to its unique breadth of scope, impact, and consideration; Mainzer (31) notes the wider range of concerns in public, as compared to private, administration; Wamsley and Zald (57) cite the unique symbolic significance of government actions; and Banfield (5) cites the opportunity to participate in large affairs, and to achieve power and glory, as incentives of greater importance in public than in business organizations. At a more operational level, an administrator experienced in both public and private organizations observed that government executives are involved in decisions which are more important and influential (59).

II. 3. Public scrutiny   Closely related to a number of propositions under preceding categories are general assertions that public administrators are subject to greater public scrutiny (1)(33) (39)(51). In a similar vein, Banfield (5) argues that government organizations are able to keep fewer secrets than businesses, and are more subject to outside monitoring. Actually, a number of the earlier arguments concerning formal and political influences could be interpreted as relevant to "public scrutiny"; they refer to mechanisms of oversight and accountability, and to the multiplicity of representatives involved in the consideration of an agency's actions.

As noted earlier, there are indications of increasing public scrutiny of large private corporations, and increasing concern with their impact on the public interest. In view of the foregoing propositions, however, it seems premature to assume that there are no differences in the public scrutiny of government agencies and private corporations.

II. 4. Public expectations   Closely related to "public scrutiny" propositions are a number of references to the unique role requirements of public organizations and public officials. According to Wamsley and Zald (57), a basic difference between public and private organizations is that public organizations are perceived as being owned by the state and citizens; citizens therefore have rights and expectations they do not have in relation to private organizations. Similarly, Caiden (10) feels that citizens expect more of public administrators in the way of "integrity, fairness, responsiveness, [and] accountability (no secrets)."

II. 5. Nature of goods produced   As basis for a number of the propositions about the effects of market exposure (I. 1. above), economists note that government and government organizations are involved primarily in production of "public" and "quasi-public" goods. With some variety in phrasing, they observe that the nature of public goods (in terms of "marketability," "excludability," "rivalness of consumption," etc.) precludes application of prices and the market mechanism. Quasi-public goods are sufficiently packageable for the application of prices, user charges, or some mechanism of individual choice in consumption, but involve "significant externalities" (26) and are provided at a cost to users which is lower than the cost of production (9)(26).

III. Internal Structures and Processes

A number of observations in the literature are more directly relevant to the internal operations and structures of organizations, such as decision making, individual authority, and motivation.

III. 1. Objectives and evaluation criteria   Probably the most frequently cited distinction between business organizations and government organization is a difference in the nature of goals and performance measures of the two types of organizations. (This difference is variously phrased as a reference to goals, objectives, values, performance measures, decision criteria, etc.) The objectives and performance criteria of public sector organizations tend to differ from those of business organizations along at least three dimensions.

1. *Multiplicity and diversity* (4)(5)(9) (12)(21)(26) (31)(35)(49)(56) (57)(59): The mix of objectives and criteria is said to be more complex. In addition to multiple formal program objectives, there are political feasibility considerations. A number of less explicit criteria such as accountability, openness, and fairness may be enforced through both formal and "political" mechanisms.

2. *Vagueness and intangibility* (5)(7)(12) (15)(20)(24) (26)(35) (48)(59): It is noteworthy that the references which were primarily concerned with application of systematic and quantitative analysis in the public sector all made a point of the unique difficulties in specifying and quantifying performance measures in the public sector (15)(26)(35). Drake (15) in particular, presents an extensive list of differences, such as the greater difficulty of actually defining the issue for analysis, and the greater difficulty of applying a quantitative model due to the complex interrelationships among government activities. (Drake apparently sees the military as similar to business in applicability of quantitative techniques.)

3. *Goal conflict* (5)(20)(35) (49)(59): Numerous references to conflicts and "tradeoffs" among objectives, values, and criteria should not be surprising in view of the multiple, complex constraints and expectations focused on government, noted earlier. Siffin (50) gives an example of the pursuit of directly conflicting objectives in the same government

PART THREE
IS PUBLIC
MANAGEMENT
SIMILAR TO OR
DIFFERENT FROM
PRIVATE
MANAGEMENT?

organization. Another example is provided by the frequent observation that in government, operating efficiency (especially in the narrow sense of cost reduction) is often deemphasized in relation to other criteria (1)(20)(31) (47)(49). One can cite origins of these "other criteria" in a number of the propositions already presented, such as the unique public scrutiny and expectations of government.

The aim in this section is not to suggest that businessmen seek only more sales and profits. Clearly they, too, are faced with a complex mix of objectives, and with the frequent inadequacies of quantitative measures as representations of the quality of performance. Nevertheless, the literature advances too many observations concerning the greater multiplicity, vagueness, and conflict of objectives of public sector organizations for such propositions to be brushed aside as not potentially significant to the practice of management and preparation for it.

III. 2. Hierarchical authority and the role of the administrator The multiple political and legal influences on U.S. government organizations are related to some particular attributes of hierarchical authority in government, which have implications for the role of the administrator. In general, observers regard hierarchical authority as weaker in the Executive Branch of government than in business organizations. Sometimes the weakness is related very generally to the fragmentation and complexity of government at all levels (5)(19)(61). More specifically, some authors relate the "lack of control" (20) to the ability of subordinates to bypass hierarchical superiors by appealing to alternative formal authorities or political constituencies (20)(21)(61), thus making for weaker, more fragmented authority than is usually found in business organizations (5)(21). Moreover, there are some assertions that public administrators have less autonomy and flexibility in making their own decisions than their private-sector counterparts (5)(7)(8) (19)(21) (31)(59). The multiple legal, statutory, and procedural controls noted earlier are an obvious source of these limitations. For example, merit principles limit the flexibility of public administrators in hiring, firing, and controlling the incentives of their subordinates (5)(7)(19). Constraints on choice of methods and spheres of operation have already been cited (I. 2. above). Other references note unique difficulties in supervision, delegation, and subcompartmentalization (into profit centers, for example) in the public sector due to the lack of specific objectives and performance measures (5)(6)(21) (32)(48). Inability to specify clear objectives and performance measures makes it harder to supervise and control subordinates, and results in reluctance to delegate, in multiple levels of review and approval, and in a proliferation of regulations (21)(58)(48). The lack of specific and quantitative criteria is said to limit the tendency of public administrators to attempt innovations, since it is difficult to evaluate the potential impact of an innovation (6)(20).

There are suggestions that the necessity to maintain constituencies, to deal with multiple external influences, and to seek appropriations in a political context have implications for the roles of the high-level manager in a government organization. Nigro and Nigro (39) cite the requirement for "exposition" as well as competence. Stockfisch (52) notes the requirement to combine "political adroitness" with professional expertise. Mintzberg (34) concludes from a study of managerial work that the requirement to deal with external coalitions and to make politically sensitive decisions make the "liaison, spokesman, and negotiator roles" more important for chief executives of public organizations.

III. 3. Performance characteristics   A number of authors have made observations concerning the performance of government organizations and administrators, usually in comparison to business, and have frequently focused on dysfunctions in government organizations. Dahl and Lindblom (12) assert that "agencies" suffer more than "enterprises" from red tape, buck-passing, timidity, and rigidity. Downs notes tendencies in "bureaus" to inertia, routinization, and inflexibility. Golembiewski (21) sees a greater tendency to procedural regularity and caution in government agencies, as compared to businesses. When Weidenbaum (58) worries that some corporations are becoming so dependent on government contracts that they are losing their "essential privateness," he apparently is referring to their innovativeness, their taking and bearing of risks. Schultz (48) says that the inadequacy of performance measures in government results in risk avoidance by individuals and institutions; success cannot be recognized easily, but mistakes can be singled out and punished. Arguments concerning the greater difficulty in evaluating a proposed innovation are noted above (III. 2.). "Scheduled disruptions" (7)(20) in the form of elections and political appointments tend to interrupt sustained implementation of plans and projects. Thus, there are a number of propositions to the effect that government organizations tend to be characterized by cautiousness, inflexibility, and lack of innovativeness.

III. 4. Incentives   The literature also contains some propositions concerning differences in incentive structures and employee valuations of incentives in public organizations, which are of potential significance to training for management and the practice of management (45)(46). Schultze (48) notes the greater difficulty in devising incentives for effective performance of government programs, largely as a result of difficulties in performance evaluation when objectives are vague. A number of proposals for introducing competition as an incentive to effective performance have been noted above (I. 1.).

There are also some indications of differences in the kinds of incentives which are available, and the kinds to which employees are responsive (5)(7)(28)(42). Banfield (5) argues that the most important incentives offered to private sector employees are material incentives, primarily money. In government, he says, nonpecuniary incentives such as job security, involvement in important affairs, and "power and glory," figure more importantly. Lawler (28) cites extensive evidence that people who work in business organizations attach more importance to pay than do persons in nonprofit organizations; a study of his own indicated such a difference between employees in industrial and government organizations. Recent findings by Rawls et al. (42) give similar indications. Thus, not only are there suggestions of greater constraints on the ability of public administrators to manipulate incentives (merit system constraints contribute to these limitations, of course), there are indications of differences in individual valuations of various incentives.

103

PART THREE
IS PUBLIC
MANAGEMENT
SIMILAR TO OR
DIFFERENT FROM
PRIVATE
MANAGEMENT?

III. 5. Individual differences   A handful of empirical studies suggest individual differences in addition to the differences in valuation of incentives suggested just above. Rawls et al. (42) found that, as compared to students planning employment in the profit sector, students planning nonprofit sector employment were more likely to have played roles as change agents in the school; their responses on personality scales were higher on dominance, flexibility, and capacity for status, and they placed lower value on economic wealth. Other studies have found indications that government managers show lower work and need satisfaction (7)(43), lower organizational commitment (7), higher need for achievement, and lower need for affiliation (22). Although one should be cautious pending further replication and corroboration of these findings, they suggest differences with important implications for research and practice, and at least provide justification for further inquiry into differences at the individual level.

IMPLICATIONS

Consensus is not "proof." Yet as much as we would like to rely on extensive, conceptually clear empirical research, we are faced with the immediate decisions as to whether the comparative question is worth pursuing; and whether there are noteworthy differences in public and private "management" which in turn have implications for management training. Since space constraints preclude elaboration of conflicts on some points (16)(53), and of possible paradoxes or conflicts among some of the propositions themselves, pending further refinement and corroboration one should be cautious about assuming the accuracy of any individual proposition and about overstating its importance. With that disclaimer clearly in mind, we must do our best to answer the immediate questions.

Implications for Research

The strong normative concerns mentioned at the outset, together with strong consensus on certain points of comparison, justify further attention to the comparative question. For instance, Weidenbaum's (58) concern over loss of entrepreneurial characteristics by firms reliant on government contracts emphasizes the importance of comparative research on innovation (III. 3.a.) in the public and private sectors (45)(46)—Is business really more flexible and innovative than government? Even if the public-private distinction is, or proves to be, less important than other major variables for organizational analysis, comparative research can provide findings on those other variables and issues. For example, investigation of the propositions presented above can provide findings relevant to the effects of different environmental constraints on organizational processes and performance, to the effects of different incentive systems, and to other issues of importance to general understanding of organizations.

Implications for Management

As a way of briefly suggesting that there are some important distinctions between public and private management, one might apply some of the propositions listed above to a few of the elements which Murray (36) sees as common to all management. He offers a quotation (p. 365) to the effect that, among other things, management always involves the following: defining purposes and objectives, planning, selecting managers, managing and motivating people, and controlling and measuring results. The points of agreement in the literature suggest that there may be distinctions within these categories which should be further considered:

1. *Purposes, objectives, and planning:* Public administrators may have less flexibility and autonomy in defining purposes (I. 2.a.). Objectives may be more diverse (III. 1.a.) and harder to specify (III. 1.b.). Planning may involve a more complex set of influences (I. 3.a.), and long-term planning may be more difficult (III. 3.b.).

2. *Selection, management, and motivation:* There may be greater constraints on a public administrator's ability to select and control subordinates (III. 2.b. and II. 2.c.). He may need to consider a different set of employee needs and motivational problems (III. 5.), which must also be considered in selection decisions.

3. *Controlling and measuring results:* A public administrator may find it not only harder to measure results (I. 1., III. 1.), but also, partially as a consequence of that difficulty, harder to attain results and effective performance (III. 2., III. 3., III. 4.).

Thus, there are strong indications of unique procedures and constraints within the broad procedural categories which characterize all management. Educational implications of these differences further underscore their significance.

Implications for Training

It is difficult to see how a core curriculum in "generic management" could extend beyond a handful of joint courses, such as organization theory and basic quantitative skills. Even in those courses, difficulties as to the mix of readings, cases, and examples may arise. Drake (15), for example, discusses unique quantitative training needs of public administration students, due to the "fuzzier" problems they may encounter. Beyond these few subjects, optimal preparation for management in the two types of organizations would call for different emphases, some of which readily come to mind—more emphasis on political institutions and processes, on government budgeting, on public policy analysis, and on administrative law instead of business law. Together with a concentration in a functional area such as criminal justice or transportation, these emphases would result in such divergence in course assignments that there seems no particular utility in establishing "generic" curricula. Moreover, one could argue the need for public service trainees to devote continuing consideration to certain aspects of public service, such as concern for the public interest, and the responsibilities of the government official. One might interpret *The President's Report* of Harvard (24), which argues the need for public service training programs due to the intangible, multiple goals of public programs, as a reference to these unique considerations. It may be that such an emphasis is most effective in a separate, or near-separate, environment.

105

PART THREE
IS PUBLIC
MANAGEMENT
SIMILAR TO OR
DIFFERENT FROM
PRIVATE
MANAGEMENT?

In sum, there are indications of a number of important differences between public and private organizations, which cannot be ignored in considerations of management research, training, and practice. More importantly, there are reasons to continue public and private comparisons, not in rejection of efforts at general understanding of organizations and their management, but in the effort to supplement it.

NOTES

[1]Although we take for granted many commonalities among organizations (53), we focus almost exclusively on "differences," to specify points of contention for further inquiry. We continually refer to public and private organizations, although we consider all the propositions relevant to "management" in those organizations. In closing we make suggestions as to this relevance, but it is a matter for continuing consideration. We sometimes substitute "government" for "public" where the literature is specific in its referent, on the assumption that government organizations represent the major core of public organizations, although "public" might be defined to include some "third sector" or quasi-governmental organizations. The term "sector" is a higher-order analytic term which refers to sets of organizations, and we use it only where appropriate in this way. Moreover, the term is associated more closely with economic than with social and political functions. However, alternative concepts are also insufficiently comprehensive, or are awkwardly unfamiliar. Promising alternatives are the terms "field" and "network," used by students of interorganizational relations. They have not explicitly addressed public-private comparisons, but such efforts would be valuable extensions for their research. See White (60) on the state of interorganizational studies.

[2]For a review of a number of references prior to the early 1960s, see R. S. Parker and V. Subramaniam, " 'Public' and 'Private' Administration," *International Review of Administrative Science*, Vol. 5 (1964), p. 30. Henry (25) and Roessner (46) also compile and characterize a number of recent references.

[3]Attention to efforts by organization theorists to devise typologies and to choose major variables for organizational analysis points to no clear resolution as to the usefulness of the public-private distinction. Generally they have not attached major importance to that distinction, but neither have they resolved the choice of typologies and central concepts (23, p. 78).

REFERENCES

1. Paul H. Appleby, *Big Democracy* (New York: Alfred A. Knopf, 1945).
2. Armen A. Alchian, "Cost Effectiveness of Cost Effectiveness," in Stephen Enke (ed.), *Defense Management* (Englewood Cliffs, N.J.: Prentice-Hall 1967), pp. 74–86.
3. Kenneth B. Bailey, "Monothetic and Polythetic Typologies and Their Relation to Conceptualization, Measurement and Scaling," *American Sociological Review*, Vol. 33 (February 1973), pp. 18–33.
4. R. J. S. Baker, "Organization Theory and the Public Sector," *Journal of Management Studies* (February 1969), pp. 15–32.
5. Edward C. Banfield, "Corruption as a Feature of Governmental Organization," *Journal of Law and Economics*, forthcoming.
6. Robert L. Bish and Vincent Ostrom, *Understanding Urban Government* (Washington, D.C.: American Enterprise Institute for Public Policy Research, 1973).
7. Bruce Buchanan II, "Government Managers, Business Executives, and Organizational Commitment," *Public Administration Review*, Vol. 35, No. 4 (July/August 1975), pp. 339–347.
8. _____, "Red-Tape and the Service Ethic: Some Unexpected Differences Between Public and Private Managers," *Administration and Society*, Vol. 6, No. 4 (February 1975), pp. 423–488. [Included in this volume as Chapter 14]
9. Jesse Burkhead and Jerry Miner, *Public Expenditure* (Chicago: Aldine, 1971).
10. Gerald E. Caiden, *The Dynamics of Public Administration* (Hinsdale, Ill.: Dryden Press, 1971).

11. James C. Charlesworth (ed.), *Theory and Practice of Public Administration: Scope, Objectives, and Methods* (Philadelphia: The American Academy of Political and Social Science, 1968).

12. Robert A. Dahl and Charles E. Lindblom, *Politics, Economics, and Welfare* (New York: Harper and Row, 1953).

13. D. G. Davies, "The Efficiency of Public vs. Private Firms, The Case of Australia's Two Airlines," *Journal of Law and Economics* (April 1971), pp. 149–165.

14. Anthony Downs, *Inside Bureaucracy* (Boston: Little, Brown, 1967).

15. Alvin W. Drake, "Quantitative Models in Public Administration: Some Educational Needs," in A. Drake, L. Keeney, and P. Morse (eds.), *Analysis of Public Systems* (Cambridge, Mass.: MIT Press, 1972), pp. 75–93.

16. Peter Drucker, "Managing the Public Service Institution," *The Public Interest,* No. 33 (Fall 1973), pp. 43–60.

17. Herbert Emmerich, "Scope of the Practice of Public Administration," in Charlesworth, op. cit., pp. 92–107.

18. John Kenneth Galbraith, *Economics and the Public Purpose* (Boston: Houghton Mifflin, 1973).

19. Louis C. Gawthorp, *Administrative Politics and Social Change* (New York: St. Martin's Press, 1971).

20. ———, *Bureaucratic Behavior in the Executive Branch* (New York: Free Press, 1969).

21. Robert T. Golembiewski, "Organization Development in Public Agencies: Perspectives on Theory and Practice," *Public Administration Review,* Vol. 29, No. 4 (July/August 1969), pp. 367–368.

22. James F. Guyot, "Government Bureaucrats are Different," *Public Administration Review,* Vol. 20, No. 3 (May/June 1960), pp. 195–202.

23. Richard H. Hall, *Organizations: Structure and Process* (Englewood Cliffs, N.J.: Prentice-Hall, 1972).

24. Harvard University, *The President's Report,* 1973–1974.

25. Nicholas Henry, "Paradigms of Public Administration," *Public Administration Review,* Vol. 35, No. 4 (July/August 1975), pp. 378–386.

26. Harley H. Hinrichs and Graeme M. Taylor, *Systematic Analysis* (Pacific Palisades, Calif.: Goodyear Publishing Co., 1972).

27. Martin Landau, "The Concept of Decision-Making in the Field of Public Administration," in Sidney Mailich and Edward H. Van Ness (eds.), *Concepts and Issues in Administrative Behavior* (Englewood Cliffs, N.J.: Prentice-Hall, 1962), pp. 1–29.

28. Edward E. Lawler, *Pay and Organizational Effectiveness: A Psychological View* (New York: McGraw-Hill, 1971).

29. Robert A. Levine, "Redesigning Social Systems," in Erich Jantsch (ed.), *Perspectives on Planning* (Paris: Organization for Economic Cooperation and Development, 1969), pp. 449–469.

30. Theodore Lowi, *The End of Liberalism* (New York: Norton, 1969).

31. Lewis C. Mainzer, *Political Bureaucracy* (Glenview, Ill.: Scott, Foresman, 1973), pp. 14ff.

32. Marshall W. Meyer, *Bureaucratic Structure and Authority: Coordination and Control in 254 Government Agencies* (New York: Harper and Row, 1972).

33. John D. Millett, *Organization for the Public Service* (Princeton, N.J.: D. Van Nostrand, 1966), pp. 10ff.

34. Henry Mintzberg, *The Nature of Managerial Work* (New York: Harper and Row, 1973), p. 108.

35. Philip M. Morse and Laura W. Bacon (eds.), *Operations Research for Public Systems* (Cambridge, Mass.: MIT Press, 1967).

36. Michael A. Murray, "Comparing Public and Private Management: An Exploratory Essay," *Public Administration Review,* Vol. 35, No. 4 (July/August 1975), pp. 364–371. [Included in this volume as Chapter 5]

PART THREE
IS PUBLIC
MANAGEMENT
SIMILAR TO OR
DIFFERENT FROM
PRIVATE
MANAGEMENT?

37. Mark V. Nadel, "Corporate Secrecy and Political Accountability," *Public Administration Review*, Vol. 35, No. 1 (January/February 1975), pp. 14–23.

38. Ralph Nader (ed.), *The Consumer and Corporate Accountability* (New York: Harcourt Brace, 1973).

39. Felix A. Nigro and Lloyd A. Nigro, *Modern Public Administration* (New York: Harper and Row, 1973), pp. 14ff.

40. William A. Niskanen, Jr., *Bureaucracy and Representative Government* (Chicago: Aldine, 1971).

41. Vincent Ostrom, *The Intellectual Crisis in American Public Administration* (University, Ala.: University of Alabama Press, 1973).

42. James R. Rawls, Robert A. Ullrich, and Oscar Tivis Nelson, Jr., "A Comparison of Managers Entering or Reentering the Profit and Nonprofit Sectors," *Academy of Management Journal*, Vol. 18, No. 3 (September 1975), pp. 616–622.

43. J. B. Rhinehart, R. P. Barrel, A. S. Dewolfe, J. E. Griffin, and F. E. Spaner, "Comparative Study of Need Satisfaction in Governmental and Business Hierarchies," *Journal of Applied Psychology*, Vol. 53, No. 3 (June 1969), pp. 230–235.

44. Rodman C. Rockefellar, "Turn Public Problems to Private Account," *Harvard Business Review* (January/February 1971), pp. 131–138.

45. J. David Roessner, "Designing Public Organizations for Innovative Behavior," paper delivered at the 34th annual meeting of the Academy of Management, Seattle, Washington, August 1974.

46. _____, "Incentives to Innovate in Public and Private Organizations: Implications for Public Policy," paper delivered at the 1975 annual meeting of the Southern Political Science Association, Nashville, Tennessee, November 6–8, 1975. [Included in this volume as Chapter 26]

47. E. S. Savas, "Municipal Monopolies Versus Competition in Delivering Urban Services," in Willis D. Hawley and David Rogers (eds.), *Improving the Quality of Urban Management* (Beverly Hills, Calif.: Sage, 1974), pp. 473–500.

48. Charles L. Schultze, "The Role of Incentives, Penalties, and Rewards in Attaining Effective Policy," In R. Haveman and J. Margolis (eds.), *Public Expenditures and Policy Analysis* (Chicago: Markham Publishing Co., 1970), pp. 145–172.

49. Harold Seidman, *Politics, Position, and Power* (New York: Oxford University Press, 1970).

50. William J. Siffin, "Business Administration ≠ Public Administration," *Business Horizons*, Vol. 5 (Winter 1963), pp. 69–76.

51. O. Glenn Stahl, *Public Personnel Administration* (New York: Harper and Row, 1971).

52. J. A. Stockfisch, *The Political Economy of Bureaucracy* (New York: General Learning Press, 1972).

53. James D. Thompson, "Common and Uncommon Elements in Administration," *Social Welfare Forum* (1962), pp. 181–201.

54. Victor Thompson, *Organizations as Systems* (Morristown, N.J.: General Learning Press, 1973).

55. Gordon Tullock, *The Politics of Bureaucracy* (Washington, D.C.: Public Affairs Press, 1965).

56. Dwight Waldo, *The Study of Public Administration* (New York: Doubleday, 1955).

57. Gary L. Wamsley and Mayer N. Zald, *The Political Economy of Public Organizations* (Lexington, Mass.: D. C. Heath, 1973).

58. Murray L. Weidenbaum, *The Modern Public Sector: New Ways of Doing the Government's Business* (New York: Basic Books, 1969).

59. Herman L. Weiss, "Why Business and Government Exchange Executives," *Harvard Business Review* (July/August 1974), pp. 129–140.

60. Paul E. White, "Intra and Interorganizational Studies: Do They Require Separate Conceptualizations?" *Administration and Society*, Vol. 6, No. 1 (May 1974), pp. 107–152.

61. Peter Woll, *American Bureaucracy* (New York: Norton, 1963).

PART FOUR

THE ORGANIZATIONAL ENVIRONMENT: MONITORING AND CONTROLLING EXTERNAL ACTIVITY

The environment of public management is frequently characterized as paradoxical. On one hand, American society gives its public bureaucracies enormous powers and responsibilities and expects managers to be energetic and efficient in providing the desired public services. On the other hand, most of the American people view their government with an abiding distrust and disdain. This paradox is epitomized by the "odd fact that society calls public managers both 'civil servants' (a rather commendatory term) and 'bureaucrats' (a pejorative)" (Whorton and Worthley).

The effects of this and other features of the environment on public management are the subject of this section, which suggests that, in fact, the external environment may be *the critical determinant* of the special content of public management. Significantly, it gives importance and credence to the view, expressed earlier by practitioners with experience in both business and government, that the decision-making processes of the private and public sectors are fundamentally different. This fundamental difference is a function of economic versus

political-economic decision criteria, of a private process versus a public process, and of invisible market regulation versus visible citizen regulation. Basic to these differences is the structure of rule in American government, where citizens, individually and in groups, are a continuing and pervasive organizational force. They shape the purposes of government activity, the means by which public managers carry out those purposes, and even how public managers come to think of themselves and their profession.

While the polity may become increasingly important to business as a result of public regulation, the publicization of business, and the growing demand that business serve social ends as well as profit, it is now of crucial importance primarily to government. This difference constitutes the critical distinguishing feature between public and private management. The importance of the polity is illustrated by Everett Carll Ladd's review of the erosion of public confidence and trust in government and the resulting implications not only for what government should do, but for what government *can* do. Americans' confidence in both business and government has declined, but the decline in public confidence has been relatively greater in recent times, with respect to government. For example, Ladd notes that in the 1950s and early 1960s, Americans felt their government was "run for the people, not for a few big interests. It could routinely be trusted to do what was right, and they accepted its general competency."

However, a profound change in the public's assessment began after 1965: "The people in increasing numbers then started saying that government was overgrown, indifferent to the common citizenry, untrustworthy, profligate, incompetent." Still, the public has not been shaken from fundamental long-held commitments to, and expectations about, government. They want to "conserve the basic institutional arrangements of their society—especially the constitutional order and the way the economy is organized—and they strongly back extensions of liberal social and economic programs." In short, it appears that Americans feel that government can and should do what it does, but should do so more efficiently and responsively.

While public sentiment generally is rational, well intended, and responsible, it nevertheless can have irrational, unintended, and irresponsible effects. For example, Ladd points to the erosion of institutions of representative democracy by recent political reforms:

> A romantic yearning for a "purer" direct democracy seems capable of generating a potentially dangerous attack on the *institutions* of representative democracy. The attack began back during the Vietnam years, aimed at political parties and spurred by Democrats who believed their party was insufficiently responsive to antiwar sentiment, as well as to the needs of women and ethnic minorities. The result was a series of "reforms" threat-

ening to undermine the roles of the political parties as intermediary institutions in nominations and elections. . . . Now it is the legislatures that are thought to be unresponsive to popular demands. This fall voters in twelve states passed propositions or amendments to take tax and spending decisions out of the hands of legislatures and subject them to formal constitutional limitations. The theory here is that if voters put a "cap" on taxes or spending, then legislatures will have to get busy and eliminate waste in order to preserve needed programs. At the national level, meanwhile, there have been hearings held on a proposed constitutional amendment to provide for federal initiatives: "The people shall have the right to enact any law which the Congress has the authority to pass, and to repeal any provision of law passed by Congress which has become law. . . ."

Joseph W. Whorton and John A. Worthley further argue that the paradoxical nature of the public's view of government puts public managers in an institutional and a psychological bind. The institutional bind stems from public demands for performance with simultaneous greater demands for control over how performance is achieved. When control becomes institutionalized in such mechanisms as budgetary constraint, civil service regulation, and legislative oversight, it tends to result, according to Whorton and Worthley, in the "rule of authority over the rule of common sense and managerial discrimination" and, in fact, to decrease performance.

The psychological bind results from the effect of the public's view, combined with the institutional controls created in response to that view, on the attitude of public managers. An atmosphere is created in which public managers come to expect that their "performance will always be something less than it could be." They can then rationalize their "inaction" as caused by the extensive constraints created by institutional controls, politics, media attention, and the public's low regard. Ironically, another product of this expectation is that public managers "who do manage" tend to discount their own accomplishments because to do otherwise would "run counter to the culture" (Whorton and Worthley). Thus, the attitudinal framework of public management tends to lower both public managers' perceptions of the possibilities of improved performance and their evaluations of their actual performance.

These paradoxes of public management reinforce Gary L. Wamsley and Mayer N. Zald's view that an understanding of the theory of government management requires a "political-economic" perspective. "Political" refers to "matters of legitimacy and distribution of power as they affect the propriety of an agency's existence, its functional niche . . . its collective institutional goals, the goals of the dominant elite faction . . . major parameters of economy, and in some instances the means of task accomplishment." In contrast, "economic" refers to the "arrangement of the division of labor and allocation of resources for task accomplishment and maximization of efficiency; and the combination of factors affecting the cost of producing and delivering a given level of services or output. If goals are well established and means routinized, an organization becomes largely an administered device, an economy" (Wamsley and Zald). The unique feature of public administration, then, is not that its goals and means are dynamic, because these change in private administration as well. Rather, what is unique is that goals and means are determined by political decision processes in which the public, or polity, plays a major role. Consequently, as also

noted by Frank H. Cassell, government and business decision-making processes are fundamentally different.

The convergence of these authors' views is striking. Wamsley is a public administrationist, and Zald, a sociologist. Cassell is a professor of industrial relations in a school of general administration. Wamsley and Zald are concerned with developing a theory that explains what is "public" about public administration, based on the notion of government as a political economy. Cassell is concerned with what current and impending changes toward greater "publicization" of business may mean for the private sector and for the education of future business managers. What is significant about these two essays is that, although the authors come at their subjects from different perspectives and for different purposes, their conclusions are basically similar. What then do they conclude about public management as differentiated from private management? What is the distinctive character of public management?

Basic to both essays is the view that the distribution of public sentiment and the power resources of individual and corporate actors are fundamental to the determination of public priorities, whereas profit is the fundamental determinant of business priorities. And it is the priorities that are the most important element of democratic control—not the means of production. Moreover, the *process of setting priorities* is different in business and government. In business, priorities are privately determined, primarily from the top down, in the interest of profit (with reluctant consideration of social values), aimed at anticipating cyclical demand, and regulated primarily by the invisible hand of the market. In government, priorities are determined from the bottom up, in the interest of social values (with tacit consideration of efficient production), through open decision-making processes potentially influenced by anyone who wants to get into the act, aimed at controlling socioeconomic conditions, and regulated by the highly visible hand of the polity.

Public sentiments and power distributions conflict, and so priorities ultimately are determined by political rather than technical criteria, through the process of negotiation and compromise among competing interests rather than through the application of tools and techniques of rational, quantitative analysis. Although such tools may aid in the determination of public priorities, they do not determine them in the same way as the profit-maximizing, single-criterion tools of business determine business priorities.

All of this points to the fact that public and private managerial elites are less interchangeable than they are often perceived to be. Despite the blurring of distinctions between public and private management and the continued interchange of managers between the sectors, fundamental differences exist in the decision processes for setting priorities. These differences often render the skills and techniques of business inappropriate for public-sector management. As noted by Cassell, the "more or less accidental (and often reluctant) involvement of business in community affairs is far from the same thing as the more fundamental ordering of priorities by community pressures. . . ." The public decision process requires managers with "the talent and temperament to plan and be comfortable with uncertainties and unknowns, who can find a consensus which must sometimes come through confrontation, and who can help adjust and readjust public and private systems to accommodate the new pressures and changing priorities. This is in contrast to the current goals of providing the

[business] executive and the planner with the tools to take the risk out of taking risks" (Cassell). Thus, public planning to meet social needs and political realities is different, not in degree, but in kind, from profit planning. Similarly, quantitative techniques, which are often useful in business planning and problem solving, are less useful in dealing with public values and sentiments. Sophisticated decision techniques may make quantitative contributions to public problem solving, but not final judgments.

It is readily apparent from the foregoing analysis that, although education for public and private management shares certain commonalities, education for the public sector must necessarily focus on the processes specific to the needs of public institutions, just as education for business must focus on the unique content of business management. This "mixed-model" of general administration and special administration, which recognizes both the common denominators and unique distinctions, is likely to become of increasing importance for the education of future managers.

Nowhere are the special character and limitations of public decision making more apparent than in the field of government regulation. John Dunlop's insightful analysis illustrates how the environment of public regulatory agencies critically shapes new regulations and simultaneously creates conditions that reduce the effectiveness and sensibility of those regulations. Dunlop's practical essay, in effect a case study of decision making and implementation in the public sector, is a fitting conclusion to this section, because it illustrates the fundamental dilemma of public management. Government agencies frequently are assigned tasks precisely because the private sector cannot or will not perform them or because the private sector has failed to perform them properly (as in the case of government regulations). However, these agencies are heavily constrained in the execution of public tasks by conflicting values, severely limited resources, and a self-defeating attitudinal framework. Given that public managers have the most difficult societal tasks to perform and the most constrained means of performance, it is extraordinarily difficult for them to be successful in restoring public trust and confidence in government. But, as Dunlop notes, creating and developing public trust is *the problem* for government in our times.

What the Voters Really Want

Everett Carll Ladd, Jr.

A professor at a large eastern university had labored throughout the semester to explain contemporary politics to his students. Now, it was final examination time, and he confronted them with but a single question.

Two hours; one hundred points

A stranger arrives from a far-distant land, totally unfamiliar with the society and politics of the country on whose soil he now stands. He talks to the natives, reads their press, attends meetings, observes an election. He learns these things:

- *Only about one in seven among the citizens claim they have a high regard for the capacities of those who govern them. Half the populace believes the government is run by people who don't know what they are doing. Two-thirds don't think their leaders can regularly be trusted to do what is right. The national legislature is held in especially low esteem.*

- *In a genuinely free, fair, and contested election, however, the voters return to office overwhelming majorities of the incumbents—throughout the provinces and nationally. Only twenty-six of 399 officeholders seeking reelection to the national legislature are defeated. The governing party finds its lead largely undiminished.*

- *The citizens think their government has become oversized and overly powerful, and that it spends to an excess. They especially resent taxes—which they regard as too high and inequitably assessed. Three-fourths of them claim to have reached the "breaking point" in the taxes they pay. They endorse draconian measures to reduce their tax burden—cuts of more than 50 percent in government levies on their property and of one third in taxation of their income.*

- *Yet, this rebellious populace looks to the government for help in resolving virtually every public problem it faces. The state should take measures to stop prices from rising and to ensure a job for everyone who wants to work. Government should guarantee that there is low-cost medical care through a national health insurance system. It should not reduce expenditures—if anything, should increase them—for schools, recreation, police, libraries, environmental cleanup, urban redevelopment, and aid to disadvantaged ethnic groups.*

Drawing upon information that you have collected this semester, construct for our hypothetical visitor a plausible explanation of the above situation. Please note: I will not entertain an interpretation based on "national insanity."

P.S. You know that every datum in the above tale has been taken unburnished from leading U.S. public-opinion polls.

What indeed are we to make of the American electorate's seemingly wayward and inconsistent mood? The people are enraged over big government and their tax burdens—and they want a lot more of the services they think government should provide. They are fed up with Congress—and they think their particular Congressman is doing just fine. When the votes were counted November 7, the results of the mid-term election had to be read as at least a superficial endorsement of the party in power. The Democrats came away with majorities of fifty-nine to forty-one in the U.S. Senate and 276 to 159 in the House. They hold thirty-two governorships and control at least sixty-seven of the ninety-eight state senates and lower houses.

Such facts pose an obvious riddle. It is true that a few well-known liberals were defeated in the Senate, and it is probably also true that the new Congress, regardless of the party labels, is a shade more conservative than the old. Some of the Democratic victors campaigned as arch foes of bloated, wasteful government. But is it really conceivable that voters militantly taking arms against the size and scale of the state would be incapable of recognizing the preeminent role of the Democratic party since F.D.R. in building the massive edifice that is modern American government?

This is not the case at all. The fact is that a good many political analysts have not been listening closely enough to the message the public has been sending for more than a decade now. This message is complex, but it is not unclear. "Cut taxes" is part of the message, but it is not the central part. Nor is "Cut government programs" the serious message. The American people have not become more conservative in their attitudes toward government. Indeed, the movement of opinion over the past decade or two is better described as liberal than as conservative. Americans have become *more* demanding of governmental services, thus more liberal in the New Deal sense. On "social issues," too, we see a liberal drift. There has been a fairly dramatic growth of the pro–civil liberties and pro–civil rights positions; and there has been an erosion of many of the old codes of personal comportment, governing a range of such matters as premarital sex, abortion, and the use of marijuana.

This is not to suggest that the public is blissfully happy about the recent course of American society and politics. Quite the contrary is true. Not since the days of the Great Depression have Americans been so complaining or skeptical about the quality and character of their country's public perfor-

PART FOUR
THE
ORGANIZATIONAL
ENVIRONMENT:
MONITORING AND
CONTROLLING
EXTERNAL ACTIVITY

mance. The people are saying something about government that is serious, substantial, and far more consequential to the future of American democracy than the simple notion of a taxpayers' revolt suggests.

Two key elements in the contemporary response to the state are of prime importance. First, confidence that government can accomplish those things the people want done has declined over the past fifteen years to a point lower than at any time in the modern era. This deterioration is diffuse and generalized, not focused and specific—with the public doubting government's overall effectiveness, rather than its performance in one or two areas.

Second, this dissatisfaction, while pervasive, has not shaken the public from some fundamental, long-held commitments—and expectations of government. Americans remain *institutional conservatives* and *operational liberals*. They want to conserve the basic institutional arrangements of their society—especially the constitutional order and the way the economy is organized—and they strongly back extensions of liberal social and economic programs. What the discontent with governmental performance has done thus far has been to intensify and enlarge symbolic protests. This means an affirmation of conservative or antistate values in public rhetoric and an inclination to chastise government—so long as all the complaining talk is not likely to seriously disrupt actual programs. We may add, then, to the above description: Americans are operational liberals, institutional conservatives, and *symbolic conservatives* as well. They will pass a Proposition 13 *and* return a liberal Democratic Congress. They will endorse reduced spending in principle—while voting for increased spending on specific programs.

Whatever the political commentators may think, the voters of today do not see anything schizophrenic about these attitudes and actions. They think they are making reasoned and objective responses to clearly evident problems. Over the past quarter century, the nation's families earning around the median income have seen the proportions of their income paid in taxes approximately double—from 11.8 percent in 1953 to 22.5 percent in 1977. Because incomes have grown dramatically, the tax increase in dollar terms has been even more alarming. These families have not perceived any comparable increase in the value of the services they receive from government. This has been enough to convince them that government at all levels wastes far too much of their money. The public has been virtually shouting: "You can make cuts in our taxes *without* reducing public services. We know you can."

Almost every major survey on the topic documents the exceptional emphasis voters place on governmental waste and inefficiency. They argue, for instance, that property taxes could be reduced by at least 20 percent without significant service reductions. So strong is this perception of a highly inefficient government that just after Proposition 13 mandated a 57 percent property-tax cut, two-thirds of the California families deriving all or part of their income from state or local payrolls said it was not likely that many of the state's public-service workers would lose their jobs. There was, of course, the special California circumstance of a huge state surplus, whose existence had led State Treasurer Jesse Unruh to describe Governor Jerry Brown as the "father of Proposition 13." But it is also clear from extensive surveys that California voters of all persuasions believe government is appallingly casual

Pollster Louis Harris has asked Americans since 1966 whether they have "a great deal of confidence, only some confidence, or hardly any confidence at all..." in the leadership of various institutions. The percentage expressing some or a lot of confidence has declined sharply, leaving no institution unscathed. Confidence in governmental leadership recovered a bit after Watergate but has plunged again this year.

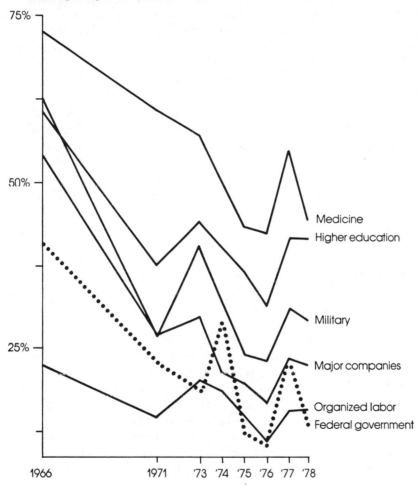

and wasteful when it comes to their tax dollars.

We find this same emphasis on waste in personal interviews conducted for *Fortune* this fall in three sections of the U.S. "You should walk down the halls of the state capitol and look into the offices. They could probably eliminate two out of every five persons that are there," a Des Moines TV repairman asserted. A San Jose housewife insisted that "if my husband's store were run as loosely as the government is, it would go bankrupt in a month." An engineer in Newton, Massachusetts, a prosperous Boston suburb, claimed to "strongly favor most of the things government here and nationally is attempting, but I sure as hell wish things could be run more efficiently. Waste plays

PART FOUR
THE
ORGANIZATIONAL
ENVIRONMENT:
MONITORING AND
CONTROLLING
EXTERNAL ACTIVITY

right into the hands of the extreme tax cutters." Such assessments are the rule—not the exception.

Do Americans really believe that property taxes can be cut 57 percent, or income taxes by a third, without a serious impact on services? Not really. The tax protest is based on a genuine belief that government can and *should* do all that it *is* doing—but much more efficiently. The protest is also symbolic—a deliberately exaggerated expression of low regard for the government's competence. This seems to Americans to be a rational way to dramatize an important problem. They see the contemporary state as a very unresponsive animal, one that will not pay attention until it gets a jolting shock. In fact, the polls show that unresponsiveness ranks right beside incompetence and waste in the catalogue of public complaints about government. As an elderly resident of Des Moines put it: "Anytime you call the government, they put you on hold."

In one sense, the Proposition 13 vote was as much about responsiveness as taxes. Over and over again in the interviews we conducted for *Fortune,* Californians complained about the big state surplus that had accumulated while voters struggled with rising property taxes. "Why didn't they do something sooner?" a retired Redwood City homeowner exclaimed in frustration. "Why did they make us use a meat axe?" The meat-axe metaphor is especially popular. Even proponents of Proposition 13 applied it to their handiwork. "It's not the right way to do things," many were saying, "but we had to show them."

This mood of the voters is relatively new. As recently as the Eisenhower and Kennedy years, government seemed to them to function a lot better than it does today. Today, Americans feel that in the 1950s and early 1960s—as they told the pollsters at the time—their government was run for "the people," not for a few big interests. It could routinely be trusted to do what was right, and they accepted its general competency.

The profound change in assessment began after 1965. The people in increasing numbers then started saying that government was overgrown, indifferent to the common citizenry, untrustworthy, profligate, incompetent. Whatever the phrasing of the questions, and whatever component of governmental performance the pollsters sought to assess, they found the same constant theme: a generalized erosion of trust and confidence. During this period, to be sure, every major institution—education, religion, business, the press, and so on—was falling in public esteem. But none fell more dramatically than government.

During these same years, of course, government was treating the public to some historic failures: a costly, "no-win" war in Southeast Asia, a "Great Society" of domestic programs that promised much and seemed to deliver little, the scandal of Watergate, and the worst recession since the 1930s. Just when confidence in government was picking up a bit, the specter of inflation reappeared, implacable in its claims on real family income, seemingly intractable, defying conventional economic wisdom and the country's political leadership, and profoundly shaking all faith in government. It is hardly surprising that the polls find dissatisfaction with governmental performance more vehement today than in the most troubled days of the Vietnam War or Watergate.

Although the doubts about government's ability to deal with major prob-

DISTRUST OF THE FEDERAL GOVERNMENT INCREASES

Government generally, but especially on the national level, now gets roundly criticized by large majorities as wasteful, unreliable, and a creature of "the interests." The growth of this pervasive distrust has gone on with no real interruption since the early 1960's. The data in the accompanying chart come from a number of different sources, but especially from the election-year surveys by the Center for Political Studies of the University of Michigan.

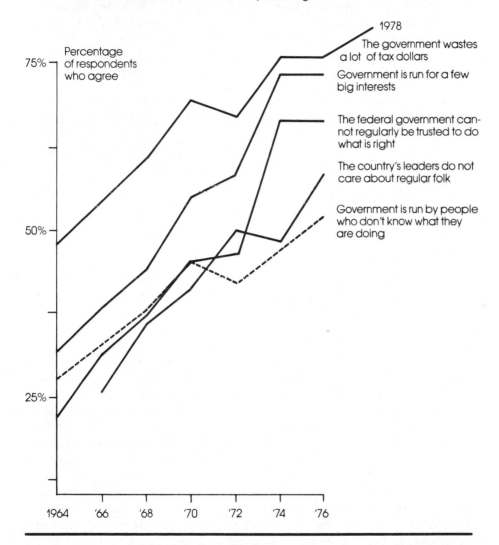

lems can be traced to those earlier failures, it seems clear that confidence will not be restored until the campaign to control inflation begins to prevail. In this respect, the public's willingness to pay whatever price may be necessary seems to have been running well ahead of government's willingness to act.

By overwhelming majorities, Americans are prepared to support a variety of different means that promise some cure for inflation. They give solid endorsement to wage and price controls. A clear majority says it would prefer to get a pay increase *lower* than the cost of living—if there were some assurance

119

PART FOUR
THE
ORGANIZATIONAL
ENVIRONMENT:
MONITORING AND
CONTROLLING
EXTERNAL ACTIVITY

that inflation would really be brought under control. Though the public thinks taxes are too high and wants some relief, it is even more anxious to have inflation licked. The CBS News/*New York Times* surveys show roughly two-thirds of the Congress in favor of some rollback of the Social Security tax increase mandated by the Ninety-fifth Congress—apparently an anticipatory response to the voters' presumed anger—while *two-thirds of the voters themselves want to keep the new taxes in place.* About 90 percent of the public maintains that "controlling inflation is more important than cutting taxes."

After their painful education with this problem over the last decade, Americans have changed their thinking about its source. In the 1950s and early 1960s, they blamed inflation mostly on labor and business. Now they are convinced that governmental actions in taxing and spending are the major cause.

They hold government responsible and have concluded, moreover, that it is incapable of acting effectively. A clear majority believes that no President and no unit of government outside the presidency will be able to "keep prices from going up all the time." Similarly, two-thirds of Americans believe that a balanced federal budget within the next few years is unattainable, no matter who their leaders are. During the 1974–75 bout with double-digit inflation, about two-thirds of the populace did not agree that inflation had become "one of the facts of life and here to stay." They thought instead that it would be halted after a while. By the summer of 1978, however, high inflation was thought to be as certain as the proverbial death and taxes. By an extraordinary 9-to-1 margin, Americans had come to believe that high inflation would relentlessly continue.

Inflation, then, is the prime cause for public doubt of the competence of big government. If either political party could convince the American people that it could be counted upon for a coherent and effective response to inflation, it would reap huge electoral dividends. Neither party, of course, has yet succeeded in this. The Republican failure is especially striking because "sound money" has been the G.O.P.'s strong suit. Today the Democrats are trusted by more people than the Republicans when it comes to handling inflation—while half the populace says there is no difference between the two. It seems clear that, electorally at least, the G.O.P. blundered with its Kemp-Roth proposal and demonstrated anew the dangers of partial knowledge. The party had been told—quite correctly—that Americans were wedded to the service state and that it was losing votes by appearing niggardly on services. So G.O.P. leaders decided to soften all talk about cuts in services and emphasize a massive tax cut. But while the people want services, they also want leadership that inspires confidence in its responsibility—especially its ability to bring inflation under control. It may be a deficiency in their appreciation of "Laffer curves," but Americans for the most part do not believe that a one-third cut in federal income taxes is a notably competent or reasoned response to an inflation caused, to some substantial degree, by government deficits.

Obviously, a "competency gap" that was fifteen years in the making will not be easily closed. Yet it also appears that all the public's seething frustrations do not yet add up to a crisis for American democracy. While Americans are intensely critical of the state, they do not bristle with resentment at its authority. They do not even want to slash its size or narrow its range of responsibility. They want rather to reform it—though they are at sea as to how this can be done. Their mood, contentious but not really rebellious, is accounted for by two fundamental features of their larger outlook on the world. They are generally satisfied with and optimistic about their personal lives. And in the political realm, they embrace rather than repudiate the progression of governmental interventions that we call the service state.

If American conservatives have committed one near-fatal blunder, it has been in failing to appreciate the depth of the popular commitment to the service state. Yet they have had fair warning. Over and over again, when Americans are asked whether they want to cut back on spending for public services, they have come down overwhelmingly in favor of sustaining or increasing current levels. (The one isolated exception is the area of "welfare," but this connotes, to the average American, a dole for those *unwilling* to work.) People in all economic groups, in all regions, and of all political perspectives have endorsed big government.

The fusion of operational liberalism with symbolic conservatism could not be more clear. Ninety percent or more of those who insist their federal taxes are too high want to maintain or increase public spending to clean up the environment, to improve the nation's health, and to strengthen the educational system. It is equally striking—at a time when much is made about the clashes between various special-interest groups—that Americans do not appear in the polls to be particularly selfish. Among those who think their taxes are too high, for example, 70 percent or more favor high spending to solve urban problems and to improve the situation of black Americans.

Nonetheless, there are some worrisome trends. A romantic yearning for a "purer" direct democracy seems capable of generating a potentially dangerous attack on the *institutions* of representative democracy. The attack began back during the Vietnam years, aimed at political parties and spurred by Democrats who believed their party was insufficiently responsive to antiwar sentiment, as well as to the needs of women and ethnic minorities. The result was a series of "reforms" threatening to undermine the roles of the political parties as intermediary institutions in nominations and elections. The most serious single step here involved the increasing recourse to direct primaries. Nearly three-fourths of all Democratic convention delegates and two-thirds of the Republic delegates were selected through primaries in 1976. The resultant near-anarchy in the political parties has weakened the capacity of representative institutions to respond in a coherent way to major problems.

Now it is the legislatures that are thought to be unresponsive to popular demands. This fall the voters in twelve states passed propositions or amendments to take tax and spending decisions out of the hands of legislatures and subject them to formal constitutional limitations. The theory here is that if voters put a "cap" on taxes or spending, then legislatures will have to get busy and eliminate waste in order to preserve needed programs. At the national level, meanwhile, there have been hearings held on a proposed constitutional amendment to provide for federal initiatives: "The people shall have the right to enact any law which the Congress has the authority to pass, and to repeal any provision of law passed by Congress which has become law. . . ."

121

PART FOUR
THE
ORGANIZATIONAL
ENVIRONMENT:
MONITORING AND
CONTROLLING
EXTERNAL ACTIVITY

GOVERNMENT IS TOO POWERFUL

	NO	YES
Do you think the federal government is too strong?	28%	72%
Would you like a smaller government providing fewer services?.	40%	60%

BUT IT SHOULD DO MORE

	NO	YES
Do you want the government to impose wage and price controls?	39%	61%
Do you want a national health-insurance program?.	33%	67%
Do you want the government to help people get low-cost medical care? . . .	15%	85%
Do you want the government to see to it that everyone who wants a job gets one?	23%	77%

Americans seem to be sending out contradictory messages. The public thinks the federal government is too strong and spends too much money—but wants it to solve a lot of intractable problems and open its pocketbook for various social causes. The data in the charts are drawn from a variety of the most reputable recent surveys of American opinion.

TOO MUCH FEDERAL SPENDING

	TOO MUCH	TOO LITTLE OR ABOUT RIGHT
Is the federal government spending	82%	17%

BUT NOT ENOUGH FOR PUBLIC SERVICES

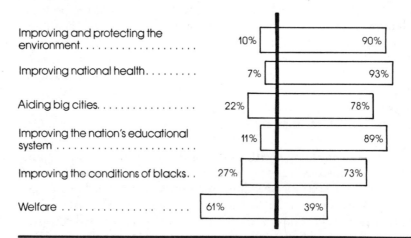

Improving and protecting the environment.	10%	90%
Improving national health.	7%	93%
Aiding big cities.	22%	78%
Improving the nation's educational system	11%	89%
Improving the conditions of blacks. .	27%	73%
Welfare	61%	39%

Although this proposed amendment is at a very preliminary stage in the approval process, it still must be taken seriously as an omen. It has at least thirty-five congressional sponsors, and it was endorsed by about 100 candidates for election to the House of Representatives in 1978. In a Gallup survey last spring, nearly three-fourths of Americans who had an opinion on the matter supported the idea of federal initiatives. That a scheme so palpably unworkable—and so threatening to the whole structure of American representative democracy—should receive serious discussion is an extraordinary sign of public exasperation with the ways and costs of government.

A study of American political behavior by a distinguished political scientist, the late V. O. Key, Jr., advanced "the perverse and unorthodox argument" that "voters are not fools." Key conceded that many citizens sometimes respond in odd or unpredictable fashion. But he still insisted that "in the large the electorate behaves about as rationally and responsibly as we should expect. . . ."

Nothing in all the current signs and measures of popular sentiment seriously contradicts this general judgment. There is nothing irrational about a public sense of grave anxiety and frustration under the converging pressures of soaring prices in the private sector and soaring taxes in the public sector. Alike for the governed and for those who govern, there are no simple ways to contain these pressures. So the complaint of the people is not simple—and should not be construed simplistically.

The heart of the indictment is a call not for *less* government but for *better* government. The urging is not for government to retreat but to reform. In a large and special sense, the problem of government looms before the voter as the most dramatic form of inflation itself. And he has responded precisely in this spirit. As a citizen-shopper in the private sector, he does not think the answer to inflation is to be found in his being forced to purchase *less*—but in his having a chance to meet his needs at a moderate price. As a citizen-voter in the public sector, similarly, he does not want the services and programs of government eliminated or curtailed. He wants their cost to be within the reach of his ability to pay.

From this, obviously, there can only follow tension between the citizenry and its government. But the essential message of 1978 is a sober call for improved performance. There is little of a blind lashing out at government, and nothing could be more unfortunate than for government to answer this call with a series of contrived responses, unrealistic promises, and exaggerated rhetoric. Such a reaction would only strengthen the doubts already felt about the government's competency and responsiveness.

The call is as unglamorous as it is important: to seek out means of reducing waste, improving services, and enhancing the capacity of representative institutions to deal coherently with broad national needs. It can be heeded, but the exercise will be a demanding test of maturity for both the voters and their leaders.

PART FOUR
THE
ORGANIZATIONAL
ENVIRONMENT:
MONITORING AND
CONTROLLING
EXTERNAL ACTIVITY

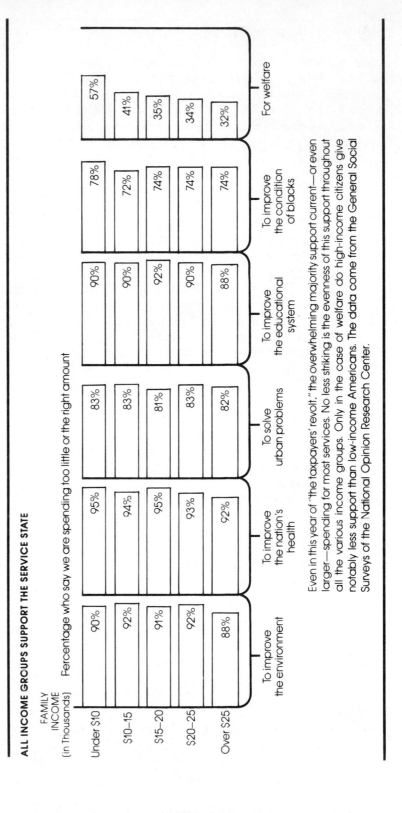

ALL INCOME GROUPS SUPPORT THE SERVICE STATE

FAMILY INCOME (in Thousands)

Percentage who say we are spending too little or the right amount

FAMILY INCOME (in Thousands)	To improve the environment	To improve the nation's health	To solve urban problems	To improve the educational system	To improve the condition of blacks	For welfare
Under $10	90%	95%	83%	90%	78%	57%
$10–15	92%	94%	83%	90%	72%	41%
$15–20	91%	95%	81%	92%	74%	35%
$20–25	92%	93%	83%	90%	74%	34%
Over $25	88%	92%	82%	88%	74%	32%

Even in this year of "the taxpayers' revolt," the overwhelming majority support current—or even larger—spending for most services. No less striking is the evenness of this support throughout all the various income groups. Only in the case of welfare do high-income citizens give notably less support than low-income Americans. The data come from the General Social Surveys of the National Opinion Research Center.

WHICH IS MORE COMPETENT—GOVERNMENT OR BUSINESS?

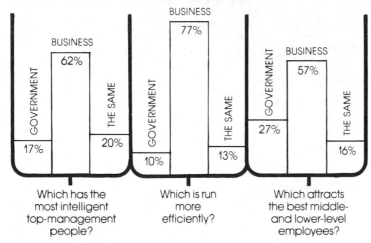

| Which has the most intelligent top-management people? | Which is run more efficiently? | Which attracts the best middle- and lower-level employees? |

Business corporations are not loved these days. But when the Roper Organization asked Americans to compare business competence with governmental competence, business received positively glowing marks. Which is run more efficiently? Business—by nearly 8 to 1.

CONGRESSMEN YES, CONGRESS NO

Do you approve of:

The job Congress is doing?

The job your Congressman is doing?

	NO	YES
The job Congress is doing?	64%	36%
The job your Congressman is doing?	25%	75%

Congress is held in notably low esteem by Americans. Logically, they should welcome any chance to throw out the incompetent rascals, right? Wrong. The people hold their own individual Congressmen in quite high esteem. It is the institution of Congress that is severely faulted for poor performance. The data are from a September, 1978, survey by CBS News/New York Times.

9 | A Perspective on the Challenge of Public Management: Environmental Paradox and Organizational Culture

Joseph W. Whorton
John A. Worthley

A striking phenomenon in American public management is the paradoxical nature of its environment. On the one hand, American society gives its public bureaucracy enormous powers and expects public managers to energetically provide desired public services. On the other hand, there is a distrust and disdain evident in the public's view of the governmental bureaucracy. Public managers are given considerable resources and broad discretion for administering programs, but are subjected to an array of laws, procedures, and norms intended to closely control their behavior. While entrusted with large amounts of money and administrative power, they are deluged with judicial rulings, "golden fleece awards," beat reporters, taxpayer revolts, and legislative investigations, not to mention freedom of information maxims, administrative procedure dictates, and performance audits. Epitomizing the paradox is the odd fact that society calls public managers both "civil servants" (a rather commendatory term) and "bureaucrats" (a pejorative).

As a result of this paradoxical environment, the world or "culture" of the public administrator is complex and challenging to say the least, and often is confounding and confusing. Efforts to improve public management have, understandably, proven to be difficult.

Although this phenomenon of paradox has long been recognized, its effect on the task and behavior of public managers has seldom been probed. In this article, we present a perspective on the phenomenon, using the concept of

Reprinted from Joseph W. Whorton and John A. Worthley, "A Perspective on the Challenge of Public Management: Environmental Paradox and Organizational Culture," *Academy of Management Review*, July 1981, 6, 357–361.

organizational culture to explore the consequences for management in the public sector. Our findings suggest that inadequate appreciation of the paradoxical phenomenon has been a significant cause of difficulty in applying modern management advances to public administration.

■ 9 ■
Joseph W. Whorton
John A. Worthley

ORGANIZATIONAL CULTURE AND PUBLIC ADMINISTRATION

The paradoxical nature of the environment of public administration can be crystallized through the concept of organizational culture developed by Redfield (1941), Margulies (1969), Evan (1974), and Pettigrew (1979). Briefly, the concept is that all organizations have a culture that affects individual and group behavior in a predictable way. To the extent that this culture affects behavior, it will determine perceptions of what the organization really is, what its prospects for success are, and who counts. Where the culture is well defined and articulated, individual expressions about the organization and its membership are suppressed. The pressure is in favor of the individual supporting the norms and beliefs of the culture rather than voicing beliefs that run counter to the culture.

For example, Barnard (1938) portrayed organizations as cooperative systems controlled in part by what he termed the "informal organization." The informal organization's effect is manifest in two ways: first, it establishes certain group attitudes, customs, norms, and roles; and second, it helps to maintain, expand, and clarify what Barnard called the "zone of indifference." Taylor (1911) had articulated a similar phenomenon when he argued that workers, through their informal organization, establish work rates and control those individuals who deviate from the group work norm. Although Barnard and Taylor provide rich descriptions of how informal organizations can work, they do not fully address the issue of the source of the norms, rules, and so forth found in both the informal and formal organization. The concept of organizational culture focuses on understanding the sources of such organizational behavior and determinants of performance.

It is our opinion that, in the public sector, the culture, or sources of organizational behavior, can be traced to the paradox—which, as outlined above, includes both a philosophical expression of high ideals and aspirations (a positive force) and a distrusting statement of constraints and limited powers (a negative force). The positive force springs from policy mandates that generate legislation designed to create administrative action directed at meeting public goals and objectives. These legislative acts often loftily define the purpose of the public agency in terms of promoting the "common good," of solving problems, and of protecting society. They do, indeed, affirm the positive possibility of public administration; they form a major cultural aspect of the environment of public management.

The other major aspect of public administration, the negative force, is characterized by constraint and limitation and is typically labelled "bureaucracy." For the public manager, bureaucracy transcends the agency as a legislated statement of the normative behavior expected of all public employees. As culture, it represents operationalization of such societal ideology as public service, accountability, protection from governmental abuse, and the like. Sunshine laws, personal financial disclosure, civil service protection, and

127

PART FOUR
THE
ORGANIZATIONAL
ENVIRONMENT:
MONITORING AND
CONTROLLING
EXTERNAL ACTIVITY

accountability procedures are all examples of attempts to control and limit the behavior of public employees. As such, they are negative statements about the intrinsic nature and propensity of the public employee, and they reflect a societal distrust of administrative agencies. Hummel (1978) and Peters and Nelson (1979) provide notable illustrations of this negative perspective.

To manage in the public sector, then, is to function in a domain of competing values and of paradox. To illustrate: competitive bidding is law based on principles of accountability and control. Public administrators are required to follow mandates for competitive bidding even though such practice may cause them to pay more for a product than would be charged on the open market. They do this while being fully aware that they may be seen by the public as, consequently, being wasteful and blindly following procedures. They are forced to trade off between accountability and efficiency.

Beyond this kind of generic dilemma, public managers are sent frequent messages to rationalize their methods and to become more efficient at their jobs. Writings and discussions on practical public administration, delivered didactically, are seldom wanting in stress on "shoulds" and on prescriptive technological approaches to management. Formalized performance evaluations, systems analysis, participatory management, and productivity improvement are often presented as magic potions that will rationalize public operations and make them more effective. Public managers are, inevitably, criticized for not fully grasping these "rational" methods.

As a result of these realities, managers face a schizophrenic existence. They wear the hat of agent for the social good as well as the hat of incipient wrongdoer. Indeed, the great majority of public managers with whom we have dealt describe their work world as bounded by the rule of law, procedure, and structure. In this culture, restraints on individual behavior take on important symbolic and methodological meaning by being elevated to an institutional status. Where the controls are institutionalized, they cease being negative statements about self-worth and become, instead, devices easily viewed by managers as limiting their ability to manage. Control-based institutions such as the budget division, civil service law, and legislative committees are ascribed great power and influence in the culture.

Perceptions of and attitudes toward these institutions provide the individual a cognitive map or rationale of how and why work is determined, organized, and accomplished. To the extent that activity spawned by these institutions is conflicting, irrational, or wholly nonproductive, the organizational culture legitimizes the rule of authority over the rule of common sense or managerial discrimination (Weick, 1977). A consequence, judging from our experience, is a particular approach to management that may help explain behavior patterns of public administrators.

CONSEQUENCES OF THE CULTURE: "IF-ONLYS" AND "THEMS"

A noticeable consequence of this culture in the public sector is an organizational lore that develops, reinforces, and maintains attitudinal and behavioral norms that form what we call the "if-only" approach to management. The work environment of public administration, replete with its myriad of constraints, is viewed in the if-only approach as exacerbating the difficulty of getting a job done. This view is expressed through such phrases as "the damned civil service rules," "the meddling legislature," "the plodding legal department," "the unending paperwork," and "the confounded computer." Obstructions are seen as relentlessly impeding the public manager's efforts to get on with the job. Concomitantly, new bromides and gimmicks designed to increase managerial competence and efficiency are viewed as implying that the task *can* be done and that the problem is with the manager.

■ 9 ■
Joseph W. Whorton
John A. Worthley

The approach to management that emerges from these views is suggested in the comments of managers who confront these situations in the practical world of public administration. The following litany is representative of public managers' responses when asked about their jobs:

"The rules tie our hands."
"If only the union weren't so powerful."
"The budget division prevents us from meeting program goals."
"Politics undermines the intent of the project."
"I can't motivate my people because of the freeze on wages."

Statements like these cloak significant managerial attitudes. They are often offered as excuses for nonmanagement or as explanations of managerial failure ("We can't do anything about it," or "They prevent us from doing what really needs to be done"). In some public organizations, the persistence of these attitudes produces a distinct managerial style that largely shapes the atmosphere of the organization. It is the "if-only" approach to management:

"If only I could fire Jones, then we could get this department in shape."
"If only the legislature would stop playing politics with our program."
"If only I could hire the best people instead of those the Civil Service and affirmative action office send me."
"If only the budget division would stop setting expenditure ceilings."

An important component of if-onlys is "thems." Thems are creatures that lurk "out there" and whose major purpose is to torment public managers and obstruct efforts to do what needs to be done. Thems spend a lot of time plotting the downfall of administrators. Sometimes they attack directly, sometimes they construct roadblocks, and—worst of all—sometimes they are totally indifferent to management. There are many thems. Some of the more prominent are the politicians, the press, the civil service system, the consumer groups, and the budget analysts. They are viewed as causes of inaction and inefficiency.

In brief, the if-only manager is characterized by the use of statements, attributable to the organizational culture, that explain or rationalize the paradoxes and inconsistencies in the environment. If-onlys are employed to reinforce perceptions of the nature of the work and to maintain legitimacy and credibility with the immediate social network. They provide a psychological "out" from a frustrating work environment. They foster an elaborate myth that insulates the organization from the environment by creating the expectancy that performance will always be something less than it could be.

PART FOUR
THE
ORGANIZATIONAL
ENVIRONMENT:
MONITORING AND
CONTROLLING
EXTERNAL ACTIVITY

When fully institutionalized as part of the culture, if-onlys and thems can produce a wholly negative focus and become defense mechanisms for resisting change and denying the possibility that new technologies might improve organizational performance. They can also be used to depict organizational subunits as adversaries. Line units tend to shift responsibility for poor performance to staff units, which are, of course, significant "thems" viewed as constantly narrowing discretion and usurping power. To listen carefully to an organization's if-onlys and thems is to hear of armed camps, warring factions, and perpetual struggles.

This is not to suggest that if-onlys and thems are solely the products of individual and organizational neuroses. Nor are they merely the products of overactive paranoid minds or of fantasy and convenience. If-onlys and thems do, indeed, have some basis in fact. Budget cuts do complicate public programs; civil service does structure hiring; legislators do meddle. Public managers' ability to maneuver is limited. Thus, to the extent that such problems occur, the if-only approach to management is a realistic managerial assessment and guideline (Dandridge, 1980).

The problem is that, though it begins with an accurate perception of reality, the if-only approach often develops in an unrealistic direction and is used to justify inaction. It is unrealistic to maintain that civil service procedures prevent any accomplishment, just as it is unrealistic to behave as though nothing can be achieved because of a budget cut. Moreover, it is simplistic to believe that "if-only the legislature would appropriate money, the program would succeed."

This leads us to a second facet of if-onlys and thems, one that is particularly disconcerting. Public managers often do manage—"despite" the legislature, "despite" the budget office, "despite" the press leak. Thems are, in fact, dealt with. That is, not only do public administrators tend to use if-onlys to lessen responsibility for action, they also use them to discount their own accomplishments! So complete is the job of reinforcement through the organizational culture that many managers cannot or will not acknowledge their own successes. To do so would run counter to the culture.

IMPLICATIONS OF THE PARADOX

The concept of organizational culture takes us beyond mere recognition of the paradoxical environment of public administration to the implications of the paradox for management. One implication is that the challenge of managing in the public sector is more complicated than managing in less paradoxical environments. The business manager may indeed have it easier than the public manager—as Curtis (1980, p. 57) and Fottler (1981, pp. 9–10) have concluded. This is not to suggest that the culture of private management is free from such complications. If-onlys and thems clearly exist in business organizations as well. Line/staff interactions, certain techniques, government regulations, and the like are significant complicating aspects of the business environment. The difference in the public sector is that the paradoxical pressures are much more prevalent, run much deeper, and produce more remarkable behavior patterns. For example, while both public and business managers face legal forces in their respective environments, in public administration there is considerably greater reliance on and vulnerability to the law. Government regulations are a challenging reality of business administration, but legalisms circumscribe and influence the operation of a public organization thoroughly. "In private management," observe Pfiffner and Presthus, "one is assured that he can do anything not specifically forbidden. In public administration, on the other hand, discretion is limited" (1967, p. 427). George Berkley portrays the difference more forcefully: "In private administration the law generally tells the administrator what he *cannot* do; in public administration the law tells him what he *can* do" (1981, p. 10). This reality, when combined with other forces, such as the continual scrutiny to which public managers are subjected, understandably prompts a different perspective.

■ 9 ■
Joseph W. Whorton
John A. Worthley

A second implication of the paradox is that public managers tend to underplay or disclaim their accomplishments because of the organizational culture. As devotees at the altar of reason, managers expect things to "make sense." The premium placed on reason makes it difficult to accept and appreciate paradox. Our experience suggests that, faced with the paradoxical nature of their environment, public managers tend to rationalize the paradox; and the process of rationalization creates the perception that it is not possible for them to accomplish as much as a business manager. In the language of psychology, the public manager caught in this situation exhibits the classic neurosis called an inferiority complex. Like the inferior personality, the public manager discounts performance and holds to a limited view of the possible; and these feelings persist even when by objective standards the individual may be performing well and achieving all that might be expected. In such cases, the message of actual performance does not get through to organization members and, perhaps more important, to the public. Self-image and public perception may consequently be distorted.

A third implication is that efforts to improve public management might benefit from understanding and addressing factors of organizational culture. Our findings suggest that knowledge of the culture and efforts to change it may be a necessary first step before new work methods and modern technologies can be successfully implemented. The area of budget techniques is illustrative. In the past twenty years, public managers have faced four "new" budget techniques. Program budgeting, PPBS, MBO, and ZBB have all been held up as new and improved medicine that would cure them of a plague of bloated budgets, waste, and inefficiency. In practice, none of the techniques has realized its promise, and all have tended to confound more than assist the work of the manager. One cause of these difficulties, we believe, is that the techniques ignore or underestimate the paradoxical environment that limits management flexibility, and the norms and attitudes of the organizational culture that, if unaddressed, produce behavior unconducive to success.

Clearly, more research is needed to properly portray the organizational culture of public administration, and to test and expand our impressions. Developments in the federal government under President Reagan, for example, are ripe for study. Our initial work does suggest that the concept of organizational culture can provide a useful prism for viewing the challenge of public management in a new light.

PART FOUR
THE
ORGANIZATIONAL
ENVIRONMENT:
MONITORING AND
CONTROLLING
EXTERNAL ACTIVITY

REFERENCES

Barnard, C. *The functions of the executive.* Cambridge: Harvard University Press, 1938.

Berkley, G. E. *The craft of public administration* (3rd ed.). Boston: Allyn & Bacon, 1981.

Curtis, D. A. Management in the public sector: It really is harder. *Tempo,* 1980, *26,* 57–61.

Dandridge, T. Organizational symbolism: A topic to expand organizational analysis. *Academy of Management Review,* 1980, *5,* 248–256.

Evan, W. M. Culture and organizational systems. *Organization & Administrative Sciences,* 1974, *5,* 12–19.

Fottler, M. D. Is management really generic? *Academy of Management Review,* 1981, 6, 1–12.

Hummel, R. *The bureaucratic experience.* New York: St. Martin's, 1978.

Margulies, N. Organizational culture and psychological growth. *Journal of Applied Behavioral Sciences,* 1969, *5,* 490–498.

Peters, C.; & Nelson, M. *The culture of bureaucracy.* New York: Holt, Rinehart & Winston, 1979.

Pettigrew, A. On studying organizational cultures. *Administrative Science Quarterly,* 1979, *24,* 568–579.

Pfiffner, J. M.; & Presthus, R. *Public administration.* New York: Ronald, 1967.

Redfield, R. *The folk culture of Yucatan.* Chicago: University of Chicago Press, 1941.

Taylor, F. W. *The principles of scientific management.* New York: Harper, 1911.

Weick, K. Enactment processes in organizations. In B. Staw & M. Salancik (Eds.), *New directions in organizational behavior.* Chicago: St. Clair Press, 1977.

10 | The Political Economy of Public Organizations

Gary L. Wamsley
Mayer N. Zald

The search for a theory of public administration often takes on aspects of a quest for the Holy Grail or a hunt for the mythical unicorn. Public administration theory has meant variously: a search for "scientific principles"; broad ruminations on what phenomena are included within "the field"; and general orientations of students of the subject, both professional and academic.[1]

Seldom has theory referred to systematic, empirically based explanations of a phenomenon; a system of related and proven propositions that answer the question "Why?" Though this article cannot begin to present such a theory, hopefully, it does more than issue another pious call for one. It is intended to set forth a framework with roots in organizational analysis that is simple but has enough heuristic power to make its application appealing to a wide range of students of public administration; that can pose questions for those areas still in need of exploration, and conceptually link them with those areas already well defined. A framework that can perform such an integrative role would represent a major step toward explanations of why individuals, groups, or organizations behave as they do in that part of the political system we have analytically abstracted and labeled public administration; and it would tell us something about how that behavior affects public policy. If we can better answer the "why" questions, we can also answer better the "how to do it," or the "what should be done" questions that have been so important to the field in the past.

Needless to say, we feel no such framework currently exists. A consensus approach to theory building is needed that can integrate knowledge not only within the field, but from different disciplines; one that focuses on the study of *public* rather than general administration, and therefore has organic links to political science and policy analysis, as well as to organizational sociology.

PART FOUR
THE
ORGANIZATIONAL
ENVIRONMENT:
MONITORING AND
CONTROLLING
EXTERNAL ACTIVITY

THE PRIOR QUESTION: IS THERE "PUBLIC" ADMINISTRATION?

After decades of debate, public administration theory is still mired down in debate over whether a meaningful distinction can be made between public and private administration. While granting that to understand the political system, it is necessary to understand public agencies, some argue that for those interested in administration-*qua*-administration, the distinction is counterproductive since it obscures important similarities. Others contend that even if the aim is to understand the political system, it is still possible to assume all administration is the same, and merely "plug in" variables and concepts borrowed from the study of private management.

Our position is that public organizations have distinctive characteristics which make it useful to study them in a separable but interrelated discipline. If we seek to understand public agencies and treat some aspect of them as dependent variables, we find that they are subject to a different set of constraints and pressures than private ones. Specific variables take on different weights in the public sector. If one treats public policies and the agencies that shape and execute them as *independent variables* affecting political effectiveness and legitimacy, he will need an understanding of public organizations quite different from that necessary to understand the effectiveness and legitimacy of private organizations.

A government is a system of rule, distinctive from nongovernmental institutions in that: (1) it ultimately rests upon coercion and a monopoly of force, and (2), if legitimate, it symbolically speaks for the society as a whole, or purports to do so. From these fundamental features flow definitions of membership, rights, expectations, and obligations in relation to the state and its agencies. Citizens and ruling elites both feel they have different "rights" and "expectations" with regard to the FBI than they have with General Motors.

The public organization is more dependent upon funds influenced by political processes or agents. The recipient of services is usually not the immediate funder;[2] and the taxpayer finds it hard to discern linkage between his taxes and any benefits accruing from organizational output. The price-utility relationship is lost, and political considerations not found in the market place result. When, for example, the British National Health Service decided to charge for prescriptions, the issue was raised in the House of Commons.

Public administration is also distinctive in the crucial role played by public organizations in shaping and executing public policy, of visibly rewarding and depriving in the name of society. Some organizations and their processes contribute to certain policy outcomes, and others facilitate different outcomes. Current concern over policy analysis calls for a theory of public rather than general administration; a theory that can be focused on the consequence of organizational structure and process for policy development and implementation. The abilities, problems, and limits of agencies in developing and carrying out policies are part of the process by which allegiances and regime support are shaped and effected.

These distinctive aspects of public organizations—symbolic significance, differences in funding, perceptions of "ownership" or rights and privileges, and resulting resource constraints—and the relationship of public organizations to public policy point to a potential unity and intellectual coherence in the field of public administration that will be useful for both analytical and normative purposes.

■ 10 ■
Gary L. Wamsley
Mayer N. Zald

THE POLITICAL ECONOMY APPROACH

Granted that the phenomenon called public administration evokes some relatively distinctive concerns, can the previous approaches to the subject which have come from a variety of sources and disciplines be unified and integrated? Elsewhere we have reviewed and criticized such approaches.[3] The political economy approach draws strongly upon the literature of "organizational analysis" or "complex organizations" (as contrasted with scientific management, bureaucratic analysis, or human relations approaches).

Organizational analysis has been most useful to us because it treats organizations as social systems—dynamic, adapting, and internally differentiated—eschews the search for a "one best" model of organization, and has been non-normative, or at least accompanied prescriptions for effectiveness, with contingency statements.[4]

Since it is a structural-functional approach, organizational analysis has tended to treat the full range of social system processes—recruitment and socialization, authority and control patterns, conflict and tension resolution, role conflict, goal adaptation, management processes, technology of task accomplishment, and adaptation to environment—as ongoing processes of an integrated social system. This breadth of approach, however, is also one of its limitations. Analysts alternately claim the greatest heuristic and analytic leverage lies in goals, communications, raw materials and technology, socialization, etc. There has been little agreement about what are the most important variables accounting for structure and change. The political economy framework, however, tries to overcome this weakness by focusing attention on precisely such key variables.

The phrase "political economy" has a long history and several different meanings. It once meant that relationship of government to the economy which promoted a competitive marketplace and thus produced efficient allocation of resources and production. Modern welfare economics uses the phrase in a normative sense to refer to the quest for that policy alternative benefiting most people at least cost. The late 1960s saw the development of a variety of techniques for analyzing policy options. We use the phrase descriptively as the interrelationship between structure of rule (polity) and a system for producing and exchanging goods and services (economy).

We suggest that just as nation-states vary in their political economies—their structure of rule authority, succession to high office, power and authority distribution, division of labor, incentive systems and modes of allocation of resources—so, too, do organizations. And political-economic variables are the major determinants of structure and change.

Throughout this article the term "political" will refer to matters of legitimacy and distribution of power as they affect the propriety of an agency's existence, its functional niche (in society, political system or policy subsystem),[5] its collective institutional goals, the goals of the dominant elite faction (if they vary from institutionalized goals), major parameters of economy, and in some instances the means of task accomplishment (if the task is

135

PART FOUR
THE
ORGANIZATIONAL
ENVIRONMENT:
MONITORING AND
CONTROLLING
EXTERNAL ACTIVITY

vague enough to raise value questions or if values change sufficiently to bring established means into question).[6]

"Economic" refers to the arrangement of the division of labor and allocation of resources for task accomplishment and maximization of efficiency; and the combination of factors affecting the cost of producing and delivering a given level of services or output.[7] If goals are well-established and means routinized, an organization becomes largely an administered device, an economy.

An organization's political economy can be analytically divided into internal and external aspects.[8] Analysis of the external political economy focuses on the interaction of the organization and its environment.

External Political Environment: Structure and Interaction

Traditional and neo-classical writings in public administration have tended to treat both external political and economic factors as given, beyond the scope of public administration theory. For us they are central concerns in efforts to develop dynamic analyses because so many of the pressures for change occur in the external environment.

Public organizations exist in an immediate environment of users and suppliers, of interested and disinterested "others." Together, the organization and its relevant others make up a policy subsystem; an arena of individuals, groups, and organizations affected by and interested in influencing, a policy for which the organization has prime responsibility and concern. These relevant others include a variety of actors in and out of government: interest groups, competing public organizations, legislative committees, control agencies. They may be competitive, hostile, overseeing, etc.; regardless, a policy subsystem shapes the conditions of existence for an agency.

An external political structure represents the distribution of sentiment and power resources among an agency's relevant others, i.e., opposition or support to the agency, its goals and programs. The distribution of sentiment and power is a reflection of: the dramaturgy or emotive element in the public organization's operations; its perceived expertise; the degree to which its impact is felt; the breadth (number of groups and individuals affected or interested) of its relevant others; the intensity of their interest; the resources they can bring to bear in exerting influence, and their ability and willingness to use resources.[9]

Sentiment distribution alone offers only a partial description of an agency's political environment. The power resources of actors, their willingness or ability to use them, and their skill in building coalitions also represent an important part of the equation. Some actors have intense interest but are relatively powerless, e.g., prisoners vis-à-vis the U.S. Bureau of Prisons; others have power resources but fail to use them because of political costs or internal conflicts over which action to take. Thus, sentiment patterns are weighted by the power resources and capabilities of relevant others.

Nor do public organizations merely accept the existing sentiment and power distribution; they also manipulate it with varying degrees of success. Administrators try to routinize the controversial by obtaining an equilibrium of interests, by benignly institutionalizing their environments.[10] The task is never complete, for the equilibrium can be upset by administrative error, changes in influence patterns and technology, or the suddenly negative attention of a latently powerful actor, e.g., the U.S. Tea Tasting Board's "discovery" and proposed abolition in 1970, or the CIA in the aftermath of the Bay of Pigs fiasco.

■ 10 ■
Gary L. Wamsley
Mayer N. Zald

External political structures tend toward rigidity. Change does not come easily in a public organization or its policy subsystem either by dint of its manipulation *or* impingements of the environment. Goals and procedures may be frozen by conditional patterns of support and hostility. A press for change mobilizes opposition. The incentive system of public organizations seldom works for change. A change agent must generate issues, mobilize a coalition of forces, and gain the support of key proximal others in a policy subsystem. Though difficult, change does occur through interaction and political exchange. Political exchanges result from conscious efforts of: (1) external actors to affect a public organization's niche and related goals; or (2) an agency to manipulate its relevant others in order to alter its legitimacy and the order of magnitude of resources, and thus its overall goals and direction. The effects can thus alter niche, the general functional goals related to it, internal political patterns, processes of task accomplishment (if they involve legitimacy), and even survival.

When we think of the external political interactions of an organization and its environment, most of us think of the obvious, such as the Nixon Administration's efforts to subtly shift the goals of the Civil Rights Division of Justice and the Office of Civil Rights for HEW from zealous pursuit of desegregation in the South to a diverse nationwide approach of lower intensity, less inimicable to the growth of Republicanism in the South.[11] But this is the obvious. The more subtle and ongoing source of interactions are the efforts by the executive cadres of organizations to alter their own domain or that of their neighbors, and thus alleviate uncertainty. Domain may include claims on future functional-level goals and the requisite resources to achieve them as well as those presently held.[12] In this ongoing political interaction over niche or domain, agencies vary along several dimensions in their sensitivity to political impingements and capacity to manipulate.

Goals, ambiguity and clarity   Where goals are clearly defined and subject to surveillance, an agency like the Social Security Administration may be left little room for choice or maneuver in goals, program objectives, and perhaps even means of task accomplishments. But if goals are ambiguous or multiple, an organization's elite may press for one definition or another and, within the bounds of political feasibility, allocate resources internally in pursuit of this choice (correctional institutions: treatment or custody).

Surveillance   Some agencies effectively avoid scrutiny by superiors and other external actors. The CIA with its budget hidden in other departments' appropriations, is the most notable example. But ambiguity of goals, hidden missions, or simply overwhelming complexity of programs and accounting information also hinder effective surveillance and diminish sensitivity.

Centrality of values   If a public organization is perceived to fulfill a central value of the political culture, its autonomy is enhanced as long as it does not

PART FOUR
THE
ORGANIZATIONAL
ENVIRONMENT:
MONITORING AND
CONTROLLING
EXTERNAL ACTIVITY

drastically alter niche goals. If the agency loses effectiveness, surveillance increases and autonomy declines. A state fire marshal's office charged with ensuring fire safety in schools, institutions, and public buildings may hardly be reviewed until a tragic fire occurs.

Personnel and funding allocation Not all agencies are equally subject to influence by external and superior actors in the matter of funds and personnel. Special, strategically placed allies like a chairman of an appropriations subcommittee can help or hurt them in terms of financial support. Or those operating on users fees, trust funds, or special funds may enjoy greater freedom from surveillance by superiors than those operating from general funds, though they are subject to special scrutiny from the clientele from which the revenues derive.

Public organizations have a relative lack of control over executive appointments. Central budget and personnel offices often have "position control" over personnel. But the nature and extent of this control varies. Some terms of appointment are long, and in the case of many boards they are staggered. Other agencies at the state level are headed by elected officials, which gives them a strong base of autonomy.

The structure of support and an established feed-back loop Autonomy increases if an organization offers a well-received product to efficacious clientele who are able to influence key, proximal others. They, in turn, enlarge the organization's share of resources and legitimacy. This requires the right balance of numbers, geographic dispersion, and of efficacy. Sometimes this means the establishment of advisory committees, propaganda aimed at relevant others, news media, and mass public, or even the actual organization of interest groups by the agency.

Political interactions and exchanges take place between an agency and relevant others at its boundary. Transactions involve such outputs as strategically timed withholding or providing of products or services, "leaks" to news media, providing of information to allies; and such inputs as interest group demands, demands of a chief executive, influence of an appropriation subcommittee chairman. Inputs or outputs are political rather than economic if they are of sufficient magnitude to alter niche, overall goals and direction, the order of magnitude of resources, or major economic parameters.

ECONOMIC ENVIRONMENTS AND EXCHANGES

An examination of a public organization's economic environment requires an analysis of costs and behavior necessary in obtaining factors of production and exchange of output at organizational boundaries. It means emphasizing what in the private sector would be called "industry structure," markets, and the elasticity of supply and demand. Special attention must be given to the degree of "industry concentration," the relationships among competitors, distinctive aspects of technology, supply of raw materials and labor, and "markets" or factors affecting the distribution network for outputs.

The industry structure of public organizations is generally ignored on the assumption that they have monopolistic or oligopolistic status. But many have competitors among other agencies and in the private sector as well. In addition, the supply and prices of the factors of production for public organizations are directly affected by events in the economy at large.

However, many phenomena which might be treated as economic in the private sector must be treated as political-economic in the public sector. Demands are aggregated, filtered, and channeled through the budget process and an agency's policy subsystem, as questions about the legitimacy of spending public funds for certain purposes are raised and as its resource needs are thrown into competition with others. The process is pronounced in the United States with its strong separation of executive and legislative functions and its weak party system, but is also found elsewhere.

The lack of market controls for a public organization and the corresponding lack of efficiency incentives have led to elaborate accounting and budgeting controls in an effort to simulate market functions. Contract clearance, position control, independent audits, control of category transfers, competitive bidding, apportionments, cost-benefit analysis, and performance budgeting are devices for controlling cost and registering preferences. Often these are purely instrumental and economic in nature, but the analyst must be aware of their political ramifications as well.[13]

The cost curves of producing and delivering a public organization's product vary considerably and can become political in nature. The steep costs of putting in a new weapons system for deterrence or damage limitation may trigger a national debate over national priorities, the risks of attacks, etc. In contrast, political crises over school costs are slower to develop because they rise incrementally rather than in "lumps" that might mobilize opposition.

What, then, is treated as strictly an external economic exchange for a public organization? Economic exchanges are neither intended to nor do they actually affect niche, functional goals, order of magnitude of resources, or major economic parameters; rather they are designed merely to implement established goals and tasks, and are seen as legitimate by both the dominant coalition of an organization, its opposition, and by relevant others. Government agencies, for example, bargain over price and quality of certain elements of production, but do so without conscious effort to manipulate their environment politically.

Often economic considerations are ignored in the literature of public administration because of a failure to conceptualize public organizations as obtaining raw materials from an economic environment and processing or converting them into products offered to consumers.[14] Even public organizations which we assume have highly charged political environments have established some niche and carry on some "production" that no longer raises questions of legitimacy. For example, the Joint Chiefs of Staff produce "products" like advice to the Joint Staff, translation of policy into strategic orders, decisions on weapon systems and force level priorities that we normally fail to recognize as products. Many of the JCS's products resemble those of a private consulting firm. They are produced by collating information and beliefs (the raw materials) through "technologies" of debate, compromise, defined disagreement, suppression of the source of raw materials, delay in processing, ambiguous decisions, agreement not to disagree, and technical loyalty to the Administration but covert disloyalty. Some products like decisions on weapon systems have definite political effects, but many of them, like advice to the

PART FOUR
THE
ORGANIZATIONAL
ENVIRONMENT:
MONITORING AND
CONTROLLING
EXTERNAL ACTIVITY

Joint Staff, no longer raise questions of legitimacy and are most meaningfully seen as economic[15] because they are relatively routine. If public organizations are viewed as procurers and processors of raw materials, and offerers of products at their boundaries, then their external economic exchange (and internal economic structures) become more readily apparent.

General economic and manpower pictures can also affect a public organization. Full employment and inflationary economy make it more difficult for public organizations to recruit personnel because of their lower status and lag in pay scales. The costs of public organizations are closely tied to labor rates because they produce services rather than manufactured goods, and it is difficult for them to substitute machines for labor. As wages rise, public costs spiral. Workloads also respond to economic and manpower outlooks. Some workloads rise as the economy declines, e.g., welfare and unemployment insurance agencies; while that of others, like Selective Service, declines as unemployed men volunteer and lower draft calls result.

Broad and diffuse changes in demand are also economic and are so perceived by agencies, e.g., the increase in camping that has vastly changed the National Park Service. Similarly, technological changes are usually perceived as economic, though they may drastically alter an agency and its exchanges with its environment—Internal Revenue Service and computers; the Army and helicopters.

Public organizations seek to manipulate their economic as well as political environments. Competitive bidding and mass central purchasing are obvious examples; but cost-plus-fixed-fee contracts, grants, loans, and leasing out of capital assets are all methods used to overcome hesitancy of contractors and suppliers.

Public agencies exist in a web of political and economic exchange structures that shape long-run functions and directions of change, as well as short-run interactions and concerns. Changes in societal values and the values of relevant others can alter an agency's functional goals and legitimacy, while cost factors and the pattern of "industry structure" affect its ability to accomplish tasks. Public administration must be able to analyze agencies' environments in order to predict change, and an understanding of public policy and changes in it calls for a political economy analysis of the organizations that are prime actors and relevant others in a policy subsystem.

NOTES

[1]Martin Landau, "Sociology and the Study of Formal Organization," in CAG Special Series No. 8, Washington, D.C., 1966. His description of a preparadigmatic field should be uncomfortably familiar to students of public administration. See p. 38.

[2]Some public organizations such as the Post Office are funded by customers, but there are still differential costs and benefits, and rates are subject to political constraints.

[3]Wamsley and Zald, *The Political Economy of Public Organizations: A Critique and Approach to the Study of Public Administration,* forthcoming. Previous work on our framework can be found in Mayer N. Zald, *Organizational Change: The Political Economy of the YMCA* (Chicago: University of Chicago Press, 1970), and in his essay "Political Economy: A Framework for Comparative Analysis," in Mayer N. Zald (ed.), *Power in Organizations* (Nashville: Vanderbilt University Press, 1970), pp. 221–261.

[4]Prominent among the contributors to the literature of organization analysis are the works of

Philip Selznick and his students upon whom we draw heavily. Representative of other "strands" are the works of Alvin Gouldner and Peter Blau and their students.

[5]The concept of *niche* is borrowed from studies of biotic communities in which each organism has a niche in an interdependent and symbiotic relationship. Similar and used interchangeably is the concept of *domain*. See Sol Levine and Paul White, "Exchange as a Conceptual Framework for the Study of Interorganizational Relationships," *Administrative Science Quarterly*, Vol. V (March 1957), pp. 444–463.

[6]Even tasks performed by lower functionaries can become political if values within and without the organization are affected by the discretion they wield. Performance of a vague task may define values, or a long-established pattern of task accomplishment may run afoul of changed environmental values.

[7]More than a few economists will be unhappy with our definition. Modern analytic economics tend to focus on maximization and resource allocation. Our definition includes them but focuses on the structure of the economy, the extent and limits of differentiation and coordination.

[8]If our framework focused solely on *internal* political economy the phrase "political-administration" or "political-managerial" might suffice, but it is also important to describe the structure of the *external* economic environment.

[9]Rourke, *Bureaucracy, Politics and Public Policy* (Boston: Little, Brown, 1969), chapters 2, 3, and 4.

[10]For example, see Gary L. Wamsley, *Selective Service and a Changing America* (Columbus, Ohio: Chas. E. Merrill, 1969), chapter 7.

[11]See L. E. Panetta and P. Gall, *Bring Us Together: The Nixon Team and Civil Rights Retreat* (New York: Lippincott, 1971).

[12]Levine and White, op. cit.

[13]Aaron Wildavsky, "The Political Economy of Efficiency, Cost Benefit Analysis, Systems Analysis, and Program Budgeting," *Public Administration Review*, Vol. XXVI (1966). For examples of accounting becoming "political," see Thomas J. Anton, *The Politics of State Expenditure in Illinois* (Urbana: University of Illinois Press, 1966), pp. 46–47, 69–70, 203–204.

[14]See Charles Perrow, "A Framework for the Comparative Analysis of Organizations," *American Sociological Review*, Vol. XXVI (1961).

[15]The JCS operate in a highly competitive milieu. Their legitimacy depends on an occasional product acceptance. They not only act as a "consulting firm" but a "coalition of normally competing firms." Each member (except the chairman) plays a role as representative of his service as well as a collegial role. Example based on analysis as of early 1960s.

11 | The Politics of Public-Private Management

Frank H. Cassell

Who would have imagined twelve years ago that the government would be running the passenger service of the railroads, or that the government would rescue a huge aircraft firm from certain bankruptcy by lending it cash and furnishing contracts to keep the business alive? Or that a conservative American government would abandon its old theories about the free market and intervene in the economics of society to manage wages and prices? Or that the same conservative government would propose guaranteed incomes for the poor, even for those who work but are so poorly paid by private enterprise that they would need public subsidy to meet the barest subsistence level of living? Who would have expected President Nixon to sign a general public employment law to employ 150,000 people in public service jobs for an investment of $2.25 billion?[1]

Who would have thought, even in New Deal days, that the federal government would be underwriting well over 50 percent of all the research and development work in the nation, thus providing much of the motive, power, and ideas for private enterprise?[2] Who would have foreseen that the traditional operations and values of the marketplace would be challenged so regularly and would be in conflict so often with the priorities and values arrived at through community action, or that free market operations often would be superseded by the planning of social and economic action needed to fulfill the needs and priorities demanded by the community?

Indeed, it is fair to ask whether there is any longer such a thing as a pure business problem. Or whether, instead, public and private, the needs of the people and of the economy, have become so crossed and intertwined that we have arrived, without our quite knowing it, at a time when few decisions of the private sector can be made without an expression by the public of its legitimate concern for the consequences of those decisions.

So pervasive has the trend become that proposals for its further extension —for even more intertwining of public and private enterprise—come from

Reprinted from *MSU Business Topics*, Vol. 20, No. 3 (Summer 1972), pp. 7–18, by permission of the Board of Trustees of Michigan State University.

surprising sources. For example, Roger S. Ahlbrandt, chairman of Allegheny Ludlum Industries, Inc., is urging the government to adopt centralized economic planning, lest the steel industry slip further behind in world competition with totally managed economies. He refers to an

> economic sickness that affects our whole nation and society. It is a sickness directly connected to the fact that our nation has not had, and still lacks, a coherent international economic policy.... America's foreign policy for generations has been influenced by *military* and *political* considerations. But we now live in a world where *economic considerations* must assume first priority.... We in this nation find ourselves now trying to compete not just with individual steel companies, for example, for both domestic and overseas markets—but with ENTIRE ECONOMIES, in which a central decision-making body determines allocation of raw materials and other resources, directs the flow of finance, determines the penetration of markets, establishes costs and prices, and—in truth—*governs* and *directs* the entire national economic entity. In those nations, government and people look upon industries as "national assets," which increase their national strength and improve their living standards. Unfortunately, this cannot be said of public and government attitudes toward business and industry in the United States.... We must recognize that the sweep of change, inside and outside our country, is not reversible. The four great economic blocs that compete with us globally will not disappear and go away. And their policies—economic, social and political—do not come out of any of *our* textbooks.[3]

Another example of a surprising proposal for much greater involvement of the public sector in private enterprise has come from the Committee for Economic Development. It reasons that all institutions are under question because of the "sluggishness of social progress." The committee also notes that some of government's tasks are being contracted out to business, and it proposes a vast extension of that process into "new hybrid types of public-private corporations . . . to combine the best attributes of government (funds, political capacity, public accountability) and of private enterprise (systems analysis, research and technology, managerial ability) in the optimum mix for dealing effectively with different kinds of socio-economic problems."[4] The CED further states:

> This emerging partnership is more than a contractual relationship between a buyer and seller of services. Fundamentally, it offers a new means for developing the innate capabilities of a political democracy and a private enterprise economy into a new politico-economic system capable of managing social and technological change in the interests of a better social order.... The government-business relationship is likely to be the central one in the last third of the twentieth century.[5]

In a later section of this article the implications of Ahlbrandt's proposal, which is aimed at government economic planning to aid industry, and the CED's proposal, for public-private corporations to handle many aspects of our lives, will be considered. Both of the proposals certainly give impetus to the idea that there is no longer such a thing as a pure business problem, and, henceforth, few private sector decisions can be made without consideration of the public's legitimate concerns. This idea even now is too little understood in its implications regarding the decision-making process. For example, what do these new facts mean for managers and administrators who are selected and trained to cope with a corporate environment they can control and influence,

143

PART FOUR
THE
ORGANIZATIONAL
ENVIRONMENT:
MONITORING AND
CONTROLLING
EXTERNAL ACTIVITY

one characterized by a high degree of predictability rather than unpredictability, and often chaotic and conflicting pressure, brought to bear by the surrounding community over which the managers have little or no control? What do they mean to men who, accustomed to working within and conforming to a system that seems to satisfy their needs, are confronted with community people who feel that system does not satisfy community needs and therefore want to change or replace it? What do they mean for managers and planners, long accustomed to think in terms of orderly processes for the achievement of well-defined objectives which have been fed in from the top of the typical business organization? What do they mean for educators and for those business schools who have charged themselves with educating managers for both the public and private sectors?

The implications of the new and growing public-private sector are so immense that the questions are only dimly understood and the answers are not available. The implications are particularly challenging to the business schools because of the time lag between an individual's training and his accession to power. Business schools currently are training students who will not be in management positions with real decision-making power for another fifteen to twenty years. But the new kinds of community pressures already exist and are baffling: they are producing consternation among the current crop of executives trained fifteen to twenty years ago.

THE BETTER MOUSETRAP?

In the private sector, historically, priorities have been determined by the profit motive. If a worse mousetrap made more profit, it would be produced. In the public sector, priorities have been determined through the political process. People in government, either elected or appointed, have sought to perceive the needs of the community and plan to meet those needs. Of course, there always has been pressure from the electorate, but formerly it was largely through the established political procedure, through the election of people who thought your way and through political lobbying to achieve your aims. Even the inevitable conniving and sly deals operated through the established political procedure. And here too the mousetrap analogy is applicable; if a worse mousetrap would get you elected, it would be invented.

Planning was involved in both private and public sectors, but it usually was ordered from the top down; planners sought to convert objectives—determined somewhere in the boardrooms, the mayor's office, or legislative halls—into an orderly and workable program.

CHALLENGES TO TRADITIONAL PLANNING

Both of these traditional methods for determining priorities, by profit in the private sector and political decisions in the public, are under wide attack. One reason is that the planning system has become circular, listening to itself and responding not to the needs of people but to the demands, goals, or needs of planning itself. Challenges from everywhere are racking all of our institutions. The institutions are finding their traditional behavior and priorities are not in tune with or capable of accommodating the demands of contesting

forces; each force wants the institutions to behave in a manner calculated to benefit them. Thus, for both public and private institutions, there are whole new arsenals of pressure, from the bottom up rather than the top down, and it is often expressed not through what we have thought were the normal channels but in many new ways of social protest. These new bottom-up pressures illustrate a conflict both of values and organizational methods, and in both cases the new pressures make the people subjected to them extremely uncomfortable. People are devising new ways to demand consideration in the making of decisions that affect their lives.

Their clamor to be heard is a sufficiently recognizable phenomenon to be finding its way into our humor. Russell Baker said in *Harper's* recently: "People who have the power to make things happen don't do what people do, so they don't know what needs to happen." True enough, no doubt, and the people with power still may not do what people do, but they are certainly going to be told what needs to happen.[6]

VARIETIES OF PRESSURE

Sometimes the new pressures serve chiefly as dramatic attention-getting devices. A community group in Chicago, distressed over the prevalence of rats in the neighborhood, summoned their alderman to a planning meeting. When the alderman did not come, the president of the group nailed a dead rat to his front door; the alderman was present at the next meeting. Another example is the Fox, an anonymous Fox River Valley (Illinois) man who is fighting pollution symbolically. He once dumped on the reception room carpet of a steel firm's local office a bucket of the foul sludge that was draining out of the company's pipelines into the once beautiful Fox River. The Fox became an instant folk hero.

Often new pressures are designed to change traditions and procedures that have proved to be unresponsive to needs. Did we ever hear of a tenants' union until a decade ago? By withholding rents until a recalcitrant landlord meets their demands, the tenants' unions are challenging what we always have thought were basic property rights of the landlord, protected through generations of common law. The tenants' unions did not fare well at first, but they are beginning to win some victories in the courtrooms as some of the old beliefs about property rights are giving way.

Other examples of pressures aimed at unresponsive procedures can be seen in the struggle for more community control over schools. Recall the devastating school strikes in New York City in 1965. They had complex causes, but at their heart was an insurgent demand by neighborhood people to have some control over the kind of education their children were getting, and to determine priorities for their children, who clearly were being short-changed by traditional methods. The result was instant conflict not only with the giant school bureaucracy but also with the contractual rights of the giant teachers' union. The neighborhood people lost their battle in New York; they lost in the school board offices, in the governor's office, and in the legislative sessions in Albany. But the struggle for community control and for schools that will be answerable to the people who use them will continue.

145

PART FOUR
THE
ORGANIZATIONAL
ENVIRONMENT:
MONITORING AND
CONTROLLING
EXTERNAL ACTIVITY

Consider pollution, which brings other challenges to unresponsive procedures. The attacks from the new insurgents are two-pronged: against the government in demands for protection against the side effects of the industrial revolution, and against the corporations, seeking board members who will place the public interest, survival itself, against, or at least alongside, the profit motive. Louis S. B. Leakey recently warned the American Association for the Advancement of Science that man is in imminent danger of extinction, perhaps within fifty years, unless he uses "his wonderful computer brain" to ward off impending disaster.[7] Many are listening to such messages and trying to act, sometimes fumbling, sometimes winning a little. These kinds of pressures are new and must be reckoned with. The line between public and private sectors in this area of environmental control is muddled, but basically the attack is on procedures, either by government or by industry, that have turned out to be threatening to the majority. Slowly, but perhaps inevitably, some political leaders are beginning to align themselves with these causes.

WHO DECIDES WAR OR NO WAR?

Perhaps the most wrenching of all the new public pressures are those that aim not at attracting attention to an injustice or challenging unsatisfactory and unresponsive procedures, but those that aim at fundamental policies. There is no better example than our society's agony over the Vietnam war. It has produced challenge after challenge, all of them aimed at basic policies and long-accepted procedures of our society: the right of the government to collect taxes, to wage war, to conscript citizens, and the right of any industry to produce any kind of product as long as it returns a profit. There have been those who refused to pay taxes for what they felt was pointless destruction of human life and the environment. There have been those who tried to prevent private enterprise from producing napalm and fragmentation bombs, contending that no governmental policy and no profit motive could possibly justify such instruments of horror. The invasion of Cambodia in the spring of 1970 brought an outpouring of infuriated young people; some were killed, many went to jail. And a significant part of our young generation simply has refused to fight such a war, in many ways challenging the government's right to be in the war at all and to force any citizen to participate. To observers of society, this unheaval is an object lesson in what can happen when people perceive that they are not a part of the deciding and planning processes but are, in fact, an object of the planning. These fundamental challenges may be leading to permanent changes in the society's authority system.

ANYONE CAN PLAY

One of the important factors about the new kinds of community demands for a share in priority planning is that anyone can play. In many cases, it has not been the sophisticated and educated people in business and government who have acted to highlight the shortcomings of the system; it has been the people who experienced the consequences, people who organized outside the system because the system had entirely excluded them from power in the first place. This included young people with no power who went to prison and into exile rather than fight an unconscionable war; black people who formed their own unions or black caucuses within unions because they were denied any impact on policy; poor people who have been cheated by credit abuses long protected by law; ethnic groups who feel they have been getting the short end of the socioeconomic stick; taxpayers and recipients of public services who are seeing their own interests trampled by powerful public employee unions claiming a greater and greater share of the public funds; and women who are deciding they are people and not possessions.

The point is that everyone is demanding a share in making the decisions that affect their own lives and seeking new ways to enforce these demands. The implication of these bottom-up public pressures are tremendous. One such implication is that untrained people are telling professional managers how to do their jobs and what is expected of them. Another is the intertwining of private and public sectors mentioned previously. Decisions that once were made privately and regulated by the profit motive now are being profoundly affected by public policy and by the political process. And politics is not orderly in the planning sense; priorities arising out of political pressures often are not in the best order of efficiency. Politics challenges integrated systems which, to operate well, depend on mathematical or planning logic for effective use of resources. These systems fall apart when the political logic leads to apparently inefficient uses of resources or to goals which make political but not planning sense. This, in effect, is a clash of systems and even a clash of life styles of the corporation people and the community.

Wherever the influence of the public interest is extended into the private sphere, and wherever the private decision-making power is turned over to the public-political process of decision making, this kind of clash is invited. There is a crucial distinction between decision making in the private and in the public sector; different rules apply. This seems to be little understood. It is this inherent distinction that makes a steel company's advocacy of greater economic planning by government and a CED proposal for public-private partnership in business both so surprising. Both proposals open the private decision-making process to public participation with its frequent and continuing conflict among a variety of communities.

In his speech Ahlbrandt sees economic advantages for American industry in the world market if government orders economic priorities but takes no note of the kinds of pressures that will be brought to bear on that government process. The CED talks of a method "to insulate the (public-private) corporation from political pressures."[8] It suggests that public accountability would be achieved through a board of directors, partially elected and partially appointed, with a tenure, perhaps of seven years, overlapping political terms. But apparently when it talks of political pressures it thinks only of those brought to bear by governmental officials. Nowhere does it mention the kinds of pressures being brought by the public, pressures to which the proposed new public-private corporations will most emphatically be opened. The CED proposal may even be a new kind of Magna Carta for those millions of people who have been frozen out of the private decision-making process, and who, whether from the right or from the left, are attempting politically to be heard.

147

PART FOUR
THE
ORGANIZATIONAL
ENVIRONMENT:
MONITORING AND
CONTROLLING
EXTERNAL ACTIVITY

CONFLICTING PRIORITIES

Let us look at some of the priorities and expectations that society seems to have of its various institutions, both public and private: (1) full employment without inflation; (2) clean air and clean water at no additional cost; (3) the right of every person to adequate medical care, perhaps in the form of cradle-to-grave health insurance, at no extra cost; (4) more recreational space without harming the living space for all forms of life, including an expanding human population; (5) more economic growth and more sophisticated technology without employee dissatisfaction and unemployment; (6) extension of the good life to the have nots without inconveniencing the haves; (7) free college education to all students with motivation and ability even though not enough jobs are available for the educated; and (8) the efficiency of an automated interchangeable society without dehumanizing the individual and making him interchangeable too.

Obviously these wants bring conflicting and contradictory pressures on both public and private institutions. They involve choices which will be difficult to make. More than that, they involve costs, which also are subject to counterpressures. Most of us prefer a choice that will cost someone else something. But the costs must lodge somewhere.[9] It has been society's habit to allocate costly, economically unrewarding tasks to government. Government, in turn, subcontracts some of those tasks back to the private sector, adding greatly to the fuzziness of the line between public and private business. Put another way, in the areas where priorities are set by the community rather than the marketplace, the job is given to government, but that job and the extent of the dollars involved will, in turn, affect the marketplace. Countless private enterprises, not only those in defense-related programs, are government subcontractors. Thus, they are an extension of government, and, consequently, their priorities are set politically rather than traditionally by profits. These subcontracted activities include military procurement, space exploration, research and development, and claims administration by Blue Cross.

Without seeming to recognize the implications of public priority setting for these subcontractors, the Committee for Economic Development calls this *privatizing* the public sector.[10] It also might be viewed, perhaps more accurately, as *publicizing* the private sector, since the most important element of control is priority, not production. Perhaps this is why large government contractors and their unions try to influence the public ordering of priorities through their lobbies. The greater the subcontracting to private enterprise, the greater the chance and incentive for the individual citizen to influence priorities, even though it may be difficult to do so.

Some idea of the extent of government subcontracting to private business can be seen in federal government expenditures for goods and services. These increased 750 percent between 1930 and 1970. In 1930, federal expenditures for goods and services accounted for 1.5 percent of the gross national product; in 1970, they accounted for 10 percent. If we include state and local government expenditures as well as federal, governmental spending accounts for 22 percent of GNP.[11] Government contracting for services and supplies in fiscal 1970 amounted to $48 billion.

THE REGULATORS

Deciding, taking action, getting results, fulfilling expectations, and evaluating performance are the usual managerial functions. But it is the deciding that must come first, before action and evaluation of action. What is different today is that people in the society are saying: "These are our priorities. We want to decide. We want them fulfilled. That is what we expect of the economic system and the manager." But the manager only can bring these changes about as he manages the reallocation of resources of manpower and capital not necessarily according to where they bring their best economic return, but where they satisfy the community's needs and expectations regardless of the level of profit.

Even this is not the whole story because, in the absence of the profit regulator, a substitute must be found to enable the community to assess and evaluate the value of services rendered or products produced against the cost. Even prior to this step is the need to provide the planning which enables the community to decide its priorities in the first place. Planning in this case is not merely a technical process; it is a political process—the means for a community to decide at the local and national levels what it considers more important and what it considers less important. Planning and assessment of costs and benefits are essential if the community is to decide effectively among the choices open to it instead of having the choice established by the market system. It is essential if the quality of the services and efficiency with which they are rendered is to be evaluated.

A business with a government contract usually has tended to evaluate value in terms of the profit it can make on such a contract, not on the value of the good or service to society. This is where the community and private enterprise collide. If the community prevails and the profit potential is too low versus other opportunity, business will require a subsidy to make the contract attractive enough for business to eschew other opportunity. The community, through subsidies, programs private enterprise to fulfill its wishes. But it is important to note that we refer to fulfilling the community's wishes, not those of private business. This is why the steel industry, if it is looking for public planning of the economy, may be shopping for a package it does not really want.

A NEW SOCIAL CONTRACT

There is increasing interest in considering quality of services and community priorities in the determination of gross national product, giving additional weight in the index to those products with greatest utility in filling social needs, and subtracting from the index the costs of disposing of the mountains of waste that are the by-products of production and marketing (called the *disproduct*).[12] It is an intriguing concept and one that may yet be useful in the ordering of priorities in our increasingly complex society. Willard Wirtz, former Secretary of Labor, recently gave a boost to the proposal for a council of social advisers by suggesting the development of a system of social accounting

PART FOUR
THE
ORGANIZATIONAL
ENVIRONMENT:
MONITORING AND
CONTROLLING
EXTERNAL ACTIVITY

as efficient and comprehensive as economic accounting.[13] Joel F. Henning, program director at the Adlai E. Stevenson Institute for International Affairs, has proposed a tandem idea; he suggests a dual system of chartering large corporations, state and national, with the national charter to be issued on "a showing of fiscal and social responsibility." David Rockefeller, chairman and chief executive officer to the Chase Manhattan Bank, foresees the day when corporations may be required to publish a "social audit," but he cautions that there may have to be new laws to assure that the more socially responsive firms will not suffer a competitive disadvantage.

What is new to the generations trained in our school of business where profit is the primary criterion of success is that priorities are going to be set increasingly by community consensus or a political decision of one form or another. These priorities will not necessarily, or even probably, be in accord with those set by the profit system. The profit regulator allows us to throw out what is unprofitable, to weed out what is inefficient but not what is worthless. The profit system can decide among efficiencies, but does not decide whether or not the service or product should be provided at all. It does not distinguish, for example, between the disposal of trash and the creation of trash.

Ultimately, of course, it will be the cost relative to the benefit of the cost that will serve as the basis for decision, both for the social utility of the service or product and where its cost is best applied. In the private sector, increased social benefits will increase the cost of goods and services. In the public sector, increased social benefits will increase taxes. In the former case, profitability competes against general consumer interests; in the latter, differing segments of the electorate will compete against each other as to whether the social good is worth the price. But if the benefits are a desired priority, their costs must lodge one place or the other.

With scarce resources of money and manpower, the community will need to order its needs and values. This will require the analytical tools of the planner, the economist, the financial expert, plus the input of the social scientists, to produce the information on costs and benefits which will assist the community to decide what service should come first, second, and third, and what should be omitted.

Profit is a single criterion of performance, therefore simple and easily understood. The criteria being used by the community to measure the performance of its institutions are often multiple, interlinked, and complex.

Suppose we add one criterion to profit, for example, a guaranteed job to each employee who successfully completes a one-year probationary period. Think of the interaction of short-term profits with this new goal and the planning that has to be done in order to accommodate both long-term profits and job security. Without this requirement, the planning of manpower revolves around the cycle of business; with this requirement, business plans (and those of the economy as well) have to be built around a stable demand, which is needed to guarantee jobs. Planning shifts from anticipating cycles to controlling them. (As the national economy balance moves from the production of goods to the production of services, planning for job tenure may be substantially easier, due to the lessened effect of business cycles on employment in service occupations.)

THE VISIBLE HAND

The implication is clear that with a competing method for ordering priorities, there also will be divergences in values, as well as in means and ends. At its very basic level, the competing method can represent a conflict of social as against pure economic values and objectives. But it also represents an effort to have the visible hand of the citizen replace the invisible hand of competition as the regulator—at least in some decision-making areas, especially those that most affect the citizen.

A NEW BALL GAME FOR BUSINESS SCHOOLS

The newer decision-making process poses a particular problem for the business schools, a problem that, for the most part, is just beginning to be faced. This decision-making process will require managers with the talent and temperament to plan and be comfortable with uncertainties and unknowns, who can find a consensus which must sometimes come through confrontation, and who can help adjust and readjust public and private systems to accommodate the new pressures and changing priorities. This is in contrast to the current goals of providing the executive and the planner with the tools to take the risk out of taking risks.[14]

There is something of a tendency for business schools to assume that planning and establishing priorities according to profit somehow also will produce the plans and priorities needed to be responsive to social needs and political pressures. This reflects a gulf between those who assume that a management tool, planning, is a tool for all purposes and times and those who feel that planning to meet social needs and political realities is different, not in degree, but in kind, from profit planning.

WHO IS RESPONSIBLE FOR WHOM?

There may be a tendency, too, for people to say: "What is so new about all this? Plenty of corporations have shown that they can accept social responsibility, haven't they?" It is true that many staff functions in private enterprise now exist not because they can be justified by their direct profit contribution, but because community priorities run over into the firm and become those of the firm because it cannot help itself. Many firms, some reluctantly, have discovered that they cannot live entirely apart from their environments.[15] It has been the fashion for a corporation to feel it has some responsibility for its local community and to allow some of its businessmen time to participate on boards such as Community Chests and the Urban League. The assumption is that business is helping to determine what is wise and good for society. But there appears to be a shift away from this business responsibility for the community idea toward community responsibility for business.

Citizens are learning that it was the community that gave the corporation its power and that it can take that power away, that the community rather than the corporation can impose standards of behavior, and that it is the community that decides what institutions are needed and how they should behave.[16] Thus, the more or less accidental (and often reluctant) involvement

151

PART FOUR
THE
ORGANIZATIONAL
ENVIRONMENT:
MONITORING AND
CONTROLLING
EXTERNAL ACTIVITY

of business in community affairs is far from the same thing as the more fundamental ordering of priorities by community pressures, the kind of new decision making with which we are being confronted. There are conflicts in values and methods and the people involved have different needs, goals, and aspirations. These differences explain why such matters are slow to find their way into the curricula of the business schools. They simply pose difficult problems for schools; to some they are a basic challenge to the established methods. But, perhaps more importantly, few have yet understood the meaning of the changes going on about us. We still tend to think in terms of the antitrust laws and government regulation from the top.

NEEDED: A NEW IMPULSE

The last great creative impulse in the area of business education occurred about twelve years ago. That was before the government began running the passenger trains, bailing out a bankrupt aircraft industry, controlling wages and prices, financing more research, and talking about guaranteed incomes.

This educational shake-up stemmed from two reports on higher education for business completed in 1959: the Gordon-Howell report, financed by the Ford Foundation, and the Pierson report, financed by the Carnegie Corporation.[17] These reports were sharp indictments of the general state of business education and, by extension, of all higher education. Although they found a wide variation in quality, they pinpointed the general weaknesses of the schools at that time: (1) excessive vocationalism (an overemphasis upon training for specific jobs) tended to block the individual's maximum intellectual growth and thus ultimately damage his career. At the same time it denied society the kinds of broad-gauged thinking needed to get at the roots of complex and interrelated problems. (2) Creeping intellectual obsolescence was reflected in rigid curricula, inadequate foundation courses, and poor teaching methods. (3) Low standards of most business schools attracted both low-caliber students and low-caliber faculty and a highly inbred faculty. (4) Poor quality and inadequate quantity of business research contributed to the absence of a stimulating intellectual atmosphere.

The reports made specific recommendations about how to correct these weaknesses, but we can see from our present vantage point that the recommendations did not (and perhaps could not) encompass all the problem areas. In neither report, for example, was there specific mention of the fields of manpower administration or labor-management relations, although studies of executive behavior even then showed these to be primary and difficult problems taking up much of the executive's time. Urban studies were not referred to in either study except under the rubric of environment—whatever that meant. And in the knotty area of decision making, the reports seemed to rest with the assumption that the decision-making processes of business were adequate for most purposes, not having anticipated the political-social enigmas that confront business today. For that matter few could have anticipated the virtual social revolution which has occurred since that time.

The curricula recommended in the Pierson report allotted only three hours, 5 percent of the total, to public control of business, and three to six hours, 5 to 10 percent of the total, to social science courses in human behavior and management. The Gordon-Howell report recommended a requirement of six hours of study in the legal, social, and political environment; that, too, represents only about 10 percent of the total core.

What seemed to be missing from the reports' findings was the knowledge and development of insight to enable a person to understand what is going on about him in the human-social-political sense, its consequences to himself, the institution which he serves, and to people who get in the way of his decisions. The sheer immensity of these changes and complexities seem to suggest the need for an updating of the Pierson and Gordon-Howell reports to evaluate progress made and formulate new paths to follow.

UPDATING THE STUDIES OF BUSINESS EDUCATION

Such an updating particularly will be needed if suggestions like those for greater governmental economic planning and new kinds of public-private corporations actually are adopted. Both Ahlbrandt in his speech and the CED in its proposal refer to significant roles for the universities in the processes they advocate. Ahlbrandt, in saying that the economic, social, and political policies of the four great economic blocs that compete with the United States globally do not come out of U.S. textbooks, goes on to say: "May I suggest, finally, that our nation's educators in economics bear, within industry, a responsibility to recommend courses of action that will solve our problems? You may find that you may even have to rewrite the old textbooks—so pervasive is change in our brave new world."[18] (Parenthetically, what textbooks? Smith, Ricardo, Mill, Marshall? Or Keynes, Hansen, Galbraith, Samuelson?)

The CED, in advocating new partnerships between government and private enterprise, says: "It by no means will be an exclusive partnership, for other private institutions, especially universities, will also play very significant roles."[19] But it apparently has not sensed just how startlingly different those roles will be.

What would the updaters of the business school reports find now, twelve years later? They would find that, in general, the business schools have been strengthened. A generation of business school graduates probably has received a better education than earlier generations. Their tools in the area of quantitative analysis are infinitely more advanced than those of earlier graduates. They likely would find a growth of educational pluralism in the schools of business which, in the long run, may be the healthiest development of all. They would see substantial experimentation. The most exciting development and the most relevant, for our emphasis, is the growth in concern for the relationships of business schools to the community. Educational researchers now would find a number of schools attempting to graft on urban studies or manpower management courses. But the main thrusts continue, even here, to be quantitative and technological, seeking to solve urban problems primarily with business and system techniques.

THE NEW HYBRID

A few schools have adopted or are moving toward the generic management approach. This approach leads to teaching management to people who may be headed toward either the public or the private sectors, people who will

153

PART FOUR
THE
ORGANIZATIONAL
ENVIRONMENT:
MONITORING AND
CONTROLLING
EXTERNAL ACTIVITY

work in public and community (urban) administration, education, and health and medical care, as well as in business and industry. This requires that the student come to understand not only what the tools are, but also whether they apply or can be adapted in different decision-making contexts as in the case of planning—the private, competitive context and the community or urban development context.

Finally, they would find a number of business and management schools currently moving beyond the mere grafting on of urban studies courses to full-fledged urban studies curricula, with at least three distinguishing orientations. These are: (1) the knowledge required to manage complex urban institutions, including the political area of decision making, and the management of the delivery of goods and services to the citizens of a community; (2) technical knowledge, including systems analysis, applied to the solving of community problems such as traffic control and highway development, pollution control, housing development, and general physical environmental improvement; and (3) development among members of the newer urban populations of the capacity to govern, the ability to achieve self-determination and economic self-sufficiency. The updaters of the business education reports would find, as we have suggested, that there have been significant shifts in the nature of business problems, particularly those that deal with increasing interrelationships between public and private sectors and with the strident demands of once-quieter people for a share in the making of decisions about priorities.

Large corporation chief executives behave increasingly as if they were public administrators and vice versa. In a sense they are becoming more alike as they exchange expertise, jobs, and private enterprise managerial technology for public management experience with its pluralistic decision making. They are becoming more alike in another way: the managerial bureaucracies of each, the public and the private, are being challenged to share their decision making and economic and social benefits with new power groups who are seeking entrance into the system and the power needed to enforce a full sharing of the fruits of production.

The burden of this article indeed suggests a blurring of distinctions between the public and private managerial elite. But it contends that, although there are common denominators, the public and private managerial elite presently are not readily interchangeable because of the fundamental differences in the decision-making process for the setting of priorities. The emerging questions cannot yet be answered because both public and private management are in states of transition, but they must be explored by those who would devise curricula to train managers to manage in an urban society. What form of management or manager will emerge during this time of fundamental change in the society?

There have been other shifts in our society in the past twelve years. The economy of the United States has shifted from goods producing to service producing. Former Secretary of Labor Willard Wirtz estimates that by 1980 two people will be in service industries for every one in production.[20]

Manufacturing employment is expected to have the slowest rate of growth, up only 21 percent between 1965 and 1980. In contrast, the fastest growing area is expected to be state and local government, all of it in the service area.

Public employment is expected to increase 66 percent from 1965 to 1980. Other large increases are expected in finance, insurance and trade, and in all those areas concerned with services designed to improve the quality of the environment and of life itself (66 percent).[21]

OPPORTUNITIES AND PREFERENCES FOR MANAGERS

New managers will be needed, but they will be largely outside the traditional career areas with which business schools have concerned themselves. They will be needed particularly in health care delivery, education, public and urban administration and finance, environmental administration, and manpower-intensive industries, and they will be heavily concentrated at state and local government levels.

The people of the nation in the 1960s and 1970s have expressed their concern for improving the quality of life in the society. Whether or not this is a transitory movement remains to be seen because we do not know yet whether man will use what Leakey called his "wonderful computer brain" to work for his own survival. We are learning that many of the best students in our society are selecting job options where they feel they have a chance to do something about man's condition. This can range from making community institutions work effectively, to providing services for the sick, poor, unemployed, and persecuted, to defending man against his efforts to destroy his environment, to eliciting a higher quality of performance from the various levels of government. Many of these careers are in the political-sociological-educational areas not usually found in business. But these careers are at the heart of the capacity to master the processes of involvement of the citizen in planning his future. They are more attuned to the society's estimate of priorities than to those of business. The business schools probably are not attracting the needed share of these future-minded students. In contrast, the number of students applying to the nation's law schools was five times greater in 1971 than it was in 1961.[22]

Since the business school reports, the schools have toughened up the curricula largely through greater emphasis upon the use of quantitative techniques in solving business problems. But, unfortunately, values cannot necessarily be quantified. Matrix decision making may show the quantitative contribution but not necessarily final judgments.

IT WILL TAKE MORE THAN TOOLS

The updaters of the business school reports might find that although the work of the late 1950s added to the quality and stature of schools of business, it also tended to simplify as seemed best fitted to help the student manage the manageable. But if the world is as we seem to think it is and will be, complex, interrelated, interdependent, and extremely difficult to manage, the student will need more than tools. More than his predecessors, he will need the psychological capacity (temperament) to manage in an atmosphere of uncertainty, unpredictability, and conflict. The limits of his control will be sharply constrained and his need to accommodate ambiguity and to negotiate arrangements with other sectors of society will be apparent even before he can apply his knowledge and his tools. For the business school administrator this

PART FOUR
THE
ORGANIZATIONAL
ENVIRONMENT:
MONITORING AND
CONTROLLING
EXTERNAL ACTIVITY

suggests implications not merely respecting curriculum but respecting admissions as well.

For example, administration of a large public hospital system, of which the United States has many and will have many more, requires not only medical and managerial expertise, but also the capacity to manage under stress and conflict arising out of opposing values, expectations, and priorities of the various publics and pressure groups which have an interest in such a system. No one group has free rein to impose its priorities, not even the administration. The political skill to resolve these conflicts in priorities and expectations will be fully as important a requirement of the medical administrator as is his skill as a doctor or his talents as an administrator.

This model of administration is more likely than not to become the rule in the private sector as well, as it strives for a viable existence in the inner cities, and as more and more firms become indebted to government or become government subcontractors or partners in public-private corporations.

A MATTER OF MANAGERIAL GENETICS

The updaters of the business school reports might conclude that the next step forward in the management of a multiracial society of immense diversity would be not the imposition of a business curriculum upon the solving of problems which span both the public and private sectors, but the evolution of a generic school of management which by its nature involves people with diverse interests both in the learning and teaching processes. Such educational arrangements would enable the participants to learn early about the nature of values and priorities and the differences among people in this regard.

Planning and management would be learned under varying conditions: where profit is the regulator, where the logic of economic development is the regulator, where the logic of human development is the regulator, where political strength is the regulator. There are common denominators of management in each, but each has its unique distinctions, too. Thus, education for management is not to blend into one what are important differences, but rather to show how the processes are specific to the needs of institutions. It is to demonstrate how as institutions blend or take over one another's functions this alters the decision-making process and even remakes it to respond to new hybrid institutions.

Planning and management would entail not only the method of arriving at the plans to be achieved but also the process for achieving them, which also may include the political process. This is not an uncommon activity of institutions today, especially public sector organizations where program planning budgeting has taken hold. These planning needs will influence the curriculum for both the public and private sector.

The central role of management and planning, as suggested in the beginning of this article, is to aid people and institutions to make decisions: to decide what is important, necessary, too costly, necessary even if too costly, useful or useless either in the context of competition or community decision making. Its role will increase as the free competition sector shrinks; a means for valuing goods and services must be maintained no matter what the competitive condition.

NOTES

[1]The Emergency Employment Act was signed by President Nixon on 12 July 1972. The idea of governmentally guaranteed work dates back to 1836 when it was proposed by Louis Blanc. Prior to Karl Marx, this public employment is what Europeans thought socialism meant.

[2]In 1971, the federal government financed 55 percent of the $26.9 billion spent nationally for basic and applied research and for development. *Annual Report of the Council of Economic Advisers* (Washington, D.C.: U.S. Government Printing Office, 1972).

[3]Roger S. Ahlbrandt, "For Whom the Steel Bell Tolls," speech before the Steel Industry Economics Seminar, Wayne State University, Detroit, Michigan, 12 April 1972.

[4]Research and Policy Committee, Committee for Economic Development, *Social Responsibilities*, New York, June 1971, p. 59.

[5]Ibid.

[6]Management schools are beginning to study this phenomenon. See G. Zaltman, P. Kotler, and I. Kaufman, eds., *Creating Social Change* (New York: Holt, Rinehart, Winston, forthcoming).

[7]Speech by Louis S. B. Leakey, 27 December 1971, in Philadelphia. Reported in *Chicago Sun-Times*, 28 December 1971, p. 3.

[8]CED, *Social Responsibilities*, p. 60.

[9]*La Peau de chagain*, Balzac's thesis that every aspiration of the heart, brain, or will that is fulfilled must in the end be paid for.

[10]CED, *Social Responsibilities*, p. 51.

[11]U.S. Department of Commerce, Office of Business Economics, Summary National Income and Product Series, 1929–70, *Survey of Current Business* 51, no. 7 (July 1971): 46, Table A, Gross National Product.

[12]A. A. Berle, Jr., "What GNP Doesn't Tell Us," *Saturday Review*, 31 August 1968.

[13]Willard Wirtz, in the Julius Rosenthal lecture series on "Labor and the Law," Northwestern University, 1, 2, 3 March 1972. In 1967, Senator Fred Harris introduced a full opportunities and national goals and priorities act, creating not only a council of social advisers but also, within Congress, a joint social responsibilities committee that would parallel the Joint Economic Committee. It was not passed. Senator Walter Mondale later reintroduced the bill which passed the Senate but died in the House of Representatives.

[14]"The Corporation and the Community: Realities and Myths," *MSU Business Topics*, Autumn 1970, p. 18.

[15]In the article referred to in ibid., the author argued that community involvement is largely a delegated function, to keep it from interfering with the main stream of corporate activity.

[16]"The concept of the corporation was developed to give government a vehicle for accomplishing activities in the public interest. Originally corporate charters were rarely granted to accomplish things the government could do for itself but chose to delegate, such as building bridges or highways, or helping to administer colonies, as the British East India Co. did for the English crown. Thus it seems obvious that government has the right to ensure that corporations operate in the public interest." Joel H. Henning, "Found a Dual System of Corporate Chartering," *Chicago Sun-Times*, 30 January 1972.

[17]Robert Aaron Gordon and James Edwin Howell, *Higher Education for Business* (New York: Ford Foundation, Columbia University Press, 1959). Frank C. Pierson, *The Education of American Businessmen* (New York: Carnegie Corporation, McGraw-Hill Book Co., 1959).

[18]Ahlbrandt, "For Whom the Steel Bell Tolls."

[19]CED, *Social Responsibilities*, p. 59.

[20]Willard Wirtz in Julius Rosenthal lectures, Northwestern University, 1, 2, 3 March 1972.

[21]*The U.S. Economy in 1950*, Bulletin 1673 and Manpower Report of the President, 1970.

[22]Robert W. Meserve, "We Are Flooded," *Illinois Bar Journal*, May 1972, p. 772.

12 | The Limits of Legal Compulsion

John T. Dunlop

In recent years, a rapid expansion of government controls has been associated with a growing dissatisfaction with the effects of regulation. Scholarly books and journals have offered detailed criticisms of specific regulatory policies, but these analyses have neither slowed the growth of formal regulation nor encouraged the development of alternative approaches to problems.

The issue confronts those involved in public policy generally. The Department of Labor, however, is an unusual vantage point from which to survey different types of regulatory programs and the arguments about their usefulness. The Department emerged from some of the same social, economic, and political concerns which were involved in the development of private collective bargaining as the predominant means of establishing the network of rules which governs behavior in the workplace and work environment. As such, its ties to industrial relations are strong.

In recent years, however, the Department has been assigned one of the most extensive sets of regulatory programs in the Federal Government. In 1940, the Department administered 18 regulatory programs; by 1960, the number had expanded to 40; in 1975, the number stands at 134. At present, the Department has responsibility for promulgating and administering complex regulations under the Occupational Safety and Health Act, the Urban Mass Transportation Act, the Consumer Credit Protection Act, the Davis-Bacon Act, the Civil Rights Act of 1964, the Equal Pay Act, the Employee Retirement Income Security Act, and many others. All of these regulatory programs establish substantive—and in many cases quantitative—definitions of acceptable conduct for employers, employees, and third parties.

The Department thus provides examples for a broader comparison between essentially private methods for rule-making within a broad and general governmental context—exemplified by collective bargaining—and the more intensive approach of governmental promulgation of mandatory regulations.

At the outset, a distinction also needs to be drawn between economic regulation of prices, rates or fees, and related conditions of entry to a market on the one hand, and social regulation, on the other, affecting conditions of work such as discrimination, health and safety, and the like. In the case of economic regulation it may often be appropriate to raise the question of whether the interests of a sector and the public may not better be served by deregulation. In the field of social regulation, while some deregulation may be appropriate, the major areas of review are likely practically to be concerned with methods of regulation, involvement of those affected by enforcement, compliance approaches, and communication to those affected. Regulation to achieve a public purpose continues, but the central concern is the methods, approaches and mutual attitudes of the regulators and the regulatees.

PRACTICAL AND EFFECTIVE

Over the years, regulation has proved to be a practical and effective approach to some social and economic problems. The inspection of meat and poultry is an obvious example and suggests the sort of concerns that prompted the development of regulation in the late eighteenth century. In the words of a foremost student of administrative law, Kenneth Culp Davis, "Practical men were seeking practical answers to immediate problems. . . . What was needed was a governmental authority having power not merely to adjudicate, but to initiate proceedings, to investigate, to prosecute, to issue regulations having force of law, to supervise." From these perceived needs developed the structure of modern regulation, an approach which is now used without significant modification as our principal policy tool for dealing with occupational disease, discrimination, dangerous toys, and pollution.

A major reason for the attraction of regulation over the years has been the belief that it is a speedy, simple and cheap procedure. It should be apparent that the administrative procedure is by no means fast or inexpensive but the prevailing belief is that it is. This misconception, in large part, is due to the fact that the constraints on the rule-making and adjudicating activities of regulatory agencies are not widely perceived or appreciated. Perhaps, too, because the majority of Congressmen are lawyers, and not business executives, labor leaders, economists, or labor mediators, they are apt to think of social and economic problems in legal terms. For these and other reasons, when a problem acquires national attention—as pollution, inflation, and occupational disease have in recent years—the natural reaction has been to create a new regulatory agency to deal with it. There are a variety of problems with this approach.

The first problem with regulation is that it encourages simplistic thinking about complicated issues. To get regulatory legislation passed in a pluralistic society often requires the evocation of horror stories and the mobilization of broad political support. To quote Professor Wilson: "Political inertia is not easily overcome, and when it is overcome, it is often at the price of exaggerating the virtue of those who are to benefit (a defrauded debtor, a sick industry) or the wickedness of those who are to bear the burden (a smog-belching car, a polluting factory, a grasping creditor)."

Second, designing and administering a regulatory program is an incredibly complicated task. How successfully and efficiently occupational disease or discrimination in hiring practices will be reduced depends not just on the kind

159

PART FOUR
THE
ORGANIZATIONAL
ENVIRONMENT:
MONITORING AND
CONTROLLING
EXTERNAL ACTIVITY

of goals set by Congress or a few key decisions by civil servants in Washington but upon tens of thousands of individual actions taken by business firms and private citizens across the country. Ensuring compliance with a regulation is far more difficult than promulgating it, though that too can be a complicated and lengthy process. There are, for example, 5 million workplaces and 1,200 OSHA inspectors. All affected parties can never be notified of a new rule's existence, and thus reasonably be expected to comply, and the means of informing regulatees of new rules (mainly through publication in the *Federal Register*) is severely inadequate.

UNINTENDED CONSEQUENCES

Third, oftentimes policies that appear straightforward will have unintended consequences which can create problems as severe as those with which the regulations were intended to deal. For example, the Wagner Act meant to encourage the development of unions and collective bargaining, but its concept of "exclusive representation"—where the employees in a unit decide which union, if any, they want to represent them in bargaining with management—contradicted the traditional union principle of "exclusive jurisdiction" —in which all workers in a particular craft or industry are legitimately represented by one union.

The Wagner Act had the effect of encouraging competition between unions for members, leading to disputes between unions and changing the internal governance of organized labor, an entirely unintended effect. Article XX of the AFL-CIO constitution was later adopted to provide a method for mitigating these disputes through limited arbitration; competitive elections, rational bargaining structures, and union jurisdiction are not entirely compatible. It is very hard for affected groups to perceive the longer term and often unintended consequences of regulation.

A fourth problem is that the rule-making and adjudicatory procedures of regulatory agencies tend to be very slow, creating conflicts between the different groups involved, and leading to weak and ineffective remedies for the people the programs aim to help. Early experience demonstrated the need for the regulatory agencies' procedures to include the same sort of safeguards to insure fairness that were present in the judicial and legislative processes. The result eventually was the Administrative Procedure Act of 1946, which established formal procedures for the promulgation of rules and the adjudication of cases. The purpose was to ensure that each party affected by a proposed rule would have an opportunity to present its views, thereby limiting the possibility that regulations or decisions would be arbitrary, unworkable, or unfair.

Common sense recognizes the importance of these procedures, but while they are designed to make regulation fair, they can also make it rigid. When a regulatory program is imposed immediately upon passage and the administrative agency lacks authority to adjust the law to fit the realities of business practice—as is the case with some requirements of the new pension law (ERISA)—the result is often rules based on abstractions which are fair and effective in some settings and pointless and burdensome in others. In the case of one ERISA provision, the Department of Labor received over 220,000 individual requests for exemption, some taking more than twelve months to process. The procedure is lengthy and complicated: If an exemption is proposed, it is then published in the *Federal Register* and comments are solicited; a public hearing can be requested and if, as a result, the exemption is modified, then the procedure may be repeated. The process is often prolonged by different groups taking advantage of procedure to advance their interests; thus, a legitimate exemption may take months to obtain.

Fifth, the rule-making and adjudicatory procedures do not include a mechanism for the development of mutual accommodation among the conflicting interests. Opposing interests argue their case to the government, and not at each other. Direct discussions and negotiations among opposing points of view, where mutual accommodation is mutually desirable, as in collective bargaining, forces the parties to set priorities among their demands, trading off one for another and creating an incentive for them to find common ground. The values, perceptions, and needs of each become apparent. And some measure of mutual understanding is a by-product.

As compulsory arbitration undermines the willingness of the parties to bargain conscientiously over their differences, so regulation lessens incentives for private accommodation of conflicting viewpoints. Public hearings encourage dramatic presentations and exorbitant demands, and the government's disclosure rules and the Advisory Committee Act inhibit private meetings between the affected parties and the agency.

CONFLICT ENCOURAGED

The regulatory agency is thus ignorant of the parties' true positions, and is forced to guess each interest's priorities and needs from the formal and often extreme public statements the parties have presented at public hearings. The regulatory process encourages conflict, rather than acting to reconcile opposing interests. Moreover, there is a sense that it is wrong for the regulatory agency to try to bring parties together and develop consensus. Reliance on public and highly formal proceedings makes the development of consensus extremely difficult, if not impossible. And unless this consensus can be developed, neither party has any stake in the promulgated rule. Thus, both are free to complain that it is biased, stupid, or misguided. Moreover, each side is free to continue the controversy in the form of endless petitions for review, clarification, and litigation before the agency and the courts. Nothing is ever settled because true settlement can come only through agreement, consent, or acquiescence.

Sixth, regulatory efforts are rarely abandoned even after their purpose has been served. As James Q. Wilson has pointed out: "Both business firms and regulatory agencies operate on the basis of a common principle: Maintain the organization ... for the public agency that means creating and managing services (or a public image of services) that please key Congressmen, organized clients, and the news media."

A parallel problem affects the agency's body of regulations; repealing or modifying those rules is a lengthy and complicated process and is rarely done. Thus the code becomes bloated with anachronistic and rarely enforced regulations that nonetheless have the force of law and could be applied at the conve-

PART FOUR
THE
ORGANIZATIONAL
ENVIRONMENT:
MONITORING AND
CONTROLLING
EXTERNAL.ACTIVITY

nience of a compliance officer. Trivial and important regulations are mixed; to the regulatee the program appears irrational and arbitrary. Also, as the body of rules expands, it becomes increasingly more difficult and expensive for the regulatees to figure out what is required of them. In this way, the agency and its rules remain in place long after their usefulness has been served.

A seventh problem involves the legal game-playing between the regulatees and the regulators. The tax law is the classic example; it is typical of regulatory programs in general. The regulatory agency promulgates a regulation; the regulatees challenge it in court; if they lose, their lawyers may seek to find another ground for administrative or judicial challenge. Congressional amendments may be developed. Between a challenge to the regulation's basic legality, pressure on the agency for an amended regulation, and administrative and judicial enforcement proceedings, there is ample opportunity for tactical strategies, allegations of ambiguity, pleas of special circumstances and the like. It should be a first principle that no set of men is smart enough to write words in which others cannot find holes when the stakes are high.

An eighth problem with regulation concerns the difficulty encountered by small and medium size firms in complying with the regulations of the various agencies, and the problems the government has in trying to enforce compliance. Many regulations do not well fit the circumstances of small enterprises. It is often difficult if not impossible for small to medium size firms to keep track of the large number of regulations issued by various agencies. And there is little reason to do so; the chances of a small or medium size firm being inspected are minute, and if it is inspected and found to be in violation fines for a first offence are usually small. Thus, it may make practical business sense for a firm to put off the expenses required to achieve compliance until after an inspection has specified those changes which have to be made.

Compliance cannot be compelled through a police effort in every workplace, given any practicable levels of funds and personnel. To a degree, "public examples"—where a company found in violation is given harsh and visible treatment—encourage other companies to come into compliance. But this tactic is generally unsuccessful for several reasons. Nearly every company—particularly if it is a small one—has a good or plausible excuse for not being in compliance (e.g., they were not aware of the regulations); thus, a large fine tends to get whittled down to a small one through the successive stages of administrative review. Also, such tactics are perceived to be unfair and generate strong resentment in public opinion and the press. They create hostility to the program and attempts to change it in the political arena.

Ninth, as the rule-making and compliance activities of regulatory agencies become routine, it grows increasingly difficult for the President and the agency to attract highly qualified and effective administrators into leadership positions. As the quality of leadership declines, problems often receive increasingly less imaginative treatment or no attention at all.

Tenth, uniform national regulations are inherently unworkable in many situations because the society is not uniform. There are significant differences between industries and sectors and regions of the country. Consequently, a regulation may be unrealistically harsh in one industry or sector or part of the country and too lenient in another.

An eleventh problem is what is called "regulatory overlap," where a number of different regulatory agencies share some of the same responsibilities. Although the creation of a new specialized agency probably heightens effectiveness in one field, the danger is that a series of uncoordinated steps, each quite sensible in itself, can set up a series of unanticipated consequences that is overwhelmingly negative. No one regulatory program is ever able to see the problems through the eyes of those subject to regulation, and the total consequences of regulatory programs on the firm or industry are never perceived. There is no mechanism in government to add up these consequences. Moreover, jurisdictional conflict among agencies, even with the best of good will, consumes vast amounts of time and energy and stimulates general disrespect for governmental agencies.

QUALITY IMPROVEMENTS

It is not realistic to expect any significant reduction in the number of Federal regulatory programs in the immediate future; in fact, it is likely that the political processes and the Congress will seek to add new ones. Regardless of the theoretical merits of regulation, it is important as a practical matter that more attention be given toward improving the quality of regulation.

In a sense, accommodation with practical reality has always occurred. While some inspectors in the field enforce the letter of the law, others develop an array of informal operating rules of thumb which drafters of the regulations never thought of, or indeed rejected. Sometimes these rules of thumb call for non-enforcement in trivial cases or where application of a rigid rule would be unreasonable. "Policy makers" would do well to address explicitly that which lower level implementers will do anyway—though unevenly—through the application of common sense or prejudice. The following suggestions are designed to make the regulatory process more responsive to the problems cited above.

First, the parties who will be affected by a set of regulations should be involved to a greater extent in developing those regulations. The way regulations are currently developed is inherently contentious and acts to maximize antagonism between the parties. The result is poorly framed rules, lawsuits, evasion, and dissatisfaction with the program by all parties. In our society, a rule that is developed with the involvement of the parties who are affected is more likely to be accepted and to be effective in accomplishing its intended purposes.

There is no single way by which the parties can be involved in the rule-making process, but a method is suggested by the Department's recent experience with section 13(c) of the Urban Mass Transportation Act. UMTA gives grants to cities to take over failing private transit systems. Section 13(c) requires that funds not be granted until the Secretary of Labor has certified that employees would not be adversely affected by the federally funded activities. This requirement has caused substantial delays and confusion as unions and private managers or city officials haggled over what constituted equitable compensation.

Rather than prepare regulations, the Department brought together union and transit representatives and got them to prepare a three year agreement as

PART FOUR
THE
ORGANIZATIONAL
ENVIRONMENT:
MONITORING AND
CONTROLLING
EXTERNAL ACTIVITY

to what protection employees should receive as a consequence of the federally funded activities. The Department mediated and provided technical assistance, helping to create the standards to apply to individual cases presented to it. Processing time will be very noticeably reduced.

This approach is not necessarily applicable without modification to, say, OSHA or ERISA. However, it represents a useful spirit of reliance on private mechanisms which sometimes can achieve a program objective most efficiently.

Second, anachronistic and unnecessary regulations should be repealed and, in the future, rules should be promulgated with greater reluctance. It is an open question as to how many regulations a business, particularly one of small or medium size, can absorb. Not only is it difficult for the regulatee to figure out what is required, but it is equally hard for compliance officers to determine violations. Often they rely on a small percentage of the rules with which they are familiar; thus the trivial rules are enforced as often as the important ones. This causes annoyance with the program without producing substantial benefits.

Third, greater emphasis should be placed on helping regulatees achieve compliance, especially through consultation. Trying to force compliance primarily through threats of inspections and stiff fines has not proved successful. It has worked against acceptance of the programs by isolating the regulators (and their expertise) from the regulatees and creating antagonism and distrust between the two.

As pointed out earlier, the chances of a small or medium size business ever being inspected are minute and the cost of coming into compliance is often high. If the business executive asks the agency for technical assistance, in effect the person is asking to be inspected; at least this is the common perception. The regulatory agencies have the expertise to deal with complicated, technical problems such as pollution and occupational disease. But because the programs appear punitive, there is little constructive interplay between the regulators and the regulatees.

Fourth, the activities of the various regulatory agencies need to be better coordinated. As it is now, a single firm may be under the purview of OFCC, OSHA, the Wage and Hour Administration and a variety of other programs. Simply the number of forms required poses a substantial burden, again encouraging antagonism for the programs. More significantly, the jurisdictions may overlap. Perhaps some consolidation and more coordination and sensitivity can be a long-range goal.

Fifth, regulations must be made to reflect differences between industries, sectors, and geographic regions. A rule that is fair and workable in New York may be excessively severe or unnecessary in Utah. Similar problems exist between industries and types of enterprises and labor organizations. Uniform, national rules may assure equity but they do not reflect the reality of the workplace.

And sixth, the actions of the various regulatory agencies need to be brought into greater harmony with collective bargaining. Many of these programs undermine relations between organized labor and management, as when issues of safety and health, apprenticeship and training, and pensions are placed under government regulation. Without limiting its responsibility to administer the law, and recognizing that some laws are designed explicitly to change the results produced by private collective bargaining, there are ways to involve the parties better to achieve practical and acceptable solutions.

CONCLUSIONS

The country needs to acquire a more realistic understanding of the limitations on bringing about social change through legal compulsion. A great deal of government time needs to be devoted to improving understanding, persuasion, accommodation, mutual problem solving, and informal mediation. Legislation, litigation, and regulations are useful means for some social and economic problems, but today government has more regulation on its plate than it can handle. As I said on the occasion of my swearing-in at the White House, in many areas the growth of regulations and law has far outstripped our capacity to develop consensus and mutual accommodation to our common detriment.

It has well been said that the recreation and development of trust is the central problem of government in our times. The development of new attitudes on the part of public employees and new relationships and procedures with those who are required to live under regulations is a central challenge of democratic society. Trust cannot grow in an atmosphere dominated by bureaucratic fiat and litigious controversy; it emerges through persuasion, mutual accommodation, and problem solving.

PART FIVE

THE INTERNAL ENVIRONMENT: INDIVIDUAL AND GROUP BEHAVIOR

The preceding set of readings shows vividly that public managers are frequently confronted with a significant environmental paradox—the American people increasingly turn to government for the resolution of difficult social problems, but they also show mistrust and contempt for the institutions and managers who try to cope with these problems. This paradox affects the innermost activities of government organizations and the feelings of individual managers about themselves and their profession. What effect does this paradox have on the bringing together of individuals into effective, functioning public organizations? More specifically, what factors help to attract individuals to government organizations? How is their commitment maintained? Can individuals be expected to provide extra effort in the pursuit of organizational goals, even when confronted by hostile environments? What binds individuals to the goals of government organizations? These questions are important in their own right, but they must also be answered in order to develop a better understanding of the special con-

text of public organizations.

At a general level, the requirements for effective individual and group behavior in government organizations look much like those in private organizations. Daniel Katz (1964) identified three behavioral requirements that are the bases for effective organizations. First, individuals must be enticed to enter and remain with an organization. This first requirement means that an organization must have a sufficient supply of human resources to carry out its tasks. Without an adequate supply of resources, no organization can function effectively.

Second, organizations must attract individuals who perform dependably. Most organizations specify roles for their members, and it is important that these roles are regularly and reliably performed. The lack of reliable role performance prevents an organization from carrying out tasks efficiently.

Finally, organizations must elicit from their members performance above and beyond the call of duty, that is, it is not sufficient for people simply to come to work and perform their major tasks or roles reliably. Organizations also need individuals who will act beyond their role requirements and spontaneously give extra effort when it is needed.

Again, at a general level, these behavioral requirements are necessary for all organizations to function effectively and to survive. But, as the readings in this section illustrate, both the specific behaviors required in government organizations and the methods for eliciting those behaviors tend to differ from those in private organizations. In the first article, James L. Perry and Lyman W. Porter assess the factors affecting the degree and type of effort that individuals exhibit in public-sector work situations. They classify motivational factors into four categories: individual characteristics, job characteristics, work environment characteristics, and external environment characteristics. Within each category, they identify factors that make the context for energizing and sustaining behavior in public organizations different from that of private organizations. Their research review suggests that: (1) the needs of government managers tend to differ from those of their business counterparts; (2) public-sector jobs typically confront public managers with dilemmas about the nature and appropriateness of performance criteria; (3) the lack of clear goals complicates the tasks of developing attachments to government organizations and generating spontaneous goal-directed activity; and (4) socionormative and political changes create significant ambiguities about the appropriate roles for members of public organizations.

These peculiarities of the motivational context in public organizations carry significant implications for the techniques and policies that are used to elicit effective organizational behavior. Perry and Porter argue that the four most common motiva-tional methods—monetary incentives, goal setting, job design, and participation—probably require special adaptations in the public sector. They suggest that, among the four types of incentive systems, goal setting holds the most promise for improving the performance of government organizations.

Not only do the motivational contexts in business and government exhibit significant differences, but, as Bruce Buchanan illustrates, our expectations of public managers are frequently grounded in myth rather than in fact. Buchanan investigates some common assumptions about the prominence of administrative red tape in public-agency operations and the existence of a service ethic that represents a special kind of involvement among public servants. Contrary to his expectations, he found that business managers perceived more red tape in their organizations than public managers did. However, public managers exhibited lower levels of job involvement than their business counterparts did.

Buchanan offers several compelling explanations for why the general beliefs about public servants were not borne out by his data. One of these reasons turns on the economies in which business and government organizations are located. Buchanan suggests that the market economy in which most business organizations are located requires a stricter adherence to operational procedures, thereby creating more sensitivity to formal structure, that is, red tape. This same market context creates deeper personal work involvement or identification. Buchanan contrasts these forces of a market economy with those in government organizations. Although government organizations generate substantial bodies of rules, civil service systems permit substantial autonomy. Furthermore, unlike industrial organizations, the greater diversity, representativeness, and openness of government organizations are likely to permit indifference (or worse) among some mid- and upper-level managers.

The final two articles by Alan W. Lau, Arthur R. Newman, and Laurie A. Broedling, and by Lyman W. Porter and John Van Maanen, are especially helpful for understanding the similarities and differences in effective managerial behavior between business and government organizations. Lau, Newman, and Broedling looked at a group of 370 U.S. Navy top executives to see how they spent their time. In their study, they used a typology originally developed by Henry Mintzberg (1973) to study the roles performed by managers: Managers perform ten different roles across three general types of activity. On an interpersonal dimension, executives tend to fill three roles: figurehead, leader, and liaison. As information facilitators, executives perform the roles of monitor, disseminator, and spokesperson. Finally, in the area of decision making, executives, according to Mintzberg's typology, perform four different roles: entrepreneur, disturbance handler, resource allocator, and negotiator.

The Lau et al. study suggests that the managerial roles performed by public executives are reasonably congruent with the results of Mintzberg and others who looked at private-sector managers. They report that the public-sector executive, like his or her private-sector counterpart, does not have time for reflective systematic planning, strongly favors oral communication, has accumulated many obligations, and serves as facilitator for the exchange of large amounts of information from the outside environment.

Even given this general similarity between executive jobs in business and government, the last two articles in this section also demonstrate some significant differences. For example, the role of technical expert, not previously documented in private-sector studies, is identified in Lau et al. This role reflects the dual obligation of many public-sector managers to perform both managerial roles and technical roles, as in directing a project while solving project-related problems.

Porter and Van Maanen, although essentially agreeing with the above similarities in how business and government managers use their time, suggest some additional, important differences. They suggest that, although government managers may perform roles similar to those of business managers, they have less control of their time, there is more intrusion of outsiders in their activities, and the time that they spend alone is allocated to different activities. These differences may again reflect the absence of product markets in the public sector and the resulting need for public managers to respond to specific requests and demands for accountability by organizational outsiders.

Despite the fact that managers in business and government may perform the same roles, Porter and Van Maanen suggest that the relationship between role performance and effectiveness may be strikingly dissimilar in the two sectors. They note that effective performers in government organizations appear to be those who make fewer attempts to control their time and therefore have the flexibility to respond to the demands of a particular situation. In contrast, task accomplishment in industrial organizations appears to be more closely related to the planning and controlling of one's time. Thus, although role behaviors may be similar, the value of these behaviors may be different in business and government.

REFERENCES

Katz, D. The motivational basis of organizational behavior. *Behavioral Science*, 1964, 9, 131–146.

Mintzberg, H. *The nature of managerial work*. New York: Harper and Row, 1973.

13 | Factors Affecting the Context for Motivation in Public Organizations

James L. Perry
Lyman W. Porter

The need to get "more for less" has been a major issue within public sector organizations during the 1970s and, if recent developments provide any clues, it promises to remain near the top of managers' agendas throughout the coming decade. Many public managers probably identify the most recent efforts to get more for less with fads that, by now, are represented by familiar "buzz" words—zero-based budgeting (ZBB), cutback management, sunset, total performance measurement, and total pay comparability. The current concern about governmental efficiency, however, also has helped to focus renewed attention on some of the basic and enduring responsibilities of public managers, among them the motivation of employees.

At the outset, it is important for the reader to be aware that although the general terms "public employees" and "public organizations" are used, the public sector encompasses many different types of organizations and roles. Some of the generalizations in the present review, therefore, may not extend to all public organizations or public sector jobs. Based on the types of organizations studied in the research from which the present evidence is drawn, the generalizations are appropriate for civil servants and civil service jobs in medium to large governmental agencies, but they may apply to public employees in other contexts also. The research agenda proposed here should help to delimit better the proper scope of any generalizations.

THE CONTEXT FOR MOTIVATION

As a hypothetical construct, motivation usually stands for that which "energizes, directs, and sustains behavior." In shorthand terms, it is the degree and type of effort that an individual exhibits in a behavioral situation. How-

Reprinted from James L. Perry and Lyman W. Porter, "Factors Affecting the Context for Motivation in Public Organizations," *Academy of Management Review*, January 1982, 7, 89–98.

ever, care needs to be taken not to equate motivation simply with sheer amount of effort. It also has to do with the direction and quality of that effort.

Any comprehensive look at the motivational bases of behavior in organizational settings must of necessity focus on the several sets of variables that influence motivation. A classification system (Porter & Miles, 1974) found useful identifies four major catetories of variables: (1) individual characteristics, (2) job characteristics, (3) work environment characteristics, and (4) external environment characteristics. If motivation is to be affected, one or more of these variables must be changed or affected. Let us look briefly at each category of variables and the special facets of motivational tasks in public organizations.

Individual Characteristics

Although it is obvious that certain characteristics (such as attitudes) can be changed after one joins an organization, the focus here is on individual characteristics *brought to* the work situation. Presently there is a very limited understanding of special considerations that involve the "raw materials" in public sector motivational processes. Of course, one reason for this deficiency is simply the belief that, if government is different from other management contexts, it is distinguished by the nature of work or the environment within which the work occurs, not by the individuals whom it attracts or employs. Given this prevailing belief, only a few studies provide an indication of the motivational characteristics of public employees. Guyot (1961) compared middle managers in the federal government and in business on their needs for achievement, affiliation, and power. He concluded, quite surprisingly, that both popular and academic images of civil servants were distorted. Government middle managers had higher needs for achievement and lower needs for affiliation than did their business counterparts, but their needs for power were roughly the same.

Few researchers have attempted to replicate Guyot's results. However, two relatively recent studies by Rawls and his associates (Rawls & Nelson, 1975; Rawls, Ulrich, & Nelson, 1975), using samples of students about to enter management careers, again uncovered differences in individual characteristics. They found that students about to enter the nonprofit sector (primarily government) were significantly more dominant and flexible, had a higher capacity for status, and valued economic wealth to a lesser degree than did entrants to the profit sector. No significant differences existed between the groups on need for power and need for security. Thus, the collective findings of the three studies cited above exhibit a fairly high degree of consistency, considering the limitations on the comparisons that may be made among them, regarding the needs of public employees and how these needs differ from individuals in other sectors.

An independent issue related to individual characteristics involves the types of individual needs that are satisfied by the activities that occur in government organizations. Several studies (Paine, Carrol, & Leete, 1966; Rhinehart, Barrell, DeWolfe, Griffin, & Spaner, 1969; Rainey, 1979a, 1979b) indicate that public managers experience significantly lower levels of satisfaction than do their counterparts in business. Among the areas in which the differences are significant is satisfaction with promotion. This finding can be contrasted with the strong need for achievement found among entrants to government organizations. However, these studies utilized deficiency scores to measure satisfaction; thus levels of satisfaction then could simply reflect more stringent norms or expectations among government managers.

■ 13 ■
James L. Perry
Lyman W. Porter

Job Characteristics

The second major set of variables that can be changed or modified to affect motivation involve what the person *does* at work—that is, the nature of the job or the collection of tasks that comprise the job. Although the unique features of government structures are generally believed, as indicated earlier, to have little impact on individual characteristics affecting public sector motivational processes, organizational structures and goals unique to government clearly influence the design of jobs in the public sector. Yet, just as the understanding of individual characteristics is deficient, motivation-relevant characteristics of public sector jobs also are not well documented in the research literature. Among the job characteristics that have been identified to be important, however, are the measurability of individual performance, degree of goal clarity, and degree of job challenge.

A frequent point of departure for many scholars attempting to identify unique aspects of public employment is the nature, both from aggregate and disaggregate perspectives, of public sector jobs. For example, Rainey, Backoff, and Levine (1976), Newman and Wallendar (1978), and Fottler (1981) have concluded that demands on higher level public managers to maintain constituencies, deal with competing external interests, and seek funding in a political environment probably differentiate their roles from managers in other economic sectors. This view is reinforced by the results of a study (Porter & Van Maanen, 1970) that compared time management and task accomplishment for public and private managers. Similarly, from an aggregate perspective, government is perceived primarily as a service provider rather than a goods producer. And, in fact, government is enormously more labor intensive than are other sectors of the American economy because it is oriented toward the provision of personal services. The implications of this phenomenon are significant for the dimension of jobs that Thompson (1967) terms the *types of assessments* levied against individuals, that is, the extent to which individuals are likely to be evaluated by maximizing or satisficing criteria. Because government organizations are predominantly service providers, with additional burdens of accountability and public responsiveness, the problems of creating performance criteria and implementing evaluation schemes are complex and difficult. The difficulties place a special burden on public managers in designating what performance shall be evaluated.

A related aspect of performance appraisal in many public organizations is what Buchanan (1975a) terms *goal crispness*. Buchanan argues that governmental organizations pursue diffuse and conflicting goals, quite unlike the tangible and relatively more specific goals of business organizations. Thus, public managers are usually confronted by a two-pronged dilemma with respect to the motivational properties of public sector jobs: (1) jobs for which performance criteria cannot be readily defined or measured and (2) conflicting criteria for superior performance.

Quite surprisingly, the consequences of these characteristics of governmental jobs do not appear to spill over into other job dimensions and, therefore, they do not further complicate motivational processes. For example, Rainey (1979a) hypothesized that the greater vagueness and intangibility of governmental goals would lead to public middle managers expressing higher mean scores on role conflict and role ambiguity. He found, however, no significant differences between government and business managers. Thus, performance in public sector jobs generally may be more difficult to assess, and the task goals of public jobs might inherently conflict, but these phenomena apparently do not produce corresponding role-related conflicts. Managers develop means for coping with problematic job characteristics such as assessing jobs in terms of standard operating procedures (Cyert & March, 1963) that simplify and avoid the difficulties of performance measurement in public service organizations.

A recent report by the National Center for Productivity and Quality of Working Life (1978) suggests that two other job dimensions, job content and job challenge, satisfy the needs of employees relatively well. Most public employees responding to a series of attitude surveys rated the content of their jobs as good (managers—84 percent; nonmanagers—64 percent), and few disagreed with a statement that their jobs made good use of their skills and abilities (managers—14 percent; nonmanagers—23 percent). Buchanan (1974a) reports results on first-year job challenge comparing business and public managers that seemingly contradict the latter result. Industrial managers in his sample scored higher, reporting significantly greater *first-year* job challenge. Because Buchanan focused, however, on first-year job challenge, it is quite plausible that differences might exist between the National Commission results and his more restrictive and retrospective concept. He offers several reasons for the lower level of first-year job challenge among government managers. One reason is that bureaucratic roles, particularly at training levels, might be difficult to infuse with excitement. This could be exacerbated by the gap that exists between the routineness of the first job and the idealism that might have drawn the manager to the public service. Buchanan notes that first-year job challenge might also be negatively affected by government's efforts to assure representation and to train unemployed individuals. These policies might unwittingly contribute to overstaffing and the dilution of training positions.

Work Environment Characteristics

Variables dealing with work environment characteristics than can be changed or modified to impact motivation can be placed into two subcategories: immediate work environment characteristics and organizational actions. Clearly, the two most critical factors in an employee's immediate work environment are: the peer group and the supervisor. Organizational actions, insofar as they affect motivation, can be classified into (a) provision of system rewards, (b) provision of individual rewards, and (c) creation of an organizational climate.

More insights have been developed about important motivational aspects of the work situation in public organizations than about the preceding two categorizations of variables, individual and job characteristics. A number of these insights relate to organizational climate and emanate from Buchanan's work (1974a, 1974b, 1975a, 1975b) on organizational commitment. Among the work situation characteristics affecting motivation is the phenomenon of *goal crispness,* discussed earlier in conjunction with job characteristics. The diffuseness of, and contradictions among, public organizational goals may be viewed as work environment characteristics as well as job characteristics. In either instance, they complicate the task of developing attachments to government organizations and generating spontaneous goal directed activities.

■ 13 ■
James L. Perry
Lyman W. Porter

Goal crispness is only one of several work environment characteristics relevant to motivation in the public sector. Buchanan (1974a, 1975b) identifies at least three other work environment characteristics that influence a manager's leverage in motivating employees: personal significance reinforcement, stability of expectations, and reference group experiences.

Personal significance reinforcement, a related aspect of goal crispness, involves the extent to which individuals perceive that they make contributions to organizational success. As Buchanan argues, it is especially difficult for many public agencies to instill employees with a sense of personal significance. One reason is that it is often difficult for public employees to observe any link between their contributions and the success of their organizations. The absence of this linkage is the result of a variety of factors, among them the sheer size of many governments, the pluralistic composition of policy implementation networks, and the lack of clear-cut performance indicators or norms. Developing the attitude among employees that they are valued members of an organization is a difficult job even in the best circumstances. However, the task becomes increasingly demanding when attitudes of personal significance must be developed within a large-scale organization in which there might be little acceptance or recognition of general standards of performance. The problems of stimulating a sense of personal significance among employees are compounded by the constitutional separation of the executive and legislative branches of government, which occasionally produces legislative-administrative conflicts that destroy attitudes of personal significance.

Goal crispness and personal significance reinforcement perhaps are the most important, but not the only, work situation characteristics affecting motivation.

A third factor, stability of expectations, is directly related to the frequency with which the dominant coalitions (Thompson, 1967) of governments change. This variable involves whether employees perceive that their organizations have a stable commitment to the mission or programs that they pursue. Of course, even "planned" changes in political leadership seriously jeopardize the development of this stability. If the directions of programs or missions change frequently enough, employees are likely to question the need to put forth maximum effort on what they come to perceive as transitory programs. The end result of such instability is that an organization "will find it more difficult to command the same intensity of loyalty that other organizations enjoy" (Buchanan, 1974a, p. 43).

Another significant work environment characteristic that influences motivation is the diversity of values and characteristics of work groups. Work or

175

similar task related groups exercise a certain amount of control over their members' attitudes. Heterogeneous or representative groups, more typical of government than of the private sector, will, in Buchanan's terms, "rarely develop intensely favorable attitudes toward their agencies or foster climates in which commitment to the agency is a group norm" (Buchanan, 1975b). This phenomenon, by reducing cohesion and consensus within the work group, diminishes the likelihood or, at the very least, increases the difficulty of eliciting spontaneous goal directed behaviors from employees.

Another interpersonal dimension of the work situation, an aspect of the immediate work environment, with significant implications for motivation is the quality of supervision. The National Center for Productivity (1978), drawing on a nonrandom sample of previous attitudinal studies, reported employee perceptions of lower supervisory quality in the public than in the private sector. One exception to this generalization was that, among managers, public sector supervisors were rated more highly than private supervisors on human relations skills. Public supervisors, in contrast to their private counterparts, suffered primarily in terms of their subordinates' evaluation of their technical competence. The quality-of-supervision differences reported by the National Center for Productivity might have a variety of causes. The evaluations of technical competence could reflect greater predominance of manager-professional conflicts in government organizations. They also might reflect less investment in training or less success in recruiting supervisory personnel. In any event, the quality of supervision is a critical element in motivational processes.

As a whole, these special work environment considerations in public organizations appear likely to constrain motivational levels significantly even when individual and job characteristics are conducive to employee motivation. Factors such as goal crispness and the quality of supervision are too integral to eliciting superior employee performance to argue otherwise. Although the accumulated research evidence permits some generalizations about the underlying processes, it does not offer any prescriptions for better managing these work environment characteristics.

External Environment Characteristics

The fourth major category of variable that can affect employee motivation is the external environment (or environments). In particular, it is changes or the anticipation of changes in the external environment that can have powerful impacts on individuals' behavior in work organizations. This category of variables, however, in contrast with the first three, is not one which any given organization can directly control. Nevertheless, that does not leave the organization helpless. It can monitor the external environment and, based on such monitoring, it can proceed to make changes internally within the organization that can influence employee motivation.

External environments can be usefully subdivided (arbitrarily, to be sure) into several major categories: socionormative, political, demographic, economic, and technological. Focus will be on the first two categories, because it is believed that they contain the variables that have the greatest differential effects on employee motivation in public sector organizations.

Socionormative changes   Public sector organizations cannot help but be impacted by what Clark Kerr has termed the "fourth period of great evolutionary change" in the labor force in the United States with respect to "its composition, its character, and the rules for its conduct" (1979, p. ix). The quest for personal self-fulfillment is regarded by Kerr, along with other social observers such as Daniel Yankelovich and Amitai Etzioni, as especially significant for the work environment—any work environment, including that of the public sector. As Kerr puts it, "We have a crisis of aesthetics, not ethics—tastes have changed, and the indulgence of psychic satisfactions has increased" (1979, p. xi).

These broad socionormative changes can directly affect motivation, by altering the orientations of those who enter public organizations, but they also might influence motivation indirectly, by modifying the attitudes and values of those whom public organizations serve. To the extent that the general public holds unfavorable attitudes about public employment and public bureaucracies, motivation-relevant employee perceptions, such as self-worth and personal significance, can be expected to be affected. Furthermore, compounding any motivational difficulties that might be associated with society's attitudes about public employment—attitudes that tend to fluctuate widely over time (White, 1932; Janowitz & Wright, 1956)—is the complexity of public attitudes about government. As Katz and his colleagues (Katz, Guteck, Kahn, & Barton, 1975) have observed, for example, there appear to be marked inconsistencies between the public's ideological and pragmatic attitudes. One manifestation of this inconsistency (so evident in the public's response to Proposition 13) is that, at an ideological level, private enterprise is perceived as more effective than government agencies, but, at a pragmatic level, government interventions into areas like pollution control and auto safety regulation are strongly supported by the public. The continued existence of these types of inconsistencies in the socionormative environment will challenge those who attempt to sharpen the goals of public organizations and may diminish managers' ability to motivate individuals who seek guidance from stable and consistent, rather than ambiguous, public expectations.

Political changes   The implications of these changes for motivation perhaps are the most difficult to characterize because they influence motivation less directly than do socionormative or demographic changes, and, in recent years, they collectively have followed no easily discernible patterns. Some of the more long-standing political trends no doubt affect employee motivation only in very general ways. Counted among these trends might be the recent (the post-Eisenhower period) instability in the American Presidency, steadily declining public trust in major political institutions, and, perhaps partially as an outgrowth of the latter trend, increasingly frequent legislative intervention into day-to-day administrative details. Except for legislative interventionism, which actually or potentially might have an impact on the task structure of government jobs, the political changes above influence motivation primarily by altering the climate—the "psychological feel"—within an organization.

Other, more discrete political changes of recent years unquestionably will affect motivation in measurable, but yet to be explored ways. Legislative mandates for citizen participation, spanning the eras of the Great Society and New

Federalism, have contributed to the dispersion of power and authority in administrative systems. This most recent manifestation and reassertion of the tenets of representative democracy (Kaufman, 1969) most certainly has affected key variables bearing on motivation. Similar consequences could be expected to flow from other current political developments: the "new" populism (including Ralph Nader, Common Cause, and Jimmy Carter), the ebb of the electorate toward greater conservatism (often equated with less government), and an era of relative scarcity within the political economy.

EFFICACY OF MOTIVATIONAL TECHNIQUES

Most organizations employ one or more methods to elicit role compliance and goal directed behaviors from their employees. These motivational techniques usually are intended to maximize benefits to the organization, but their relative utility varies considerably. The list of motivational techniques presently used by employers is extensive: monetary incentives, goal setting, flexitime, job enlargement, job enrichment, behavior modification, participation, award and recognition plans, discipline, and counseling. However, as a recent review (Locke, Feren, McCaleb, Shaw, & Denny, 1980) illustrates, most research has focused on four basic (but not mutually exclusive) motivational methods: monetary incentives, goal setting, job design, and participation. In fact, most motivational methods are derived from these basic techniques.

Monetary Incentives

Locke et al. (1980) concluded from their review of field studies of monetary incentives that significant performance improvements resulted from the use of these techniques. The median performance increase found in the field studies they reviewed was 30 percent. This median increase, however, may overestimate the value of money as an incentive, because monetary incentives typically are accompanied by some form of methods analysis, goal setting, or other technique that contributes to motivating performance. Until quite recently, monetary incentives, with the exception of output-oriented merit increases, have not been adopted widely in the public sector. A 1973 survey (National Commission on Productivity and Work Quality, 1975) of 509 local governments reported that 42 percent of the respondents used merit increases, only 6 percent employed performance bonuses, and 1 percent used shared savings or piecework systems. On the basis of a very limited amount of information, government's success with monetary incentives prior to the Federal Civil Service Reform Act of 1978 (CSRA) has, at best, been mixed. For example, the National Commission on Productivity stated:

> Some reported output-oriented merit increases were, in fact longevity increases or focused more on personal characteristics rather than output. Indeed, even truly output-oriented merit increases often became routine and are taken for granted by employees after they have been in operation for a while (1975, p. 44).

It should be noted, however, that CSRA is intended to remedy these types of shortcomings associated with the use of monetary incentives in the federal government. Whether or not the reforms achieve this goal is a matter for future inquiry.

At a conceptual level, the designs of monetary incentives must clearly deal with some of the motivational considerations discussed earlier. Perhaps the most important consideration is the values of employees. As noted previously, there is some indication that individuals entering the public sector value economic wealth to a lesser degree than do entrants to the profit sector. If this is indeed true, the motivational potential of monetary incentives might be limited in contrast to experiences elsewhere. It is quite possible, however, that greater emphasis on monetary incentives will begin to attract individuals who value economic wealth more highly. This development might lessen the attraction of the public service to more idealistic types. These concerns may be moot considering that even with the addition of monetary incentives public managers probably will receive much lower monetary rewards than will managers in other economic sectors (Fogel & Lewin, 1974; Smith, 1976).

The successful use of monetary incentives in government also is threatened by the extent to which performance differences can be measured with precision and an equitable formula can be developed that ties rewards to performance. Definition and measurement of performance criteria obviously will affect the acceptability and results of such incentive systems. The extent to which competing goals of an agency are mirrored in performance criteria also will complicate incentive systems.

Goal Setting

Goal setting essentially involves establishing observable standards for employee performance and offering feedback to the employee about the extent to which the standards have been achieved. Techniques for goal setting, like monetary incentives, come in a variety of formats, including performance targets, management by objectives, and work standards. Goal setting techniques have been used widely in government, and the early conceptual and practical development of some techniques, like MBO, owe a great deal to governmental experience (Sherwood & Page, 1976).

From their review of 17 field studies of goal setting, Locke et al. (1980) attribute a 16 percent median improvement in performance (with a range of 2 percent to 57.5 percent) as a result of goal setting. They also emphasized that feedback about progress vis-à-vis goals is essential for goal setting to regulate performance effectively. One reported use of goal setting in the Bureau of Census (Hornbruch, 1977), which gave regular feedback about performance against work standards, achieved a 52 percent improvement in output.

The design of goal setting techniques for public organizations must take into account a myriad of considerations that might moderate their success. The most important of these obviously is the vague and conflicting nature of governmental goals. An important issue is whether goal setting techniques will encourage more concrete goal explication, or whether there are countervailing influences that assure that government goals will remain inherently vague and conflicting. Although examples supporting the belief that goal setting can indeed improve employee understanding of tasks and objectives might readily be obtained, the practical difficulty of creating concrete and precise goal statements in many situations is not altered. Also, there is the problem that attempting to make goals more concrete (crisp) may run the risk of making them more trivial. Given these considerations, it might be necessary to create highly flexible, decentralized goal setting techniques so that the task characteristics of the focal agency receive adequate attention. It also might be necessary to state goals in terms of organizational inputs or activities rather than outputs because of the difficulty of measuring achievement.

The vagueness of the goals of public organizations is perhaps the most challenging problem confronting the success of goal setting, but it is not the only issue with which public managers and policy makers must be concerned. The diversity of internal and external constituencies will increase the effort that must be devoted to goal setting and could possibly increase the likelihood of political attacks upon administrators. It may be necessary to protect administrators from these inefficiencies or risks of goal setting techniques to assure that they will fully support their use.

Although the difficulties of implementing goal setting successfully in public organizations appear substantial, these difficulties must be weighed against several considerations. First, goal setting often is an important prerequisite of effective performance appraisal and monetary incentives. Second, goal setting offers one of the primary routes to personal significance reinforcement because it creates a mechanism by which individuals can observe their contributions to organizational success. Third, goal setting is an attractive alternative to monetary incentives, which, in the long run either could fail for lack of adequate financial rewards or might detract from public interest values. Fourth, goal setting might be an efficient alternative to monetary incentives in that it offers a high rate of return for quite limited investments. This is an important factor in light of declining budgets and resource scarcity. Thus, because goal setting is an integral aspect of other motivational techniques and possibly is more efficient than other methods, it may be more likely to be incorporated effectively by public organizations.

Job Design

Job design involves the structuring of various aspects of the job content (Hackman, 1977). For example, job design might involve increasing job responsibilities, the variety of tasks, or employee autonomy. Although job design has been popular since the early 1960s, the 1973 Urban Institute survey for the National Commission on Productivity (1975) reported that only 73 of 509 local government organizations had used some form of job rotation, redesign, or teamwork technique.

Evaluating the effectiveness of job design is more difficult than evaluating the effectiveness of other motivational techniques because it usually is implemented in conjunction with feedback and other structural changes (Locke et al., 1980). As Locke et al. suggests, if the performance contributions of the goal setting component of job design programs are controlled, job design might have no further effects on performance. Thus, the contributions of job design to public sector performance are somewhat problematic. Many cases of successful job design are described in the National Commission report (1975), but no rigorous evaluation of applications of the technique is available. Furthermore, the primary thrust of job design has been toward changing job content, but, as already indicated, this is not a widespread source of dissatisfaction among public employees. This indicates that there might be only a selective need for job design, possibly confined to those situations in which a direct cause-effect relationship exists between satisfaction with job content and service quality or output, or in cases in which an employee is being underutilized.

Another threat to the success of job design involves the ability of managers to alter variables significantly—variables such as self-direction or responsibility—when these aspects of the job are controlled by legislators or program constituents. At the very least, this problem might restrict the applicability of job design to jobs embedded both vertically and horizontally within an organization. One selective use for which job design might clearly pay dividends is in training positions. The problem of first-year job challenge is clearly amenable to solution by the use of job design.

Participation

Participation involves some type of shared or joint decision making between superiors and subordinates at the work group, program, or organizational level. A few instances of its use in state and local governments are described in the National Commission report (National Commission on Productivity and Work Quality, 1975). Of course, collective bargaining, already widespread in the public sector, is one variant of participation.

Because of the limited understanding of the effects of participation, it is extremely difficult to judge its probable efficacy as a motivational tool in government. At a superficial level, questions might be raised about participation's consequences for "who governs," but this does not appear to be a significant impediment to the instrumental use of participation. Intuitively, one might expect that participation would contribute positively to motivational considerations like perceptions of personal significance and quality of supervision. Its utility for moderating the effects of other variables, such as work group diversity, is less clear.

CONCLUSIONS

This paper has reviewed a diverse set of topics focused around motivational processes in public organizations. Now is proposed an agenda for research, composed primarily of questions that have been raised implicitly in this paper. The issues enumerated below are illustrative of those that might be addressed.

1. *The individual-organization match:* Considerable research attention has been addressed to how organizations choose individuals, but much less attention has been paid to the reverse: how individuals choose organizations and how organizations attract individuals. Insufficient research attention also has been given to a related aspect of the individual-organization match: How the attitudes, beliefs, and interests that an individual brings to organizational settings impact motivation. An understanding of these questions seems particularly important in light of research evidence that indicates that public organizations attract somewhat different types of individuals than do private organizations. The practical payoff from such a line of inquiry might be to increase the extent to which individuals entering government are satisfied with their organization and the extent to which the organization is able to secure effective behaviors from its members.

2. *Measurability of individual performance:* One of the most immediately pressing needs for research attention involves the measurability of individual performance in typical public sector jobs. For example, it might be necessary to make some conceptual advances before a public manager's "ability to deal with competing external interests" can be adequately measured. Because the performance of many public employees probably will be measured despite the lack of availability of generally accepted criteria, research on performance appraisal methods most appropriate for such circumstances also is needed.

3. *Goal clarity:* A better understanding of the sources of goal clarity (or lack of it) is needed so that remedies can be designed or a certain degree of murkiness in the goals of public organizations may have to be generally accepted. It is necessary to develop a better understanding of the ways in which the political environment reduces goal crispness and displaces goal directed activity. Research on how people adapt to situations in which goals are inherently unclear might contribute to developing methods for encouraging effective behaviors in such situations.

4. *Job security:* Differences between job security practices are a source of continuing, and often unfavorable, comparison between the public and private sectors. As noted earlier, the findings of several studies suggest that the security needs of public employees do not differ from those of private employees. However, knowledge about the motivational effects of the use of job security as a system-wide reward in public organizations is minimal. Research might focus on developing a better understanding of the motivational "costs" and "benefits" of current public job security practices and designing alternative means for protecting political neutrality.

5. *Moderators of motivation techniques:* Another research issue might be the identification of key moderators of the effectiveness of the various motivational techniques. For example, Locke et al. (1980) indicated in their review that, although participation had demonstrated only about a 1 percent *median* performance increase in a group of 16 field studies, half of the field experiments exhibited positive results, one as high as 47 percent. The critical research question is: Did the eight field sites in which participation was successful share characteristics that were absent in those sites where participation failed? This search for the factors that moderated the effectiveness of participation could be generalized to all the motivational techniques and should be a central concern of evaluative studies in public organizations.

Generally, the literature on motivation tends to concentrate too heavily on employees within industrial and business organizations. The comparative perspective used in the present study has been valuable for showing the limitations of knowledge about the context for motivation in public organizations. With approximately 20 percent of the American work force employed in the public sector, it clearly is important to develop better insights about what accounts for motivational variance in public organizations. Exploration of the questions proposed here should contribute measurably to a better understanding of the variables that play an especially important part in public sector motivational processes.

REFERENCES

Buchanan, B., II. Building organizational commitment: The socialization of managers in work organizations. *Administrative Science Quarterly,* 1974a, *19,* 533–546.

Buchanan, B., II. Government managers, business executives, and organizational commitment. *Public Administration Review,* 1974b, *35,* 339–347.

Buchanan, B., II. Red tape and the service ethic: Some unexpected differences between public and private managers. *Administration and Society,* 1975a, *6,* 423–438. [Included in this volume as Chapter 14]

Buchanan, B., II. To walk an extra mile: The whats, whens, and whys of organizational commitment. *Organizational Dynamics,* 1976b, *4,* 67–80.

Cyert, R. M., & March, J. G. *A behavioral theory of the firm.* Englewood Cliffs, N.J.: Prentice-Hall, 1963.

Fogel, W., & Lewin, D. Wage determination in the public sector. *Industrial and Labor Relations Review,* 1974, *27,* 410–432.

Fottler, M. D. Management: Is it really generic? *Academy of Management Review,* 1981, *6,* 1–12.

Guyot, J. F. Government bureaucrats are different. *Public Administration Review,* 1961, *22,* 195–202.

Hackman, J. R. Work design. In J. R. Hackman & J. L. Suttle (Eds.), *Improving life at work.* Santa Monica, Calif.: Goodyear, 1977, 96–162.

Hornbruch, F. W., Jr. *Raising productivity.* New York: McGraw-Hill, 1977.

Janowitz, M., & Wright, D. The prestige of public employment. *Public Administration Review,* 1956, *16,* 15–21.

Katz, D., Guteck, B. A., Kahn, R. L., & Barton, E. *Bureaucratic encounters.* Ann Arbor, Mich.: Survey Research Center, Institute for Social Research, University of Michigan, 1975.

Kaufman, H. Administrative decentralization and political power. *Public Administration Review,* 1969, *29,* 3–15.

Kerr, C. Introduction: Industrialism with a human face. In C. Kerr & J. M. Rostow (Eds.), *Work in America: The decade ahead.* New York: Van Nostrand, 1979, ix–xxvii.

Locke, E. A., Feren, D. B., McCaleb, V. M., Shaw, K. N., & Denny, A. T. The relative effectiveness of four methods of motivating employee performance. In K. D. Duncan, M. M. Gruneberg, & D. Wallis (Eds.), *Changes in working life.* London: Wiley, Ltd., 1980, 363–383.

National Center for Productivity and Quality of Working Life. *Employee attitudes and productivity differences between the public and private sector.* Washington, D.C.: U.S. Civil Service Commission, 1978.

National Commission on Productivity and Work Quality. *Employee incentives to improve state and local government productivity.* Washington, D.C.: U.S. Government Printing Office, 1975.

Newman, W. H., & Wallendar, H. W., III. Managing not-for-profit enterprises. *Academy of Management Review,* 1978, *3,* 24–31.

Paine, F. T., Carrol, S. J., Jr., & Leete, B. A. Need satisfactions of managerial personnel in a government agency. *Journal of Applied Psychology,* 1966, *50,* 247–249.

Porter, L. W., & Miles, R. P. Motivation and management. In J. W. McGuire (Ed.), *Contemporary management: Issues and viewpoints.* Englewood Cliffs, N.J.: Prentice-Hall, 1974, 545–570.

Porter, L. W., & Van Maanen, J. Task accomplishment and the management of time. In B. M. Bass (Ed.), *Managing for accomplishment.* Lexington, Mass.: Lexington, 1970, 180–192. [Included in this volume as Chapter 16]

Rainey, H. G. Perceptions of incentives in business and government: Implications for civil service reform. *Public Administration Review,* 1979a, *39,* 440–448.

Rainey, H. G. Reward expectancies, role perceptions, and job satisfaction among government and business managers: Indications of commonalities and differences. *Proceedings of the Thirty-Ninth Annual Meeting of the Academy of Management,* 1979b, 357–361.

Rainey, H. G., Backoff, R. W., & Levine, C. H. Comparing public and private organizations. *Public Administration Review,* 1976, *36,* 223–244. [Included in this volume as Chapter 7]

Rawls, J. R., & Nelson, O. T., Jr. Characteristics associated with preferences for certain managerial positions. *Psychological Reports,* 1975, *36,* 911–918.

Rawls, J. R., Ulrich, R. A., & Nelson, O. T., Jr. A comparison of managers entering or reentering the profit and nonprofit sectors. *Academy of Management Journal,* 1975, *18,* 616–622.

Rhinehart, J. B., Barrell, R. P., DeWolfe, A. S., Griffin, J. E., & Spaner, F. E. Comparative study of need satisfaction in governmental and business hierarchies. *Journal of Applied Psychology,* 1969, *53,* 230–235.

Sherwood, F. P., & Page, W. J., Jr. MBO and public management. *Public Administration Review,* 1976, *36,* 5–12. [Included in this volume as Chapter 22]

Smith, S. P. Pay differences between federal government and private sector workers. *Industrial and Labor Relations Review,* 1976, *29,* 179–197.

Thompson, J. D. *Organizations in action.* New York: McGraw-Hill, 1967.

White, L. D. *Further contributions to the prestige value of public employment.* Chicago: University of Chicago Press, 1932.

14 | Red Tape and the Service Ethic: Some Unexpected Differences Between Public and Private Managers

Bruce Buchanan II

Comparing public and private organizations has long been a favorite pastime of public administration, but such comparisons have often been self-serving. Most have stressed conceptual or normative arguments—oriented largely toward justifying the separate study of public administration. Few have undertaken to establish an empirical basis for their claims. One of the strongest cases made thus far against such comparative efforts is by Parker and Subramaniam (1964). They note particularly the lack of common standards of description and analysis typical of these comparisons, the tendency to compare "great conglomerations of miscellaneous phenomena," and the absence of an agreed-upon model of an administrative organization. They might have, but did not, stress that nonempirical comparisons of this sort tend to appear in public administration textbooks with the implicit but clear purpose of justifying special attention for public as distinct from other administrative settings.

Self-interest is an inadequate ground for scholarly advocacy, particularly when such advocacy proceeds largely from normative rather than empirical bases. These problems are magnified by the conceptually and empirically porous quality of "public" and "private" as administrative categories. Such categories are simply not the mutually exclusive, theoretically perceptive containers that social scientists usually seek for purposes of comparative organizational research. A large number of more sophisticated schemes for classifying organizations have been suggested, any one of which is theoretically superior to the public-private dichotomy (see Blau and Scott, 1962; Etzioni, 1961; Parsons, 1960; Katz and Kahn, 1966; Perrow, 1967; Rushing, 1966).

If better strategies are available, why should the public-private distinction command further attention? One reason is that it is imbedded in the institutional fabric of society as "government" and "business." This distinction recently has come to stand for alternative approaches to problem-solving. Business organizations typify efficiency and rationality, while government bureaucracies symbolize red-tape, a ponderous, often ineffective administrative style. These images can be related to certain characteristic assumptions about business and government organizations. It is often argued, for example, that public agencies lack crisp, operational goals and are not disciplined by the need to create a profitable demand for their outputs in a competitive market economy (Radnor et al., 1970). Such views have prompted the development of a critical literature aimed at formulating substitutes for the purifying influence of the market test in the public sector (see Ostrom, 1973; Niskanen, 1971; Downs, 1967). In this sense the distinction between public and private organizations is clear and prominent in the minds of citizens as well as scholars. Such images have operational implications. Thus, certain technological work is "farmed out" by government to private industry; government "corporations" like TVA are created; the postal service is streamlined along "business" lines—all because of real or imagined distinctions in the character and competencies of business and government organizations. These factors cannot help but focus some scholarly attention on institutional contrasts, however conceptually inadequate the distinction seems.

Another reason, more germane to this discussion, has to do with the empirical footing of scholarly comparisons of business and government organizations. Despite a prevailing assumption by organizational sociologists and psychologists that there are no significant differences, evidence is accumulating which lends substance to claims of important distinctions between the two sectors. These data stem from the research of those in and outside public administration and are less easily dismissed than some of the efforts criticized by Parker and Subramaniam. Much of this work has been reviewed elsewhere (Buchanan, 1974a). Additional efforts, worthy of consideration in the same light, include a comparative study of business and government executives conducted by Guyot (1960), and a comparative analysis of policy implementation in business and government organizations (Radnor et al., 1970).

The present study was designed to contribute to this growing body of comparative data. Its purpose was to subject two rather prevalent assumptions about public organizations and public servants to a preliminary empirical test. The tested assumptions concern the prominence of administrative red tape in public agency operations and the suspected existence of a service ethic, a special kind of involvement with duty among public servants.

THE PUBLIC SERVICE ETHIC

The notion of a public service ethic, particularly at middle and upper hierarchical levels, is prominent both in scholarly literature and conventional wisdom. Mosher (1968) indicates that the nature of public employment is presumed to demand, on the part of individual employees, a unique sense of loyalty, both to duty and to the government as a whole. Such expectations derive from the state's representation of the sovereign power and public servants, nonelected trustees of portions of this power, wielding it with special sensitivity to the public interest. Efforts have been made to encourage such an ethic throughout the federal civil service. Mindful of the flagship prestige and professional dedication characteristic of the public services in certain European countries, the Civil Service Commission has instituted special recruitment efforts, training programs, elite supergrade cadres, all aimed at enhancing the self-image and dedication of public servants. There is some evidence to suggest that feelings of identification and involvement with the service do characterize middle- and high-level bureaucrats. Warner et al. (1963) found that their sample of interviewees placed a high value on their public service occupations, felt they were participating in something particularly worthwhile, and perceived similar careers in business as dull and uninteresting by comparison. Stanley (1964) found that his sample of higher public administrators felt a desire for recognition as members of an elite service group. He also reports that the numbers which designate supergrade status in the federal General Personnel Schedule (e.g., 16, 17, 18) have themselves become symbols of aspiration among mid-level careerists.

These studies suggest that a service ethic may indeed characterize middle- and upper-level bureaucrats, but they provide no basis for assessing its depth or intensity. Such a basis can only be provided by comparative research, in which such attitudes are systematically contrasted with those of similarly placed individuals in nonpublic organizational settings. The present study undertook such a comparison between public servants and business managers along the lines described. The attitude measured was job involvement, selected to represent the kind of personal immersion in all aspects of the work role that might fairly gauge the extent of a special sense of dedication among public servants (see sample items below). The prediction was that the strong expectations for loyalty and dedication purported to characterize the public service as a whole would result in our sample of public managers reporting significantly greater job involvement than business managers.

A related image of the federal bureaucracy is its supposed obsession with rules and procedures. This perceived characteristic may be seen to have a number of roots. One positive view is that rule emphasis is a logical extension of the service ethic because scrupulous attention to procedural and administrative due process is an important vehicle for protecting the rights of citizens. The traditional scholarly literature has contributed to this image of the public bureaucracy as justifiably rule and constraint conscious. Most public administration textbooks, for example, echo the sentiment expressed by Morstein Marx (1957: 171) that,

> Running through the organization theory of private enterprise is an emphasis on ready achievement of results. By contrast, the organization theory of government puts all action under strong safeguards to keep authority in bounds and subject to precise accountability.

A more pragmatic reason for expecting an emphasis on formal procedures stems from the relationship between Congress and the bureaucracy. Operating funds and continued existence depend on the ability of agencies to justify plans and performance before congressional appropriations committees. As Fenno observes (1966), few congressmen are technically proficient enough to

187

evaluate the substantive performance of most agencies. This, combined with the scarcity of empirical and substantively relevant performance criteria for agencies, results in congressional oversight which tends to stress procedural rather than substantive performance standards. Since Congress cleaves to procedure and since the bureaucracy is extraordinarily sensitive to Congress, one might expect to find close adherence to procedures as a means of justifying behavior at all bureaucratic levels.

A third source of the red-tape image combines public sentiment with sociological explanation. This view holds that rule consciousness results from indifference to the needs of agency clients rather than from a concern for protecting their rights. The sociological rationale is supplied by Merton's (1957) notion of goal displacement. By infusing organizational members with a special feeling for the sanctity of rules and procedures beyond the technical requirements of the task at hand, the organization promotes a transference of rules into ends-in-themselves, with greater weight than the goals they were intended to advance. The result is bureaucratic arteriosclerosis of the sort that fuels the public image of the federal bureaucracy.

Finally, it can be argued that the relative absence of clear and precise goals, plus the absence of a market test for agency output, contributes to structural proliferation in the public sector. Imprecise goals make it difficult to identify and separate administrative procedures which are clearly goal-relevant from those which are not strictly necessary. And the lack of market competition for profits might undermine the motivation to ferret out and to eliminate costly administrative excesses.

These perspectives collectively paint a picture of public agencies and their managers enmeshed in administrative constraints and procedures far surpassing those confronted by their industrial counterparts. Again, however, there is a dearth of comparative data which would give the image a convincing empirical foundation. To make a preliminary comparative test of this assumption a special questionnaire scale was constructed to tap the extent to which individual managers in business and government organizations perceived a pronounced emphasis on rules and procedures in their respective milieus. This scale, the job involvement scale, and other details of the study are the subjects of the next section of this paper.

METHOD

Two-part questionnaires were distributed among middle-management personnel in four business organizations and four federal agencies. The selection of "middle" management as the focus reflects the view that bureaucratic orientations and procedures of the sort measured here are best represented at this level. As White (1955: 90) observes, "The importance of middle management is obviously great. Here it is that the spirit and tempo of the public service and its reputation are largely made." The operational definition of middle management in the public agencies was GS 9-13. In the private firms it was "above the foreman level but below the vice-presidential level."

Each of the eight organizations stipulated that it remain anonymous as a condition of participation. The agencies, located in Washington, D.C., represent a broad range of domestic governmental functions. Each of the four is an operating subdivision of one of the great departments of the executive branch. The private organizations are manufacturing and service firms located in the industrial northeast, and the participating subdivisions roughly match the public agencies in size.

Distribution of questionnaires was arranged through personnel officers in each organization. Each officer developed a list of managers who met the middle-management criterion and the work-role criterion described below. Truly random selection of managers proved impossible, as participation was voluntary and the declination rate was fairly high. It is fair to claim, however, that all eligible managers in each organization had an equal chance of being invited to participate. Approximately thirty managers from each organization were invited to participate.

An additional criterion for invitation was the nature of the work assignment a manager held. The effort was made to secure an even distribution between line and staff personnel in each organization. This was achieved in seven of the eight organizations. In the eighth, a government agency, the distinction was meaningless and was ignored. In general, the objective was to ensure that respondents from both sectors were middle-level executives charged with policy implementation and supporting staff work, rather than policy making.

Questionnaires were distributed through the in-house mailing system in each organization, but were completed privately and returned directly to the researcher by mail. Organizational officials saw the results only in tabular form. They were not given the opportunity to examine individual responses. The total number of questionnaires distributed was 250; 145 analyzable instruments were returned, for a response rate of 62%. Of the respondents, 76 were managers in government agencies and 69 were managers in industrial firms.

MEASURES

Table 14-1 contains sample items from the two questionnaire scales employed in this project. The structure salience scale was developed to measure individual impressions of the salience (prominence, significance, conspicuousness, importance) of formal bureaucratic routines in the administrative climate. "Structure" was defined as general rules and procedures, specific job descriptions, and formal authority relationships. The items were worded to reveal the extent to which respondents perceived that close adherence to these structural constraints was customary and expected in the organizational activities of which they were part. Is it appropriate or inappropriate to deviate from procedures for good cause? What is more important, getting the job done or doing things by the book? Collective answers to such questions can suggest the bureaucratic tone of a given administrative climate.

The structure salience scale was refined by submitting successive drafts of item pools to groups of behavioral science faculty and students for evaluation in terms of face validity. The final 25 items received the highest possible validity ratings from three-fourths or more of the evaluators. Reliability was assessed with the split-half technique, which after the Spearman-Brown adjustment yielded a coefficient of .68. While adequate for present purposes, the

TABLE 14-1
Sample Items for Structure
Salience and Job Involvement Scales

Structure Salience Scale (25 items)

My supervisor is more concerned that I follow rules and procedures than he is that I do an effective job.

I feel that rules, regulations, and procedures are very important in this organization.

I always check things carefully with my boss before making important decisions.

Rules, administrative details, and red-tape make it difficult for new and original ideas to receive attention.

The formal job descriptions and specifications do not really describe what people do in this organization.

It is considered inappropriate in this organization to try to deal with a problem without taking it through proper channels.

Job Involvement Scale (21 items)

I feel a sense of pride in working for this organization.

I usually show up for work a little early, to get things ready.

If I had my life to live over again, I would still choose to work for this organization.

The major satisfaction in my life comes from my job.

---

magnitude of this coefficient does reflect a relative lack of internal consistency for the structure salience concept as a whole. This is partly explained by the threefold conception of structure (rules, roles, and authority) used in its development.

The job involvement scale was developed by Lodahl and Kejner (1965). Its value for gauging the intensity of an individual's dedication to or immersion in his work role is suggested by the following characterization:

> Job involvement is the internalization of values about the goodness of work or the importance of work in the worth of the person, and perhaps it is thus a measure of the ease with which the person can be further socialized by an organization. (1965: 24)

Subjects responded to items in both measures by indicating the extent of their agreement on a one-to-seven scale. Individual scores were obtained by summing responses to each scale. Mean organizational and public-private scores were obtained in a similar manner. For convenience in scoring, items were summed in such a way that low scores indicated high structure salience and high job involvement, as noted in Figures 14-1 and 14-2. T-tests were employed to assess the statistical significance of differences between means.

RESULTS

Figure 14-1 contains a schematic representation of the findings for both variables. As indicated, there are significant differences between the samples of business and government managers, but not in the expected direction on

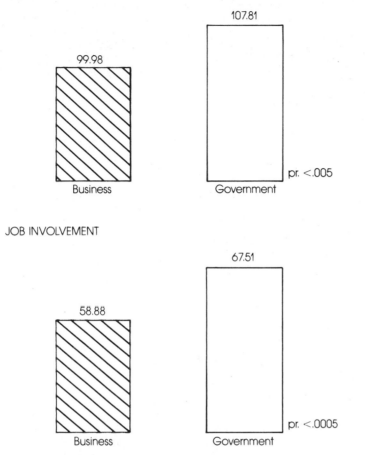

FORMAL STRUCTURE SALIENCE

107.81

99.98

Business   Government   pr. <.005

JOB INVOLVEMENT

67.51

58.88

Business   Government   pr. <.0005

Note: High scores indicate lower structure salience and job involvement.

FIGURE 14-1.
*Combined Mean Scores for Business and Government Samples on Measures of Formal
Structure Salience and Job Involvement*

either variable. Business middle managers ascribed significantly more salience
to formal structure than the government group (p < .005), and significantly
greater job involvement as well (p < .0005). A more comprehensive picture of
the nature and extent of the differences is given in Figure 14-2, which displays
bar-graph distributions of the eight organizational means for both variables.
These data show clearly that the mean differences between the public-private
categories reflect a genuine clustering of organizational types, rather than
simply the distorting influence of one or two markedly deviant organizations.
One public agency, labeled "a" in Figure 14-2, is a significant deviant from its
category on the structure salience variable, but in the direction of the business
group. Thus, its impact on the public mean is to minimize rather than to
artificially enhance the differences.

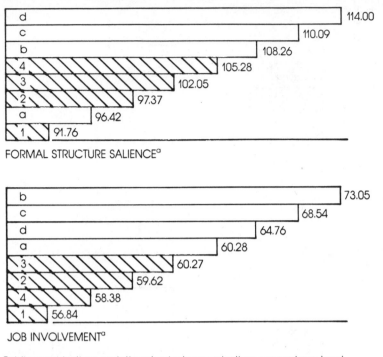

FORMAL STRUCTURE SALIENCE[a]

JOB INVOLVEMENT[a]

Note: Public organizations are lettered; private organizations are numbered and shaded.
[a]High scores indicate lower structure salience and job involvement.

FIGURE 14-2.
Distribution of Organizational Means

An additional test of the internal consistency of the public-private results is found in Tables 14-2 and 14-3. These contain organization-by-organization comparisons of mean differences for each variable. All instances in which organizations within the same category differed significantly from one another are enclosed in boxes. With the exception of organization "a," already noted as a deviant, the structure-salience mean differences reveal a fair intra-category consistency (Table 14-2). The boxed differences between organization one and organizations three and four in the business group seem best described as indications of the range of variability within that category rather than internal inconsistency, since they are the polar extremes for the group. The same situation characterizes the boxed differences between organization "a" and organizations "b" and "c" on the job involvement scale, Table 14-3.

DISCUSSION

Two questions require attention in order to make sense of these results. Why are they contrary to expectations? And what significance do they have?

The finding that this sample of business managers was more structure conscious than their government counterparts seems surprising given the preponderant view of the bureaucracy as rule-bound and procedure-conscious throughout. Such is the case despite the tentative nature of these results. There

TABLE 14-2
Differences Between Organizational Means:
Formal Structure Salience

	1	A	2	3	4	B	C	D
1	0	4.66	5.61	10.29[d]	13.52[c]	16.50[b]	18.33[a]	22.24[a]
A		0	0.95	5.63	8.86[d]	11.84[b]	13.67[b]	17.58[b]
2			0	4.68	7.91	10.89[b]	12.72[b]	16.63[b]
3				0	3.23	6.21	8.04[d]	11.95[d]
4					0	2.98	4.81	8.72
B						0	1.83	5.74
C							0	3.91
D								0

Note: Public organizations are lettered; private organizations are numbered.

Source: Table design suggested by Winer (1962, 114).

☐ Indicates significant differences between organizations of the same category.

[a]Indicates significance at the .0005 level.
[b]Indicates significance at the .005 level.
[c]Indicates significance at the .01 level.
[d]Indicates significance at the .05 level.

is no question that the public sector is characterized by structural complexity and does emphasize the deliberate operation of formal organizational processes, but it is conceivable that similar propensities in economic organizations have been deemphasized unduly by comparison. There is a plausible explanation for the differing perceptions of structure reported here, and it is

TABLE 14-3
Differences Between Organizational Means:
Job Involvement

	1	4	2	3	A	D	C	B
1	0	1.54	2.78	3.43	3.44	7.92[d]	11.70[b]	16.21[b]
4		0	1.24	1.89	1.90	6.38	10.16[c]	14.67[b]
2			0	0.65	0.66	5.14	8.92[d]	13.43[b]
3				0	0.01	4.49	8.27[d]	12.78[c]
A					0	4.48	8.26[d]	12.77[c]
D						0	3.78	8.29
C							0	4.51
B								0

Note: Public organizations are lettered; private organizations are numbered.

☐ Indicates significant differences between organizations of the same category.

[a]Indicates significance at the .0005 level.
[b]Indicates significance at the .005 level.
[c]Indicates significance at the .01 level.
[d]Indicates significance at the .05 level.

rooted in the nature and extent of an organization's capacity to control its employees. Business organizations clearly have a greater capacity to exert such control, and by implication to heighten individual sensitivity to the structural instruments of control. Such organizations may coerce compliance, if necessary up to the point of discharging an employee. While seldom used and largely implicit, this is a critical power. A middle manager in an economic organization is accordingly under constant competitive pressure to produce results and to display the norms and values prevailing in his administrative climate. Security, advancement, and ultimate success are conditioned on acceptable performance and behavior throughout the managerial career. There is thus little opportunity for coasting or withdrawal. One is likely to find few of Presthus's (1962) "indifferents" at the middle or upper reaches of industrial management.

Government agencies, on the other hand, must control largely by persuasion rather than coercion. This is because mid-level bureaucrats have abundant resources for resisting the structural constraints on their behavior, particularly in comparison with their industrial counterparts. The key resource is the tenure system, civil service "status," which after a few years prohibits dismissal without significant cause. With moderate exertion in the early career years, an individual can place himself in a virtually impregnable position.

Another source of autonomy can be developed by cultivating relationships with the powerful lobbies and interest groups which constitute an important segment of any agency's constituency. The influence such groups have in Congress gives them the capacity to influence internal agency operations to the extent of reaching in and protecting those willing to promote their interests. Not all public servants are positioned to exploit these relationships, but such ties are by no means uncommon even at middle levels.

A third potential source of autonomy emerges from the nature of work in the public sector. Many civil service jobs permit a wide latitude of acceptable performance simply because their relation to the agency mission is less clear-cut than is usually the case with a business manager's job (Radnor et al., 1970). When goals and jobs are broadly and loosely defined, it is considerably more difficult to establish the kind of strict accountability that would make the control structure a pervasive force within an organization.

Finally, there are extensive appeal routes and procedures available through the Civil Service Commission to any public servant who feels unjustly used by the rules or practices of his agency. The fact that these exist and are not infrequently used promotes a special sensitivity to the procedural due process rights of individuals and may thus detract from any emphasis on the internal agency structure that could be interpreted as unduly inhibiting or constraining of individual autonomy. It is likely of course that most large business organizations of the sort sampled in this study have provisions for the protection of individuals against capricious misuse by the organization. But it seems clear that the scope and complexity of such provisions cannot match those available on a government-wide basis to any public servant. To an extent simply not matched in business, the government bureaucrat can resist organizational pressure without risking either his livelihood or his status. This fact cannot help but influence the shape of whatever norms emerge within an agency concerning the importance of organizational structure.

Also unexpected was the finding that business middle managers were more involved with their jobs than government managers. Government-wide pressures for a service ethic, plus the results of such studies as Warner et al. (1963) and Stanley (1964) suggested that public servants well might develop a superior sense of job and career involvement. It cannot be concluded on the basis of a single study that business managers are on the whole more work involved, but the findings of other studies suggest similar conclusions. One study conducted by the author employed the Lodahl-Kejner job involvement scale, plus questionnaire measures of organizational experiences believed to affect the intensity of the job involvement attitude (Buchanan, 1974b). A different sample of 279 managers was drawn from eight business and government organizations other than those studied here. In most respects the characteristics of the two samples were similar. Mean public and private scores revealed significant differences on the experience and job involvement scales in the same direction as those reported here (p < .01). More important for present purposes, however, was the result of a multiple regression analysis in which the involvement scale was regressed on the experience scales. It was found that three organizational experiences explained nearly 60% of the variance of the job involvement scale. These were colleague group attitudes toward work, job challenge, and disappointment resulting from a discrepancy between personal expectations and organizational reality. The implication is that these experiences made the greatest contribution to the intensity of the job involvement attitude.

Since the business and government samples in that study differed significantly on the experiences which help shape involvement, analysis of such experience would seem a useful approach to explaining the involvement differences in the present study. The question, then, is why business and government managers might be expected to undergo different levels of experience in the three areas related to involvement.

The persuasive power of a cohesive work group has been well documented (Cohen, 1964), but it is not obvious why business groups should stimulate greater work involvement than government groups. The reason, it seems, is that business groups are more likely to be cohesive and to sustain positive general feelings toward organization and work. This stems from the likely demographic characteristics of group members in the two sectors and the nature of their primary loyalties. The potential affiliation of middle-level bureaucrats with external interest groups has been mentioned. Other potential loyalty conflicts exist within agency work groups which might undermine cohesiveness and involvement norms. There are, for example, tendencies toward increased minority representation and greater acceptance of women into traditionally masculine work roles. Membership in any of these categories might lessen the basic commitment of an individual to his agency or his job simply because important personal attachments exist elsewhere. In addition, the above-mentioned resources for organizational resistance available to the bureaucrat can also be used to insulate him from his peers, if he so desires. Industrial management groups, conversely, appear much more likely to comprise like-minded individuals with similar demographic attributes who are greatly dependent on the organization and hence more likely to become psychologically immersed in both the group and the job. There are likely to be fewer minorities, fewer women, and fewer opportunities to build the kind of personal external alliances that could undermine group solidarity and job involvement.

It is logical that challenging jobs would be more involving, but less obvious why industrial jobs should be more challenging. Two possibilities are that (a) government agencies are more likely to be overstaffed, with the result that a given mid-level work assignment could be diluted in substance, thus reducing the potential for involvement; and (b) agency missions are often conceived in broad, unspecific terms as was mentioned earlier (e.g., "promote the general welfare," "promote full development of the economic resources of the United States," to cite extreme examples). This might mean that the relation of mid-level jobs to the overall goal is too tenuous or indirect to impart a full measure of involvement or challenge. Business jobs, in contrast, are typically linked directly to a performance measure—production or sales, for example— which is itself firmly attached to the organization's central purpose. Because this implies direct personal accountability for results, it might explain why the industrial group experienced more challenge and involvement.

The third experience, disappointment resulting from a discrepancy between personal career expectations and organizational reality, seems much more likely to strike agency than corporation managers. This is because of the idealism believed to shape the expectations of the most promising candidates for public service careers. Such people hope to make personal contributions to the lofty aims which attracted them to the service and instead may find themselves rotating through a series of minor training assignments which seem trivial by comparison. Such experience in the early career years could certainly undermine the growth of involvement. The same fate would not typically be in store for the business executive, if only because the nature of industrial work is less likely to stimulate grandiose hopes for contributing to the improvement of society. There is also a greater chance that the business manager would be able in fact to realize his hopes for the substance of his work, if not for rapid hierarchical advancement.

These explanations for the structure salience and job involvement distinctions, while speculative and somewhat overdrawn for emphasis, nonetheless seem plausible. It remains, finally, to consider the significance of the findings in the context of similar scholarly research efforts.

The scope of the sample which produced the structure salience result is clearly not sufficient to justify a claim that it fairly represents either the government or economic sector as a whole. Its significance rests with its suggestiveness and counter-intuitiveness. It was noted that the prevailing image of the federal bureaucracy is one of heavy emphasis on structural constraints. It cannot be denied that these exist and are important in the public sector, but the present finding would suggest that their impact on the attitudes and potential behavior of public servants may be less pervasive than suspected. The industrial sample that reported greater structural salience suggests that government agencies have no monopoly on red tape, and that the image may be simplistic or inaccurate.

The involvement finding also contradicts the recorded research and impressions reviewed earlier. But its primary significance rests with the tendency to corroborate the results of several other studies and thus contributes to a growing body of evidence that the organizationally stimulated attitudes of career public servants are on the whole less favorable than those of similarly placed individuals in economic organizations. The attitudes on which differences have been reported include organizational commitment (Buchanan, 1974a) and several measures of intrinsic need satisfaction (Paine et al., 1966; Rhinehart et al., 1969). These studies collectively lend weight to the suspicion that the service ethic among public managers, as gauged by work and agency-related attitudes, may be more of an aspiration than a reality.

CONCLUSION

It is worth noting that the results of this study may be seen to reflect some attitudinal and potentially behavioral consequences of the market test. So viewed, the indication is that the market environment may promote stricter attendance to operating procedures and deeper personal work involvement among managers inside economic organizations. The assumption is often made that the market test influences economic organizations in largely positive ways (see Ostrom, 1973; Niskanen, 1971), but these results suggest a qualification. Intense work involvement will be organizationally beneficial in most cases. But heavy rule emphasis can have undesirable consequences. It may promote goal displacement, a transference of rules into ends-in-themselves. It may retard innovative risk taking and encourage the avoidance of personal responsibility. And it may undermine the adaptive flexibility of organizations by fostering undue rigidity in operations. If the results of the present study are borne out by subsequent research, a more critical assessment, particularly of the behavioral consequences of the market test, may be called for.

REFERENCES

Blau, P. M., and W. R. Scott (1962). *Formal Organizations: A Comparative Approach.* San Francisco: Chandler.

Buchanan, B. (1974a). "Government managers, business executives and organizational commitment." *Public Administration Rev.* (July/August).

———— (1974b). "The correlates of job involvement." (unpublished).

Cohen, A. R. (1964). *Attitude Change and Social Influence.* New York: Basic Books.

Downs, A. (1967). *Inside Bureaucracy.* Boston: Little, Brown.

Etzioni, A. (1961). *A Comparative Analysis of Complex Organizations.* New York: Free Press.

Fenno, R. F. (1966). *The Power of the Purse.* Boston: Little, Brown.

Guyot, J. F. (1960). "Government bureaucrats *are* different." *Public Administration Rev.* (May/June).

Katz, D., and R. L. Kahn (1966). *The Social Psychology of Organizations.* New York: John Wiley.

Lodahl, T. M., and M. Kejner (1965). "The definition and measurement of job involvement." *J. of Applied Psychology* 5, 49.

Merton, R. (1957). "Bureaucratic structure and personality," in R. Merton et al. (eds.), *Reader in Bureaucracy.* New York: Free Press.

Morstein Marx, F. (1957). *The Administrative State.* Chicago: Univ. of Chicago Press.

Mosher, F. C. (1968). *Democracy and the Public Service*. New York: Oxford Univ. Press.

Niskanen, W. A. (1971). *Bureaucracy and Representative Government*. Chicago: Aldine-Atherton.

Ostrom, V. (1973). *The Intellectual Crisis in Public Administration*. University: Univ. of Alabama Press.

Paine, F. T., S. J. Carroll, and B. A. Leete (1966). "Need satisfactions of managerial level personnel in a government agency." *J. of Applied Psychology*, 5, 50.

Parker, R. S., and V. Subramaniam (1964). " 'Public' and 'Private' Administration." *International Rev. of Administrative Sci.* 5, 30.

Parsons, T. (1960). Structure and Processes in Modern Societies. New York: Free Press.

Perrow, C. (1967). "A framework for the comparative analysis of organizations." *Amer. Soc. Rev.* 5, 32.

Presthus, R. (1962). *The Organizational Society*. New York: Vintage.

Radnor, M., A. H. Rubenstein, and D. A. Tansik (1970). "Implementation in operations research and R & D in government and business organization." *Operations Research* (November/December).

Rhinehart, R. P., A. S. Barrell, J. E. Dewolfe, and F. E. Spaner (1969). "Comparative study of need satisfactions in governmental and business hierarchies." *J. of Applied Psychology* 5, 53.

Rushing, W. A. (1966). "Organizational rules and surveillance: propositions in comparative organizational analysis." *Administrative Sci. Q.* 5, 11.

Stanley, D. T. (1964). *The Higher Civil Service*. Washington, D.C.: Brookings.

Warner, L. W., P. P. Van Riper, N. H. Martin, and O. F. Collins (1963). *The American Federal Executive*. New Haven: Yale Univ. Press.

White, L. D. (1955). *Introduction to the Study of Public Administration*. New York: Crowell, Collier, & Macmillan.

Winer, B. J. (1962). *Statistical Principles in Experimental Design*. New York: McGraw-Hill.

15 | The Nature of Managerial Work in the Public Sector

Alan W. Lau
Arthur R. Newman
Laurie A. Broedling

The passage of the 1978 Civil Service Reform Act constitutes the first major overhaul of the federal civil service since the system was created in 1883. Included in the reform act is the establishment of a Senior Executive Service (SES) consisting of approximately 8,000 individuals at the GS-16 through Executive IV levels. Under the reform act, the compensation of these executives will be based on individual and organizational performance, not on length of service. Pay for top level executives will be set at one of six levels, with the possibility of lump-sum bonuses being awarded to some of the executives.

The reform act abolishes the previous government-wide executive performance appraisal system and charters individual agencies to develop appraisal systems that specify performance requirements and link personnel actions (such as merit pay increases) more closely to individual performance. Performance standards are to be based on objective, job-related criteria and systematic identification of managerial competencies associated with carrying out the tasks and functions of executive positions. Other provisions of the reform act charge the Office of Personnel Management (OPM), the agency which replaces the Civil Service Commission, with the responsibility of ensuring that federal agencies establish programs for the training and development of current and prospective SES candidates.

Since the reform act has mandated new systems for executive selection, development, and performance appraisal, the importance of describing the public sector job and identifying what executives actually do in accomplishing the requirements of their jobs has become a critical issue.

Although there is a large body of literature on what constitutes management and how to select and develop effective managers and executives, little can be applied to the current problem. First, much of the management litera-ture has developed with the private sector manager in mind. Executive activity has received considerably less systematic attention in the public sector. Sec-ond, much of what has been written on management since Fayol[1] first intro-duced the notion of POSDCORB (Planning, Organizing, Staffing, etc.) consists of speculation regarding what managers and their subordinates say they do, could do, or should do. Relatively little of this information is empiri-cally based on studies of managerial job activities. Third, little of the literature pertains specifically to top executives; either it pertains to middle or first-level supervisors, or it treats management as a function that is the same across all hierarchical levels or functional areas. Fourth, much of the research has dealt with only one aspect of management, namely, leadership. There are numerous aspects to management (e.g., decision making, resource allocation, negotia-tion) which have received relatively less attention. Finally, management and leadership theories have traditionally been short-range and atomistic, focusing on leader-group relations and not leader-group-system relationships. In order to describe and understand managerial functioning, it is necessary to under-stand the complex organizational context in which executives operate.[2]

While a large number of studies have examined the personal styles and characteristics of managers, relatively few have investigated the behavioral requirements of these positions, i.e., what managers or executives actually *do* in accomplishing job requirements. Moreover, most of the studies cited below have relied on a single methodology (e.g., questionnaires, work activity diar-ies, observations) to describe managerial jobs rather than on a multimethod approach.

A few major investigations have used self-descriptions to identify behavior-al requirements of the managerial job. Hemphill[3] described the similarities and differences in a variety of executive jobs by asking executives to complete a 575-item questionnaire concerning the extent to which job elements (e.g., selection of new employees) were a part of their jobs. This research, though well known, has not stimulated many others to use his questionnaire or to undertake similar studies. Recently, however, a number of researchers have used self-report questionnaires to develop a behaviorally based system for describing and comparing managerial jobs.[4]

Other researchers have used a work diary method to collect data on the work activities of managers. In this method, managers keep track of their time using precoded activity diaries.[5] It was found that managers spend much of their time in informal "face-to-face" communication and that the consider-able number of distractions in their job leaves them with little time to reflect and plan. A review and summary of observational and work diary studies of managerial work also report that managers spend considerable time with their subordinates, have little time alone, and experience frequent interruptions and fragmentation of their work.[6]

One particularly interesting and important study of managerial activities was conducted by Mintzberg.[7, 8] After analyzing extensive records of types of mail received by executives and individually observing five executives over a period of one week, Mintzberg proposed ten basic managerial roles within three areas that were common across executive jobs:

■ 15 ■
Alan W. Lau
Arthur R. Newman
Laurie A. Broedling

1. *Interpersonal:* Figurehead, liaison, leader.
2. *Informational:* Monitor, disseminator, spokesman.
3. *Decisional:* Entrepreneur, disturbance handler, resource allocator, negotiator.

Mintzberg also concluded that "job pressures drive the manager to be superficial in his actions—to overload himself with work, encourage interruption, respond quickly to every stimulus, seek the tangible and avoid the abstract, make decisions in small increments, and do everything abruptly" (1974, p. 60). Mintzberg found that executive jobs were remarkably similar and could be described by common sets of behavior or roles.[9] Evidence from a number of recent studies supports the general validity of Mintzberg's roles and indicates that the relative amount of time spent in these roles is related to managerial and organizational effectiveness criteria.[10]

Our intent in this article is to describe what top level public sector executives in the Navy do on their jobs, both in terms of (a) job content, i.e., the roles and functions they perform and (b) job characteristics, i.e., how executives accomplish these functions within the organizational context of the federal environment.[11] The study has action implications for the selection, development, and performance appraisal systems for public sector executives. It is argued that an accurate description of the content and characteristics of public sector executive work is a critical prerequisite for developing effective selection, development, and appraisal programs. The present study builds on Mintzberg's research by using his framework and description of managerial activities and provides an opportunity to evaluate the similarity of public and private sector managerial jobs.

Two basic sets of research questions guided the present study:

1. Do managers in the public sector engage in activities that correspond to Mintzberg's managerial role descriptions? What are the major role functions in the public sector? Are these role functions the same in the public and private sectors?
2. What are the characteristics of the public sector managerial job? Are they similar to those in the private sector?

METHODS

Sample

The study was conducted on an executive population in the federal government—the highest graded civilians working for the U.S. Navy, defined as those who hold GS-16, 17, 18 or equivalent Public Law positions (N = 370).

Two-thirds of these executives are in a research and development career field such as science or engineering. An additional 14 percent are in weapons systems acquisition, 8 percent are in financial management, and the remaining 12 percent are in personnel administration, intelligence, or logistics. Sixty percent of the group hold advanced degrees, generally in the physical sciences or engineering.

Data Collection Methods

While most studies of managerial activities have relied upon a single method to describe executive jobs, the present study is somewhat unique and allowed us to support conclusions derived from questionnaires with data from other sources. Methods included interviews, observations, work activity diaries, and structured questionnaires. The first three methods were used on a subsample of the population, while the questionnaires were sent to all Navy career civilian executives. Data were collected between July 1977 and March 1978.

Interviews   Structured interviews were conducted with a representative cross-section of 57 civilian executives. Interviews averaged 1¼ hours.[12]

Work activity diaries   A representative cross-section of 19 civilian executives was asked to describe their activities over a two-week period using an Executive Work Diary Form. A work sampling technique was used so that executives recorded activities performed on alternate four-hour morning or afternoon time blocks. For each activity (e.g., phone call, meeting, conversation), the executive was asked to record the amount of time taken and to indicate the type of activity conducted, where it had taken place, and its purpose. Purpose was categorized in terms of the ten executive roles developed by Mintzberg. An eleventh role, that of "Technical Expert," was added based on feedback from executives during the interviews. The definitions of these roles, as provided to executives, are shown in Table 15-1.

Observations   Four civilian executives were observed individually doing their job over a two-day period. Two of these executives were from laboratories, one was from a system command, and one was from a headquarters organization. The observer used the Executive Work Diary Form to record each activity in which the executive engaged.

Questionnaires   Using Mintzberg's framework and description of managerial roles, 50 items describing work content were developed. Executives were asked (1) how much time they spent on the average in each activity, and (2) how important each activity was to them in the successful conduct of their work. Responses were made on an 8-point scale, where 0 = "None" and 7 = "Great Deal." In addition to job content, there were 15 items which assessed perceived job characteristics.

The population of 370 civilian executives was mailed a questionnaire. A total of 210 questionnaires were completed and returned (a return rate of 57 percent). Those who returned the questionnaire were representative of the full population in terms of GS level, occupational series, and organizational affiliation.

RESULTS

Job Content

The responses on the importance scale to the 50 items in the job content section of the executive questionnaire were analyzed with an information re-

TABLE 15-1
Summary of Executive Roles

Role	Definition[a]	Identifiable Activities from Study of Chief Executives
	INTERPERSONAL	
Figurehead	Symbolic head; obligated to perform a number of routine duties of a legal or social nature.	Ceremony, status requests, solicitations.
Leader	Responsible for the motivation and activation of subordinates; responsible for staffing, training, and associated duties.	Virtually all managerial activities involving subordinates.
Liaison	Maintains self-developed network of outside contracts and informers who provide favors and information.	Acknowledgment of mail; external board work; other activities involving outsiders.
	INFORMATIONAL	
Monitor	Seeks and receives wide variety of special information (much of it current) to develop thorough understanding of organization and environment; emerges as nerve center of internal and external information of the organization.	Handling all mail and contacts categorized as concerned primarily with receiving information (e.g., periodical news, observational tours).
Disseminator	Transmits information received from outsiders or from other subordinates to members of the organization; some information factual; some involving interpretation and integration of diverse value positions of organizational influencers.	Forwarding mail into organization for informational purposes, verbal contact involving information flow to subordinates (e.g., review sessions, instant communication flows).
Spokesman	Transmits information to outsiders on organization's plans, policies, actions, results, etc.; serves as expert on organization's industry.	Board meetings, handling mail, and contacts involving transmission of information to outsiders.
	DECISIONAL	
Entrepreneur	Searches organization and its environment for opportunities and initiates "improvement projects" to bring about change; supervises design of certain projects as well.	Strategy and review sessions involving initiation or design of improvement projects.
Disturbance Handler	Responsible for corrective action when organization faces important, unexpected disturbances.	Strategy and review sessions involving disturbances and crises.
Resource Allocator	Responsible for the allocation of organizational resources of all kinds—in effect, the making or approval of all significant organizational decisions.	Scheduling; requests for authorization; any activity involving budgeting and the programming of subordinates' work.
Negotiator	Responsible for representing the organization at major negotiations.	Negotiation.
Technical Expert	Providing expertise to projects. Serving as a consultant to internal or external projects.	Directing a project or subproject; solving project-centered problems.

[a]Definitions for all roles but "Technical Expert" based on *The Nature of Managerial Work* by Henry Mintzberg (New York: Harper and Row, 1973).

duction technique called factor analysis. This technique investigates the underlying pattern of relationships within a set of responses by combining similar items into a minimum number of factors. The factors are generated such that the maximum amount of differences between factors is preserved while eliminating information that is redundant. In this analysis, four factors were found that accounted for 76 percent of the differences in responses to the 50 items.[13]

Since the analysis done on the time dimension yielded essentially the same factors and was consistent with an analysis of the importance dimension, only results from the latter are described in this article. Items that combined to form these four factors are listed in Table 15-2. Each factor is described below.[14]

Factor I: Leadership and supervision (9 items)   This factor alone accounted for 54 percent of the differences in executive job content. In the leadership and supervisory role, the executive is responsible for guiding and motivating

TABLE 15-2
Factor Analysis of Executive Job Content

Factors and Items	Factor Loadings[a]			
	I	II	III	IV
Factor I: Supervision				
1. Evaluating the quality of subordinate job performance and providing recognition, encouragement, or criticism.	.75			
2. Attending to the training and development needs of your employees.	.64			
3. Keeping members of your unit informed of relevant information through meetings, conversations, and dissemination of written information.	.59			
4. Attending to staffing requirements in your unit such as hiring, firing, promoting, and recruiting.	.57			
5. Integrating subordinates' goals with the command's work requirements.	.56			.46
6. Providing guidance and direction to your subordinates.	.54			
7. Maintaining supervision over planned changes to improve your unit.	.49			
8. Participating in EEO activities and responsibilities.	.44			
9. Programming work for your unit and assigning people to work on it.	.43			
Factor II: Information Gathering and Dissemination				
1. Staying tuned to what is going on in outside organizations, including the professional and scientific communities.		.65		
2. Gathering information from or about sponsors and consumers.		.63		
3. Keeping sponsors, consumers, or other important governmental groups informed about your unit's activities and capabilities.		.61		
4. Keeping professional colleagues informed about your unit.		.58		
5. Making yourself available to "outsiders" who want to go to the "person in charge."		.55		
6. Attending outside conferences or meetings.		.54		
7. Exploiting or initiating opportunities to improve or expand as a unit.		.47		
8. Developing new contacts by answering requests for information.		.47		
9. Joining boards, organizations, clubs, or doing public service work which might provide useful, work-related contacts.		.43		
10. Keeping abreast of who is doing what in your unit or command.		.43		

subordinates and for integrating individual and organizational goals. This role also includes staffing, programming work for the unit, maintaining supervision over planned change, and keeping subordinates informed of relevant information.

Factor II: Information gathering and dissemination (10 items) This factor accounted for an additional 10 percent of the differences. Items involve a variety of interrelated interpersonal and informational roles concerning the ability to deal with the external environment, keeping up with current events, and keeping sponsors informed about unit activities. These roles correspond to Mintzberg's categories of figurehead, liaison, monitor, and spokesman. Access to information places the executive in a strategic position related to communication flows between the organizational unit and the external environment. The executive uses this information to coordinate activities of the various organizational units and to guide the total organizational effort in a way that is in keeping with external events.

	Factor Loadings[a]			
Factors and Items	I	II	III	IV
Factor III: Technical Problem Solving				
1. Providing technical quality control through the review process.			.71	
2. Identifying and solving complex engineering or scientific problems yourself.			.68	
3. Judging the accuracy of approach and utility of technical programs and proposals.			.66	
4. Consulting with others on technical matters.			.63	
5. Directing a technical project or subproject.			.53	
Factor IV: Executive Decision Making, Planning, and Resource Allocation				
1. Participating in defining command strategies and policies.				.60
2. Transmitting ideas and information from your outside contacts to appropriate people inside your command.		.49		.53
3. Implementing the directives of higher authorities.				.52
4. Attending business meetings or social gatherings as an official representative of your unit or command.				.52
5. Evaluating the outcomes of internal improvement projects.				.50
6. Monitoring output of formal management information systems.				.48
7. Resolving conflicts either within your unit or between your unit and other organizational components.	.40			.46
8. Touring your own command's staffs and facilities, including field activities.				.46
9. Allocating your own time.				.45
10. Preventing the loss or threat of loss of resources valued by your unit.				.45
11. Participating alone or on a team in atypical negotiations with outsiders.				.45
12. Taking immediate action in response to a crisis or "fire drill."				.44
13. Determining the long-range plans and priorities of your unit.				.40

[a]Only items having factor loadings of at least .40 are included.

Factor III: Technical problem solving (5 items) This factor accounted for 7 percent of the differences. Although technical problem solving is an integral part of Navy management, especially in the R&D setting, the vast majority of executive jobs do not involve the actual identification and solution of complex engineering or scientific problems. Rather, they involve such scientific processes as judging the usefulness of technical programs and proposals, maintaining close relationships with subordinates over technical projects, and technical management and administration over functions that fall within their career fields.

Factor IV: Executive decision making, planning and resource allocation (13 items) This factor accounted for 5 percent of the differences in executive job content. Although activities included under this role are somewhat heterogeneous, they generally involve command strategies and policies or decisions on expansion of organizational efforts. These activities involve a variety of interrelated decisional roles as described by Mintzberg—entrepreneur, disturbance handler, and resource allocator. While serving in these roles, the executive determines which departments or activities will expand and which will diminish. Resource allocation, particularly where the executive participates in defining organizational strategies, determines long-range plans, and authorizes actions on internal improvement projects, is the cornerstone of effective public sector management.

Average importance scores were calculated for the item sets that loaded on each of the four factors. In terms of overall importance, the leadership and supervision factor was rated as the most important to successful conduct of public sector executive jobs (5.0 on a scale ranging from 0 to 7), followed by executive decision making, planning, and resource allocation (4.5), technical problem solving (4.2), and information gathering and dissemination (4.0).

Mintzberg reported that the content of executive jobs could be described by common sets of roles. In our study of executives, we examined job content by line and staff position, organizational location (headquarters vs. field), and job function (R&D vs. non-R&D management). Like Mintzberg, we found that executive jobs share many more common than unique characteristics. Since questionnaires were anonymous, however, it was not possible to examine job content by organizational level (i.e., GS-16, 17, 18).

Job content information collected from interviews, work activity diaries, and behavioral observation was compared to questionnaire information. A content analysis of interview information disclosed that executives described their jobs as requiring activities in the following main categories: (1) leadership, supervision, and personnel administration; (2) resource allocation; (3) monitoring and disseminating of internal and external information; (4) technical consultation; and (5) planning, decision making and influencing policy. These activities are consistent with information obtained from the questionnaires.

When executive activities documented by work diaries and observations were categorized under the 10 Mintzberg roles, it was found that 30 percent of the work diary activities and 35 percent of the observed activities involved two or more interrelated roles. An analysis of the work diaries indicated that 34 percent of executives' time was spent in interpersonal roles, 22 percent in informational roles, and 13 percent in decisional roles. Other activities were combinations of the various roles (e.g., leader-resource allocator).

■ 15 ■
Alan W. Lau
Arthur R. Newman
Laurie A. Broedling

In general, there was a reasonable amount of congruence between time spent in the various role activities as measured by interviews, work activity diaries, observations, and questionnaires. Findings concerning this congruence would appear to strengthen the generalizability of the study.

Job Characteristics

Mintzberg found that managerial activities are characterized by brevity, variety, and discontinuity. This drives the manager to overwork, to perform many tasks superficially, and to strongly favor verbal communication (e.g., telephone calls, informal meetings) over formal management information systems. In the present study, information from the interviews, questionnaires, observations, and work diaries was used to examine whether similar job characteristics influenced the way in which public sector executives performed their jobs.

During the interviews, it became apparent that the job environment of the public sector executive had a strong influence on his or her behavior. Four important environmental characteristics emerged from an analysis of the interviews:

1. The extraordinary amount of complexity in the Navy shore organization and the important implications this complexity has for executive functioning, selection, and development.
2. Increasing centralization of decision making and proliferation of controls.
3. Personnel shortages and the slowness and rigidity of civilian personnel administration.
4. The high degree of job sharing between civilian executives and their military counterparts.

A number of executives summarized the influence of these environmental characteristics. One commented:

> The greatest impediment to effective performance is the lack of clear-cut responsibility. Almost any action can be undercut by factors not under my control. There is an utter dearth of effective long-range planning.

Another said:

> Your questions really don't address the real problems encountered by a line manager, i.e., the total frustration with personnel, contracts, and legal support offices who assume that line organizations exist to serve them. Also, hiring freezes, high ceilings, additional staffs and layering of organizational levels. I can commit vast sums of taxpayer money, but can't get an operable typewriter for my secretary.

Almost 90 percent of respondents to the executive questionnaire reported that there is either moderate or great pressure on them to produce; none reported that there was no stress in their jobs. All of them, however, reported that they could handle job stress moderately well or completely. Principal sources of job stress reported include: (1) frustration in the slowness of accomplishing anything (70 percent checked this source); (2) lack of efficient

207

in-house personnel (52 percent); and (3) pressure from organizations external to the Navy (48 percent).

Another characteristic investigated was the degree to which executive jobs are fragmented and hectic. From an analysis of questionnaire responses, we found that the majority of executives report their daily work routine is fragmented with interruptions and unscheduled events (72 percent agreed), that the greatest block to doing their jobs is "the constant barrage of fire drills" (71 percent), that it is virtually impossible to set a work schedule and stick to it (64 percent), and that meetings burn up an unnecessary amount of time (63 percent). The data gathered by observing executives also reflect the hectic and fragmented nature of their jobs. On the average, 43 activities per day were observed. Except for meetings, which were coded as a single activity, these activities typically were very brief (e.g., review of in-coming and out-going correspondence, and making and answering phone calls). In general, executives indicated insufficient time to devote to leadership activities, long-range planning, and/or definition of organizational goals. Many react to this situation by putting in long hours—an average of 52 hours per week at the office and an additional eight hours per week at home.

A final characteristic investigated was how executives distribute their time among various activities. Executives reported that they spend over 70 percent of their time interacting with other individuals. Of this, 45 percent is spent in scheduled meetings and 17 percent in unscheduled meetings. Other interpersonal activities involve telephone calls (7 percent) and observations of personnel and their work activities (7 percent). Executives spend only 24 percent of their time alone, generally performing desk work such as reading correspondence.

DISCUSSION

The results of this study suggest that both public and private sector executives perform the same kind of activities, both in terms of complexity of job content and roles, and in terms of job characteristics, i.e., the fragmented, high pressure, quick reaction nature of executive positions. They also suggest that public sector executives engage in activities that correspond to Mintzberg's managerial role descriptions, and that the major role functions are similar in both sectors. Further corroboration of this hypothesis comes from a recent study of 225 managers in a variety of private sector firms.[15] A comparison of the average rankings of Mintzberg's ten managerial roles from this study with the average rankings in the present study of public sector executives showed a remarkable degree of similarity between the two sectors. A more direct test of this hypothesis clearly suggests that generalizations regarding differences between public and private sector managers and executives may frequently be overstated.[16] Moreover, with continued changes toward a process which fits a Management by Objectives philosophy, one can anticipate even closer parallels between the two sectors.

With respect to job characteristics, the public sector executive, like his or her private sector counterpart, does not have time for reflective, systematic planning, strongly favors the verbal media (telephone calls, meetings), is overburdened with obligations, and serves as a nerve center of the organizational unit by processing large amounts of information from the external environment.

■ 15 ■
Alan W. Lau
Arthur R. Newman
Laurie A. Broedling

As a result of pressures, job demands, and bureaucratic requirements, executives in the public sector perceive discrepancies between what they are doing and what they should be doing. An analysis of the executive questionnaire indicates that executives have insufficient time to devote to leadership activities, long-range planning, and/or the influence and definition of organizational policies and goals. Many put in long hours, feel overworked, and are unable to follow pre-planned work schedules. Much time is spent reacting to short-term crises, to demands imposed by superiors, and to what executives regard as unnecessary meetings, red tape, and bureaucratic trivia. Observational findings also indicated that the executives work at an unrelenting pace with little free time, and that their activities are characterized by variety, interruptions, and unscheduled events.

During this study, it became progressively apparent that, in order to describe and understand executive behavior, one also had to understand the functioning of the entire Navy shore organization and its organizational context. Anyone undertaking research in a large, public sector organization should be aware of the need to describe and deal with the complexity of functioning that probably pervades all public sector bureaucracies.

Bennis[17] predicted that what constitutes public and private sector management would become more similar, merging over time. While researchers have generally examined the private sector for models of management functioning and development, it may be more warranted to look to the public sector for models. It seems justified to say that the private sector is becoming more like the public sector in terms of complexity, number of regulations, and multiplicity of constraints, rather than the opposite. To some degree, the effect of government requirements has probably influenced the increasing convergence of the two sectors.

IMPLICATIONS FOR ACTION

Executive selection, development, and performance appraisal processes within the public sector are frequently conducted independently of one another, with differing sets of criteria being employed. A better understanding of the job activities and the underlying required skills, knowledge, and abilities of public sector executives has implications for evolving personnel systems required under the reform act. Some implications of the present study to enhance public sector executive selection, development, appraisal, and utilization are presented below:

- Technical qualifications should be treated as necessary but not sufficient selection criteria. At the executive level, there should be increased emphasis upon human and conceptual skills in the selection process. This reflects the fact that tasks at this level are primarily administrative and managerial.

- Training and development and performance appraisal programs should be based on identified job activities and roles required of the executive job.

- The complexity of the executive's job environment should be recognized in the new appraisal process. In the current climate of scarce personnel resources, it is difficult to set realistic performance goals. If executives cannot control these resources, the appraisal process should be modified.

• Implementation of the SES in the Department of Defense (DoD) should recognize the unique element introduced by the large cadre of rotating military executives. Within the DoD, with such a high degree of military mobility, there is a need for people who maintain continuity and corporate memory.

NOTES

[1]Henri Fayol, *Administration industrielle et generale* (Paris: Dunod, 1916).

[2]For further evidence on these points, see Morgan W. McCall and Michael M. Lombardo (eds.), *Leadership: Where Else Can We Go?* (Durham, N.C.: Duke University Press, 1978).

[3]John K. Hemphill, "Job Descriptions for Executives," *Harvard Business Review*, 37 (1959), pp. 55–67.

[4]See Walter W. Tornow and Patrick R. Pinto, "The Development of a Managerial Taxonomy: A System of Describing, Classifying, and Evaluating Executive Positions," *Journal of Applied Psychology*, 61 (1976), pp. 410–418; and John J. Morse and Francis R. Wagner, "Measuring the Process of Managerial Effectiveness," *Academy of Management Journal*, 21 (1978), pp. 23–35. Relevant studies in the public sector include David T. Stanley, *The Higher Civil Service* (Washington, D.C.: Brookings Institution, 1964); and R. L. Ellison, C. Abe, and D. B. Fox, *The Job Activities Description (JAD) Questionnaire: An Analysis of Time Spent on and Importance of Managerial Duties* (Salt Lake City, Utah: Institute for Behavioral Research in Creativity, 1978).

[5]See T. Burns, "Management in Action," *Operational Research Quarterly*, 8 (1957), pp. 45–60; J. H. Horne and Tom Lupton, "The Work Activities of Middle Managers," *Journal of Management Studies*, 1 (1965), pp. 14–33; and Rosemary Stewart, *Contrasts in Management* (London: McGraw-Hill, 1976).

[6]Morgan W. McCall, A. M. Morrison, and R. L. Hannan, *Studies of Managerial Work: Results and Methods* (Technical Report No. 9), Greensboro, N.C.: Center for Creative Leadership, 1978.

[7]Henry Mintzberg, *The Nature of Managerial Work* (New York: Harper and Row, 1973).

[8]Henry Mintzberg, "The Manager's Job: Folklore and Fact," *Harvard Business Review*, 53 (1974), pp. 49–61.

[9]Several researchers have found that the importance of Mintzberg's roles varies significantly according to the manager's level in the hierarchy and functional area. See Larry D. Alexander, "The Effect Level in the Hierarchy and Functional Area Have on the Extent Mintzberg's Roles are Required by Managerial Jobs," *Academy of Management Proceedings* (1979), pp. 186–189.

[10]See Athol M. Harrison, "The Operational Definition of Managerial Roles," Doctoral Dissertation, University of Cape Town, September 1978; Morse and Wagner, op cit.; and William T. Whitely, "Nature of Managerial Work Revisited," *Academy of Management Proceedings* (1978), pp. 195–199.

[11]The full study is described in the following two documents, the first being a summary of the study and the second being the detailed technical report on the study: (a) L. A. Broedling and A. W. Lau, *Executive Summary: Navy Civilian Executive Study* (NPRDC SR 79–10), San Diego: Navy Personnel Research and Development Center, January 1979; (b) A. W. Lau, L. A. Broedling, S. K. Walters, A. Newman, and P. Harvey, *The Nature of the Navy Civilian Executive Job: Behavior and Development* (NPRDC TR 79–27) San Diego: Navy Personnel Research and Development Center, July 1979.

[12]For a description of interview findings see Laurie A. Broedling, A. W. Lau, and S. K. Walters, "The Job of the Navy Civilian Executive in Headquarters," *The Bureaucrat*, 8 (1980), pp. 12–18.

[13]A principal component solution was obtained. Orthogonal rotation to the varimax criteria yielded four major factors with eigenvalues exceeding 1.00. Factor analysis generally requires that

the ratio of participants to questionnaire items be at least as large as 5:1 for adequate reliability to be obtained. The entire sample (N = 210) was split into two random samples and separate factor analyses were conducted. The two factor structures were then compared using procedures developed by D. Veldman, *Fortran Programming for the Behavioral Sciences* (New York: Holt, Rinehart and Winston, 1967). Correlations between the factor variables derived from the two analyses ranged from .89 to .99, indicating a stable factor structure across both groups.

[14]A fifth factor, negotiation, included only three items and accounted for an additional 5 percent of the variance. Items referred to activities involved in negotiating labor-management agreements or dealing with union representatives, and handling formal grievances.

[15]Alexander, op cit.

[16]The same items used in the present study of job content and job characteristics were administered to a sample of 220 private sector managers and executives in Southern California. See Alan W. Lau, Cynthia M. Pavett, and Arthur R. Newman, "The Nature of Managerial Work: A Comparison of Public and Private Sector Jobs," forthcoming in the *Academy of Management Proceedings* (August 1980).

[17]Warren Bennis, "Organizations of the Future," *Personnel Administration*, 30 (1967), pp. 7–19.

■ 15 ■
Alan W. Lau
Arthur R. Newman
Laurie A. Broedling

16 | Task Accomplishment and the Management of Time

Lyman W. Porter
John Van Maanen

"_____is of the essence."

"_____is money."

"_____waits for no man."

The number and pervasiveness of such familiar sayings as those above testify to the importance of it.[1] A prominent management consultant (Drucker, 1966) has recently referred to it as "the scarcest resource." As he goes on to point out, ". . . one cannot rent, hire, buy, or otherwise obtain more" of it. Its supply is absolutely inelastic. "No matter how high the demand, the supply will not go up. There is no price for it, and no marginal utility curve for it. Moreover, [it] is totally perishable and cannot be stored . . . . [It] is totally irreplaceable . . . there is no substitute for [it]." Furthermore, everyone in an organization, whether he be the president or the janitor, has an equal amount of it. It is as critical to a nonprofit governmental or educational organization as it is to the most profit-hungry business company. "It" is time.[2]

Given the unique properties of time, it seems clear that its effective management would have a great deal to do with the successful completion of task and organizational accomplishments. Drucker, in fact, states that "Nothing else, perhaps, distinguishes effective executives as much as their tender loving care of time." (It should be noted, however, that this is an assumption; it is based on his own—admittedly shrewd—observations of the particular sample of executives with whom he has had contact.) An article in the *Wall Street Journal* (1968) quotes a number of executives on the tremendous importance they attach to attempts to make themselves more effective by employing various stratagems to conserve time and allocate it constructively. Still another

Reprinted from Bernard Bass (Ed.), *Managing for Accomplishment,* 1970, by permission of the publisher, Lexington Books, Inc.

recent management-oriented article (Jones, 1968) emphasizes the rapidly increasing cost, and hence, value of executive time.

In addition to the possible development of prescriptions concerning how time should be allocated, the study of how managers in fact go about *attempting* to allocate and manage their time should provide valuable analytic information concerning organizational processes. It is one approach to determining the nature of some of the key ingredients in managerial and supervisory effectiveness. It also should provide some clues to the perceived demand characteristics of different parts of the organization as they impinge on managers in particular positions in organizations. In short, it is one way of learning more about the phenomenal organizational world in which the manager operates and with which he has to cope.

Despite its apparent vital importance to task and organizational accomplishment, the management of time has not been extensively studied by students of organizations. This statement is particularly true if one distinguishes the study of the decision-making process of attempting to allocate time, from research on the mere recording of how time is actually spent in specified situations. Investigations of the former are notable by their absence; there are, however, a small number of studies of the latter type, and these will be reviewed briefly below. In the meantime, it should be stressed that the focus of this paper is on the former: the decision-making aspects of the manager's efforts to manage his time.

Systematic studies of the distribution of executives' time date back to Carlson's (1951) investigation of ten managing directors (chief executives) of Swedish firms. This study relied chiefly on a method—*self* recording of time spent on various activities—of data collection that has featured most of the subsequent research of this type. Other studies using some version of the self-recording technique include those by Burns (1954), Dubin and Spray (1964), Hinrichs (1964), Horne and Lupton (1965) and Lawler, Porter, and Tannenbaum (1968). An alternative methodology was employed by Ponder (1958) and Kelly (1964), in which observers recorded supervisors' and managers' actions at specified points in time. It is worth noting, incidentally, that most of the above investigations utilized extremely small samples (N's of 4, 8, 9, etc.) with the exceptions of Horne and Lupton ($N = 66$), Lawler, Porter, and Tannenbaum ($N = 105$) and Hinrichs ($N = 232$). Conclusions, consequently, must be of a limited nature. Also, there was considerable variation in the nature of the samples obtained, in terms of the organizational positions held by the subjects. At the broadest level of generalization concerning their findings, these studies seem in most frequent agreement about the essentially verbal nature of the average manager's job—that is, the fact that he spends a high proportion of his time interacting with other people, whether in a meeting, in a one-to-one informal conversation or by phone. The converse of this finding is that the typical manager spends relatively little time alone (and, presumably, relatively little time in individualized *thinking*). (As a management consultant quoted in the previously referred to *Wall Street Journal* article has said: "Many executives waste time doing things that don't justify their high-priced attention just because they're afraid to be seen sitting with their feet up on the desk planning and thinking." The consultant goes on to say that when he pointed this out to one executive, the reply was: "But I just can't

213

spend all my time thinking.") The other generally appearing finding from several of the studies was the substantial (and, to those investigators, surprising) amount of time managers devote to interacting with their peers (as opposed to superiors and subordinates). This latter finding serves to emphasize, as Dubin (1962) has noted, the horizontal as well as the vertical nature of the manager's job.

As we have pointed out earlier, the studies cited above have investigated the way in which managers spend their time. They do not provide data on how managers think they *should* spend their time. It may be that managerial *intentions* are more critical for understanding and analyzing organizational pressures and processes than are records of actual time spent. Proceeding on this assumption, the remainder of this paper will describe an exploratory and comparative study designed to investigate some of the decision-making facets of the management of time problem. The study will center on two major comparisons in this respect: differences in attempted time management between managers employed in one type of public organization (in this case, city governments) and those in private industry, and differences between managers judged to be relatively highly effective and those identified as relatively less effective.

THE PILOT STUDY

Methodology

A structured questionnaire was the method utilized to collect data for this study. Prior to the construction of the questionnaire, some two dozen semi-structured interviews were conducted in order to formulate the precise items to be used in the questionnaire. These interviews were carried out with small samples of managers from industry, from local governmental situations and from educational institutions. One feature of the interview results, in particular, influenced the design of the ultimate study: the apparent differences between industrial managers and those employed in city government administrations concerning the amount of attention devoted to planning for the management of time. Managers in industrial firms appeared to have given considerably more thought to this than had the managers in the local government sector.

The questionnaire that was developed consisted of six parts:

Part I: Eight questions concerning the *manager's attitudes and opinions toward aspects of planning his time.* "In planning for the *use* of your time during the work week, how much planning would you like to do?" "To what degree are you successful in implementing your plan of weekly activities?" etc.)

Part II. *Perceived control over the amount of time spent* in six activities (scheduled formal meetings, scheduled one-to-one interactions, informal unscheduled interactions, telephone conversations, time spent alone, and time spent outside the immediate work environment on a business-related activity).

Part III: *Perceived degree of planning of time* for six activities (same as those listed in Part II).

Part IV: *Estimates (percentage of 100) of time spent* in six activities (same as those in Part II).

Part V: *Perceived degree of importance of* six *factors in making decisions to allocate time.* The six factors were: formal requirements of the job; needs and demands of superiors; needs and demands of peers; needs and demands of subordinates; needs and demands of those outside the organization (the public, customers, salesmen, etc.) and, "your own individual views about how to allocate your time."

Part VI: *Hypothetical "problems" in the allocation of time.* Five such problems were presented; for each problem, three possible solutions were offered, and the respondent was asked to rate each solution in terms of its "goodness" from his point of view. An example of such a hypothetical problem was the following:

> You are headed for a scheduled meeting with two of your subordinates when unexpectedly your superior telephones to request an immediate conference with you. What would your response be?
>
> Solution A: Call your subordinates and ask them to wait until you had finished meeting with your superior and then you would meet with them.
>
> Solution B. Call your subordinates and cancel your meeting with them, making arrangements to reschedule your meeting later.
>
> Solution C: Tell your superior that you will be unable to meet with him at that particular time and attempt to rearrange another time for the requested conference with him.

Sample

Given the limited resources (especially, time!) available to the researchers, it was decided to sample forty managers from city governments and forty from industrial companies. Within each of these two samples, the aim was to obtain 50% who were rated as relatively "most effective" and 50% rated relatively "least effective" by the respondent's superior. In other words, the design could be thought of as a 2×2 paradigm (see Table 16-1). (The total response rate was $97\frac{1}{2}\%$; two managers—one "most effective" and one "least effective"—in the industrial sample did not return the questionnaire; hence, the actual cells in these two instances have an N of 19 instead of the planned 20.)

TABLE 16-1

| | | Effectiveness | |
		Most Effective	Least Effective
Domain of Organization	City Government Administrators	N = 20	N = 20
	Industrial Managers	N = 20 (actual N = 19)	N = 20 (actual N = 19)

In obtaining respondents for the samples, only those individuals who held essentially line middle managerial positions were selected as respondents. That is, they could not be the top person in their organizational unit; on the other hand, they must have at least one level of supervision reporting to them. The governmental (we shall frequently use this phrase as a shorthand term for the city government sample) and industrial samples were obtained as follows:

City government sample: In order to obtain respondents who would have jobs that emphasized the "public" nature of their work, we decided to sample department managers in city governments. This was done by contacting ten city managers and asking them to nominate two of their "most effective" department heads, and two of their "least effective" department heads. Four department heads from each of ten city governments served as the respondents in completing the time allocation questionnaires. In obtaining the nominations of "most" and "least" effective subordinates from the city managers, no mention whatsoever of the actual purpose of the study was made until after the city manager had made his nominations. In other words, when the city managers made their nominations they did not know that this was a study of time management. They were merely told that this was a study of "modes of operation of administrators." They were asked to select "most" and "least" effective department heads in terms of who is "the most and least efficient, competent, and productive, with respect to all aspects of their jobs." The department heads nominated covered a wide range of duties, including parks and recreation, water, planning, police, fire, finance, etc.

After the nominations had been obtained, a researcher visited the four department heads and asked each if he would be willing to complete a brief quesionnaire concerning administrative methods. (It was explained that the city manager had given permission for the quesionnaire to be distributed.) In some cases the questionnaires were completed in the presence of the researcher; usually, however, they were returned by mail to the researchers at the university within the next few days.

Industrial sample: The methods of obtaining the industrial sample were essentially the same, except that five rather than ten (as in the governmental sample) organizations provided the samples of respondents. In each of these five companies, all of them local industrial-manufacturing firms, two upper-middle level managers were asked to nominate their two most effective subordinate managers and their two least effective subordinates. Eight respondents were obtained from each company. Other methodological procedures followed those outlined above for the respondents from the city governments.

Results

Since the study reported here is strictly exploratory, with samples relatively limited by their size and their representativeness of two organizational domains (city governments and industrial firms), no attempt will be made to present precise statistical tests of differences. Rather, comparative trends in the data will be emphasized in order to suggest the general direction of the results and to provide fruitful hypotheses and leads for future and more elaborate research.

In discussing the results, we shall first focus on the city government-industrial comparison without regard to effectiveness differences within each sample (keeping in mind that each sample was composed of an equal percentage of effective and ineffective managers), and then on comparisons within each sample on the effectiveness dimension.

Managers from City Governments vs. Industrial Organizations

As mentioned earlier, our preliminary interviewing had indicated that managers operating in city government administrations seemed to give less attention to attempts to manage their time and also appeared to feel that they had relatively low control over how their time was allocated. To us, this suggestive finding could be attributed to the perceived role demands on the part of the city government managers. Consequently, in the major questionnaire phase of our study we drew one-half of our total sample from department heads in city governments, judging that they would be relatively high on contacts with individuals (e.g., members of the general public) outside of their immediate work organization compared with contacts with those inside their organization (i.e., other individuals employed in their own city government). What we are stressing here, then, in our city government-industrial comparisons are not the "publicness" vs. "privateness" per se, but rather organizational positions that appear to require a relatively large number of "outside of organization" contacts compared to positions that are more inwardly (organizationally speaking) oriented. (Almost all our respondents from the private sample were primarily on the "interior" of the organization, rather than having jobs [such as sales] dealing with "exterior" relationships.)

Before proceeding to detail the findings on the city government-industrial comparisons, it may be useful to say a further word about the nature of the organizations for which the city government department heads worked. All ten of the city governments sampled in this study were of a particular administrative form, namely, council-manager. Banfield and Wilson, in their recent book (1963), summarize the nature of this type of city government as follows: "The council-manager form, which from its inception in 1910 has been favored by municipal reform groups, carries the separation of powers a step further by placing all 'administrative' authority in the hands of a professional manager who is hired by the elected council. . . . Under this plan there is a mayor, but his duties are purely ceremonial" (p. 81). They further point out that: "From its beginnings to the present, the municipal reform movement has had the goals of eliminating corruption, increasing efficiency, and making local government in some sense more democratic" (p. 138). The council-manager form of government was viewed as the best way of accomplishing this task. Additionally, "[it is] a characteristic expression of the 'good government' point of view . . . that the interest of the community 'as a whole' should be determined in disinterested ways and then be carried into effect expeditiously and efficiently by technicians" (p. 170).

The essence of the above description of the particular type of city governments we sampled is that they "should be run in a businesslike way." As Banfield and Wilson quote from a newspaper supporting the establishment of such a form of city government: "Why not run [the city] on a *business* schedule by *business* methods under *businessmen*? . . . The city manager plan is after all only a *business* management plan . . ." (p. 170).

The reason for stressing that our sample of middle level managers in city governments all worked under council-manager plans, is to point out that such local government organizations attempt to operate as much like "efficient" business companies as possible. Had we sampled from city government administrations operating under different organizational plans we might have obtained radically different responses to time management questions. (The presumption here is that our sample of city government department heads is on the whole more oriented to "efficient operations"—including time planning—than would be a sample drawn from differently organized city governments.)

In Parts I and II of the questionnaire, which concerned attitudes toward time, planning and perceptions of the degree to which control can be exercised over time allocations, a very definite trend is evident (and which was forecast from the results of the preliminary interviews): The governmental managers feel that they have considerably less control, compared to the industrial managers, over how they allocate their time, particularly in the areas of telephone conversations, time spent alone, and (to a slightly lesser extent) time spent outside the immediate work environment on a work-related activity. Accompanying this feeling of relatively lower control on the part of the government manager is the related view that the average 8-hour workday does not provide adequate time for the accomplishment of task and work responsibilities. Likewise, the governmental managers report feeling much more "rushed," with "not enough time to get the things done you want to do." It would seem from these results that the outside, unpredictable world is indeed intruding on the department manager in a city government organization much more than it is on the average manager in a private industry manufacturing-type organization. This finding, if confirmed by future research, raises some interesting questions concerning the psychological nature of the managerial job within the two types of organizations, and also poses some questions concerning the nature of environmental and ecological demands made on the two types of organizations.

Somewhat contrary to our preliminary and less structured interview findings, the questionnaire results did not show significantly greater perceived *attempts* by the industrial managers to plan the allocation of their time. However, the most sizable difference occurring in Part III—the degree of planning of time to devote to each of six activities—did show that the industrial managers reported giving more attention to scheduling "time spent alone" compared to the city government managers. This particular activity—time spent alone—and efforts to control and plan for it appears to be a major distinguishing feature between the two types of organizational situations.

Estimates of the percentage of time spent among six types of activities (refer to description of Part IV of the questionnaire) showed that the relatively greatest differences between the governmental and industrial samples occurred in two areas: telephone conversations and time spent alone. The governmental managers reported spending 17% of their total time on telephone activity, while the percentage for the industrial managers was only about half of this, 9%. For the "time spent alone" category, on the other hand, the industrial managers reported spending 25% on this activity while the city government managers said they spent only 18% of their time this way. While such absolute values of the estimates may deviate somewhat from "objective reality" (see the articles by Hinrichs, 1964, and Horne and Lupton, 1965, for data on this point), the *relative* values may very well be accurate. (Again, see Hinrich, 1964, and Horne and Lupton, 1965.) Independent confirmation of public agency vs. industrial "telephone" differences, obtained by an entirely different and more "objective" data collection method, can be found in the Lawler, Porter, and Tannenbaum (1968) study. It could be inferred from such "telephone" differences that the local government managers are receiving considerably more communication inputs from extraorganization sources. While telephone calls can of course be from either inside or outside the organization, it is a reasonable assumption that a major cause of the higher percentage of telephone conversations reported by the governmental managers is the outside calls added on to the usual inside ones. (Again, our preliminary interviews indicate that such outside-the-organization phone calls were a major time-spending activity for the manager in certain kinds of public agencies.)

Still another support for the thesis of far greater necessity to respond to external-to-the-organization demands on the part of the city government managers comes from Part V of the questionnaire. In this part, the respondents were asked to rate the importance attached to each of six factors in influencing "your determination of how to spend your time." Differences between the governmental and industrial samples were relatively small on "internal" factors, such as needs and demands of bosses, subordinates and peers, but were relatively large on "your own individual views about how to spend your time" and were exceptionally large on "needs and demands of those outside your organization." The industrial managers put more weight on their own individual views, while the governmental managers attached far greater importance than did the managers in business firms to the needs and demands of outsiders. Although this latter finding is not unexpected, it does serve to reinforce the general picture of city government-industrial differences in time allocation decision making obtained elsewhere in the questionnaire.

It will be recalled that the final part of the questionnaire contained five hypothetical time allocation problems. While space (and time) prevents a detailed discussion of the findings from this part, two trends that did appear will be briefly noted. On the question dealing with an unexpected call from the boss while the manager is on his way to a previously scheduled meeting with his subordinates, the industrial managers were more inclined than the governmental administrators to favor the solution of telling the boss that "you will be unable to meet with him" and asking him to attempt to arrange another time for the conference. This may indicate somewhat more attention to formal hierarchical arrangements on the part of the managers in city governments. On two other questions dealing with "outside" intrusions (an unexpected visitor, in one case, and telephone calls, in the other), the managers in the city governments reflected their apparently beleaguered situations with respect to time demands from outsiders by favoring solutions that attempted to "dispose of" the intrusion (making the visitor wait until a scheduled in-progress meeting is over, asking the secretary to redirect as many phone calls as possible) rather than dealing immediately and directly with it. Putting these latter findings together with all the other reported city government-industrial differences leads to the conclusion that the governmental managers feel much more acutely the problem of demands from outside the organization, would like to be able to reduce such demands, but generally feel they are not able to do so (at least in comparison to how the industrial managers feel about dealing with similar demands).

More Effective Managers vs. Less Effective Managers

In reporting results in which managers from the public city government organizations and the private industrial firms are compared on the effectiveness dimension, it is important to stress that our criterion of effectiveness is of a particular type: namely, the superior's judgment. It is readily acknowledged that other measures of effectiveness might produce a different pattern of findings from that to be discussed below. Nevertheless, we would defend the organizational importance and relevance of the criterion utilized in this investigation because it is the one on which a number of major organizational actions are often based. (Again, the reader is reminded that superiors' identifications of more and less effective subordinates were made without knowledge that this was a study of time management.)

A word about hypotheses: On the basis of impressions gained from the small number of preliminary interviews, and on the basis of our own general analysis of managerial behavior, we made the following overall hypothesis: Managers rated as more effective by their supervisors will report exercising more formal planning of, and control over, time allocation than will managers rated as less effective.

Furthermore, we expected that such "effective vs. ineffective" (shorthand terms for the more accurate but longer terms of "more effective" and "less effective") differences in this direction would be greater within the industrial sample than within the city government sample.

A quick overview of our findings with respect to these hypotheses shows the following: The major hypothesis was substantially confirmed for the industrial sample. Effective managers reported more planning and individualized control over time allocation than did ineffective managers. Furthermore, the differences *in this direction* were, indeed, greater in the industrial than in the governmental sample. What we did not expect was the fact that the effective-ineffective differences within the governmental sample often tended to be in the opposite direction. That is, within the governmental sample, it was the *less effective* managers who tended to report more planning of their time allocations. Interestingly enough, our chief hypothesis was confirmed for only one of the two organizational domains.

In more detail, the findings look like this: On the eight attitude-toward-planning questions comprising Part I of the questionnaire, there were relatively large differences between the effective and ineffective industrial managers for six of the questions, and moderately large differences on the other two. The effective industrial managers reported doing more actual planning, greater desire to try to plan, greater feelings of control over time scheduling, greater feelings that the eight-hour day is adequate for accomplishing responsibilities, *less* allocation of time "on the spur of the moment," and *less* of a feeling of being rushed "with not enough time to get things done you wanted to do." The pattern of responses on Part I within the governmental group was somewhat different. For the city government managers, it was the *less effec-*

tive managers who reported doing more actual planning and desiring to do more planning of time. On the other hand, on the items dealing with the adequacy of the eight-hour working day and feelings of being rushed, the direction of effective vs. ineffective differences within the government sample was the same as for the industrial sample. On these two items, the less effective governmental managers responded in the same general direction as the less effective industrial managers: that is, they felt the eight-hour day was inadequate and they felt more rushed.

■ 16 ■
Lyman W. Porter
John Van Maanen

The findings on Part II—ratings of the amount of control over time spent in various activities—tended to follow the patterns of Part I. The effective industrial managers felt they had relatively greater time control with respect to most activities, except for formal meetings and the telephone, than did the ineffective managers. Within the governmental sample, there were relatively small differences between effective and ineffective managers on these perceived control-over-time items. The less effective city department heads did report, however, that they had greater control over time spent outside the immediate work environment on business-related activities.

On Part III where ratings were provided for the amount of time spent in planning each of six types of activities, the effective industrial managers did not indicate greater planning activity (and, in fact, on one activity—formal interactions with other persons—they showed definitely less planning) compared to the ineffective managers. (While the failure of items on this part to distinguish between the two groups of industrial managers is somewhat surprising considering the results for similar items for Part I, it should be noted that this particular question format also tended not to produce differences between the total industrial and public samples even though such differences were obtained on other parts of the questionnaire.) Returning to effective-ineffective comparisons, the differences within the governmental sample on this part were also relatively small, but they were consistent with the differences on similar questions in Part I: the less effective managers reported more planning (except for telephone conversations).

Estimates of time actually spent in six different activities (Part IV) by effective vs. ineffective administrators showed several interesting contrasts. The activity that produced the largest differences (relatively speaking) was informal interactions: the more effective industrial managers and the *less* effective governmental managers reported spending *less* time on this activity than their respective counterparts. On telephone conversations, the more effective managers in both samples spent *less* time on this activity. Other activities tended to produce insignificant effective-ineffective differences in estimated time usage within both samples.

Perhaps the most striking effective-ineffective differences of all were obtained on Part V, in which respondents indicated the relative importance they attach to various factors in allocating their time. Within the industrial sample, the more effective managers attached greater importance to all of the factors —except the formal requirements of the job—than did the less effective managers. Within the governmental sample, a reversal pattern was found: The more effective managers attached *less* importance to most of the factors as determinants of their time allocation. The largest and most striking differ-

221

ences—and reversal—occurred on "needs and demands of peers." The more effective industrial managers and the less effective governmental managers attached relatively much greater importance to this factor than did the other sets of managers.

Finally, the results from the five hypothetical time allocation problems contained in Part VI showed few clear-cut trends. There was, though, some tendency within both the industrial and the governmental samples for the more effective managers to utilize a subordinate's (in this case, a secretary's) discretion in helping them handle incoming messages.

CONCLUSIONS

The study that has been reported on the preceding pages is only the beginning of research approaches to the understanding of how and why time is allocated the way it is in managerial-type jobs. Nevertheless, as an initial attack on the problem it provides some fruitful leads for further investigations which, eventually, may provide some prescriptions for ways in which managers in particular types of organizations *ought* to manage their scarcest of all resources—time.

Our findings point to the following: The nature of the organization, at least in terms of whether it is essentially externally oriented vs. internally oriented, would seem to play an important role in task accomplishment by means of time management strategies. In our particular samples of managers, it appeared to be the city government administrators who had to be prepared to face the unexpected (and undesired?) intrusion into one's own time. Within this milieu, interestingly enough, the more effective performers (as rated by superiors) appeared to be those who attempted *less* time control and who consequently "rolled with the time punches" as it were. Task accomplishment in this type of organizational environment seemed to be related to abilities to accommodate to demands not under one's own control and perhaps not of one's choosing. On the other hand, task accomplishment in the more traditional work environment of the industrial organization seemed to be correlated with a relatively high sensitivity to time planning and to attempts to control time allocation. The industrial managers on the whole tend to report that their time situation is more controllable, and success (as defined by high ratings from superiors) is associated with those who report the greatest degree of control.

In interpreting the findings summarized above, it is well to reemphasize the nature of the criterion of managerial effectiveness that was utilized in this study: namely, ratings by the immediate superior. Though such a criterion is limited in that it represents only one of a number of possible criteria, it nevertheless is important from an organization point of view because of the many personnel decisions that are often based on it. In terms of the specific results of the present study, it may be that the raters in the city governments used bases for judging effectiveness that were somewhat different from those used by the raters in the industrial organizations. That is, it is possible that the very qualities in subordinates that resulted in high ratings in the city government situations may be those that caused low ratings in the industrial companies, and vice versa. Our findings may tell us as much about the "criteria of effectiveness" as they do about the respondents' perceptions of how they spend their time. In future research of this type, it would be useful to obtain additional information from the raters (whether superiors or others in the organization) concerning their *reasons* for rating subordinates high and low on effectiveness. With this information we would have a clearer picture of whether effective subordinate behavior was different between the two situations (e.g., city government and industrial) with the criteria constant, or whether subordinate behavior in the two situations was similar but the criteria of effectiveness differed.

Future research also will need to investigate much more extensively the impact of different types or organizational environments on decision-making aspects of time management. By systematically varying sampling across specified types of organizations, we should be able to add to our store of comparative organizational knowledge as well as to our understanding of how this particular resource can best be utilized. Another research need is to combine the type of study reported here that focuses on perceived decision-making approaches to time management with the types of studies (mentioned in the introduction) that report on actual time allocation. Such combined studies should serve to improve the analysis of the "why" of time allocation beyond the mere recording of what the allocation was.

The most pressing research need, however, with respect to time management as a factor in task accomplishment, is to conduct experiments wherein distinctly different allocation plans are put into practice for reasonably extended periods of time. As just one example, it is intriguing to speculate on the results that might be obtained if an experimental group of subjects rigidly adhered to a plan of allocating two consecutive hours a day to a completely uninterrupted (no long-distance telephone calls, no secretaries asking questions, no colleagues dropping in to pass the time of day, etc.) block of time to spend on (heaven forbid!) THINKING. The results from such an experiment might prove a useful antidote to the recently quoted lament of a top executive —a lament that is probably common among many managers, not to mention professors and researchers. This executive stated that when he gets home at the end of the day and his wife asks him how he spent the day, he frequently admits to something like the following: "I don't know what I did. It was just a mass of nothings."

There would appear to be a felt need for imaginative research on that scarce, inelastic, nonsubstitutable, and completely perishable resource called time. There is no _____ like the present to begin.

NOTES

[1] The authors wish to acknowledge the helpful comments of Edwin Locke and Fred Fiedler on an earlier draft of this paper.

[2] Perhaps it is necessary to acknowledge that, in a sense, time is an abstraction representing (according to the dictionary definition) a "system of those relations which any event has to any other," and that one does not allocate time per se but rather allocates activities during the passage of time. Nevertheless, it is both convenient and useful to think in terms of allocating and managing "time."

Lyman W. Porter
John Van Maanen

REFERENCES

Banfield, E. C., & Wilson, J. Q. *City politics*. New York: Random House, 1963.

Burns, T. The directions of activity and communications in a departmental executive group. *Human Relations*, 1954, 7, 73–97.

Carlson, S. *Executive behavior*. Stockholm: Strombergs, 1951.

Drucker, P. F. *The effective executive*. New York: Harper and Row, 1966.

Dubin, R. Business behavior *behaviorally* viewed. In G. B. Strother (Ed.), *Social science approach to business behavior*. Homewood, Ill.: Irwin-Dorsey, 1962.

Dubin, R., & Spray, S. L. Executive behavior and interaction. *Industrial Relations*, 1964, 3 (2), 99–108.

Hinrichs, J. R. Communications activity of industrial research personnel. *Personnel Psychology*, 1964, 17, 193–204.

Horne, J. H., & Lupton, T. The work activities of 'middle' management—An exploratory study. *Journal of Management Studies*, 1965, 2, 14–33.

Jones, C. H. The money value of time. *Harvard Business Review*, 1968, 46,(4), 94–101.

Kelly, J. The study of executive behavior by activity sampling. *Human Relations*, 1964, 17, 277–287.

Lawler, E. E., Porter, L. W., & Tannenbaum, A. Managers' attitudes towards communications episodes. *Journal of Applied Psychology*, 1968, in press.

Ponder, Q. D. The effective manufacturing foreman. *Proceedings of the Tenth Annual Meeting, Industrial Relations Research Association*, 1958, 41–54.

Wall Street Journal. August 13, 1968.

PART SIX

MANAGEMENT TOOLS

I t has become increasingly apparent in the last decade that a knowledge of management techniques and skills and their creative use is as important for public managers as is substantive knowledge about the internal and external environment of public organizations. Frequently basic to the introduction of management techniques to government is the problem of their transferral from the business sector where they were developed. How appropriate are business techniques to public-sector management? And what assumptions and conditions are required for their appropriate transfer? Earlier sections on the internal and external environment of public management clearly indicate that government is different. As a consequence of this difference, techniques developed for profit maximization, for profit planning, and for private decision making may not be appropriate for the public sector or, at the least, may not be directly transferable. However, there is increasing evidence, based on successful applications in the public sector, that many techniques are appropriate, if used with sensitivity to their assumptions, theoretical

principles, and requirements for adaptation to the context of public decision making.

Most important to this adaptation is the recognition that management tools and techniques are not apolitical. Their use has political, control, and other effects, which may not be immediately discernible but which, when apparent, are certain to give rise to questions about the motivation for their use, the inherent bias built into the techniques, and the resource redistributions directed by their results. Perhaps the clearest evidence for the political character of the use of these techniques is the fact that they are almost always introduced into public management in the name of "reform." The notion of reform clearly implies some desired change in the existing ways of allocating resources or dealing with client groups and, therefore, in the actual allocations of public goods, services, and values among interested and often competing groups. Sometimes, the aim of reform is less direct, that is, it is aimed at changing the ways in which political and bureaucratic decision making is conducted —at increasing the explicitness of public decision making—rather than at changing

225

specific decision outcomes. Here it is hoped that reform in the *process* of decision making will produce changes in political outcomes.

The political character of the application of management tools in government helps to explain why such techniques have advanced less rapidly in government than in business. It also helps to explain why successive attempts to introduce new techniques, such as in the area of public budgeting, have consistently failed to stick or to bring about the desired changes. Despite the remarkable lack of success of management techniques in government, their use continues to be advocated even by their harshest critics. Consequently, this section examines seven major areas where management techniques have been applied in the public sector and, by so doing, suggests, at least indirectly, both the possibilities and the conditions for their effective use. These areas are accounting and financial reporting, managerial finance, marketing, management science, organizational development, management by objectives, and collective bargaining.

Governmental accounting and financial reporting are perhaps the oldest and the best-developed management tools in government. However, Frank M. Patitucci argues that accounting and financial reporting practices in the public sector lag seriously behind private-sector practices and are in urgent need of reform. Patitucci focuses on municipal accounting and financial reporting in the public sector. He argues that the key problem with current practices is that they generate confusing and misleading information for government managers, policy makers, and the public.

The importance of accounting and financial reporting practices is illustrated by two examples—one from business and one from municipal accounting. Patitucci notes that in the 1960s many corporate conglomerates flourished because of a then-accepted accounting and financial reporting practice that allowed corporations to report acquisitions in such a way that the earnings per share of stock of the conglomerate appeared to be growing rapidly. Although these were only "paper" calculations, they were interpreted by both stockbrokers and corporate managers as reflecting real growth and value, and the result was a rapid rise in stock prices. By the late 1960s, a close examination of these conglomerates revealed that, after a merger, the growth-and-profit patterns of acquired companies actually did not change much from what they had been before. The growth in earnings was mainly on paper, and there was no justification for the high values and continued rise in stock prices. As a result, the accounting profession was called on to change the rules for reporting acquisitions and combinations; when this occurred, the stock prices of the conglomerates tumbled.

Similarly misleading information is produced as a result of municipal accounting and financial reporting practices. For example, municipalities do not equate current tax revenues with the current costs of providing services. This practice results in distorted taxing and spending policies that allow "free" benefits from past expenditures to present taxpayers or put off the burden of costs to future taxpayers. Moreover, municipal practices that separate expenditure data according to revenue source make it difficult, if not impossible, to see how revenues from a variety of sources come together to provide a single service. And, as Patitucci argues in his article, they also make it difficult to pinpoint the final expenditures for which a single manager should be held accountable.

Given the important impact of such

practices, Patitucci compares public- and private-sector accounting practice as a means of identifying specific problem areas in municipal accounting. He notes that there are two major differences between municipal and corporate accounting. The first is that municipal accounting is largely fund accounting, "a practice largely unknown in the private sector." Fund accounting treats separate sources of revenue independently of one another and of organization structure. Moreover, different accounting practices are used for each type of revenue and, therefore, completely different financial statements result. It is nearly impossible, then, for the users of municipal financial statements to obtain a comprehensive picture of a municipality's financial status.

The second difference between municipal and corporate accounting is that different municipalities use different accounting principles, whereas corporations use a comprehensive and consistent approach to developing and reporting financial information. Municipal accounting and financial reporting practices differ from state to state, from municipality to municipality within a state, and from service to service within a municipality. And these differences are both caused and aggravated by the federal and state government financial reporting requirements placed on municipalities.

Patitucci identifies seven major problems in current municipal accounting and reporting practices and then urges specific reforms for dealing with these problems. The first reform, which must occur at a national level through intergovernmental cooperation and coordination with the accounting profession, is the "establishment of a uniform set of generally accepted accounting principles for the public sector and a body to revise and update these

principles and practices." The second, which must be accomplished by individual governments themselves, is the development of "flexible and responsive accounting and financial systems, using basic, state-of-the-art computer and systems technology." Such systems would permit the construction of better budget documents (e.g., by relating line-item budgets to program budgets) and would facilitate both accountability and performance without complexity or rigidity.

Managerial finance, which has become the premier tool of business managers since the 1960s, is examined by David Methe, Jerome Baesel, and David Shulman. They note that public-sector educators and practitioners confronting investment and financing decisions are increasingly adopting the private-sector tools of managerial finance, but they also note that these tools cannot be readily used without adaptations, because the theory, assumptions, and rules for their application in the private sector and the public sector are different. To illustrate their point, the authors examine the applicability of four areas of managerial finance—working capital management, capital budgeting, capital structure, and operations budgeting—and conclude that, of the four, only the principles of working capital management are directly transferable to the public sector.

However, the authors note that even the principles of working capital management are rarely transferred properly "because the tools are often not fully understood." They cite as an example the now well-known fact that New York City rolled over an ever-increasing short-term debt without having the current asset base to support it and, consequently, experienced de facto bankruptcy. Whether New York's insolvency was due to the lack of under-

227

standing of working capital management principles is questionable, however. As much as anything, the New York City bankruptcy illustrates the role of political motivations and behavior in public financial decision making. Some observers indicate that the city knew the financial risks it was taking all along, but city officials continued to finance long-term capital investments through short-term debt instruments because they were unable to obtain voter approval for long-term debt financing and did not require such approval for short-term financing. Moreover, the banks and other financial institutions underwriting the city's short-term debt were fully aware of the risks involved in the practice, but they concurred because they benefited from the higher interest payments and shorter rollover periods on the short-term debt. Thus, for years, city officials and their financiers employed practices known to be risky until it became apparent to everyone that the city soon would not be able both to meet its operating budget requirements and to pay off the short-term debt, and the whistle was blown on the entire scheme.

Kenneth L. Kraemer and James L. Perry look at management science as an approach to decision making in the public sector and examine the applicability of specific management-science techniques. They conclude that the general approach of management science, which emphasizes systematic analysis of different kinds of public-sector problems, is clearly as applicable to the public sector as to the private sector (where it has been more extensively used). However, they also note that the development of management science applications lags considerably and that the development of techniques that specifically take into account the multiple-criteria nature of public decision making lags even further. Finally, they note the features of

the public sector that constrain the application, implementation, and use of management science techniques. Chief among these features are the character of policymaker involvement, the organizational impacts resulting from the use of management science, and the complexity of the governmental setting, as illustrated by the frequent lack of correspondence between problem and jurisdictional boundaries, the necessity for involvement of citizen constituencies, and the difficulty of defining public goals.

Philip Kotler and Sidney J. Levy next look at a management tool that is often considered to be the sole province of the private sector—marketing. In a stimulating essay, these authors look at marketing as a generic organizational function that originally developed in business, but that they feel is equally applicable to the public sector. Kotler and Levy point out that all organizations are concerned about their product and image and are searching for methods to enhance them.

Basic to their contention about the applicability of marketing to the public sector, however, is a special conception of marketing. Kotler and Levy note that marketing usually conjures up two meanings in the minds of people who use the term. One, which is the most frequent meaning, is the selling, influencing, and persuading of people to buy certain products regardless of whether they want them or whether the products are "good for them." Another meaning, which is weaker in the public mind and in the minds of people who employ marketing techniques, is that marketing is "sensitively serving and satisfying human needs." Thus, to Kotler and Levy, marketing is that function of an organization that can keep in constant touch with its clients, read their needs, develop products to serve those needs, and built a communication program to express the organization's purpose. Basically, this concept holds that the problem of all organizations is to develop client loyalties and satisfaction; the key to this problem is to focus on client needs. Although the short-run goal of many organizations is to sell people existing products, the long-run goal is to create products that people clearly need. It is this client- rather than product-oriented conception of marketing that is potentially useful in the public sector.

Tim R. V. Davis presents an interesting case study of organizational development (OD) intervention in a state welfare agency. This case simultaneously illustrates the usefulness of this management tool in the public sector and, harking back to earlier themes in this book, how differences between the public and private sectors affect the applicability of management tools derived from the private sector. Davis identifies the five general features of public-sector organizations that complicate attempts to use management tools, such as organization development, as compared to similar attempts in the private sector. The first is that there are many and diverse internal and external sources of influence on individual and organizational behavior in the public sector. The second is that public organizations are more vulnerable to these influences. Shifts in the external environment produce changes more readily and more often in public organizations than in business organizations. Moreover, such shifts are likely to affect features of the internal government directly. For example, Davis says:

> How closely the chief operating executive's position is linked to the seat of political influence will be a critical factor affecting the leadership and direction of the organization. The appointed official close to political sources of influence is placed in the difficult

position of assessing the external climate of political forces . . . and attempting to manage the internal resources of the organization to meet these demands. . . . Frequently, the organization head who seeks to make changes comes into conflict with the organization staff (the career civil servants).

Third, the potential for purposeful or rational change is more limited in government. It is limited by the diversity of service specialities, the vagueness of goals and performance criteria, the myriad rules and procedures, and the civil service laws regulating the hiring, firing, and promotion of personnel. Fourth, public-sector organizations vary greatly among themselves, and, therefore, each requires special attention to different sets of situational concerns—New York City is not the same as a medical school or a public health care system. Finally, the performance characteristics of public-sector organizations are obscure (sometimes deliberately so) and hard to assess. This feature makes it extremely difficult, according to Davis, for the OD consultant to "assess what is going on, let alone decide what should be going on."

Based on his experience in introducing OD into the state welfare system, Davis concludes that the foregoing features of public-sector organizations importantly affect the nature of such OD interventions. Two examples indicate the nature of these effects. First, the assumption, borrowed from the private sector, that the chief executive should set goals and make clear commitments "appears naive." Davis found that the division chief in the state welfare system was oriented to the supply of funds and sources of external political support, but the rest of the welfare agency staff was more oriented to service outputs and the demand for program improvements. The division chief's interests seemed better served by avoiding specific commitments, maintaining ambiguity, and keeping options open rather than by committing to specific welfare-program improvements. Second, the diversity of services within even this small organization was extreme in comparison to that in most private organizations. An office staff of twenty-two people was responsible for twenty-one different services, many of which did not overlap. Thus, the "incentive for cooperation and collaboration among the service specialists was minimal, while the competition for limited program support . . . was maximal."

Frank P. Sherwood and William J. Page review the use of management by objectives (MBO) within federal executive agencies during the Nixon era, when MBO was gospel for the Harvard Business School-dominated Washington bureaucracy. Their review is especially interesting because it illustrates how the values and aims of the implementers affect the implementation and use of the technique. Basically, Sherwood and Page are positive toward MBO as an idea. For example, they say that the "idea of MBO (as distinguished from ritualized process) must always be central to management action and thought," and they conclude that MBO is an "advantageous strategy in its goal clarity, in eliciting achievement motivations as objectives become clear, in its tracking wherein high achievers can see results of work, in improved capability to exercise data-based control, and in increased capability to provide rewards . . . in terms of demonstrated performance."

But Sherwood and Page also note that the "analogy of MBO to private business seems least applicable in public goal setting. Deep differences in the role and function of public and private organizations exist, and substantive rationality in govern-

ment may produce behavior that is quite removed from an MBO view of instrumental rationality. . . ." For example, a basic assumption in the model of MBO is that human behavior is rational. This rational model accepts macro-policy decisions as the parameters for analysis and decision making about objectives and determines the value of specific activities in terms of their consistency with broad objectives. However, as Sherwood and Page point out, it is difficult to identify authoritative macro-policy decisions (or decision makers) in the public sector. Public policy begins with statements of purpose from legislators and executives, but these policy statements are not necessarily accepted national goals. The American system of government tends to operate on the consensual establishment of goals supported by a majority, which may be "effectively resisted by a particular geographic area or interest group." Moreover, the goals of a policy or program may not be the real goals. Thus, a basic problem with the private-sector model of MBO is that it is based on top-down goal specification, which in its pressure for precision, quantification, and measurement may produce goal statements that are susceptible to precise expression, even though they may not be the important or the real goals of public policy and action.

Sherwood and Page conclude that MBO finds its greatest expression as a tactic in a hierarchical strategy of leadership. But they also argue that it could be used as a tactic in a different strategy of leadership—one that reflects multiple values and interests in an organization, that recognizes the importance of consensus and cooperation in arriving at decisions, and that gives at least equal importance to commitment to decisions as to the quality of decisions reached. This latter leadership strategy reflects the reality of management in the public sector and, consequently, the conditions for successful implementation of MBO as a management tool.

Lee C. Shaw and R. Theodore Clark examine differences in collective bargaining as a management tool in the public and private sectors in the last essay in this section. They argue that collective bargaining in the public sector exhibits certain practical differences as well as differences resulting from political considerations. These differences relate to responsibility and accountability for bargaining, the motivation of managers to bargain, and the basic bargaining philosophy employed. Although the authors conclude that public-sector managers can learn much from the private-sector bargaining experience, they also conclude that differences between the sectors make for significant differences in the nature of bargaining in government.

The differences in responsibility and accountability for bargaining illustrate this disparity. Many corporations are divided into distinct divisions, with the head of each held responsible for the division's profitability. Each division head is expected to stay within budget and is rewarded according to the division profits. Because labor costs constitute a major proportion of the total costs of any division, it is to the benefit of every division head to minimize them; thus, each is assisted by a personnel director who negotiates with unions and administers the union contract on a day-to-day basis. The future of the personnel director in the company depends on how effectively labor negotiations and relations are managed. In addition, the personnel director and division head have a management group to aid them in collective bargaining matters, including safety engineers, salary-administration experts, employee-benefit personnel, and legal advisers. The result is a sizable management

effort toward a well-ordered strategy concerning labor relations.

In contrast, many public-sector organizations still do not see the need to establish a distinct labor-relations staff as a part of their organization. Responsibility for collective bargaining is not fixed; no individuals are assigned the specific obligation to promote and protect management's interest; individuals who are thrust into labor-relations roles are expected to perform their normal duties in addition to this function; managers are not prepared by training or background to deal with collective bargaining. Moreover, in some cases, the responsibility for labor negotiations is assumed by the ultimate policy body—city council, school board, or county commissioners—which is composed of part-time lay officeholders who are ill-equipped to negotiate a collective bargaining agreement with professional union representatives. Even when these practical issues are resolved, labor negotiations in the public sector are highly susceptible to political "end runs." Shaw and Clark note that this involves an "attempt by the union to circumvent the collective bargaining process and make a direct appeal to the legislative body that is responsible for making the final decision." Such end runs are especially frequent where one or more members of the legislative body have strong political ties to labor groups or where one or more members of the legislature come from organized labor.

An irony of the debate about the applicability of private-sector techniques to the public sector is increasingly apparent today. Many advocates of the transfer of private-sector techniques criticize public management for its failure to integrate rational process and technique into public decision making and conclude that this failure is a major reason for the general lag in performance of the public sector compared to the private sector. The irony is that these analysts would impose private-management practices on the public sector at the same time that they are looking for new practices to replace those that they are attempting to transfer to the public sector.

The danger in the transfer of private-sector techniques to the public sector is similar to the danger in the transfer of Japanese management techniques to American business. In a recent review of two books on the Japanese way of management appearing in the *New Republic,* Robert A. Reich (1981) argues that the danger is that business leaders may seek to emulate the social reality of the Japanese workplace "through the mere implementation of new management techniques." The sharp distinction between the cultures of the Japanese and American workplaces "will remain intact but will be camouflaged by cosmetic devices—quality circles, work groups, collaborative teams, encounter groups, meetings of all sorts and kinds—which serve to soften or blur the underlying structure of management control." To Reich, it is the fundamental difference in the structure of management control that must be addressed if such transformation is to improve the outcome—the productivity of American industry. In short, the right process transplanted without attention to the corresponding change in the workplace will not achieve the desired outcome.

Reference

Reich, R. A. The profession of management. *New Republic,* June 27, 1981, pp. 27–32.

17 | Government Accounting and Financial Reporting: Some Urgent Problems

Frank M. Patitucci

This paper discusses current practices of municipal accounting and financial reporting, outlines the problems caused by these practices, and suggests what might be done about them. While such a topic may once have been considered dismal, in my view it is no longer so. In fact, it ought to arouse considerable public interest and concern. By way of analogy, economics was once called "the dismal science," but in the last 15 years, rampant inflation, the gold crisis, high interest rates, and price controls have shown its dramatic importance in such a way that much of the public now understands and is concerned with economics.

Similarly, while municipal accounting and financial reporting were until recently seldom seen as worthy of political concern or reform, the stage is set for change. Members of the public and administrators are beginning to see how municipal accounting and financial reporting practices adversely affect the policy and managerial decisions that officials must make. The financial crisis in New York two years ago was only the first of the major confrontations that are bringing politicians and the public face-to-face with the inadequacies of government accounting and reporting practices.

CONGLOMERATES AND CONFUSION: HOW INFORMATION CAN MISLEAD

A private-sector example demonstrates the important impact of accounting and financial reporting practices on managerial decision making. In the 1960's, a phenomenon called the "conglomerate" appeared in the business

Frank M. Patitucci, "Government Accounting and Financial Reporting: Some Urgent Problems," *Public Affairs Report*, Vol. 18, No. 3 (June 1977) (Berkeley: Institute of Governmental Studies, University of California). Copyright © 1977 by the Regents of the University of California.

world.[1] This entire "industry" was established and flourished in large part because of a then-accepted accounting and financial reporting practice: It allowed corporations to report acquisitions in such a way that the earnings per share of stock of the combined company appeared to be growing rapidly. These were only paper calculations, but were interpreted by the stock market and corporate managers alike to reflect real growth and value. The result was a rapid rise in stock prices. This in turn forced additional decisions needed to keep stock prices artificially high.

For a while many people made money—at least those who got in early and got out in time. Eventually, in the late 1960's, the bubble burst. Close examination of the conglomerates showed that after the merger, the growth and profit patterns of acquired companies actually did not change much from what they had been before. In short, the growth in earnings was mostly on paper. There was no justification for the high values and continued growth in stock prices.

Eventually, at the urging of the Securities and Exchange Commission, the accounting profession changed the rules for reporting acquisitions and combinations. Stock prices tumbled. The glamor of the conglomerates dissipated, and investors came to realize that a dollar of earnings from a conglomerate was basically the same as a dollar of earnings from an ordinary, single-product company.

INADEQUATE REPORTING OF THE GOVERNMENT'S FINANCIAL PERFORMANCE

What does this have to do with municipal accounting and financial reporting? I believe that current municipal accounting and financial reporting practices produce information that can be as misleading to the public and public decision makers as the reporting systems used for conglomerates. For example, present practices do not equate current tax revenues with the current costs of providing services. This allows distortions by permitting present taxpayers to enjoy "free" benefits from a past expenditure or, worse, to put off the burden of costs to future taxpayers. Further, present practice is to separate expenditure data according to the source of revenue. This makes it difficult if not impossible to see how revenues from a variety of sources come together to provide a single service. It is also difficult to pinpoint the final expenditures for which a single manager should be held accountable.

Present practices do not encourage simplified financial reports that could present the financial condition of the entire governmental entity. This makes it difficult for the average citizen or political leader to interpret the impact of current decisions on overall financial health. In short, present practices produce misleading information that causes political leaders, municipal managers and the public to draw wrong conclusions about local government performance, and may prompt bad public decisions. Until accepted practice is restructured into a rational and comprehensive system that accurately reflects and communicates government's financial performance, even the most conscientious public officials are likely to make some misguided public decisions, for lack of better information.

Private-sector accounting practice is used here as a standard of comparison to help identify the principal problem areas in municipal accounting and financial reporting. Admittedly private-sector practices also leave something to be desired. Nevertheless, financial and accounting professionals in that sector have rationalized a comprehensive and consistent approach to financial information reported by corporations and, most importantly, have established a method for revising and keeping their approach current.[2] So far, the public sector falls short of these two accomplishments.

■ 17 ■
Frank M. Patitucci

The following discussion has three phases: First, it defines municipal accounting and financial reporting. Second, it treats seven problem areas caused by current practices. Third, it outlines some recommendations for reform.

WHAT IS MUNICIPAL ACCOUNTING AND FINANCIAL REPORTING?

Municipal accounting can be defined in much the same way as private sector accounting: It is the means by which an entity's financial transactions are recorded and reported to provide an accurate and consistent financial record for a variety of users. While the ensuing discussion highlights some of the differences between municipal accounting and private-sector accounting, two major differences are fundamental and should be emphasized at the outset.

First, municipal accounting is largely "fund accounting," a practice generally unknown in the private sector. Fund accounting is the practice of accounting for various sources of revenue as if each fund represented a totally separate and independent entity. Thus, a fund has its own revenue, expenses, assets, liabilities, and equity and, except for interfund transfers, is independent of other funds. Further, a fund is a *financial* entity only, and may be totally independent of or unrelated to a government's management or organizational structure.

Under this concept, the type of revenue dictates the accounting practices. For example, general fund accounting will be employed for a general tax revenue (i.e., property tax).[3] On the other hand, enterprise fund accounting methods apply if the revenues come from fees received for providing services (i.e., water sales).[4] Thus these two types of funds use different accounting practices, producing completely different financial statements and reports for decision makers and the public.

Second, the public sector uses different accounting principles than the private sector. Three primary sources of these principles include: the National Council on Government Accounting (NCGA), the American Institute of Certified Public Accountants' (AICPA) Committee on Government Accounting and Auditing, and government itself at all levels. More about this later.

Financial reporting merely presents accounting information in a report for one or more user groups. Such user groups include: the public, elected and appointed officials, creditors (bond-holders), employees and other levels of government. The major issue is: What information do the user groups need? Many of the problems discussed below result from different answers to this question.

LACK OF UNIFORMLY ACCEPTED PRINCIPLES
AND A MECHANISM TO KEEP THEM CURRENT

The first major problem is the lack of a *uniform body of generally accepted accounting principles to guide public sector financial record keeping and reporting*. Until 1974, the National Council on Governmental Accounting (NCGA)—closely affiliated with the Municipal Finance Officers Association (MFOA)[5]—was the only organization attempting to set forth a comprehensive set of accounting principles for governments.

NCGA periodically issues a guidebook, *Governmental Accounting, Auditing and Financial Reporting*,[6] affectionately known as "GAAFR." Most local directors of finance consider this book the "Bible" of governmental accounting. The 13 principles in the most recent edition's first chapter are basically the same principles that have guided municipal accounting and financial reporting for the past 50 years.

State-imposed reporting requirements offer a challenge to the NCGA's supremacy. Increasingly, state legislatures are establishing reporting requirements for their own local jurisdictions. Rather than enunciating accounting principles, however, these state laws typically prescribe detailed accounting systems that *must* be used by local jurisdictions.[7]

The NCGA's most serious challenge, however, comes from the public accounting profession. In 1972, the American Institute of Certified Public Accountants (AICPA) formed a Committee on Governmental Accounting and Auditing. In 1974, the committee produced its own guide for financial reporting, accounting, and auditing of public sector institutions.[8] While the AICPA did not attack the principles of the NCGA head-on, they did note significant differences in approach.[9]

Few local governments comply with all of these standards. Even within the same state there is often little or no uniformity of financial reporting from one local jurisdiction to the next. Independent audits are required in less than half of the major U.S. cities.[10] Many local governments do not even produce an annual financial report, whether audited or unaudited.

Another dimension of this problem is the absence of a *central body—like the Financial Accounting Standards Board in the private sector—to establish and revise standards and resolve issues relating to them*. Through its various committees, the MFOA has tried to provide a self-regulating system. Annually, it issues a "certificate of compliance" to local governments that prepare financial reports in the GAAFR-prescribed format.[11] Fewer than 100 governmental units and special districts receive such certificates annually out of a total of 70,000 that could comply.

LACK OF FOCUS ON COSTS
OF SERVICES: "MODIFIED ACCRUAL"

The second major problem is caused by an inadequacy of accrual methods —the primary deficiency of current principles. Governments focus almost solely on dollars coming in and going out in a given period, with little concern for the true *cost* of governmental services. This is so in large part because municipal finance and accounting practices generally call for the use of the "modified accrual" method in accounting for costs. In contrast, private businesses use the "full accrual" method. A private corporation must always depreciate a capital asset for reporting purposes, i.e., the cost must be spread over its useful life.

A long-lived public-sector capital asset, however, can be depreciated in municipal accounting practice only under certain conditions, the criteria being determined by fund accounting. These practices lead to such public-sector situations as sanitary sewer investments being depreciated, while storm sewer investments in the same right-of-way are not depreciated. Inconsistencies in applying the "modified accrual" method lead to inaccurate reporting of the true costs of services, difficulties in comparing one government to another, or in comparing various operations within the same governmental unit.[12]

The "modified accrual" practice also makes it difficult to distinguish between who pays for and who receives governmental services. Purchasers of water from local government may pay close to the actual cost of the water they use, because water is usually provided through an enterprise fund. In this type of fund, a local government employs accounting techniques similar to those of a private business. Even so, many water utilities owned by local governments use buildings and facilities (i.e., City Hall) that were purchased with direct appropriations from taxes paid by the general taxpayer. These costs do not show up in the cost of water, and the general taxpayer is unknowingly subsidizing the water utility.

In the general fund, this situation can be much worse. For example, many local governments buy capital equipment and other fixed assets only when it is politically feasible to appropriate the purchase money. The entire cost of such assets is thus borne by the taxpayers in the year of acquisition. In subsequent years, taxpayers only pay annual operating expenditures—they do not bear any share of the capital cost of the assets from which they benefit.

FRAGMENTATION OF SYSTEMS

The third problem relates to *the fragmentation of accounts, accounting systems, and accounting entities*. In a local government's financial report, it is not unusual to find various departments and agencies using completely different, often incompatible accounting systems, usually in response to federal or state requirements. For example, federally subsidized transportation agencies are required to keep their books in a manner prescribed by the U.S. Department of Transportation. If such an agency is part of a local government, its accounting system will have to differ from that of the government's other departments.

In short, fund accounting—plus federal and state requirements—has led to the financial separation of entities that are actually part of the same organization. For example, one afternoon a week the Santa Clara County Board of Supervisors meets as the Santa Clara County Transit District. The transit administrator reports directly to the county executive, and the county executive is considered the chief administrative officer of the transit district. Moreover, the transit district is coterminous with county boundaries. But the transit district's revenues and expenditures do not show up in the county's budget or financial reports because it is considered a separate entity in fiscal and regulatory terms.

This kind of informational fragmentation and confusion is virtually unique to government. It is difficult to imagine a private business with a wholly owned subsidiary, that would not be required to include the latter's data for financial reporting purposes. But questions of the legal, managerial and financial "boundaries" of governmental entities, and how they should be tied together, are not addressed by current public-sector accounting practices.

PERFORMANCE VS. CUSTODIANSHIP

A fourth problem is *lack of a performance orientation in municipal finance and accounting.* A private corporation's balance sheet and income statement is organized on the assumption that the users will be concerned with financial health and performance. *Financial health* is determined from the balance sheet, and by comparing consistently presented balance sheet values over a period of years. The readers can thereby assess the entity's ability to meet its obligations at different times. *Financial performance* is determined from the income statement, and by comparing income statement accounts over a period of years. These tell whether or not the entity's ability to keep revenues at or above costs has stayed ahead (profit) or fallen behind (loss) during the most recent period.

Municipal financial reports lack such a performance or managerial orientation. Instead, the primary purpose of municipal financial reporting is fund *custodianship,* i.e., tracking of dollars from their sources through to their ultimate uses, giving assurances that all legal restrictions and requirements have been met. By contrast, a *performance or managerial* approach would emphasize how accounting and financial information can affect, guide, and support administrative and public decisions.

For example, a department of a city government might be financed by two sources of revenue: (1) a local property tax and (2) a federal program revenue. Custodianship accounting would track each of these in separate funds. All auditing standards would be met, but neither the department head nor the city council would see a report showing how both of these sources combine to provide a single service to the public. Thus, typical local financial reports, while demonstrating compliance with custodianship responsibilities, tell the reader little or nothing about the institution's financial performance, i.e., whether revenue covered the true costs of services provided during the reporting period.

FOCUS ON THE BUDGET, NOT THE INCOME STATEMENT

In government the budget, not the income statement, is the major focus of decision-making attention. The financial performance of a private business is determined by how well it does on its income statement—"the bottom line." All financial transactions, whether periodic expenditures or capital investments, are interpreted by their effect on profit, the difference between income and expenses.

In a local government, however, the budget is the financial document of most concern. The budget is *not* an income statement, but is more akin to a flow-of-funds statement[13] of a private business.

A government expenditure budget does not represent the costs of services in the way a private business income statement shows the cost of goods sold or services provided in a particular period. The income statement of a simple, one-product private business permits the total costs as shown to be divided by the number of products sold, yielding the unit costs of the product for that year. This is not the case with a government budget.

This point cannot be emphasized strongly enough: *Budget surpluses are not the same as business profits, and budget deficits are not the same as business losses.* Attempts to overcome this distinction have created complicated conceptual problems, one example being "program budgeting." Many who advocate "program budgets" are really asking for an "income statement" approach to budgeting, rather than a "flow-of-funds" approach. They want to know how revenues compare with the true costs of services, *not* how many dollars happen to be coming in and going out in a particular time period. The public sector has no standard practice for relating a line item budget to a program budget, analogous to the private sector's ability to relate a corporate flow of funds statement to an income statement. There is, however, some promising work going on in this area.[14]

COMPLEXITY AND RIGIDITY OF SYSTEMS

The sixth problem is the *complexity and rigidity of local governments' accounting and financial reporting systems.* Local governments are at the bottom of the governmental totem pole. They are affected by policies of every level of government above them. Moreover, each local government imposes its own special requirements. In quest of uniformity in local accounting and reporting, many states have recently prescribed *specific accounting systems* to be used by local governments. (Employing a *set of principles* as a means of control is usually discarded in the mistaken belief that requiring more detail automatically means more control.) In the process, local accounting systems have become more and more complex, detailed, and rigid, and consequently more and more fragile. Many systems are like houses of cards—even minor changes could cause them to fall apart completely.

This is occurring at a time when systems ought to be made more flexible rather than less so.[15] We can safely predict one thing: The future is not going to be like the past. System flexibility is essential.

LEGAL COMPLIANCE VS. RESPONSIBLE REPORTING

The seventh problem is *an overemphasis on legal compliance.* In government, emphasis on legal compliance often interferes with responsible accounting and reporting practices. Local finance departments generally respond to legal requirements first, and second to the requirements for financial information desired by the administration or the public. In many cases, the only financial information available from a finance department is what must be reported to meet a federal grant requirement or a state reporting law. The administrators' problem is like trying to understand or manage a private business using only its annual tax return, or the forms that are filed with government regulatory agencies.

(I caution the reader not to be overly critical of local governments' finance directors and finance departments in this matter. They have recently faced mushrooming reporting requirements imposed by state and federal laws and regulations. Meeting these is an extremely difficult and expensive task.)

WHAT SHOULD BE DONE?

What should be done about these problems, when, and by whom?

The quest for answers to these difficult questions is complicated by the large number of people, groups, and institutions involved. These include local finance officers and treasurers; local, state, and federal elected officials; accounting professionals; government managers; and municipal bond purchasers, to name a few. All have agendas for reform, or strong reasons for maintaining the status quo. My recommendations are made within this context.

When are solutions needed? As soon as possible. There can be no more delay. The rapid growth in the size, scope and impact of state and local governments gives them a major role in our economy and personal lives. We can no longer afford the risk of making financially irresponsible public decisions based on inadequate accounting and financial information.

What should be done and by whom? In trying to find answers, I believe the first four problems outlined above can be taken together. Their solution calls for *establishment of a uniform set of generally accepted accounting principles for the public sector, and of a body to revise and update these principles and practices.* The generally accepted accounting principles for municipal accounting, and the resulting financial reporting must, at a minimum: (1) provide for adequate accrual methods, so the true costs of government are known, reported, and paid for by present taxpayers; (2) eliminate the fragmentation of accounts and accounting systems, forcing consolidation and requiring consistent accounting methods within and among governmental jurisdictions; and, most importantly, (3) provide for reports that present an entity's financial performance and financial health, rather than focusing solely on custodianship.

Two groups should take principal responsibility for these reforms: (1) state and federal governments, and (2) the accounting profession. Some segments of the accounting profession have already begun to push for one major reform: the application of private sector accounting and reporting principles to government as a short cut to reforming municipal accounting and financial reporting.[16] The federal government has also begun to consider the regulation of accounting and financial reporting, primarily by requiring disclosure of specific financial information before the sale of tax-free municipal bonds is authorized. State governments, unfortunately, are continuing to require more and more detailed compliance with state-prescribed accounting systems and reports, often violating responsible accounting principles.

State and federal government officials alike should consider giving the accounting profession a period of time—say three years—to develop a set of generally accepted accounting principles and financial reporting formats for state and local governments. During this period, the profession should also be required to establish a mechanism[17] to write, update, and revise these principles. If the principles were developed, and the system put in place by the end of the period, federal and state governments could then require all jurisdictions to have an annual independent audit made in accordance with these principles, much the way private businesses do today. Further, federal and state governments could begin to rely on the information prepared for these audits to meet their various departmental and programmatic requirements. Thus, everyone could eventually be working from the same basic accounting and financial information, to satisfy a variety of reporting and auditing needs.

The fifth and sixth problems identified above—relating to the meaning of the budget and the rigidity of accounting and financial reporting systems—can only be solved by individual local governments themselves. Municipal governmental budgeting practices, unlike financial reporting practices, are evolving rapidly. Many local governments are taking innovative and interesting approaches to the budgeting area.[18] The number of efforts, however, must be increased and reform extended to the financial practices that relate to budgeting. Further, private-sector technology and expertise are available to develop flexible and responsive accounting and financial systems, using basic, state-of-the-art computer and systems technology.[19] Complexity and rigidity can be dealt with if local finance officials and managers are willing to re-examine their existing systems and replace them with more recent technology.

Finally, only the state and federal governments can solve the problem of overemphasis on compliance with legal requirements. If a set of generally accepted accounting principles were in common use, requiring consistent and comparable reporting for all governmental jurisdictions, there would be less need to impose special requirements for information and special audits (e.g., of the transportation and community development programs) on local government. While we wait for this to happen, state and federal governments should be encouraged to seek ways to reduce mushrooming demands for detailed information from subsidiary governments, and to find ways to use the same basic information to satisfy a variety of needs. The state and federal governments could start on this task immediately.

CONCLUSION

Something needs to be done, and soon. Otherwise the well-intentioned individual actions that have already been taken, plus likely future measures to solve narrow accounting or reporting problems, will create an undecipherable overall accounting and financial reporting mess in state and local government.

We need to look at the total picture and develop a system of accounting and financial reporting principles on which all governmental levels, and the general public, can rely for current, accurate and comparable financial information. Basically, good information can alert decision makers and the public and provide an early warning of developing dangers and the need for timely action. Otherwise, many more local governments and perhaps some of our states will suffer from the same sort of tactics that left many oblivious to the real situation in New York City two years ago. One such experience should be enough.

NOTES

[1]Conglomerates were epitomized by such firms as Litton Industries, Gulf and Western, TRW, and other corporations whose names told nothing about the companies' products. These companies claimed that their rapid growth through corporate acquisition should be reflected in a higher stock price, because they could provide better overall management. They allegedly would create a kind of "synergy" by combining two mundane companies, such as one making steam engines and another manufacturing fire-fighting equipment, and quickly set up a combination that was more valuable than the sum of its two parts.

[2]The Financial Accounting Standards Board (FASB) has been established by the accounting profession to continually review and update generally accepted accounting and reporting standards for private enterprises.

[3]General fund accounting uses a modified accrual method, and does not permit depreciation or the incorporation of assets into the general funds accounts.

[4]Enterprise fund accounting practices are much more similar to those found in a private business than general fund accounting.

[5]The MFOA is an organization made up primarily of practicing Directors of Finance.

[6]See *Governmental Accounting, Auditing and Financial Reporting* (Chicago: National Committee on Governmental Accounting [NCGA], MFOA, 1968). NCGA is currently updating this publication. An exposure draft (March 1977) is now available for review. In the writer's view, these proposed revisions will not to any significant degree address the problems discussed in this paper.

[7]See "Improving Local Government Financial Information Systems," Jan M. Lodal, 1976 *Duke Law Journal*, 6:1133–1155. See 1148–1152.

[8]See *Audits of State and Local Governmental Units* (New York: American Institute of Certified Public Accountants [AICPA], 1974).

[9]For example, the AICPA challenged the concept of legal compliance for public reporting. They held that a public report should adhere to the principles even if these conflicted with what a state or local law required. The difference between the principle and the legal requirement was to be footnoted.

[10]See *Sound Financial Management in the Public Sector* (Arthur Anderson & Co., 1976).

[11]I say prescribed format because it is the format of the reports that is important, not whether the principles have been adhered to.

[12]See *Financial Disclosure Practices of the American Cities: A Public Report* (Coopers and Lybrand & Co., University of Michigan, 1976), p. 36.

[13]A flow-of-funds statement presents a summary of those transactions (i.e., sources and uses of funds) that change the working capital or cash position of the entity.

[14]As an example, the reader is referred to the budget and reporting reform process now underway in Santa Clara County government under the supervision of the County Executive Office; and a similar effort being undertaken by the Director of Finance in the City of Dallas.

[15]See Lodal, n. 7 above.

[16]See *Financial Reporting by State and Local Government Units*. Sidney Davidson et al. (Center for Management of Public and Nonprofit Enterprise, Graduate School of Business, University of Chicago, Illinois, 1977). See also Coopers and Lybrand, n. 12 above.

[17]This could be accomplished by modifying the makeup of the Financial Accounting Standards Board to include public members.

[18]See n. 14 above.

[19]See Lodal, n. 7 above.

18 | Applying Principles of Corporate Finance in the Public Sector

David Methé
Jerome Baesel
David Shulman

During the past two decades, tremendous strides have been made in the development of corporate finance theory. Tempered by empirical work, this theory has evolved into a comprehensive set of decision-making tools for the corporate financial manager. There has been no parallel development in the public sector. Much of what is referred to as public finance originates from macro and welfare economics and is not concerned with micro-financial decisions in the public sector. Consequently, public-sector managers have tended to adopt decision rules borrowed from the private-sector literature without considering the numerous restrictions under which many of the rules have been developed.

This article is primarily concerned with the identification of financial policy issues, their theoretical underpinnings in the private sector, and the question of the transference of this theory to public-sector decision making. The article is intended to complement existing public finance literature rather than substitute for it. A secondary objective is to provide individuals interested in other aspects of public-sector decision making a perspective on financial-policy issues from a micro-economics standpoint.

THE BUDGETING PROCESS

A budget is a document that records the intended allocation of financial resources in order to fulfill the desired goals of decision makers as expressed in various programs. The procedure by which the budget document is drawn up, approved, and implemented is called the budgetary process.

Although organizations in both the public and private sectors prepare budgets, there are several differences in the process. In the private sector, business firms set up budgets for their respective divisions to cover periods from three months to a year. These budgets are used to determine the progress toward a particular goal set by central management. Data are collected on cost and revenue, and programs and managers are evaluated on performance in meeting their goals.

In the public sector, budgets are done once a year and usually provide the entire funding for the operation of the agencies. In addition, there are two more steps to the budgeting process in the public sector. As with the private sector, agencies or divisions draw up budgets based on some overall policy. However, in the public sector these budgets are then collected and reviewed by the executive. In the federal government this is done by the Office of Management and Budget. The executive has the option to change priorities for an agency by cutting one program and increasing another. Although large multidivisional firms in the private sector may have an executive clearance process that is similar, this is a relatively new phenomenon and is not as pervasive as in the public sector. Executive clearance occurs at all levels of government, federal, state, and local.

The next step in the public-budgeting process is legislative approval. Once the chief executive, governor, or city manager has completed the budget it is sent to the legislature, the ultimate holder of the purse strings, for approval. These two structural differences in the budgeting process introduce the next major difference.

Because the legislature must approve a budget before it can be put into effect, it can act as a court of last resort for the agencies that are displeased with the changes the executive has made in their budgets. Because the legislature must balance many competing interests, the principle of compromise is a major tool for generating a budget. However, the political rationale of compromise is often in direct conflict with the economic rationale of efficiency (Shick, 1973).

Although organizational politics exists in the private sector as well, it is of a different type (Porter, Allen, & Angle, 1981). As such, the budget process in the private firm is likely to be characterized by the dominance of the economic rationale over the political rationale. In the public-sector organization, the political rationale is more likely to dominate over the economic rationale in the budgeting process. As a consequence, some surprising inconsistencies are maintained. For example, subsidies are provided to tobacco growers, while support also is given to research on the effect of smoking on cancer (Wildavsky, 1978, pp. 165–167).

The discussion thus far has centered on the macro-organizational aspects of public and private budgeting. There is a difference at the micro or managerial level as well. The manager in a private organization carries out tasks that, in many cases, do not appear different from what public-sector managers do. However, there is a critical difference. The private-sector manager's activities generate revenues and costs because of the pricing mechanism, which governs the markets in which private-sector firms operate.

In the public sector, revenues are not generated by the activities of managers but are collected as taxes. Managerial activities in the public sector generate costs and benefits, but, as we shall see in the capital budgeting section, this is a much weaker symmetry than that which exists in the private sector. It is sufficient to say here that this weak symmetry leads to measurement difficulties and, hence, to manager and program evaluation difficulties.

We have outlined some major differences between private- and public-sector budgeting. The first is that the public sector is more commonly character-ized by multiple power centers. The second is that political rationales tend to dominate economic rationales in the public sector, whereas the opposite holds in the private sector. The third is that managerial activity in the public sector is asymmetrical in that it generates costs without equally concrete revenues or benefits, which leads to measurement problems.

WORKING CAPITAL MANAGEMENT

Theoretical Issues in Private Finance

Practicing financial managers tend to spend large portions of their time managing current assets, such as cash, marketable securities, accounts receiva-ble, and inventory, and current liabilities, such as accounts payable, notes payable, and accruals. Current assets and liabilities are short-term in that assets can be converted into cash rapidly and liabilities must be paid off with-in at most several months after they have been incurred. The more rapidly a current asset can be changed into cash to pay off a current liability, the more liquid it is. Cash is the most liquid.

Two concepts which play an important role in working-capital manage-ment are maturity matching—paying for current liabilities with current assets —and the recognition that the risk-return tradeoff found in other areas of finance is also extant in working capital management.

Application to the Public Sector

With maturity matching it is important to have enough current assets that can be liquidated into cash to pay for current liabilities that come due. This principle was not followed in the New York City bankruptcy. New York City rolled over an ever-increasing short-term debt (current liabilities) without having the current asset base to support it. As a result, when the short-term liabilities came due there was not enough cash on hand, nor could enough assets be liquidated to pay the holders of the liabilities. Insolvency was the result.

Risk-return is related to maturity matching. Return is revenue over cost and can also be considered profit, or, in the public sector, current assets. Because the public sector manager is concerned with cost generation rather than revenue or profit generation, is risk-return still relevant? Much of the analytical work done in the private sector tends to focus on cost minimiza-tion, which is the other side of the coin of profit maximization, rather than on what financial analysts accept as the objective, that is, shareholder wealth maximization. Thus, a manager can increase return by either increasing the revenue from, or decreasing the cost of, some activity. This fact, that cost reduction can also lead to an increase in return, makes risk-return consider-ations important in the public sector also.

Risk is the potential that an agency or firm will go insolvent, as New York did. Generally, the more liquid the assets of a firm, and the more of them, the less the risk of insolvency. An example of risk-return is with inventory con-trol. If the inventory of goods necessary for production, such as iron ore for steel making or pens and paper for an accounting firm or government office, is allowed to grow too large, there is a greater risk of insolvency, because this material cannot be rapidly converted into cash when current liabilities come due. However, if the manager buys these materials in large enough quantities, their cost is reduced. Hence the risk-return tradeoff.

Given the demands imposed on a manager by the need to monitor working capital, it is not surprising to find extensive literature in public finance that is concerned with cash and current-asset management (Forbes, 1978). Although no major theoretical stumbling blocks exist to the direct application of private-sector tools in this realm, in practice, the tools are often not fully understood. Private-sector working-capital management tools in principle can be useful in the public sector, provided the two concepts of maturity matching and risk-return are kept in mind (Weston & Brigham, 1978, pp. 172–195).

CAPITAL BUDGETING

Theoretical Issues in Private Finance

One of the major theoretical advances of private-sector finance has been in the area of capital budgeting. Capital budgeting is the process by which long-term assets are acquired. These assets are called long-term because they are expected to yield a return to the firm for longer than one year.

Two important principles of capital budgeting are the separation and the unanimity principles. The separation principle, often called Fisher Separation for its developer, Irving Fisher, states that, for perfect and complete capital markets, the production/investment decision for the owners of a firm is separate from their consumption decision. (Perfect capital markets are those that have no transaction costs, are perfectly competitive in product and securities markets, have no information costs, and in which all individuals are utility maximizers; see Copeland & Weston, 1979, p. 197.) The firm chooses the set of production opportunities that will bring in the maximum return to the owners. This is accomplished by engaging in projects up to the point where the return on the last project undertaken is equal to the market rate of return. This obtained wealth can then be borrowed on or lent by the owners of the firm, depending on the individual owner's time preference for consumption.

If Fisher Separation holds, then the individual owners need not be concerned with making the decisions on each and every production project the firm faces. These decisions can be given to the managers of the firm. The owners know that, regardless of whether they prefer consumption now or consumption in the future, as long as the managers invest in every project up until the marginal return on the last project equals the market return, their wealth will be maximized. Once this is done, the owners can borrow if they prefer consumption now or lend if they prefer consumption in the future. Because all shareholders implicitly agree to this decision criterion when they invest in a firm, this is called the unanimity principle. Thus, the managers do not have to consult the owners on every decision because all owners agree that the goal is the maximization of their wealth. If a project increases shareholder wealth, all will be in favor of it. Further, the separation principle implies that the decisions made to maximize wealth are the same ones that would have been made if shareholders had decided to maximize the total

246

value of lifetime consumption, discounted back to present terms.

■ 18 ■
David Methé
Jerome Baesel
David Shulman

As it did in working-capital management, the direct relationship between risk and return exists in capital budgeting. The important difference between the two is that capital-budgeting projects have a longer time frame, one year or more. Thus, the discount rate is that rate of interest that allows you to equate one dollar now with one dollar at some future date, in terms of purchasing power. When a project has no risk, the discount rate only takes into consideration the time value of money. The closest approximation to a riskless investment is a government security. As the amount of risk increases in terms of potential failure of a project and the loss of the investment, so too does the discount rate. Thus, as the amount of risk increases, so must the amount of return, in order to compensate investors for the possibility of partial or complete loss of their investment. The shareholder wealth-maximization criterion is analytically implemented by accepting all projects for which the cash inflows minus cash outflows, each discounted to their present value, are positive. This criterion is the net present value (NPV) investment decision rule. Consequently, the maximization of the shareholder wealth-maximization objective contains risk-return tradeoffs in this analytical process.

Application to the Public Sector

In applying the private-sector financial management techniques of capital budgeting, it is crucial to find a context in which the separation and unanimity principles hold. Communities that meet many of the special conditions necessary to invoke separation and unanimity have been formally introduced by Charles Tiebout (1956, p. 419). First, consumer-voters need be fully mobile. This requires not just the absence of moving costs in the common sense of that term, but also the absence of any limitations to labor mobility. For example, there must be no concern for the lack of pension-fund vesting in the decision. Citizens are assumed to have complete knowledge of all expenditure and revenue patterns in all communities under consideration. Constant returns to scale are required in the provision of each service by each community, and each community must be equally efficient in the provision of each service. Communities that offered little in the way of services would have low taxes; those that offered much would have high taxes. Consumer-voters have a choice over a complete range of communities that offer combinations of services and taxes.

Given a full set of communities that meet these conditions, Tiebout outlined a set of conditions under which consumers of public goods would reveal their preferences as if a direct-market mechanism existed. In this pure Tiebout world, citizens vote or register preferences with their feet. The act of relocating or failing to relocate is critical. It replaces the usual market test of willingness to buy a good and reveals the citizen's demand for public goods. Thus, each locality has a revenue and expenditure pattern that reflects the desires of its residents (Tiebout, 1956, p. 420). Separation holds because community managers can make decisions independent of elections. Citizens will "adjust their portfolios," or collection of goods, by moving. Unanimity will also hold as each citizen will want decisions made to handle resources as efficiently as possible so that his or her house will have its maximum value.

Although a direct mapping of the private-sector financial theory may seem

247

appropriate, another consideration, the type of good offered by governmental entities, must be taken into account. These goods, termed public goods, differ from private goods in two important ways. The first is that the consumption of the good by one individual does not exclude the consumption of it by another individual. This is called the nonexclusive condition. The second is that it is difficult to place a unit price on the good. This is called the nonpricing condition. If both these conditions exist, then a pure public good is said to exist. Fire protection is an example. When some fire protection is purchased by one individual, the benefits are shared by all in the community.

In order to capture returns on these goods, it must be possible to preclude enjoyment of the benefits. Public goods are commonly available to any member of a community and typically take the form of a nonmonetary good. Two considerations arise in applying traditional financial decision-making tools: the measurements of the benefits of the projects are difficult, and controversy surrounds the appropriate discount rate to apply to projects. In order to apply the net present-value discounting concept, it is necessary to place a monetary value on the consumption stream. How to estimate this value is the problem of measurement. Invoking the concept of utility is possible, but moving from utility to money is difficult without the existence of a market. In public finance, the willingness to be taxed substitutes for the willingness to buy. This leads to the rule that public managers should accept any project for which the citizens are willing to be taxed an amount sufficient to cover the costs. Applying this concept requires taking a funding vote for each project, or a package of projects called a budget, which implies that the capital-budgeting decision is not independent of the consumption decision. Thus, the first of the principles of private-sector finance, the separation principle, does not hold.

The public financial manager, in considering a project, may attempt to estimate benefits. However, even if benefits could be straightforwardly identified with money, it is inherently difficult to identify benefits. Benefits exist in many forms, primary (direct), secondary (indirect), external and internal, tangible and intangible (Haveman & Weisbrad, 1977). All of these categories must be evaluated and placed in money terms. The literature on how to evaluate them is extensive and beyond the scope of this article. Suffice it to say that the estimation of benefits is more involved for public projects than for most private projects.

In order to avoid a continuous voting process, the community may allow the manager to predict or guess whether the citizens are willing to pay taxes sufficient to cover the costs of certain classes of projects. In a pure Tiebout world, as long as the value of each house rises by the value attributable to the project, the project should be undertaken. Because anyone not wanting to consume the new public good may costlessly move from the community, the only way someone can be made worse off by the project's being undertaken is for the value of that person's house to fall before he or she can sell. Citizens remaining in the community, obviously, are at least as well off with the project as without it. Thus, in a pure Tiebout world, the objective of maximizing the value of the homogeneous houses corresponds to shareholder wealth-maximization in corporate finance.

In principle, comparing the present value of the benefits from a project to the present value of the costs is straightforward. However, the appropriate rate to apply in the discounting process is a topic of controversy. Two schools of thought exist. Kenneth Arrow argues that the appropriate rate is the risk-free rate (Arrow & Kurz, 1970). Jack Hirshleifer proposes the market rate appropriate for the risk of the project (Hirshleifer & Shapiro, 1977). The essence of the disagreement is whether the pooling of all government projects has the portfolio effect of the projects' being riskfree. A portfolio is a collection of projects, or investments, that are grouped together in order to minimize the collective risk of the projects. Arrow originally relied on the notion of a large number of independent projects being undertaken by government, resulting in the well-known insurance effect of making the portfolio riskfree. More recently, he has allowed that "if the benefits are uncertain, large in relation to other income of beneficiaries, and uninsured, then the benefits are indeed valued by society by risk-averting individuals and should be valued by society at less than the expected value" (Arrow & Kurz, 1970, p. 9). This suggests that the risk of the project should indeed be taken into account when selecting the appropriate discount rate.

Both Arrow's and Hirshleifer's arguments are aimed at the national government. When examining local government, the arguments for a risky discount rate seem even stronger. The caveat offered by Arrow above is especially appropriate to local government.

Accepting the idea of using a risk-adjusted rate, there is some controversy regarding how the rate should be determined. Hirshleifer suggests using the market rate for the project that would be used if the project were undertaken by a private organization (Hirshleifer & Shapiro, 1977). William Baumol (1977) and E. J. Mishan (1975) argue for an opportunity cost approach. The opportunity cost of a project would be the foregone return that the money invested in that project would have earned in other projects. Baumol and Mishan contend that the proper discount rate should be a weighted average of the foregone return on private investment and consumption. Again, risk would be figured into the private investment and would thus enter the social discount rate.

It seems clear that Hirshleifer's approach is to be preferred for two reasons. First, only information about the project under consideration need be taken into account. Second, there is no compelling reason to believe the projects foregone by the private sector in order to accept the project in the public sector have the same risk level. Thus, using a rate from the projects foregone may inaccurately adjust for risk.

One further comment on public-sector capital budgeting is necessary. Often, legal restrictions limit the amount that a municipality can budget for capital expenditures (Moak & Hillhouse, 1975, p. 103). In this case, the capital budgeting process must be considered to be performed under capital rationing. The appropriate analysis under this situation differs from that discussed above. In this situation, the discount rate appropriate for analysis is the rate of return on the most attractive project foregone by the budget constraint. It is well known that discounting by this rate may result in the acceptance of a portfolio of projects that differs from that using the market rate, risk-adjusted. Public-sector financial literature contains two techniques that correspond to private-sector literature. The net present value technique goes under the guise of the net benefits approach and the profitability index tech-

■ 18 ■
David Methé
Jerome Baesel
David Shulman

nique (the ratio of the present value of benefits to the present value of costs) is referred to as the benefit-cost ratio. Under capital rationing, the net benefit and the benefit-cost ratio may give conflicting signals. The net benefits approach gives the correct solution, because this will add the most to the value of the community. (See Weston & Brigham, 1978, p. 332, and Singer, 1976, pp. 309–312.)

CAPITAL STRUCTURE

Theoretical Issues in Private Finance

The fourth area of interest is capital structure, which, along with capital budgeting, is an area of important theoretical advances in private-sector finance. Capital structure is concerned with the financing of the projects undertaken in capital budgeting. Capital structure is the proportion of debt to equity that the firm has to use to pay for its capital-budgeting investments. Debt is raised external to the firm by borrowing from banks or other financial institutions. Equity is ownership in the firm, and dollars from this sector are raised by selling stock in the firm.

In the capital-structure discussion, the underlying concern is whether the investment, that is, the capital-budgeting decision, can be made independent of the financing or capital-structure decision. As is clear from the investment-decision discussion, the choice of investments will depend on the discount rate used. In the capital-structure question, the focus is not on whether borrowing and lending rates differ, but on whether the discount rate, appropriately mixing the cost of debt in terms of return to debtholders and cost of equity in terms of return to owners, varies as the proportion of funds coming from the sources varies. If it does, then the financing package must be known in order to make the investment decision. This complicates the decision because, in order to attract debt and equity, a project must be shown to have a positive return. This, in turn, requires knowing the discount rate, which cannot be known until the amount of debt and equity in the financing package is determined. This is circular decision making, where one decision depends on another.

Application to the Public Sector

In public-sector finance, the issue that corresponds to the capital-structure question in corporate finance is whether the tax policy (bonds versus current assessment) of the community matters. In a pure Tiebout world, the argument for independence of the discount rate from the tax policy is similar to that for capital structure in the private sector. This has been cogently discussed by Albert Breton (1977, pp. 21–22). He observed that, if local government finances an incremental dollar of expenditures through the sale of a bond, the taxes that will be levied in the future will be capitalized by actual and prospective residents. People with a low marginal rate of time preference, that is, a greater relative preference for consumption in the future, will contemplate moving to communities that finance through current taxes. High time-preference citizens will move to communities with bond-funding policies. This potential mobility will lower the price of property in jurisdictions with debt relative to properties in communities with current tax policies. If municipal bonds are riskfree, the difference in the value of the property in the two communities can be no more nor less than the value of the taxes. Otherwise people will move.

Breton argues that the potential arbitrage could be carried out in the municipal bond market. Arbitrage occurs whenever two markets are separated and the prices of a good differ. Then someone can buy the good in the market where its price is low and sell the good in the market where the price is high, provided transport costs are less than the difference in the two prices. In the capital-structure case as described by Breton, personal mobility will lower the price of property in the jurisdiction that uses debt financing and raise it in communities with tax financing. This, in turn, will alter the anticipated yields on bonds and on the property tax base and will cause lenders to modify the composition of their portfolios. They will do this by selling lower-yielding bonds and acquiring higher-yielding ones. Consequently, the values of communities will remain unchanged. Further, citizens will not have to move into different communities because the action of investors "undoes" the decision of local government (Breton, 1977, p. 22).

This argument is similar to the "home-made leverage" argument of Merton Miller and Franco Modigliani (1948). Their argument states that, if two companies are alike except for their capital structure and market value, investors will sell shares in the overvalued firm and buy shares in the undervalued firm, thus driving their market value to equality. This is accomplished through the investor borrowing money and investing in the firm that has no debt. The investor has substituted "home-made" debt for corporate debt (Weston & Brigham, 1978, p. 748). The mechanism that brings about the independence of the cost of capital from capital structure is the same in both cases: It is the arbitrage of investors that ensures independence. The assumptions under which independence exists in the Breton model are quite strict. As in the private-sector case, some form of compromise between strict independence and strict dependence is the most likely case (Weston & Brigham, 1978, p. 758).

Problems with the Tiebout Framework in Capital Structure

The existence of a pure Tiebout community, as defined in this paper, is unlikely. By definition, it can only exist at the local level. It is difficult to imagine a state government embodying the characteristics outlined above. Size of population or geographical area are not the only inhibiting factors. Even within a local government, forces are at work that would tend to destroy the concept of unanimity.

With public-sector projects, rarely do returns fall equally or in direct proportion to "ownership" (Hirshleifer, 1958). In the private sector, returns do fall in proportion to ownership of stock. Often public-sector projects are directed toward a specific clientele. Although all in the community may receive some benefits from a training program, those undergoing the training are likely to be the major beneficiaries.

Therefore, clientele effects are more likely to occur in the public sector than in the private sector. This is the source of the voluminous discussion of interest-group politics in the political science literature.

The public sector is also charged with the responsibility of ensuring equity in distribution of output (Musgrave & Musgrave, 1973, p. 10). There has been a long-recognized tradeoff between efficiency and equity (Okun, 1976). As a result, the equity dimension must be taken into consideration when evaluating government projects. Recent examples of the necessity to consider distributional issues can be seen in discussions of energy policy, particularly as it relates to price and income effects of oil and natural gas deregulation and subsidies for solar and other alternative fuel sources (Joskow, 1980). There is no universally accepted equitable distribution of output. When this is coupled with the interest group or clientele effects enumerated above, it spells certain collapse of the unanimity principle. Both in theory and in practice, there will exist minorities who are not satisfied with present or proposed projects.

Closely related to questions of distribution are questions of the incidence of taxes and expenditures. It is an accepted philosophy that our tax system should be progressive in terms of income. Much has been written as to the actual progressivity of the system. What determines the progressivity is the incidence of the taxes levied. Who bears the burden? The answer is beyond the scope of this article, but the de jure burden is often different from the de facto burden of the tax. Thus, potentially attractive projects can and are rejected because a majority of the voters fear the costs will be disproportionately placed on them.

A similar question can be asked in regard to expenditures: On whom does the benefit fall? The benefits of government programs can be distributed between the owners of labor and capital in such a way that, under certain conditions, groups not originally designated for benefits receive them (McClure, 1972). The proposition flows from general equilibrium analysis. In general equilibrium analysis, all of the owners of capital benefit from governmental expenditure programs that are capital-intensive, such as defense. On the other hand, all of the owners of labor benefit from labor-intensive programs, such as education. This is a result of the government expenditures changing the factor prices of capital and labor relative to one another.

The result of this discussion is the assertion that the separation and unanimity principles are less likely to hold in the public sector than in the private sector. This implies that the questions of capital budgeting and capital structure are more complicated in the public sector and appropriate techniques possibly different in principle from those called for in the private sector. Essentially, the analysis suggests that the appropriate discount rate is unlikely to be independent of the financing decision.

A Possible Solution to the Nonindependence Problem

Stewart C. Myers examines, in a private-sector context, the NPV rule in the case of nonindependence of the discount rate from the financing decision (1976). In general, for projects of long life and nonregular benefit flows, the weighted average cost of capital is inappropriate as a discount rate. Although the errors in calculating the rate are not large, they do exist. Further, the error rate is highest for high-risk projects that can be heavily debt-financed. The errors in calculating the discount rate are magnified in calculating NPV. Myers advocates using a decision technique called adjusted present value (APV), which includes using NPV with a discount rate that is the "rate at which investors would capitalize the firm's expected average after-tax income from currently held assets, if the firm were all-equity financed" (1976, pp. 349–350). APV would then add to that value the amount that a particular project would add to the debt capacity of a firm (1976, p. 349).

A similar analysis could be applied to the decisions of a community. The equivalent of the all-equity financed firm is the tax-and-pay-as-you-go community. It would be possible to determine a discount rate for such a community and then adjust the finding of the traditional net benefits approach by the amount the project adds to the community's debt capacity. A guidepost could be the evaluations given by the various bond-rating services. The lower the rating, the more the project should be tax-financed.

SUMMARY AND CONCLUSIONS

This paper has examined four areas of finance common to private and public organizations. They are the budget and the budgetary process, working-capital management, capital budgeting, and capital structure.

In the section on the budgeting process, some of the crucial differences between the two sectors were outlined: multiple power centers, the dominance of the political over the economic rationale, and the asymmetry between costs and revenue/benefits that occur in the public sector. These underlying differences have been responsible for the failure of many budgetary reforms that originated in the private sector and were brought over to the public sector (See Wildavsky, 1978, and Shick, 1973.)

In the second section, on working-capital management, it was shown that there are no major theoretical stumbling blocks for the use of private-sector techniques in the public sector. The major caveats were that the maturity matching and risk-return principles be observed. Where the techniques are applied without consideration of these principles, serious financial difficulties can and did result, as illustrated by the New York City bankruptcy.

In the third section, capital budgeting was discussed. Two theoretical principles important to private finance, the separation and unanimity principles, were considered. Because these are crucial to the functioning of private-sector capital-budgeting techniques, a framework in which they held would have to be found for the public sector before transference of these techniques could take place. A theoretical framework of this nature was developed by Charles Tiebout. Within this framework, private-sector capital-budgeting techniques, such as net present value, can be used.

However, the practical application of such techniques is difficult because of the exigencies in measuring benefits and the controversy over a proper discount rate. Because the issue of benefit determination must wait for more sensitive methods of quantifying the intangibles that public-sector decision makers must contend with, little could be offered by way of solution. However, with regard to the discount-rate debate, a possible solution was offered. From a theoretical standpoint, the market, risky rate is most appropriate.

It was also suggested that an appropriate maximizing criterion for the public sector is the value of housing. These last two points, the discount rate and maximizing criteria, hold especially for local governments.

In the fourth section, the capital-structure question of how to finance capital projects was discussed. Both the concepts of debt and equity found in the private sector can be applied to the public sector. The analog of equity in the public sector would be the tax base of a community.

Some serious challenges to the Tiebout framework introduced in the capital-budgeting section were raised. Only local government entities, such as cities, can fulfill the Tiebout conditions. Even with local entities, problems exist. These problems arise out of factors inherent in government activities. Two such factors are incidence and justice or equity as it is identified in the public economics literature. The incidence of both taxes and services do not fall in direct proportion to ownership in a community. This contributes to the strength of interest-group politics in the public sector. Furthermore, government is concerned with issues of justice or equity that do not exist in the private sector. As a result, there is a breakdown of independence between the capital-budgeting and capital-structure decisions. One must know the one in order to decide the other. Because this is often not possible, important decisions cannot be made or are made solely on subjective criteria. To provide a basis for using objective criteria, the system developed by Myers was proposed. This procedure can be used even when the capital-budgeting and capital-structure decisions are not independent.

One further comment on the dependence of capital-budgeting and capital-structure decisions is in order. When faced with a particular project, a voter will often cast his or her ballot not on the merit of the project, but on the financing of the project. It would thus be advantageous to offer voters several investment-financing packages among which to choose. Although this might raise decision-making costs, the benefit derived for the citizen is a clearer understanding of the choice. The benefit to policy makers is a definitive mandate from citizens.

REFERENCES

Arrow, K. J., & Kurz, M. *Public investment, the rate of return and optimal fiscal policy.* Baltimore: Johns Hopkins University Press, 1970.

Baumol, W. J. On the discount rate for public projects. In R. H. Haveman & J. Margolis (Eds.), *Public expenditures and policy analysis* (2nd ed.). Chicago: Rand McNally, 1977.

Breton, A. Local government finance and debt regulation. *Public Finance*, 1977, *32* (1), 16–28.

Copeland, T. E., & Weston, J. F. *Financial theory and corporate policy.* Menlo Park, Calif.: Addison Wesley, 1979.

Forbes, R. W. State and local government cash management practice. In J. E. Petersen, C. L. Spain, & M. F. Laffy (Eds.), *State and local government finance: A compendium of current research.* Chicago: Municipal Finance Officers Association, 1978.

Haveman, R. H., & Weisbrad, B. A. Defining benefits of public programs: Some guidance for policy analysts. In R. H. Haveman & J. Margolis (Eds.), *Public expenditures and policy analysis* (2nd ed.). Chicago: Rand McNally, 1977.

Hirshleifer, J. On the theory of optimal investment decision. *Journal of Political Economy*, August 1958, *66*, 329–352.

Hirshleifer, J., & Shapiro, D. L. The treatment of risk and uncertainty. In R. H. Haveman & J. Margolis (Eds.), *Public expenditures and policy analysis* (2nd ed.). Chicago: Rand McNally, 1977.

Joskow, P. America's many energy futures. *Bell Journal of Economics*, 1980, *11*, 377–398.

McClure, C. E. Jr. The theory of expenditure incidence. *Finanzarchive*, 1972, *30*, 432–453.

Mishan, E. J. *Cost-benefit analysis: An informal introduction* (2nd ed.). London: George Allen and Unwin, 1975.

Moak, L. L., & Hillhouse, A. M. *Concepts and practices in local government finance*. Chicago: Municipal Finance Officers Association, 1975.

Modigliani, F., & Miller, M. H. The cost of capital, corporation finance and the theory of investment. *American Economic Review*, June 1948, *48*, 125–160.

Musgrave, R. A., & Musgrave, P. B. *Public finance in theory and practice* (2nd ed.). New York: McGraw-Hill, 1973.

Myers, S. C. Interactions of corporate finance and investment decisions—Implications for capital budgeting. In S. C. Myers, (Ed.), *Modern developments in financial management*, pp. 347–371. New York: Praeger, 1976.

Okun, A. *Efficiency versus equity: The big trade-off*. Washington, D.C.: Brookings Institution, 1976.

Porter, L. W., Allen R. W., & Angle, H. L. The politics of upward influence in organizations. *Research in Organizational Behavior* (JAI Press), 1981, *3*, 109–149.

Shick, A. A death in the bureaucracy: The demise of federal PPB. *Public Administration Review*, March/April 1973, *33*, pp. 150–151.

Singer, N. M. *Public microeconomics: Introduction to government finance* (2nd ed.). Boston: Little, Brown, 1976.

Tiebout, C. M. A pure theory of local expenditures. *Journal of Political Economy*, October 1956, *64* (5), 416–424.

Weston, J. F., & Brigham, E. F. *Managerial finance* (6th ed.). Hinsdale, Ill.: Dryden Press, 1978.

Wildavsky, A. *The politics of the budgetary process* (3rd ed.). Boston: Little, Brown, 1978.

19 | Implementation of Management Science in the Public Sector

Kenneth L. Kraemer
James L. Perry

Management science is oriented toward the use of scientific method in moving to solve problems of public importance. It is an approach to helping decision makers choose a course of action and carry out that course. It does this by investigating decision problems, searching out objectives and alternatives, and comparing objectives and alternatives in the light of their consequences—using a constructed framework (a model) to bring the decision makers' judgment and intuition to bear on the problem. The aim is to develop guidelines, so that the public and private actions necessary to solve problems can and will be initiated and will ultimately result in improvements in the lives of citizens.

MANAGEMENT SCIENCE

There are four essential characteristics of management science as it is emerging today: (1) a comprehensive or systems approach, (2) scientific tradition and method, (3) the use of mixed teams, and (4) an action orientation. (See, e.g., Quade & Boucher, 1968; Quade, 1975; Majone & Quade, 1980; and Schulman, 1980.)

The systems approach is simply a way of thinking about complex phenomena. The idea is that, in order to evaluate any decision or action, it is necessary to identify all the significant interactions in the decision situation and to evaluate their combined impact upon the performance of some system or operation as a whole. It involves deliberately expanding and complicating the statement of a problem until all significantly interacting components are contained within it. This approach consists of looking at the entire area under the decision makers' control rather than concentrating only on one special area. It also involves looking outside the area of the decision makers' control to other systems and operations that affect what the decision makers are trying to do.

Along with the systems approach, management science is characterized by the tradition of science and the experimental method. Scientific tradition holds that results be replicable, that data and methods be subject to review, and that analysis be "intendedly" objective. Experimentation in management science is symbolic rather than physical. The management scientist builds a mathematical or other model, which represents the structure of some real system of operation, and then experiments with the model—holding some properties of the model constant while varying others and, in this way, determining how the real system as a whole would be affected if the simulated changes actually did occur.

The mixed-team approach of management science stems from the idea that one individual seldom possesses all the knowledge, skill, or experience to analyze decision problems. Although this may not be the case with relatively simple and routine problems, it is almost always the case with complex problems—the kind that decision makers are most likely to encounter in government. The mixed-team approach also stems from the fact that research, knowledge, and skills tend to be organized along disciplinary and professional lines rather than around the character of decision problems. The need for mixed teams, therefore, is related to the fact that historical divisions of research, knowledge, and skills exist and influence the ways in which various people approach problems. The greater the variety of ways of viewing and structuring a problem, the greater the likelihood that one approach, or some combination of approaches, will include all the important aspects of the problem and will yield a satisfactory solution.

The final characteristic of management science is its action orientation—a concern with actual improvements as a result of the analysis conducted. In essence, this means that the management scientist is concerned not only with helping to decide what to do but with the doing as well. It means that the recommendations of management scientists include specific action proposals for effectuating a decision that take into account what is to be done, how, and by whom. It also means that the management scientist is concerned with the implementation of recommendations and the evaluation of their success. Despite the most thorough advanced planning and analysis, something that was not anticipated always comes up in application—for example, difficulties in the task of implementation or unexpected results of implementation. Moreover, complex problems have a way of never being totally "solved," and major objectives are almost never reached before they are changed. Consequently, management science is aimed at building a process that will evolve and continually improve the way in which situations are met, policies and programs developed, and problems solved within the institutional setting under study. Thus, management science is, by necessity, action-oriented.

GOVERNMENT DECISION PROBLEMS

Management science can be applied to government problems ranging from the routine day-to-day operations of the various departments and subunits to critical one-time decisions. This spectrum of decision problems may be divided into the following categories: (1) operational; (2) programming or management; and (3) developmental or planning. This division is an arbitrary one and may involve considerable overlapping in specific instances. It represents a continuum from a lower to a higher level, or from specific to general policy.

Table 19-1 summarizes some of the distinctions found in these three types of decision problems.

Operational Problems

This category of decision problems includes those generally found in day-to-day operations of government. The questions of concern relate to efficiency in the immediate future—for example, "How can an existing system (person, machine, facility) be more useful" or "How can an existing operation be better performed?" These problems are relatively simple in that they involve only a small number of interdependent factors. Objectives are singular, known (or readily definable), and agreed upon. The criterion for the choice of one system or operation over another is fairly obvious and straightforward.

Analysis of these problems is subject to fairly rigorous quantification. Except for the specific context of government, much of the analysis is essentially like that used for decision making in business, industry, or defense. In other words, a general characteristic of problems in this category is that they are, or can be, well structured. Thus, decision makers can be helped simply by applying systematic computational routines to a "generic" model that can be made relevant to a wide variety of operations merely by modifying certain features. Several standard models and techniques have been developed for many such problems. When new techniques are developed, they are most readily transplanted. Examples of problems in this category are buying policy and inventory control, personnel assignment (to jobs, training, or locations), distribution routing, replacement and maintenance, waiting lines, location of facilities, and search or detection.

Programming (Management) Problems

This category includes problems involving the integration of various systems and operations to attain some overall objective. The questions of concern are those regarding the effectiveness and appropriateness of a system beyond the immediate future—for example, "How can an existing system be redesigned (or a new one designed) to function better as a whole?" or "How well do alternative systems (including existing ones) achieve some overall objective?" These problems involve many interrelated factors, and the choice of which to include in analyzing a problem is a key issue. Further, because these problems are concerned with the future, uncertainties become important. And the more extended the future time period is, the greater are the number and degrees of uncertainties. These uncertainties may be about planning factors (such as service demands or revenues), the strategic context or environment, technological development, or change elements in the real world.

Multiple and conflicting objectives and criteria for choice also characterize management problems. The selection of objectives and criteria is frequently the central issue—for example, "What do we really want our systems to accomplish?" and "How do we test the alternative systems to see which accomplishes our objectives best?" Time phasing is also important here, for what is appropriate for one time period may not be for another. For example, "Should governments go into operation now with some particular computer configuration, or should they wait until better computer systems are developed?" Configuration A may be suitable for 1980 but not especially workable for 1985, whereas the reverse may be the case with configuration B.

The analysis of programming problems is rarely subject to complete quantification and solution by mathematical techniques, although various parts of a problem may be. Often, all one can do is develop an imitation of the system and work toward a solution by trial-and-error techniques of simulation. The models used will, therefore, most often be ad hoc. That is, they will be models developed to represent a specific system rather than general models, which fit a wide variety of contexts. However, they may be used again and again in the context of the specific system modeled.

Illustrative problems in this category include budgeting (whether capital, operating, or program), organization design, scheduling and control of projects and operations, operations management, financial management, facility layout, and some planning problems.

Development (Planning) Problems

This category of problems includes those that involve determining objectives for future systems, inventing alternatives, and planning the composition of alternative systems. The questions of concern are "What needs will exist in the future?" and "How can systems be invented and designed to meet those needs?" These problems, then, are essentially long-range "planning" problems. Development problems share the characteristics of management problems, but in more acute form. The factors involved are numerous, uncertainty about the future is great, time phasing is critical. Because development problems are concerned with systems that presently do not exist, a key task of the analysis is to seek appropriate objectives and to "invent" alternative system designs.

Most often quantitative techniques will not be helpful to either the definition of objectives or the creation of alternatives. Qualitative techniques, such as brainstorming and scenario writing, can be helpful. Further, when alternative systems have been developed, simulation techniques can be used to compare them. Finally, subparts of the systems designed may be subject to quantitative treatment.

Examples of problems in this category are: development of transportation, building and other physical systems; and development of policies for education, health, welfare, public safety, and other governmental activities. Thus, developmental problems may focus on physical systems or on "systems of policy," which eventually result in physical actions in a specific context.

APPLICATION OF MANAGEMENT SCIENCE TO DECISION PROBLEMS

The Process of Analysis

There are various steps in the process of analysis used by management science, but they can be described simply as involving four interrelated activities: perception, design, evaluation, and implementation. In perception, the issues are clarified, the extent of inquiry is limited, and the objectives identified in a way that is helpful to picking an alternative. Design involves the identification of existing alternatives, the creation of new alternatives, and the gathering of information for comparison of alternatives. In evaluation, the alternatives are examined for feasibility and compared in terms of their bene-

TABLE 19-1
Characteristics of Operational, Programming, and Development Problems

Dimensions for Comparison	OPERATIONAL	PROGRAMMING (MANAGEMENT)	DEVELOPMENT (PLANNING)
Objectives	Single objectives; known or readily defined; agreement easy; efficiency-oriented objectives	Multiple objectives; difficult to define; conflicting; consensus difficult to achieve; effectiveness-oriented objectives	Setting objectives is key problem; values-oriented objectives
Criteria	Single criterion can usually be defined and quantified and indicates best solution	Multiple criteria; choice may depend on intuitive evaluation of net benefit from costs and benefits	Evaluation of alternatives largely intuitive but may be aided by expert advice or by qualitative models
Alternatives	Many alternatives available and usually easy to identify	Alternatives limited; new alternatives often not very different from existing ones; inventing alternatives is difficult	Inventing alternatives is key problem
Models	Standard models exist and can be applied to many situations; machine or man-machine models	Same as operational problems plus ad hoc (computer and gaming) models; man-machine or behavioral models	Same as management problems plus verbal models; political and social models
Techniques	Mathematical, statistical, economic	Same as operational problems plus qualitative techniques, e.g., simulation and gaming	Same as management problems plus Delphi, scenarios, paradigms, etc.
Quantification	Quantifiable	Quantitative-qualitative	Largely qualitative; may involve quantification of parts of the problem
Time	Short-term	Mid-range	Long-range
Uncertainty	Uncertainty statistically describable	Ranges of uncertainty describable	May only be able to indicate that uncertainty exists

Solutions[a]	Solutions can be derived analytically; usually a best one	Solutions usually derived by trial and error or approximation; sometimes solution not possible—best obtainable may be aid to logical thinking about a problem	Same as management problems; often only insight, understanding, elucidation sought—not solutions
Examples	Stock control; personnel assignment; distribution routing; replacement; maintenance	Budgeting; organization design; scheduling; financial and operations management; certain planning problems	Policies planning; transportation, building and other systems development; alternative futures

[a]As used here, solution refers to the notion of a single best answer.

fit and cost, with time and risk taken into account. Finally, in implementation, the chosen alternative is executed in policy and action, and the results of execution are evaluated for their conformance to expected outcomes.

The application of management science seldom proceeds in this simplified and orderly fashion. Often the objectives are multiple, conflicting, and obscure; the alternatives are not adequate to attain the objectives; the measures of benefit do not really gauge the extent to which the objectives are attained; the predictions from evaluation models are full of uncertainties; other criteria that look almost as plausible as the ones chosen may lead to a different order of preference; execution is imperfect because the policies and actions chosen to implement the preferred alternative fail to produce the desired magnitude of effects; and evaluation of actual outcomes in comparison to predicted outcomes is difficult because human and organizational factors confound empirical measurement of results.

When this happens, a modification of the above approach is required, for a single pass or attempt at a problem is seldom enough. In such an instance, the key to successful application of management science is a continuous process of formulating the problem, selecting objectives, designing alternatives, collecting data, building models, weighing costs against benefits, examining implementation policies and actions, evaluating outcomes, and so on, until a satisfactory solution is obtained.

Models in the Analytic Process

Models are a critical element in management science. They are a central feature of all phases of analysis and are particularly important in the evaluation phase.

A model is an idealization, an abstraction, a simplification of real-world phenomena. The phenomena of interest to government policy makers and analysts are our cities, governments, or departments, the activities carried out in them, and the relations between these activities and desired improvements. To emphasize the wholeness and interrelatedness of these things, they are conceived as systems. A model is a representation of the structure of such systems. And it is generally an incomplete representation of the real system. However, this incompleteness is both a virtue and a necessity.

The complexity of most real systems is so great that the total structure can be represented only in the actual system itself. In model-building the aim is to reduce this complexity, to identify the key elements in the system, and to understand the relations between or among these elements so that decisions can be made about those elements which policy makers can control.

A model, then, is an imitation of reality. It is made up of those elements that are relevant to a particular situation and the relations among them. Questions are asked of the model (in experiments), and the answers hopefully provide some clues, which serve as guides in dealing with that part of the real world to which the model corresponds. This definition of a model would therefore include: a collection of mathematical equations or a program for a high-speed computer, a game, a scenario, an organization chart, a land use map, a city charter, a budget, or an architectural model. However, the models discussed here will be those that use symbols (mathematical, logical, verbal) instead of physical analogs to represent the real world.

Physical and Symbolic Models

■ 19 ■
Kenneth L. Kraemer
James L. Perry

A model is a representation of the structure of a system. Structure refers to the relationships between or among the elements, components, or parts of the system. In the language of model-building, these elements are referred to as variables. The representation used to depict relationships between or among variables may be physical or symbolic. The most common type of physical representation is the scale model, such as an architectural model of a building. However, a pilot plant or project (a school building or a low-income housing demonstration project) may also be a physical model in that it represents a small-scale version of some planned activity in which the aim is to try out various ideas as a means of deciding whether or not, and how, to implement some larger activity.

There are several important limitations to such physical models. Generally, the number of relationships that can be represented is limited; for example, the usual architectural model can show form, shape, mass, and some exercise detail but cannot indicate the internal physical structure, room arrangement, support system flows (heating, cooling, lighting, water), or flows of people. If additional models were built to represent these things or if a pilot structure were built that encompassed all of them, the cost would probably be prohibitive. Even if the cost were not prohibitive, the number of items that could be varied or manipulated in any such pilot structure at any one time would be extremely limited. Thus, such experimentation would be slow and ultimately costly. Finally, there would be many activities and processes that could not be represented in such a pilot structure. For example, while it might be possible to have several families live in the structure and to observe their behavior to find out how well the structure meets their needs, there might be no reasonable way of studying how their needs change over time as they pass through various stages in the family life cycle. The point here is that sooner or later one runs up against limitations in trying to carry out experiments with physical models. When this happens, another form of experimentation is needed.

Symbolic models are the major alternative to physical models. They are considerably more abstract but offer several important advantages: (1) The number of relationships can be represented explicitly; (2) the elements or variables in the model can be manipulated and modified more readily, and therefore the number of things that can be tried is greater; (3) experiments with such models can be conducted more rapidly; (4) the cost of such models is often far less than that of a counterpart physical model; and (5) the models can be used to represent and try out things that cannot be done using physical models.

The most common type of symbolic representation is that of mathematics, where various symbols are used to represent the elements and relationships in a system. Increasingly, however, the symbolism of computer programming is being used to represent relationships.

Models and Purposes

Models and purposes are interrelated. As the previous discussion suggests, the nature of a model depends on the nature of that part of the real world with which it is concerned. It also depends on the questions that decision makers and analysts wish to ask of the model—the decisions to be affected by the model's results. Robert Specht illustrates this interrelation of models and purposes as follows:

> If you are driving from Santa Monica to San Francisco and have not yet decided on a route, then an adequate model of this part of California may be a road map. If you are a trucker concerned about maintaining a schedule between here and San Francisco, then an adequate model may be a timetable that tells you, among other things, when you are due to pass Pismo. If you are a highway planner who must recommend a freeway route between two cities, then quite a different model or set of models is necessary—road maps, topographic maps, maps of land use and value, traffic charts showing origin and destination, and a model, implicit and subjective, of the behavior of a population surfeited with taxes, attached to their real estate, and not altogether enchanted with freeways. Each is unrealistic in its own way, but each is useful when shaken well and taken as directed. (1969, p. 212)

The purposes of models may be classified as: (1) description, (2) prediction, and (3) planning. Very often decision makers and analysts need a device to help them understand the forces at work in a system, develop theory about how the system works, or organize and short-cut fieldwork in efforts to test theory and find out how a system actually works. This is the aim of description—to lay out or describe the relevant elements or variables of a system and to indicate the form of the relationships between or among them. However, in description the relations between or among the variables generally are not made explicit, and the resultant model cannot be manipulated to study the effect of changes in the variables. A geographic map, which can be prepared in whatever detail and scale necessary to convey an intended description, is an example of a descriptive model.

In other cases, decision makers and analysts are interested in the future state of a system if it continues as presently or changes following some possible but uncertain event outside their control. This is the aim of prediction—to specify the future state of a given system. Prediction does not require understanding of why a system behaves as it does, but only that it behaves in a particular way under certain conditions. Thus, in prediction it is sufficient to note that two variables, X and Y, co-vary (e.g., that the variable Y has the value $5X$). A model with prediction as its aim would respond to questions in the form: "If X occurs, then Y will follow." The likelihood of X's occurrence may also be specified, as may other events that may reinforce or counteract the effects of the hypothetical change in X. Models to forecast government revenues, population, employment, traffic, or land use would be predictive models. The emphasis in predictive models is on forecasting the future state (level, amount, or other characteristics) of revenues or population and not on the reasons why revenues or population may increase or decrease.

In still other instances, decision makers and analysts are interested in making changes in an existing system. They not only want to forecast population, employment, land use, and traffic, but they seek greater understanding of the interrelation of these things to one another and to government action, so that they can develop policies, plans, programs, and actions designed to handle the forecast states of each of these sets of variables. In this instance they are seeking explanations, that is, they are seeking not only greater understanding of what the variables are or their future states, but how and why they interrelate with one another. They need a framework or a model in which they can manipulate the elements or variables representing the system in question so that they can try out in the abstract different ways of changing the actual system. Thus, the kind of model they seek is one that explicitly indicates the relationships among the variables in the system and that permits the decision makers and analysts to manipulate the variables.

■ 19 ■
Kenneth L. Kraemer
James L. Perry

Models and Simulation

The derivation of a model by mathematical analysis fits many operational problems of governments. However, often the mathematics breaks down before the sheer complexity of many real-life problems. Consequently, the management scientist must find some way of experimenting in another abstract form. He must do so in such a way that there is a close relationship between the makeup of his experiment and the real-life situation, so that the real-life situation is not affected by the experiments. Such methods are called simulation.

Simulation is the process of imitating, without using formal analytic techniques, the essential features of a system or operation and analyzing its behavior by experimenting with the model. Simulation is a broadly inclusive term used to describe various physical or analog devices, such as a computer program. The method is explained by Russell Ackoff and Patrick Rivett as follows:

> Suppose we want to know the chance that a hand of cards at bridge will contain all four aces. . . . Suppose now that we could not lay our hands on a pack of cards and were not able to solve the mathematics of the problem. One way of estimating the result would be to place 48 white balls and four black balls in a hat and take our four random samples of 13. If we then replaced the balls and carried on with this experiment we could take the proportion of times which we get four black balls as being the estimate of the proportion of bridge hands, which would contain four aces. As will be seen, we have now moved away from the direct experiment (i.e., taking the real-life situation of a pack of cards and representing it by a bag of balls). In fact, we have simulated real life and carried out an experiment. (1963, p. 27)

By simulating a governmental decision-making situation, e.g., the budgeting process, we can determine the values of the controlled variables that optimize the performance of the system.

MANAGEMENT SCIENCE TECHNIQUES

There is no sharp distinction between analytic techniques and simulation techniques or the models they employ. What difference there is lies primarily in the degree of generality or abstractness of the models employed in the techniques and the way in which the models are manipulated. Analytic techniques employ models that are abstract and deal with aggregated entities expressed by a set of equations that can be solved. The analytic model is formulated primarily for the purpose of finding a best solution to the equations. For example, an analytical model could be used to find an optimal strategy, such as an assignment of trips over all possible routes so that time is minimized. The trips could be work, shopping, and pleasure trips on a highway network, or garbage collection trips, or police, ambulance, or fire call response trips on a city's street network.

In simulation, a computer model and a set of rules for determining what happens in the model under various circumstances are used. Simulations are used to investigate specific cases, such as the outcome of assigning a specific trip to a specific route. Each trip and route combination must be individually explored and some criterion applied to determine which is best. Thus, simulation is likely to be used in an experimental fashion, to generate specific case studies or instances from which a best solution can be determined, whereas analytic techniques will be used to directly compute a single best solution.

The analytic techniques discussed here include some standard ones but the list is far from all-inclusive. The techniques in order of discussion are: mathematical programming, inventory theory, queuing theory, and operational simulation.[1]

Mathematical Programming

Basically, programming is a method of determining the optimum allocation of available resources for a number of interdependent activities, actions, or jobs. Historically a program is a schedule of the quantity, timing, and partial distribution of the various actions in a plan—actions that involve the use of resources. The problem is to find, from a large number of feasible action/resource combinations, the combination that either minimizes the total cost or maximizes the total return. The costs to be minimized may include such things as physical loss, time, or expenditure. The returns to be maximized may include service, investment, or income. Thus, the central feature of mathematical programming problems will be a concern with allocation. There are several standard allocation problems.

The first, assignment problems, involve the allocation of one resource to each job, under the following conditions:

1. There is a set of jobs (of any type) to be done.
2. Enough resources [people, equipment, supplies] are available for doing all of them.
3. At least some of the jobs can be done in different ways and hence by using different amounts and combinations of resources.
4. Some of the ways of doing these jobs are better than others (e.g., less costly or more profitable).
5. There are not enough resources available, however, to do each job in the best way. (Ackoff & Rivett, 1963, p. 38)

Therefore, the problem is to allocate the resources to the jobs in such a way that the overall effectiveness is maximized, e.g., total cost is minimized or total service maximized. For example, the resources may be classrooms and the jobs may be the housing of students; or the resources may be garbage trucks of different types and sizes and the jobs may be collection routes of varying characteristics; or the resources may be highway networks (existing or planned) and the jobs may be various kinds of trips. The problem becomes more complex if some of the jobs require more than one resource and if the resources can be used for more than one job. This variation is referred to as the distribution problem.

■ 19 ■
Kenneth L. Kraemer
James L. Perry

The second type of allocation problem arises when there are more jobs to be done than available resources permit. Thus, a selection of jobs must be made as well as a determination of how they are to be done. Most budgeting problems are of this type, but as yet no one has been able to formulate a government budgeting problem (not even capital budgeting) in a way that permits the use of mathematical programming. The evaluation of alternative transportation networks in transportation planning is another example: Here the effort has been successful.

The third type of allocation problem arises when one has control over the amount of resources but must determine how resources should be distributed. The location of new facilities and budgeting problems are of this type.

A variety of programming techniques have been developed to try to account for various real-world features of programming problems. The basic technique is linear programming. As the term suggests, it can be used when the relationships between or among the elements (variables) in a decision problem can be treated in a linear fashion, that is, when they can be represented by a straight line. Nonlinear programming is used for that class of problems in which the relations between or among the elements cannot be treated linearly but must be represented by a more complex function, e.g., a curve or a series of curves. Integer programming is a technique to be used where the values describing the elements must be expressed as a whole number. Stochastic programming treats situations where the values of the elements are known to be probabilistic in nature rather than assured of taking only one value. Dynamic programming is a way of treating decision situations that involve multistage processes and in which the stages are all mathematically similar.

Mathematical programming has been used in regional land use and transportation planning. For example, the Penn-Jersey transportation study used linear programming in its household allocation model.[2] The resources in this case were sites (of various types and locations), and the jobs were households (of various incomes and family size). The assumption was that different households have certain specific amounts that they can budget for the bundle of public and private services associated with a particular type of house. The model was aimed at seeking a market-clearing solution in which households and sites would be matched. The solution was found by a linear program that assigned households to sites so as to maximize the aggregate rent-paying ability of the region's population.

Mathematical programming has also been used in various decision problems of local schools. One such use is in the assignment of students to classrooms, given a previously developed master schedule of class meeting times. Another use is in the development of the master schedules themselves.[3] Here the problem is more complex and may be stated as: Given a set of students with a set of course requests, a set of teaching staff members, and a certain limited set of physical facilities, find a master schedule of meeting times in which (1) all students receive their requested course; (2) the requirement for staff does not exceed those available and uses them optimally; and (3) the requirement for facilities does not exceed those available and uses them optimally.

267

Another use of mathematical programming in the local school situation is that of establishing school attendance areas, i.e., assigning students to various schools within a school district. Because population shifts occur continuously in urban school districts, schools are frequently overcrowded in one area and underpopulated in another. A related problem is that of school rezoning to achieve racial balance. Both situations can be viewed as resource allocation problems. The problem is to achieve an optimum balance between students and school facilities, taking into account such things as travel time and cost, racial mix, school capacity, and the total number of students to be served. Linear programming is one method of determining school attendance area boundaries, whether the aim is desegregation or better use of existing resources.[4]

Finally, mathematical programming has been applied to a variety of other problems faced by governments. Among these applications are political redistricting (Hess et al., 1965), where heuristic programming was used to draw nonpartisan political districts in Delaware and Connecticut; refuse collection and waste disposal (Beltrami & Bodin, 1974; Krolak, Felts, & Nelson, 1972); fiscal policy (Woodward, 1968);[5] synchronization of traffic signals (Little, 1966);[6] and ambulance allocation (Jarvis, Stevenson, & Willemain, 1975; Toregas et al., 1971).

Inventory Theory

Inventory theory is concerned with the problem of idle resources. An inventory consists of usable, but idle, resources. The resources generally of concern to local government policy makers are people, property (land, structures, equipment, material), and money. In simplest terms, an inventory problem arises because there are costs associated with keeping resources in inventory and there are also costs associated with running out of these resources. The costs of idle resources are basically storage costs but may include spoilage and obsolescence costs. The costs of running out of resources are basically those of failing to meet some need, including the cost of time delays. In such instances, the objective is to minimize total expected cost. The problem in doing so is to find the quantity and/or frequency of resource acquisition so that the sum of these two costs is minimized.

The most common occurrence of inventory problems is in supply systems. (See, e.g., Ward, 1964.) However, education and training problems are another instance. The question here is, "How often should a class be run and how large should each class be?" Cash management also involves an inventory problem, i.e., "How much operating capital should a government keep available?" If too much capital is kept available, earnings from possible investments of the excess are lost—an inventory carrying cost. If too little is kept available, additional capital will have to be borrowed at premium rates —a shortage cost. There are also costs associated with preparing, processing, and closing out government debt financing.

Queuing Theory

Queuing theory deals with problems of congestion at service facilities, that is, waiting-line problems. The waiting line is called a queue. Queuing problems arise when service demands exceed the rate at which the required service can be provided, and these problems are complicated by the fact that people usually arrive at random at irregular intervals to receive a service. This situation characterizes many government services: dispatching of emergency vehicles to answer calls for service, air traffic control operations, vehicle maintenance operations, telephone switchboard operations, and numerous over-the-counter services administered by government at all levels.

A queuing problem arises because, on one hand, there are costs associated with having waiting lines, and, on the other hand, there are costs associated with having idle service facilities. The costs of waiting lines are basically those associated with loss of time, for example, the suffering of a patient waiting for ambulance service. The costs of idle facilities are basically those of personnel or labor to man the facilities and the facility costs themselves. The objective in such cases is to minimize the total of these two types of costs.

Usually the decision makers have little control over the arrival of customers, but they can control the number of service facilities. Thus, the problem is to determine the number of service facilities needed to meet some level of service in the handling of arriving customers. What queuing theory does is to provide a way of predicting the probable length and delay of a waiting line formed by the random arrival of customers at a servicing facility of a given capacity. The decision makers can choose either to accept the waiting line or to increase the number of service facilities to reduce the waiting line, i.e., to increase the level of service.

It should be noted that there are several different types of queuing problems. They can be categorized broadly as (1) jam-ups or bottlenecks, (2) idle or below-capacity usage, or (3) special service demands. Certain services or facilities are jammed up at particular hours of the day or night and create operational bottlenecks. These are referred to as peak-hour bottlenecks and occur routinely in such places as airports and tollgates on highways, bridges, and tunnels.

At other times, services or facilities are relatively idle or are not used to their full capacity. There may also be variation in their usage at times during off-peak hours. Problems at idle times are frequently met with on transportation and communication facilities, in recreation and park facilities, and in schools, where the traffic (demand for service or usage) drops to the lowest ebb during a substantial time period, particularly at night and on certain days of the week.

Another aspect of queuing or waiting-line problems emerges from special activities or occasions in which existing facilities are inadequate and need supplementation, e.g., court proceedings, claim processing, and police and fire services during and in the wake of civil disorders. The provision of services under such special demands can be enhanced by hiring additional help on a temporary basis, personnel or other adjustments within the organization, or cooperative arrangements with other organizations. However, there are many other temporary or emergent special activities and occasions that require a substantial increase in the level of service for short periods. At the same time, the nature of these services is such that it is not readily possible to increase their level or capacity. These situations require a built-in mechanism in the overall system or organization to provide for such special demands. This kind of problem is readily observable in a nationally reputed football match that draws, say, 90,000 to 100,000 people. In such a case, traffic jams, parking problems, lines at ticket booths and other facilities, and all related aspects are congested, extend up to several hours, and put onerous stresses and demands on the overall system.

The classic application of queuing theory was made by the New York Port Authority in improving the management of toll collection operations on its six interstate tunnels and bridges, and for both improving service and reducing the costs of its bus terminal telephone information service (Edie, 1954, 1957). It has also been applied to facility location, redistricting in urban emergency services, and congestion at airports. (See, e.g., Larson & Stevenson, 1972; Larson, 1975; Odoni, 1969; Carter, Chaiken, & Ignall, 1972; Kolesar, 1975.)

Operational Simulation

The foregoing techniques involve highly generalized or "standard" models. Thus, the techniques can be applied to various classes of problems in widely different contexts. Queuing theory, for example, can be applied to any of a class of problems in which the objective is to provide a reasonable level of service to a demand whose timing cannot be predicted exactly.

However, problems often cannot be forced into one of the standard types. Or, even after all acceptable simplifications, a problem may be so large or complicated that the equations describing it cannot be solved. Simulation is a technique developed to handle such situations. Simulation is essentially a technique that involves setting up a model or representation of a real situation and then performing experiments on the model. Simulation could be applied to a civil defense field exercise, a group of subjects in a laboratory where the individuals play various roles, or a computer routine that describes the year-by-year changes in the physical structure, population, political structure, or economy of a community. In all of these cases, the real object of interest is difficult or impossible to study directly. A representation of the process or system, one that is similar to the real system in its essential properties, is investigated instead, and inferences are made to the real world from the results of manipulating the representation.

Discussion here is limited to a few cases of simulation.[7] Simulation models that "physically" resemble the process or system of interest and models in which human subjects play the analog role or in which human judgment and decisions influence the course of a simulation exercise are not discussed. Rather, the focus is on cases in which the representation is an all-computer model.

Simulation consists of the step-by-step imitation of the behavior of a system or process described by a model. When linked to computers, this process of imitation can be performed swiftly and thereby "live through" many weeks of experience in a situation in a few minutes or hours. For example, John P. Crecine has developed an all-computer simulation model of municipal budgeting (1967, 1969). This model reproduces the output and procedures of municipal budgeting through a computer program that represents the structural form of (1) the decision processes (i.e., the sequence of decisions); (2) the functional form of individual decision rules (i.e., equations representing actual decision rules); and (3) the decision parameters (i.e., values of constants or empirically determined variables embedded in the structure and functional relations of the model). The model considers three separate decision processes: (1) departmental requests, as formulated by the department heads in city government; (2) the mayor's budget for consideration; and (3) the final appropriations as approved by the city council.

■ 19 ■
Kenneth L. Kraemer
James L. Perry

The mayor's model is written in the form of a computer program. Into it are fed numerical estimates of revenues, departmental budget requests (both current and past), actual previous appropriations and expenditures in various account categories, salaries and wages for employees, estimates of allowable increase over current appropriations, and the like. Further, the model contains procedures for various types of calculations relating to the numerical estimates (preliminary calculation of total budget, check of preliminary total against revenue estimate, etc.). Finally, there is a series of decision rules describing the behavior of the mayor with regard to departmental budgets (e.g., if the departmental request is less than current appropriations, it is tentatively accepted).

When data representing various numerical estimates are fed into the computer, the program executes the various steps involved, makes calculations, and applies decision rules as indicated at each step, imitating the decision process of the mayor in preparing his budget recommendation. The output is a final budget.

This model can then be experimented with to determine, for example, what happens when expected revenues are high or low, when outside funds (e.g., federal or state) become available in some functional area, or when a different set of rules is applied at various points in the process. In this way, it is possible to study the effects of changes in revenues or changes in policies on the budgeting process.

Limitations of Management Science Techniques

The foregoing techniques, derived mainly from operations research rather than from all the fields encompassed by management science, share certain problems that currently limit their applicability in the public sector. The first is that they are unable to deal effectively with multiple objectives. Unless decision problems can be reduced to a single simple objective, most of the analytic techniques simply cannot be applied. While progress has recently been made in management science toward dealing with a clearly ordered set of objective preferences, the limitations of technique remain formidable. The simple fact is that many management science models and applications don't deal with objectives at all. They merely simulate the behavior of a system or operation under certain assumed conditions and leave it to the decision maker to supply the link, if any can be made, between an array of outcomes and possible decision objectives.

A second problem is that management science techniques rarely are able to deal with social and political variables, which comprise a critical part of many public sector problems. Such variables usually must be handled outside the models by whatever means are available to decision makers. One unintended result of this situation is that excessive reliance is placed on the results of the models when they agree with the policy makers' positions, and no reliance is placed on the model results when they disagree with the policy makers' positions.

A third problem of management science techniques is that they usually require further theoretical work for proper application to public-sector problems and enormous data gathering to supply the data required for the operational specification of the theory in a model. Such efforts frequently involve major research and development, model-testing, and model-validation before their results can be considered reliable. Yet, such efforts are often portrayed to decision makers as operational decision models that can be relied on for decision and action.

A fourth problem is related to the third—the timeliness of results from management science applications. Given the time and effort involved in theoretical development, data gathering and model construction, it is frequently the case that decision and action must be taken by policy makers before the results of the models can be applied to the decision problems for which they were intended. For operational problems, this limitation seldom exists, but for management and planning problems it is the rule more than the exception.

ORGANIZATIONAL AND BEHAVIORAL PROBLEMS IN APPLYING MANAGEMENT SCIENCE

The application of management science in government, as elsewhere, is potentially full of conceptual analytic and technical pitfalls that confound analytical efforts. Moreover, there are organizational and behavioral issues that must be considered in its application. Chief among these issues are (1) the role of the policy makers in the process, (2) the organizational impacts of using analysis, and (3) the features of government that complicate the process of analysis.

Policy Makers and Management Science

One of the most important issues in applying management science in government is the role and involvement of the policy makers in the process. Policy makers have a basic responsibility to come to an understanding of policy analysis—what it is, how it can be used, what its limitations are. In addition, they may be required to perform certain specific roles.

One such role is helping to define the task of analysis, i.e., the problems to be solved or the opportunities to be used. In this capacity, policy makers may be acting as initiators and sponsors of a study and/or direct participants in a study initiated by themselves or by others. Definition of the analysis task (problem formulation) is essentially a statement of the objectives and is critical to the outcome of management science applications. If this is left entirely to the analysts or to other professionals in the organization, then the policy makers should not be surprised if someone else's problem rather than their own is solved.

Because many management science studies are performed by organizations outside government, two additional roles may be involved. One is as evaluators of studies made by outside organizations. More than one government has contracted for studies involving large sums of money only to discover that (1) they were the training ground for some consultant organization's staff; (2) the problem to be studied was of little consequence—although the initial study proposal may have spelled impending disaster; or (3) the basic approach and study design omitted consideration of the social, political, and economic realities of government decision and action.

Another role is that of monitor and controller of studies conducted by outside organizations. It is insufficient to turn an organization loose on a problem and wait for the results. Policy makers must be intensively involved if the study is to be useful to them. A key reason for this is that public problems are social in nature and are vastly different from the physical problems with which many outside or nongovernmental organizations have worked. Another reason is that the actions recommended in such studies have impacts on organization and on people—impacts which the outside organization can ignore, but which the policy makers cannot.

These impacts must be spelled out and accounted for in management science studies. Unless the policy makers are sufficiently involved in a study to indicate which impacts must be considered and which can be ignored, chances are that the wrong factors will be considered—if any such impacts are considered at all.

Whether analysis is performed in-house or by contract, policy makers will also need to be facilitators of the studies they sanction. Access to people and information and social support are critical to most policy studies (assuming reasonable financing). Policy makers also have a role to play in implementation. Assuming a study has been done well and the implementation actions have been spelled out, the necessary organizational arrangements must still be created to facilitate concerted action. This may be as simple as lending support to existing organizational units or as complex as creating new units or a new organization of units to carry out implementation actions.

Thus, policy makers may have any or all of several roles in the conduct of policy studies: initiator and sponsor, proposal evaluator, participant, facilitator, and implementor. Obviously, few of these roles can be fulfilled directly or continuously by the highest-level policy makers. How many of these roles and which of them are handled directly depends on the type of decision problem and the arrangements made for the conduct of analysis. At minimum, the responsibility of the policy makers will be to define the necessary roles in specific decision contexts and to secure their effectuation. For many decision problems, this is done by the delegation of continued responsibility to an analysis group or unit in the organization. However, on extremely consequential issues, most policy makers may want to consider these questions in the light of the specific situation.

Organizational Impacts of Using Management Science

Management science inevitably results in changes in an organization, either directly through the implementation of recommendations for change developed as a result of analysis or indirectly through its effect on the behavior of the individuals and groups who use it or who are affected by its use by others. Since policy makers must deal with these indirect impacts, several points are in order.

1. Management science is a new way of structuring decision processes. As such, it represents a threat to the power and influence of those not well versed in its language and techniques. Generally, well-organized and technically sophisticated individuals and groups gain power at the expense of those less well-equipped to engage in, use, and react to the output of management science. Further, if the latter groups concede that management science is a useful way of addressing public policy making, they are in fact conceding an advantage to those who are better versed in it. (See, e.g., Downs, 1967, p. 208.)

2. Explicit analysis of policy alternatives represents a communication and decision-justifying process that is alien to many participants in the policy-making process. That is, one can distinguish between the use of analysis in reaching a choice and setting out the explicit rationale for that choice. The former involves a synthesis of goals and alternatives and the finding of insights into the relationships between the two. The latter is more a demonstration (to others) of the connections between the chosen (or recommended) alternative and the boundary conditions of the decision. Both activities are involved in management science (Whitehead, 1967, pp. 93–105). Difficulties arise when a conflict occurs between the way people actually reach a decision and the way in which they must justify it. As long as people need not be too explicit about their justification, this conflict can be ignored. However, because management science places such great emphasis on decision justification, it is difficult to ignore. As a result, many people may be made quite uncomfortable by having to justify their positions on ground rules different from those they used to reach the decision in the first place.

3. By its emphasis on explicitness, management science forces people to face issues they were able to gloss over previously without even being aware that they were doing so. Because management science forces decision participants to be explicit and objective about assumptions and measures, there is a possibility that the analysis will produce results contrary to some of the predispositions of the participants. Some people will view this as a useful result, because it provides a basis for improving and sharpening their judgment. But others will interpret it as a challenge to their judgment and hence to their competence and status (Whitehead, 1967, pp. 104–105).

4. By calling explicit attention to the uncertainties involved in a decision situation, management science emphasizes the limited basis for decision. Many policy makers find this situation uncomfortable, especially when they have a sincere desire to reach the best decision possible. It is dissatisfying to many people to speak of tradeoffs among objectives because that implies compromise with what is really needed. Further, by stressing the uncertainties, policy analysis may weaken the decision makers' confidence in the rightness of their decision (Whitehead, 1967, p. 106).

5. Management science helps clarify objectives and ends-means relationships but by doing so may create increased disagreement within an organization. As long as ends and means are vague, basic conflicts between individuals and groups in an organization remain submerged. Further, by

couching their thinking and their defense of decisions in technical, problem-solving terms rather than in terms of fundamental tradeoffs among objectives, the participants in the decision process avoid a sense of personal responsibility and vulnerability. They are then vulnerable to criticism only by those few people in a position to question technical competence and value choices (Whitehead, 1967, p. 106).

6. In management science, judgments are regarded as part of the decision problem. Emphasis is placed on clarifying specific judgments that must be made and on using analysis to relate such judgments to one another. The more common approach to decision analysis is to present the facts of the problems and let the decision makers make a lumped judgment. The net result of this difference is that, with management science, it is much more difficult for the decision makers to foresee the tangible implications of their judgments, because they are made sequentially over a number of subareas in the policy study. Under the "lumped-judgment" approach, the policy makers seemingly have full control over the outcome of the analysis. This control may be used to ensure that a favored alternative comes out ahead, but it is probably more commonly used as insurance against unreasonable results from the analysis. People simply are able to assess the implications and acceptability of concrete alternatives better than they can assess the outcome of judgments separated from analysis. Because a major function of the decision makers is to integrate diverse considerations rather than to delve into the details of each, this shift of the locus of judgment may make it difficult for them to justify a valid but vaguely formulated overview in the face of an analysis that factors the decision problem into a number of subareas (Whitehead, 1967, pp. 107–108).

7. By cutting across established organizational boundaries, management science increases the uncertainty about how a particular individual, unit, or organization will fare in the final decision. This uncertainty tends to increase the ambivalence that most people feel about using management science and may generate opposition (Downs, 1967, p. 209).

The most general implication of these points is that, when management science is introduced into an organization, it will result in gains for some people and losses for others. Therefore, it will generate opposition as well as support. This organizational strife may be a salutary thing. Disagreement can be a help in avoiding the trap of specious analyses and can provide impetus for the development of better alternatives.

The Nature of Government and Its Problems

A final set of behavioral issues in using management science relates to the difficulties presented by the government environment. Chief among these are (1) the lack of correspondence between problem and jurisdictional boundaries; (2) the necessity for involvement of the constituency; and (3) the difficulty of defining goals.

Boundary problems   An area of difficulty in applying management science to the problems of government lies in defining the boundary of the system in which a problem occurs. The difficulty arises in trying to determine which things must be included in thinking about a problem and which can be excluded, which things can be controlled by the policy makers and which must be accepted as givens. Many problems are so interrelated they seem to defy all attempts to bound them, however the boundaries are defined. For example, assuming a programmatic definition, problems of poverty intersect with those of education, employment, and welfare; under a functional definition, police problems overlap with those of welfare, education, planning and building, and recreation; in a race definition, the problems of the black relate to those of the Chicano and Puerto Rican. Thus, the choice of an appropriate way to bound policy problems may be exceedingly difficult.

In the choice of levels and boundaries of the intervention (decision) system, a similar difficulty occurs. Is the particular problem something that can be dealt with at the local level, or does it require state or federal decision and action? Within any particular government, there is a further problem of choosing among alternative specifications of the appropriate intervention system. For example, in dealing with problems of poverty, the relevant systems may be the public programs for employment, welfare, education, or housing —or all of these.

Finally, many problems overlap legal-jurisdictional boundaries. At the local government level, many aspects of police, fire, building, planning, recreation, and other governmental problems are resolvable largely within the territorial limits of a single jurisdiction. However, other aspects of these and certain other problems (air and water pollution, transportation, refuse disposal) can be handled only on a multijurisdictional basis. Yet rarely do governmental entities exist that are able to decide and act on these types of problems. There are some cooperative mechanisms (councils of governments, regional agencies, etc.), but few of them possess the power to secure concerted action from their members. Thus, a compounding feature of many government decision problems is that the boundary of the system (e.g., the metropolitan or urban area) in which the problem occurs does not correspond to the system that seeks to deal with the problem (the municipality).

The constituency or client of management science   In government there are many possible choices of clients (including citizens, public administrators, and politicians)—each choice bringing a different problem definition—who are considered to be the decision makers, and therefore how the decision problem is stated determines in large part what will be done, how, and with what results. But the "decision makers" include more than the political leaders and government professionals: They include all those affected by particular decisions and actions in some important way. Although the actual conduct of management science may involve a much smaller number than this vast set of decision makers, it must be done with full consideration of the points of view of these others.

The increasing demand by citizens for participation and involvement in decisions that have important effects on their lives complicates the whole process of analysis in the government context. The critical problem often revolves around the way in which participation and involvement are structured rather than the way in which the technical analysis is structured. In fact, in many instances, professionals, analysts, or politicians may feel they know what should be done. The problem then is to communicate this perception so as to elicit a useful response from other relevant parties. That is, the problem is to create a forum in which issues are debated, alternative goal statements tested, and possible solutions tried out with those who will be affected by a choice among the issues, goals, and solutions.

This situation is exacerbated when issues cross jurisdictional, class, race, or other lines, but it cannot be ignored, because the best technical analysis is useless if the preferred solution fails to consider the appropriate mix of interests involved. Indeed, it would be extremely useful if management science studies were viewed as incomplete and inadequate where these considerations are not integral to the whole process of analysis and/or not covered in the resultant recommendations.

Goals and objectives   Determining goals and objectives is closely related to determining the client, that is, "Whose objectives are to be served?" Once the client is defined, an additional task is to determine the real objectives of the client. This is difficult because governments are complex social organizations with a wide mixture of goals. Further, as expressed by the citizens and political leaders, these goals are often inconsistent, contradictory, or downright unrealistic. Finally, these people may be unable to express their goals clearly, if at all.

Although there may be no single set of goals and objectives that will be agreed upon by all the interested parties or the formal client, it is important in the conduct of analysis that at least a satisfactory set be identified. As Ida Hoos says:

> What the analyst conceives as the system's objectives molds his ideas, weighs his conceptions, and has impact on so seemingly quantitative an operation as cost/benefit comparisons. Whose cost becomes whose benefit is not a matter of undisputable accounting but rather an issue for interpretation within a given framework. (1967, p. 5)

In a sense, all of this has been said before. What cannot be emphasized clearly enough is that management scientists and policy makers cannot escape from the task of determining goals, whatever the process used. The statement of objectives is the key to subsequent phases in analysis. It is in essence the process of formulating the questions that the analysis is to answer. It is not sufficient to conduct an analysis in the hope that, or on the assumption that, the model developed will be suitable for evaluating the goals on which the policy makers and others eventually agree.

NOTES

[1]Our discussion of techniques is purposively brief. For a more extensive discussion of these and other management techniques, see Larson & Odoni (1981), Beltrami (1977), and Gass & Sisson (1975).

[2]This early application of mathematical programming is described in Laubal (1967) and Herbert & Stevens (1960).

[3]These applications were first described in Blakesley (1969) and Allen (1967).

[4]Early applications were described in, e.g., Clarke & Surkis (1968), Heckman & Taylor (1969), Koenigsberg (1968), and Ploughman, Darnton, & Heuser (1968).

[5]Woodward (1968) developed a linear programming model to assist the Metropolitan Water District of Southern California in determining the optimum mix of various fiscal policies, e.g., levying taxes, selling water, issuing bonds, so as to minimize the cost of providing water to the citizens of the area served.

[6]Little (1966) dealt with the problem of synchronizing traffic signals so that a car, starting at one end of a main artery and traveling at preassigned speeds, can go to the other end without stopping at a red light. The application is theoretical.

[7]Other examples are contained in Ignall, Kolesar, & Walker (1978), Keeney (1972), and Kelling et al. (1974).

REFERENCES

Ackoff, R. L., & Rivett, P. *A manager's guide to operations research.* New York: John Wiley, 1963.

Allen, D. W. Computer built schedules and educational innovation. In D. D. Bushnell & D. W. Allen (Eds.), *The computer in American education*, pp. 51–58. New York: John Wiley, 1967.

Beltrami, E. *Models for public systems analysis.* New York: Academic Press, 1977.

Beltrami, E., & Bodin, L. Networks and vehicle routing for municipal waste collection. *Networks*, 1974, 4, 65–94.

Blakesley, J. F. Administration-integrated records and procedures. In R. W. Gerard (Ed.), *Computers and education*, pp. 183–228. New York: McGraw-Hill, 1969.

Carter, G. M., Chaiken, J. M., & Ignall, E. Response areas for two emergency units. *Operations Research*, 1972, 20, 571–594.

Clarke, S. H., & Surkis, J. Applications of electronic computer techniques to racial integration in school systems. *Journal of Socio-Economic Planning Sciences*, July 1968, 2, 259–272.

Crecine, J. P. A computer simulation model of municipal budgeting. *Management Science*, July 1967, 13, 786–815.

Crecine, J. P. *Governmental problem solving: A computer simulation of municipal budgeting.* Chicago: Rand McNally, 1969.

Downs, A. A realistic look at the final payoffs from urban data systems. *Public Administration Review*, September 1967, 27, 208.

Edie, L. C. Traffic delays at toll booths. *Operations Research*, May 1954, 2, 107–138.

Edie, L. C. Planning and control of service operations. *Proceedings, Operations Research in Industry Symposium*, June 1957, University of Michigan, Ann Arbor.

Gass, S. I., & Sisson, R. L. (Eds.). *A guide to models in governmental planning and operations.* Washington, D.C.: Sauger Books, 1975.

Heckman, L. B., & Taylor, H. M. School rezoning to achieve racial balance: A linear programming approach. *Journal of Socio-Economic Planning Sciences*, September 1969, 3, 127–133.

Herbert, J. D., & Stevens, B. H. A model for the distribution of residential activity in urban areas. *Journal of Regional Science*, Fall 1960, 2, 21–36.

Hess, S. W., et al. Nonpartisan political redistricting by computer. *Operations Research*, November 1965, 13, 998–1006.

Hoos, I. R. *Systems analysis in government administration: A critical analysis.* Berkeley: Space Sciences Laboratory, University of California, 1967.

Ignall, E. J., Kolesar, P., & Walker, W. E. Using simulation to develop analytic models: Some case studies. *Operations Research*, 1978, 26, 237–253.

Jarvis, J. P., Stevenson, K. A., & Willemain, T. R. *A simple procedure for the allocation of ambulances in semi-rural areas.* Cambridge, Mass.: MIT Operations Research Center, 1975.

Keeney, R. L. A method for districting among facilities. *Operations Research*, 1972, 20, 613–618.

Kelling, G. L., Pate, T., Dieckman, D., & Brown, C. E. *The Kansas City preventive patrol experiment: Summary report.* Washington, D.C.: The Police Foundation, 1974.

Koenigsberg, E. Mathematical analysis applied to school attendance areas. *Journal of Socio-Economic Planning Sciences*, August 1968, *2*, 243–258.

Kolesar, P. A model for predicting average fire engine travel times. *Operations Research*, 1975, *23*, 603–613.

Krolak, P., Felts, W., & Nelson, J. A man-machine approach toward solving the generalized truck-dispatching problem. *Transportation Science*, 1972, *6*, 149–170.

Larson, R. C. Approximating the performance of urban emergency service systems. *Operations Research*, 1975, *23*, 845–868.

Larson, R. C., & Odoni, A. R. *Urban operations research*. Englewood Cliffs, N.J.: Prentice-Hall, 1981.

Larson, R. C., & Stevenson, K. A. On insensitivities in urban redistricting and facility location. *Operations Research*, 1972, *20*, 595–612.

Laubal, P. S. The evaluation of alternative transportation networks. In P. M. Morse & L. W. Bacon (Eds.), *Operations research for public systems*, pp. 95–126. Cambridge, Mass.: MIT Press, 1967.

Little, J. D. C. The synchronization of traffic signals by mixed-integer linear programming. *Operations Research*, July 1966, *14*, 568–594.

Majone, G., & Quade, E. S. (Eds.). *Pitfalls of analysis*. New York: John Wiley, 1980.

Odoni, A. R. An analytical investigation of air traffic in the vicinity of terminal areas. Ph.D. dissertation, Massachusetts Institute of Technology, 1969.

Ploughman, T., Darnton, W., & Heuser, W. An assignment program to establish school attendance boundaries and forecast construction needs. *Journal of Socio-Economic Planning Sciences*, July 1968, *2*, 243–258.

Quade, E. S. *Analysis for public decisions*. New York: Elsevier, 1975.

Quade, E. S., & Boucher, W. I. (Eds.). *Systems analysis and policy planning*. New York: Elsevier, 1968.

Schulman, P. R. *Large-scale policy making*. New York: Elsevier, 1980.

Specht, R. The nature of models. In E. S. Quade & W. I. Boucher (Eds.), *Systems analysis and policy planning: Applications in defense*. New York: Elsevier, 1969.

Toregas, C., Swain, R., Revelle, C., & Bergman, L. The location of emergency service facilities. *Operations Research*, 1971, *19*, 1363–1373.

Ward, R. A. *Operational research in local government*. London: George Allen and Unwin, 1964.

Whitehead, C. T. *Uses and limitations of systems analysis*. Santa Monica, Calif.: The Rand Corporation, 1967.

Woodward, C. B. Optimization of long-range municipal multiple-resource fiscal policies. *Journal of Socio-Economic Planning Sciences*, July 1968, *2*, 273–282.

20 | Broadening the Concept of Marketing

Philip Kotler
Sidney J. Levy

The term "marketing" connotes to most people a function peculiar to business firms. Marketing is seen as the task of finding and stimulating buyers for the firm's output. It involves product development, pricing, distribution, and communication; and in the more progressive firms, continuous attention to the changing needs of customers and the development of new products, with product modifications and services to meet these needs. But whether marketing is viewed in the old sense of "pushing" products or in the new sense of "customer satisfaction engineering," it is almost always viewed and discussed as a business activity.

It is the authors' contention that marketing is a pervasive societal activity that goes considerably beyond the selling of toothpaste, soap, and steel. Political contests remind us that candidates are marketed as well as soap; student recruitment by colleges reminds us that higher education is marketed; and fund raising reminds us that "causes" are marketed. Yet these areas of marketing are typically ignored by the student of marketing. Or they are treated cursorily as public relations or publicity activities. No attempt is made to incorporate these phenomena in the body proper of marketing thought and theory. No attempt is made to redefine the meaning of product development, pricing, distribution, and communication in these newer contexts to see if they have a useful meaning. No attempt is made to examine whether the principles of "good" marketing in traditional product areas are transferable to the marketing of services, persons, and ideas.

The authors see a great opportunity for marketing people to expand their thinking and to apply their skills to an increasingly interesting range of social activity. The challenge depends on the attention given to it; marketing will either take on a broader social meaning or remain a narrowly defined business activity.

Reprinted from *Journal of Marketing*, "Broadening the Concept of Marketing," by Philip Kotler and Sidney J. Levy, Vol. 33 (January 1969), published by the American Marketing Association.

One of the most striking trends in the United States is the increasing amount of society's work being performed by organizations other than business firms. As a society moves beyond the stage where shortages of food, clothing, and shelter are the major problems, it begins to organize to meet other social needs that formerly had been put aside. Business enterprises remain a dominant type of organization, but other types of organizations gain in conspicuousness and in influence. Many of these organizations become enormous and require the same rarefied management skills as traditional business organizations. Managing the United Auto Workers, Defense Department, Ford Foundation, World Bank, Catholic Church, and University of California has become every bit as challenging as managing Procter and Gamble, General Motors, and General Electric. These nonbusiness organizations have an increasing range of influence, affect as many livelihoods, and occupy as much media prominence as major business firms.

All of these organizations perform the classic business functions. Every organization must perform a financial function insofar as money must be raised, managed, and budgeted according to sound business principles. Every organization must perform a production function in that it must conceive of the best way of arranging inputs to produce the outputs of the organization. Every organization must perform a personnel function in that people must be hired, trained, assigned, and promoted in the course of the organization's work. Every organization must perform a purchasing function in that it must acquire materials in an efficient way through comparing and selecting sources of supply.

When we come to the marketing function, it is also clear that every organization performs marketing-like activities whether or not they are recognized as such. Several examples can be given.

The police department of a major U.S. city, concerned with the poor image it has among an important segment of its population, developed a campaign to "win friends and influence people." One highlight of this campaign is a "visit your police station" day in which tours are conducted to show citizens the daily operations of the police department, including the crime laboratories, police lineups, and cells. The police department also sends officers to speak at public schools and carries out a number of other activities to improve its community relations.

Most museum directors interpret their primary responsibility as "the proper preservation of an artistic heritage for posterity."[1] As a result, for many people museums are cold marble mausoleums that house miles of relics that soon give way to yawns and tired feet. Although museum attendance in the United States advances each year, a large number of citizens are uninterested in museums. Is this indifference due to failure in the manner of presenting what museums have to offer? This nagging question led the new director of the Metropolitan Museum of Art to broaden the museum's appeal through sponsoring contemporary art shows and "happenings." His marketing philosophy of museum management led to substantial increases in the Met's attendance.

The public school system in Oklahoma City sorely needed more public support and funds to prevent a deterioration of facilities and exodus of teachers. It recently resorted to television programming to dramatize the work the public schools were doing to fight the high school dropout problem, to develop new teaching techniques, and to enrich the children. Although an expensive medium, television quickly reached large numbers of parents whose response and interest were tremendous.

Nations also resort to international marketing campaigns to get across important points about themselves to the citizens of other countries. The junta of Greek colonels who seized power in Greece in 1967 found the international publicity surrounding their cause to be extremely unfavorable and potentially disruptive of international recognition. They hired a major New York public relations firm and soon full-page newspaper ads appeared carrying the headline "Greece Was Saved From Communism," detailing in small print why the takeover was necessary for the stability of Greece and the world.[2]

An anti-cigarette group in Canada is trying to press the Canadian legislature to ban cigarettes on the grounds that they are harmful to health. There is widespread support for this cause but the organization's funds are limited, particularly measured against the huge advertising resources of the cigarette industry. The group's problem is to find effective ways to make a little money go a long way in persuading influential legislators of the need for discouraging cigarette consumption. This group has come up with several ideas for marketing anti-smoking to Canadians, including television spots, a paperback book featuring pictures of cancer and heart disease patients, and legal research on company liability for the smoker's loss of health.

What concepts are common to these and many other possible illustrations of organizational marketing? All of these organizations are concerned about their "product" in the eyes of certain "consumers" and are seeking to find "tools" for furthering their acceptance. Let us consider each of these concepts in general organizational terms.

Products

Every organization produces a "product" of at least one of the following types:

Physical products. "Product" first brings to mind everyday items like soap, clothes, and food, and extends to cover millions of *tangible* items that have a market value and are available for purchase.

Services. Services are *intangible* goods that are subject to market transaction such as tours, insurance, consultation, hairdos, and banking.

Persons. Personal marketing is an endemic *human* activity, from the employee trying to impress his boss to the statesman trying to win the support of the public. With the advent of mass communications, the marketing of persons has been turned over to professionals. Hollywood stars have their press agents, political candidates their advertising agencies, and so on.

Organizations. Many organizations spend a great deal of time marketing themselves. The Republican Party has invested considerable thought and resources in trying to develop a modern look. The American Medical Association decided recently that it needed to launch a campaign to improve the image of the American doctor.[3] Many charitable organizations and universities see selling their *organization* as their primary responsibility.

Ideas. Many organizations are mainly in the business of selling *ideas* to the larger society. Population organizations are trying to sell the idea of birth control, and the Women's Christian Temperance Union is still trying to sell the idea of prohibition.

Thus the "product" can take many forms, and this is the first crucial point in the case for broadening the concept of marketing.

Consumers

The second crucial point is that organizations must deal with many groups that are interested in their products and can make a difference in its success. It is vitally important to the organization's success that it be sensitive to, serve, and satisfy these groups. One set of groups can be called the *suppliers*. *Suppliers* are those who provide the management group with the inputs necessary to perform its work and develop its product effectively. Suppliers include employees, vendors of the materials, banks, advertising agencies, and consultants.

The other set of groups are the *consumers* of the organization's product, of which four subgroups can be distinguished. The *clients* are those who are the immediate consumers of the organization's product. The clients of a business firm are its buyers and potential buyers; of a service organization those receiving the services, such as the needy (from the Salvation Army) or the sick (from County Hospital); and of a protective or a primary organization, the members themselves. The second group is the *trustees* or *directors,* those who are vested with the legal authority and responsibility for the organization, oversee the management, and enjoy a variety of benefits from the "product." The third group is the active *publics* that take a specific interest in the organization. For a business firm, the active publics include consumer rating groups, governmental agencies, and pressure groups of various kinds. For a university, the active publics include alumni and friends of the university, foundations, and city fathers. Finally, the fourth consumer group is the *general public.* These are all the people who might develop attitudes toward the organization that might affect its conduct in some way. Organizational marketing concerns the programs designed by management to create satisfactions and favorable attitudes in the organization's four consuming groups: clients, trustees, active publics, and general public.

Marketing Tools

Students of business firms spend much time studying the various tools under the firm's control that affect product acceptance: product improvement, pricing, distribution, and communication. All of these tools have counterpart applications to nonbusiness organizational activity.

Nonbusiness organizations to various degrees engage in product improvement, especially when they recognize the competition they face from other organizations. Thus, over the years churches have added a host of nonreligious activities to their basic religious activities to satisfy members seeking other bases of human fellowship. Universities keep updating their curricula and adding new student services in an attempt to make the educational experience relevant to the students. Where they have failed to do this, students have sometimes organized their own courses and publications, or have expressed their dissatisfaction in organized protest. Government agencies such as license bureaus, police forces, and taxing bodies are often not responsive to the public because of monopoly status; but even here citizens have shown an increasing readiness to protest mediocre services, and more alert bureaucracies have shown a growing interest in reading the user's needs and developing the required product services.

All organizations face the problem of pricing their products and services so that they cover costs. Churches charge dues, universities charge tuition, governmental agencies charge fees, fund-raising organizations send out bills. Very often specific product charges are not sufficient to meet the organization's budget, and it must rely on gifts and surcharges to make up the difference. Opinions vary as to how much the users should be charged for the individual services and how much should be made up through general collection. If the university increases its tuition, it will have to face losing some students and putting more students on scholarship. If the hospital raises its charges to cover rising costs and additional services, it may provoke a reaction from the community. All organizations face complex pricing issues although not all of them understand good pricing practice.

Distribution is a central concern to the manufacturer seeking to make his goods conveniently accessible to buyers. Distribution also can be an important marketing decision area for nonbusiness organizations. A city's public library has to consider the best means of making its books available to the public. Should it establish one large library with an extensive collection of books, or several neighborhood branch libraries with duplication of books? Should it use bookmobiles that bring the books to the customers instead of relying exclusively on the customers coming to the books? Should it distribute through school libraries? Similarly, the police department of a city must think through the problem of distributing its protective services efficiently through the community. It has to determine how much protective service to allocate to different neighborhoods; the respective merits of squad cars, motorcycles, and foot patrolmen; and the positioning of emergency phones.

Customer communication is an essential activity of all organizations although many nonmarketing organizations often fail to accord it the importance it deserves. Managements of many organizations think they have fully met their communication responsibilities by setting up advertising and/or public relations departments. They fail to realize that *everything about an organization talks.* Customers form impressions of an organization from its physical facilities, employees, officers, stationery, and a hundred other company surrogates. Only when this is appreciated do the members of the organization recognize that they all are in marketing, whatever else they do. With this understanding they can assess realistically the impact of their activities on the consumers.

CONCEPTS FOR EFFECTIVE MARKETING MANAGEMENT IN NONBUSINESS ORGANIZATIONS

■ 20 ■
Philip Kotler
Sidney J. Levy

Although all organizations have products, markets, and marketing tools, the art and science of effective marketing management have reached their highest state of development in the business type of organization. Business organizations depend on customer goodwill for survival and have generally learned how to sense and cater to their needs effectively. As other types of organizations recognize their marketing roles, they will turn increasingly to the body of marketing principles worked out by business organizations and adapt them to their own situations.

What are the main principles of effective marketing management as they appear in most forward-looking business organizations? Nine concepts stand out as crucial in guiding the marketing effort of a business organization.

Generic Product Definition

Business organizations have increasingly recognized the value of placing a broad definition on their products, one that emphasizes the basic customer need(s) being served. A modern soap company recognizes that its basic product is cleaning, not soap; a cosmetics company sees its basic product as beauty or hope, not lipsticks and makeup; a publishing company sees its basic product as information, not books.

The same need for a broader definition of its business is incumbent upon nonbusiness organizations if they are to survive and grow. Churches at one time tended to define their product narrowly as that of producing religious services for members. Recently, most churchmen have decided that their basic product is human fellowship. There was a time when educators said that their product was the three R's. Now most of them define their product as education for the whole man. They try to serve the social, emotional, and political needs of young people in addition to intellectual needs.

Target Groups Definition

A generic product definition usually results in defining a very wide market, and it is then necessary for the organization, because of limited resources, to limit its product offering to certain clearly defined groups within the market. Although the generic product of an automobile company is transportation, the company typically sticks to cars, trucks, and buses, and stays away from bicycles, airplanes, and steamships. Furthermore, the manufacturer does not produce every size and shape of car but concentrates on producing a few major types to satisfy certain substantial and specific parts of the market.

In the same way, nonbusiness organizations have to define their target groups carefully. For example, in Chicago the YMCA defines its target groups as men, women and children who want recreational opportunities and are willing to pay $20 or more a year for them. The Chicago Boys Club, on the other hand, defines its target group as poorer boys within the city boundaries who are in want of recreational facilities and can pay $1 a year.

Differentiated Marketing

When a business organization sets out to serve more than one target group, it will be maximally effective by differentiating its product offerings and communications. This is also true for nonbusiness organizations. Fund-raising organizations have recognized the advantage of treating clients, trustees, and various publics in different ways. These groups require differentiated appeals and frequency of solicitation. Labor unions find that they must address different messages to different parties rather than one message to all parties. To the company they may seem unyielding, to the conciliator they may appear willing to compromise, and to the public they seek to appear economically exploited.

Customer Behavior Analysis

Business organizations are increasingly recognizing that customer needs and behavior are not obvious without formal research and analysis; they cannot rely on impressionistic evidence. Soap companies spend hundreds of thousands of dollars each year researching how Mrs. Housewife feels about her laundry, how, when, and where she does her laundry, and what she desires of a detergent.

Fund raising illustrates how an industry has benefited by replacing stereotypes of donors with studies of why people contribute to causes. Fund raisers have learned that people give because they are getting something. Many give to community chests to relieve a sense of guilt because of their elevated state compared to the needy. Many give to medical charities to relieve a sense of fear that they may be struck by a disease whose cure has not yet been found. Some give to feel pride. Fund raisers have stressed the importance of identifying the motives operating in the marketplace of givers as a basis for planning drives.

Differential Advantages

In considering different ways of reaching target groups, an organization is advised to think in terms of seeking a differential advantage. It should consider what elements in its reputation or resources can be exploited to create a special value in the minds of its potential customers. In the same way Zenith has built a reputation for quality and International Harvester a reputation for service, a nonbusiness organization should base its case on some dramatic value that competitive organizations lack. The small island of Nassau can compete against Miami for the tourist trade by advertising the greater dependability of its weather; the Heart Association can compete for funds against the Cancer Society by advertising the amazing strides made in heart research.

Multiple Marketing Tools

The modern business firm relies on a multitude of tools to sell its product, including product improvement, consumer and dealer advertising, salesman incentive programs, sales promotions, contests, multiple-size offerings, and so forth. Likewise nonbusiness organizations also can reach their audiences in a variety of ways. A church can sustain the interest of its members through discussion groups, newsletters, news releases, campaign drives, annual reports, and retreats. Its "salesmen" include the religious head, the board members, and the present members in terms of attracting potential members. Its advertising includes announcements of weddings, births and deaths, religious pronouncements, and newsworthy developments.

Integrated Marketing Planning

The multiplicity of available marketing tools suggests the desirability of overall coordination so that these tools do not work at cross purposes. Over time, business firms have placed under a marketing vice president activities that were previously managed in a semi-autonomous fashion, such as sales, advertising, and marketing research. Nonbusiness organizations typically have not integrated their marketing activities. Thus, no single officer in the typical university is given total responsibility for studying the needs and attitudes of clients, trustees, and publics, and undertaking the necessary product development and communication programs to serve these groups. The university administration instead includes a variety of "marketing" positions such as dean of students, director of alumni affairs, director of public relations, and director of development; coordination is often poor.

Continuous Marketing Feedback

Business organizations gather continuous information about changes in the environment and about their own performance. They use their salesmen, research department, specialized research services, and other means to check on the movement of goods, actions of competitors, and feelings of customers to make sure they are progressing along satisfactory lines. Nonbusiness organizations typically are more casual about collecting vital information on how they are doing and what is happening in the marketplace. Universities have been caught off guard by underestimating the magnitude of student grievance and unrest, and so have major cities underestimated the degree to which they were failing to meet the needs of important minority constituencies.

Marketing Audit

Change is a fact of life, although it may proceed almost invisibly on a day-to-day basis. Over a long stretch of time it might be so fundamental as to threaten organizations that have not provided for periodic reexaminations of their purposes. Organizations can grow set in their ways and unresponsive to new opportunities or problems. Some great American companies are no longer with us because they did not change definitions of their businesses, and their products lost relevance in a changing world. Political parties become unresponsive after they enjoy power for a while and every so often experience a major upset. Many union leaders grow insensitive to new needs and problems until one day they find themselves out of office. For an organization to remain viable, its management must provide for periodic audits of its objectives, resources, and opportunities. It must reexamine its basic business, target groups, differential advantage, communication channels, and messages in the light of current trends and needs. It might recognize when change is needed and make it before it is too late.

IS ORGANIZATIONAL MARKETING A SOCIALLY USEFUL ACTIVITY?

Modern marketing has two different meanings in the minds of people who use the term. One meaning of marketing conjures up the terms selling, influencing, persuading. Marketing is seen as a huge and increasingly dangerous technology, making it possible to sell persons on buying things, propositions, and causes they either do not want or which are bad for them. This was the indictment in Vance Packard's *Hidden Persuaders* and numerous other social criticisms, with the net effect that a large number of persons think of marketing as immoral or entirely self-seeking in its fundamental premises. They can be counted on to resist the idea of organizational marketing as so much "Madison Avenue."

The other meaning of marketing unfortunately is weaker in the public mind; it is the concept of sensitively *serving and satisfying human needs*. This was the great contribution of the marketing concept that was promulgated in the 1950s, and that concept now counts many business firms as its practitioners. The marketing concept holds that the problem of all business firms in an age of abundance is to develop customer loyalties and satisfaction, and the key to this problem is to focus on the customer's needs.[4] Perhaps the short-run problem of business firms is to sell people on buying the existing products, but the long-run problem is clearly to create the products that people need. By this recognition that effective marketing requires a consumer orientation instead of a product orientation, marketing has taken a new lease on life and tied its economic activity to a higher social purpose.

It is this second side of marketing that provides a useful concept for all organizations. All organizations are formed to serve the interest of particular groups: hospitals serve the sick, schools serve the students, governments serve the citizens, and labor unions serve the members. In the course of evolving, many organizations lose sight of their original mandate, grow hard, and become self-serving. The bureaucratic mentality begins to dominate the original service mentality. Hospitals may become perfunctory in their handling of patients, schools treat their students as nuisances, city bureaucrats behave like petty tyrants toward the citizens, and labor unions try to run instead of serve their members. All of these actions tend to build frustration in the consuming groups. As a result some withdraw meekly from these organizations, accept frustration as part of their condition, and find their satisfactions elsewhere. This used to be the common reaction of ghetto Negroes and college students in the face of indifferent city and university bureaucracies. But new possibilities have arisen, and now the same consumers refuse to withdraw so readily. Organized dissent and protest are seen to be an answer, and many organizations thinking of themselves as responsible have been stunned into recognizing that they have lost touch with their constituencies. They had grown unresponsive.

Where does marketing fit into this picture? Marketing is that function of the organization that can keep in constant touch with the organization's consumers, read their needs, develop "products" that meet these needs, and build a program of communications to express the organization's purposes. Certainly selling and influencing will be large parts of organizational marketing; but, properly seen, selling follows rather than precedes the organization's drive to create products to satisfy its consumers.

CONCLUSION

It has been argued here that the modern marketing concept serves very naturally to describe an important facet of all organizational activity. All organizations must develop appropriate products to serve their sundry consuming groups and must use modern tools of communication to reach their consuming publics. The business heritage of marketing provides a useful set of concepts for guiding all organizations.

The choice facing those who manage nonbusiness organizations is not whether to market or not to market, for no organization can avoid marketing. The choice is whether to do it well or poorly, and on this necessity the case for organizational marketing is basically founded.

NOTES

[1]This is the view of Sherman Lee, director of the Cleveland Museum, quoted in *Newsweek*, Vol. 71 (April 1, 1968), p. 55.

[2]"PR for the Colonels," *Newsweek*, Vol. 71 (March 18, 1968), p. 70.

[3]"Doctors Try an Image Transplant," *Business Week*, No. 2025 (June 22, 1968), p. 64.

[4]Theodore Levitt, "Marketing Myopia," *Harvard Business Review*, Vol. 38 (July–August, 1960), pp. 45–56.

21 OD in the Public Sector: Intervening in Ambiguous Performance Environments

Tim R. V. Davis

A gradually expanding literature documents organizational change in the public sector (Golembiewski, 1969; Costello, 1971; Ross & Hare, 1973; Giblin, 1976; Zawacki & Warrick, 1976) and how it differs from organizational change in the corporate sector. Although public-sector organizations share many features in common with corporations, certain distinguishing features generally increase the complexity of change attempts in the public sector. These have frequently been reported separately in the literature. Few contextual frameworks or models exist that pull together aspects of the setting most likely to affect public-sector OD. This lack of models decreases the potential for conceptual understanding of change processes in public organizations and lessens the likelihood of devising interventions that can be adjusted to the setting.

This paper presents an orienting framework comprising some of the most frequently cited variables that tend to affect public-sector OD. This framework is used to develop and evaluate an intervention in a division of a state welfare system. Methods and procedures are adopted that attempt to adjust the intervention to the influence variables operating in the setting. The implications of this approach and the methods used are then discussed for other public-sector change attempts.

INFLUENCE VARIABLES AFFECTING PUBLIC-SECTOR ORGANIZATIONS

Some of the variables most frequently cited in the literature that affect the operation of public-sector organizations are presented in Figures 21-1 and 21-2. Although it is by no means comprehensive, this framework distinguishes

Reprinted from J. E. Jones and J. W. Pfeiffer (Eds.), *Group & Organization Studies, 4* (3), San Diego, Calif.: University Associates, September 1979. Used with permission.

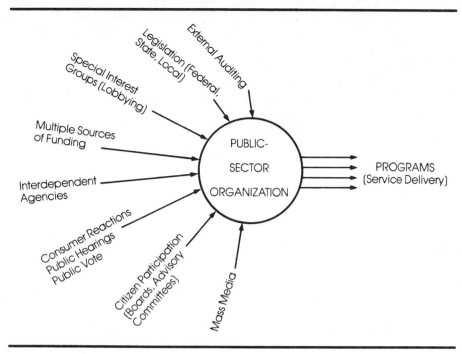

FIGURE 21-1.
External Environment of a Public-Sector Organization

those factors that frequently impact on the organization from the external environment from those that may be considered internal to the organization. Both sets of factors operate interdependently and have a mutually determining influence on organizational behavior. Included among the key external sources of influence are the legislature, special-interest groups (Golembiewski, 1969), multiple sources of funding (Wildavsky, 1964), interdependent agencies (Ross & Hare, 1973), external auditors (Warrick, 1976), citizen boards and advisory committees (Wolman, 1972), the media (Bower, 1977), and the general public. Among the key internal sources of influence typically felt in public-sector organizations are the nature of the chief operating executive's appointment (Costello, 1971) and the type of external reporting relationship(s); the importance of political goals (program visibility, rapid results, re-election, etc.) (Imundo, 1975); the level of diversity and contrasting ideology of the service specialist (Sikula, 1973; Wynia, 1974); the effects of vaguely defined programs and performance criteria (Gardner, 1974); the impact of the civil service personnel system (Giblin, 1976); and the effects of the regulations and procedures of the bureaucracy (Kharasch, 1973; Sharkansky, 1970).

The different forms of influence shown in Figure 21-1 indicate how open and vulnerable public-service organizations are to their external environments. Shifts in the environment produce changes in public agencies far more readily than in business firms. These constant shifts of input provide the external political environment for the public-sector organization. The internal environment of the agency (Figure 21-2) is strongly affected by the external political context. How closely the chief operating executive's position is

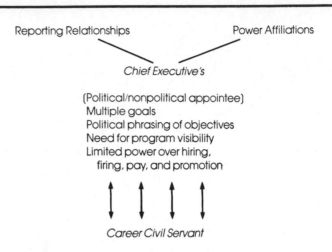

Reporting Relationships   Power Affiliations

Chief Executive's

(Political/nonpolitical appointee)
Multiple goals
Political phrasing of objectives
Need for program visibility
Limited power over hiring,
    firing, pay, and promotion

Career Civil Servant

Vague programs and performance criteria
Rigid regulations and procedures
Multiple service specialties
Varied ideological identifications
Previous program commitments
Civil service regulations

FIGURE 21-2.
Internal Environment of a Public-Sector Organization

linked to the seat of political influence will be a critical factor affecting the leadership and direction of the organization. The appointed official close to political sources of influence is placed in the difficult position of assessing the external climate of political forces (the inputs in Figure 21-1) and attempting to manage the internal resources of the organization to meet these demands (Figure 21-2). Frequently, the organization head who seeks to make changes comes into conflict with the organization staff (the career civil servants). The career civil servant has commitments to previous programs as well as vocational and ideological ties to a particular specialty. The diversity of service specialties in many public agencies, the vagueness of goals and performance criteria, the myriad rules and procedures, and the civil service laws regulating the hiring, firing, and advancing of personnel tend to limit the chief administrator's or, for that matter, the OD consultant's potential for introducing purposeful or rational changes in public-sector organizations.

Several qualifications need to be made concerning this orienting schema for viewing change processes in public-sector organizations. First, there are major differences, for example, between a change attempt instigated in New York City government (Costello, 1971) and in a medical school or health-care system (Beckhard, 1974). Both may involve public-sector change programs, but both require attention to different sets of situational concerns. The lack of research in public-sector OD makes it important to thoroughly investigate differences between settings. However, the framework proposed here provides a general orienting device to some of the influence variables that most frequently have an impact on public-sector organizations.

A second qualification concerns the notion of purposeful or rational change in public-sector organizations. Performance characteristics of public-sector organizations are frequently obscure and hard to assess,[1] and this makes it difficult for the OD consultant to understand what is going on, let alone decide what *should* be going on. Notable exceptions to this are the Post Office, public garbage collection, and public transport, which may be considered more quantifiable public services (Hofstede, 1978). Generally, however, the outputs of many public-sector agencies are vague, even when performance is evaluated close to service delivery; distinguishing performance outputs becomes still more difficult at points inlaid in the bureaucracy. The chief executive in many public agencies may be pushing for action without knowing exactly what is required. Alternatively, performance may intentionally be kept obscure. Phrasing objectives in general ways to appease a heterogeneous community may, in some cases, be an adaptive strategy for the public manager. The net result is that performance in the public sector can be totally subjective (individually defined) and change processes can be either completely irrational with no particular direction (Costello, 1971; Lindblom, 1959) or completely illusory, involving no real change, merely "symbolic action" (Edelman, 1971).

INTERVENING IN A STATE WELFARE SYSTEM

The Organization

An OD intervention was undertaken in a division of a state welfare system located in the Midwest. The division had a staff of twenty-two, consisting of a chief, assistant chief, two senior administrators, various program planners, resource developers, and program support personnel. The position of division chief was not a political patronage position. However, the division chief reported directly to a political appointee who was responsible to the state governor. This, coupled with other external pressures imposed by private advocacy groups that partially funded the division, other public agencies, the local media, and concerned citizens, made the position one of considerable political heat. The division staff was hired under a state merit plan that makes it unlikely that a person will be fired except in cases of extreme negligence and makes it difficult for any employee to be promoted over another with more seniority, even in cases of exceptional performance.

The variety of services administered by the agency meant that the staff consisted of a diverse assortment of service specialists, all trying to promote their own service areas. The public agency was not rigidly controlled through legislative action; the division merely had to keep within certain funding parameters and general guidelines for the broad service areas. Apart from this, there was considerable latitude for determining the services that could be provided and deciding on the procedures and routines of the office. The division did not have an interface with the public. Delivery of services was the responsibility of various regional and local field representatives. The division served a staff function; it did not have line management control over the field representatives. The objectives of the service areas were vaguely stated, with virtually no quantitative effectiveness criteria.

Organization Entry

As Rubin et al. (1974, p. 123) indicated, the most effective way of entering an organization is "to be asked in." When the consultant is in the position of "asking to be let in," it is less likely that he/she will be able to diagnose and define the problem(s) that will be confronted. In this particular case, the consultant was invited in. After an initial meeting with the division chief, the consultant addressed the entire staff in the presence of the division chief, partly to give legitimacy to the project and partly to provide an opportunity to publicly disavow any political ties with those in positions of authority.

Diagnosis

The diagnostic phase of the intervention consisted of: (a) a briefing with the division chief; (b) individual interviews with all staff members; and (c) administration of a diagnostic questionnaire.

Briefing with the division chief   The initial meeting with the division chief briefed the OD consultant on the division's programs, operating procedures, external political relationships, and internal service personnel. The division chief considered the main difficulties to be internal. He felt that communication and relationship problems existed among some of the staff and that this was affecting performance. The division chief's definition of "performance" was largely subjective, including such things as quality of programming, coordination of services, and the level of cooperation among the staff. When asked about more quantifiable criteria, he stated that the division provided a service function that could not be reduced to precise units of output.

The division chief's appraisal of the situation formed the starting point for the study. On the face of it, the comment that the division had communication and relationship problems was not very informative, especially when no real criteria indicated what the communication and relationships were supposed to achieve. The following questions emerged after the interview with the division chief:

1. Was performance based solely on appearances or, possibly, on the quality of interpersonal relationships among certain members of the staff?
2. Given the ambiguity of the performance environment, what were the relationship networks that formed the underlying structure of the division? Were there grounds for treating the relationship system as the performance system?

Individual interviews   An interview questionnaire was developed to identify specific performance problems and to ascertain the main organizational relationship networks. Structured individual interviews were held with each member of the division staff.

The interviews surfaced a large number of performance problems (e.g., missed special project due dates, missed suspense times, and rush work turned in without routing slips). A master list of critical incidents was drawn up from the interview data. The interviews also provided the data from which the organizational network linkages (see Figure 21-3) were constructed.[2] As can be seen from Figure 21-3, the results showed two clusterings: one cohesive network (b) involving top-level and middle-management personnel and one weakly linked network (c) involving operating-level personnel. The rest of the program-planning, supervisory, and operating-level staff had no recognizable membership in an interrelated network of relationships.

Administration of diagnostic questionnaire   Following the individual interviews, a diagnostic questionnaire was developed that examined aspects of communication and "perceived" performance effectiveness. Responses to the questionnaire revealed considerable dissatisfaction with aspects of the division's operations. For instance, the operating-level personnel (clerks, clerk typists, etc.) indicated that much of the work was poorly planned and coordinated. The middle-level program-planning and resource-development personnel showed dissatisfaction with poorly planned meetings and conferences. There was also considerable evidence that organization members did not feel able to speak freely with their superiors and that it was often difficult to obtain needed information. Interviews and questionnaire data indicated that the majority of the staff were prepared to confront the issues and problems creating difficulties in the division. It was decided to proceed with two sets of data-feedback meetings: one comprising division members of roughly equal rank who constituted a *work group* and another comprising the operational networks of mixed status that constituted a *communication group*.

Work-Group Data-Feedback Meetings

The data derived from the individual interviews and questionnaires were fed back to the work groups during a series of problem-confrontation and issue-consensus meetings. Following the recommendations of Giblin (1976), the consultants worked from the bottom up and focused on operational issues or critical incidents. The meetings were, therefore, primarily task oriented, but gave persons of equal status the opportunity to air their feelings and test their assumptions about the main operating problems. In the meetings with the operating-level personnel, each critical incident involved specific behaviors that could be subjected to a frequency tally. The affected staff members were asked to self-monitor the frequency of occurrence so that specific, quantified evidence could be provided showing the magnitude of the problem.

Predictably, the data-feedback sessions with upper-level staff did not produce such concrete issues. In these sessions, the communication network proved to be a useful tool in helping to confirm or disconfirm some of the issues and accusations that surfaced. For instance, the foster care coordinator and two of the resource-development specialists (all female) complained that they were not being adequately informed by upper-level management. They saw it as sexual discrimination by the division chief. The communication networks showed that these three people—the foster care coordinator and the two resource-development specialists—were relative isolates and gave credence to the view that they may have been cut off from needed information. However, their point concerning discrimination was not borne out by the

COMMUNICATOR	Div. Chief	Asst. Chief	Ad. Adult Serv.	Ad. Ch. Fam. Yth.	Cont. Mgr.	R.M.D. Mgr.	P.&P. Spec.	Fst. Care Co.	R.D. Spec.	R.D. Spec.	Lic. Cons.	Acct. II	Secretary II	Clerk IV	Clerk Typist III	Clerk Steno II	Clerk Typist III	Secretary I	Clerk Typist III	Clerk II	Clerk Typist II
Division Chief		X	X	X	X	X	X														
Assistant Chief	X		X	X	X	X	X														
Admin. Adult Serv.	X	X		X				X		X											
Admin. Ch. Fam. Yth.	X	X	X		X	X	X														
Data Control Mgr.	X	X		X		X	X					X									
Res. Mob. Devel. Mgr.	X	X		X	X		X		X		X										
Prog. and Plan. Spec.	X	X		X	X	X			X		X										
Foster Care Coord.		X							X						X	X					
Resource Devel. Spec.						X	X			X											
Resource Devel. Spec.		X							X	X											
Lic. Consultant						X	X							X							
Accountant II					X									X							
Secretary II												X									
Clerk IV													X						X		X
Clerk Typist III																					
Clerk Steno II						X										X					
Clerk Typist III						X											X				
Secretary I														X							
Clerk Typist III																					
Clerk II												X		X							
Clerk Typist II														X					X		X
Clerk Typist III																				X	

FIGURE 21-3.
Organizational Network

network diagrams, as two of the people in the cohesive top management cluster (Figure 21-3) were female. One of these women, the program planning specialist, was fairly low down the formal organizational chart, but evidence from interviews and group meetings indicated that she may have been the second most influential person in the organization after the division chief.

The most frequently heard complaint during the upper-level group meetings was the lack of information. Many of the upper-level staff members wanted one-to-one meetings with the division chief. However, few of them could provide specific descriptions of the content areas they wished to discuss at these meetings. What the upper-level staff appeared to be seeking was a clearer definition of the division chief's values and priorities.

Communication-Group Meetings

The follow-up meetings involved organization members of mixed status who together formed key communication networks within the division. (The

FIGURE 21-3. *(continued)*

■ 21 ■
Tim R. V. Davis

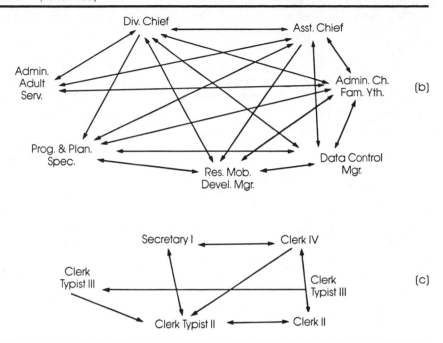

previous meetings had involved persons of equal status who belonged to common work groups.) Communication networks involved people in different horizontal and vertical positions within the organization. Following the previous format, these meetings were again conducted from the bottom up starting with the typing, clerical, and word-processing staff. Some of the results of the previous operating-level meetings had been felt prior to the actual communication-group meetings. The word was out that certain behaviors were being monitored, and this led to the immediate extinction of some of the dysfunctional responses noted earlier. The previous meetings produced a certain amount of solidarity among the operating-level employees, which led to an increased willingness to speak out. Action plans were developed for most of the remaining issues.

The upper-level meetings with top administrative staff, program planners, and resource developers did not result in such clear resolutions. Again, even before the sessions, several persons who had requested meetings with other members of the staff had already made the necessary arrangements. Both administrators expressed enthusiasm for the meetings and mentioned greater access to and more mutual understanding with the division chief. Nonetheless, none of these meetings served to pinpoint the precise issues that the respective parties needed to deal with. The issues were considered so broad and numerous that they could not be reduced to delimitable categories.

The meetings held with those persons earlier classified as "isolates" provided the opportunity for these people to stake their claims for inclusion in a network that could provide needed information. In most cases, the behavioral step was instigated, but only the continuity and long-term effects of these revised network arrangements would be evidence of their work-related utility.

Post–Test Questionnaire Administration

After allowing time for changes to be felt after the last of the action-planning meetings, the questionnaire examining aspects of communication and perceived performance effectiveness was readministered. These summative or end-point measures of change provided indications of perceived improvement.

The difficulties and frustrations attributed to poorly planned and coordinated work diminished significantly ($t = -2.70$, $p < .01$). The perceived incidence of misunderstandings concerning the interpretation of information was significantly different ($t = -2.69$, $p < .001$) and less of a problem. Also, a significant difference ($t = -3.15$, $p < .001$) was found with the extent of dissatisfaction generated by poorly planned conferences, committee meetings, etc. Again, the responses indicated improvement.

The pre-post results also indicated that vertical communication, including superior-subordinate relations, had improved. The responses concerning the ease with which information was obtainable from above were significantly different ($t = -2.94$, $p < .01$). Similarly, fewer staff members ($t = -3.00$, $p < .01$) indicated job-related difficulties with their immediate boss.

Evaluation[3]

At the operational level, critical incidents were defined and the monitoring apparatus was put in place to measure behavioral change. Differences in behavior were observed during the intervention. At the upper level, issue consensus and required behavioral change was much less substantive, but certain new networks were formed to facilitate the flow of needed information and to increase the level of "in-group" belongingness. Post-measures and personal testimonies provided evidence that changes were perceived to have taken place in the communication system and that improvements had occurred in vertical (superior-subordinate) relations, work planning, and coordination.

Evaluating the intervention in the light of the orienting framework derived from the literature described earlier shows that this study focused primarily on the internal environment of the organization. Limited access prevented a more comprehensive study of the external environment. The internal variables noted in the literature did impact on this public agency. The division chief's noncommital political behavior, the broad diversity of the service specialists, and, most important, the ambiguity of the performance environment influenced the intervention. Each of these is discussed in the following paragraphs.

First, the assumption that the chief executive should set goals and make clear commitments appears naive. In this case, the division chief appeared more oriented to *inputs*—the supply of funds and sources of external political support—while the rest of the staff was more oriented to service *outputs* and the demand for program improvements. Given the condition peculiar to the public sector that the agency does not go out of business for failing to reach a given profit objective, it would seem to be in top management's interests to avoid specific commitments, maintain the ambiguity, and keep the options open.

A second feature of this intervention was that, in private-sector terms, one small organization consisting of an office staff of twenty-two people was responsible for twenty-one products (services). A large number of these service areas did not overlap. Therefore, the incentive for cooperation and collaboration among the service specialists was minimal, while the competition for limited program service support (administrative and accounting) was maximal.

Third, what makes sense legislatively often makes little sense administratively. The public-sector specialist is left with the daunting task of translating complex legislation into workable programs. In this case, the vagueness of welfare legislation and the noncommital position of the division chief combined to produce a highly ambiguous performance environment. In this atmosphere of uncertainty, many of the meetings consisted of division members sincerely trying to represent what they believed to be the problems but, at the same time, rigorously avoiding anything that might give the slightest impression of their own incompetence.

CONCLUSION

The strategy adopted in this public-sector OD intervention focused mainly on the communication and relationship system. It is one thing to focus on communication and relationship processes in organizations with clear goals and quite another to focus on communication and relationships in organizations with virtually no operationalized goals. In the latter case, there may be good grounds for treating the communication system as the performance system—especially when the organization members and those in authority do the same thing.

In this case, an attempt was first made to isolate the organizational communication networks and to place people in those operational groupings that most closely approximated their work-related interactions. No attempt was made to build teams or to proselytize organization members into adopting OD values. The meetings were centered on issues, but bringing organization members together in their operational teams increased the level of communication. Increased communication per se is not to be valued. However, increased interaction may produce desirable behavioral effects (such as the critical incidents in this study); it may reduce the level of political ambiguity (such as the top-level briefing meetings with the division chief); it may increase the organization members' tolerance for ambiguity (see Boje & Rowland, 1977); it may lead to improvements in work planning and information processing (as indicated by the attitudinal data in this study); and it may increase the level of vertical or horizontal relationship satisfaction. All of these outcomes may be highly desirable in the public sector.

NOTES

[1]Although ambiguous performance situations are certainly not unique to the public sector, the extreme vagueness of goals and performance criteria in many public agencies makes this a distinguishing feature of a large number of public organizations.

[2]For a comprehensive discussion of communication-network analysis, see Farace et al. (1977, pp. 227–247).

[3]Since neither a control group (Campbell & Stanley, 1966) nor a comparison group (Lawler, 1977) was available, the research design component of this study may seem wholly inadequate. However, the consultant, rather than rejecting this public agency and others like it as unfit for research, used methods and measures that were available and seemed appropriate in the setting.

REFERENCES

Beckhard, R. ABS in health care systems: Who needs it? *Journal of Applied Behavioral Science,* 1974, *10,* 93–106.

Boje, D. M., & Rowland, K. M. *Spatial and temporal patterns as sense-making devices in organizational development: The role of symbols, metaphors, and myths.* Academy of Management Meeting, Kissimmee, Florida, 1977.

Bower, J. L. Effective public management: It isn't the same as effective business management. *Harvard Business Review,* 1977, *55,* 131–140.

Campbell, D. T., & Stanley, J. *Experimental and quasi-experimental design for research.* Chicago: Rand McNally, 1966.

Costello, T. W. Change in municipal government: A view from the inside. *Journal of Applied Behavioral Science,* 1971, *7,* 131–145.

Edelman, M. *Politics as symbolic action.* Chicago: Markham, 1971.

Farace, R. V., Monge, P. R., & Russell, H. M. *Communicating and organizing.* Reading, Mass.: Addison Wesley, 1977.

Gardner, N. Power diffusion in the public sector: Collaboration for democracy. *Journal of Applied Behavioral Science,* 1974, *10,* 367–372.

Giblin, E. J. Organization development: Public sector theory and practice. *Public Personnel Management,* 1976, *5,* 108–119.

Golembiewski, R. T. Organizational development in public agencies. *Public Administration Review,* 1969, *29,* 367–378.

Hofstede, G. The poverty of management control philosophy. *Academy of Management Review,* 1978, *3,* 450–461.

Imundo, L. V. Ineffectiveness and inefficiency in government management. *Public Personnel Management,* 1975, *4,* 90–95.

Kharash, R. N. *The institutional imperative.* New York: Charterhouse, 1973.

Kramer, F. A. Public accountability and organizational humanism. In R. A. Zawacki & D. D. Warrick (Eds.), *Organizational development: Managing change in the public sector.* Chicago: IPMA, 1976.

Lawler, E. E. III. Adaptive experiments: An approach to organizational behavior research. *Academy of Management Review,* 1977, *2,* 576–585.

Lindblom, C. E. The science of 'muddling through.' *Public Administration Review,* 1959, *19,* 79–88.

Ross, J. D., & Hare, G. (Eds.). Organizational development in local government: Results of an IPA grant. *First tango in Boston.* Washington, D.C.: NTL Institute, 1973.

Rubin, I., Plovnick, M., & Fry, R. Initiating planned change in health care systems. *Journal of Applied Behavioral Science,* 1974, *10,* 107–124.

Sharkansky, I. *The routines of politics.* New York: Van Nostrand, 1970.

Sikula, A. F. The values and value systems of government executives. *Public Personnel Management,* 1973, *2,* 16–22.

Warrick, D. D. Applying OD to the public sector. *Public Personnel Management* 1976, *5,* 186–190.

Wildavsky, A. *The politics of the budgetary process.* Boston: Little, Brown, 1964.

Wolman, H. Organization theory and community action agencies. *Public Administration Review,* 1972, *32,* 33–42.

Wynia, R. L. Federal bureaucrats' attitudes toward a democratic ideology. *Public Administration Review,* 1974, *34,* 156–162.

Zawacki, R. A., & Warrick, D. D. (Eds.). *Organizational development: Managing change in the public sector.* Chicago: IPMA, 1976.

22 | MBO and Public Management

Frank P. Sherwood
William J. Page, Jr.

Look at the right book, film, or government directive, and the message will be clear: management by objectives (MBO) is the answer to your managerial problem. Advocates argue that it is the successor to Taylor's "Mental Revolution"—a new way of thinking about, and engaging in, collective effort.

In 1973 and 1974, MBO was gospel for a Harvard Business School–dominated Washington bureaucracy. MBO would produce better strategies, higher quality decisions, less red tape, enhanced motivation, and a better ability to control things by the governmental executive.

Enthusiastic adherents (first in planning, programming, budgeting, then in MBO) felt a way had been found to cope with complexity, rigidity, and other regularly identified ailments. Now, a time has come for a more balanced view. MBO does have its attractions: it can make its contributions to more effective management of public services. However, it is not a "whole" system for managing. It is an instrument with basic elements of planning, coordination, and appraisal of performance. In public and private organizations, MBO is used primarily for short-range (tactical) planning of operations.

MBO is a relatively neutral instrument, whether in decentralized or centralized systems of managerial control. It is applicable in conditions of scarce or plentiful resources, and has utility in such vastly different arenas as public social services, water resources development, and industrial production.

MBO as a tactical and instrumental means of dealing with certain managerial needs is fairly straightforward. Important to MBO are: specificity in stating objectives, establishment of feasibility, short time frame (not usually more than one year), measurability of progress and results, definitive resource allocations in terms of operational plan, tracking and evaluation, and reassessment and replanning of objectives.

MBO must be seen in terms of its use as a managerial tactic, not as a management system. In our analysis we will be concerned with gaps between promise and performance, while specifying the assumptions of an "ideal world" that are preconditions to escalation of MBO into a whole system.

BACKGROUND

A number of ideas set the stage for the coming of MBO. The history of ideas relating to MBO can be traced at least as far back as the work of Frederick Taylor. Taylor's interest in quantification with its heavy emphasis on the capacity to state an objective in unambiguous terms and to measure progress toward it can be seen as one of these ideas.

The public sector was fairly heavily involved in MBO-type activity in the 1930s when serious efforts at activity measurement were undertaken. The Ridley and Simon monograph, *Measuring Municipal Activities,*[1] laid great stress on the definition of objectives as the rationale for measurement. Similar undertakings were undertaken by certain federal agencies, notably the Forest Service and the then-new Social Security Administration (SSA).

The SSA's program for evaluating and rewarding individual performance was an early effort in the government to build MBO ideas into the fabric of an organization. The system attempted to encompass the total goal constellation of the agency and to provide a functional base for the measurement of the performance of the individual employee, rather than narrow efficiency and/or economy criteria. As a result, SSA developed an image as a humane and helping organization.

The performance budgeting movement, launched by the First Hoover Commission in 1948, was unlike the later program budgeting in that it was not primarily an approach to allocating resources. Like MBO, it emphasized defining objectives and measuring progress toward anticipated results. Performance budgeting tended to be tactical, whereas program budgeting tended to be concerned with strategies of allocation. A famous example of performance budgeting in the early 1950s in municipal administration concerned the painting of light standards. The issue was not *how many* light standards should be painted but rather one of definitiveness of goals, resource allocation consistent with goals, and measurement of results achieved.

In 1954, Peter Drucker's *Practice of Management* was published. With his popularization of the term management by objectives in that book, MBO was now on track. It is important to realize that the tenets of the *Practice of Management* were empirically derived, mostly from General Motors and Sears Roebuck. However, in Drucker's opinion (correctly, we believe), MBO's early conceptual and practical development owes more to governmental than private experience.

MBO's heirs are numerous. George Odiorne has become management's modern healer. John Humble, a British consultant, has sought to enlighten Americans with his Bureau of National Affairs material, and has also introduced MBO to India. His book, *Improving Business Results,* is called "the definitive work on Management by Objectives."

Drucker's message came through to the public sector most clearly in California. Under Neeley Gardner, the California State Training Office began to push MBO (called program management) in the mid-1950s. A major goal then was to free the manager to be accountable for *results* and not just the number of paper clips used. The drive sought to create processes whereby the top manager could feel himself in control (through results) without having to check time reports. MBO was conceived as an ongoing management process; it was not a strategy for allocating and organizing resources.

In 1970 a seminar on MBO was held at the Federal Executive Institute. From the various federal executives there, it was found that MBO was then utilized by a number of federal agencies, among them the Internal Revenue Service, the General Accounting Office, the National Park Service, and the Federal Aviation Agency; the Social Security Administration used MBO tactics to control error rates and other aspects of claiming and processing benefits. Tactical planning was a major part of the SSA's response to revision of benefit payments.

One major resource of the seminar was Al Kelly, then Midwest regional commissioner of the IRS. Interestingly, Kelly essentially renounced measurement and specificity as the guiding beacons of MBO. Kelly indicated IRS was already awash with numbers and computers. His concern was to find a place for humans in IRS. Kelly engaged in lengthy sessions with his subordinates, and expected them to do likewise.

THE NIXON MBO

The Nixon term seems to mark the point at which MBO took on whole system pretensions in the federal government. It was part of an orientation that found societal good in the private sector and evil in the public. Harvard Business School became newly glorious. The attitude of the Nixon top management was one of low trust and contempt toward civil servants. Control and dominance of the system became particularly central concerns in his second term. There was a drive to introduce managerial techniques to assure continued control of policy, money, and manpower according to the classic business model. The second phase of the strategy was to obtain legislative and staffing changes to institutionalize and make permanent the new look.

It was in the Department of Health, Education, and Welfare that MBO became an allocation strategy, rather than only a tactic. Under Deputy Under Secretary Fred Malek, MBO received considerable notoriety as the answer to streamlined federal grants-in-aid programs. MBO's success in HEW was reported in the *Harvard Business Review* by Rodney Brady, who served briefly as successor to Malek as assistant secretary. Brady claimed that, in 1973, his Department had "one of the most far-reaching management by objectives . . . systems in operation anywhere."[2] However, the program, labelled "Operation Planning System," was getting mixed notices in the department itself. Four basic problems were cited: (a) enormous paperwork burden, (b) application of resources consistent with stated objectives difficult to achieve, (c) objectives out of time phase with the budget; and (d) heavy dependence on state and local governments for delivery of services while objectives were set unilaterally by the federal government.

Brady did concede that MBO could get off the track. But that was essentially a people problem. He saw the "primary constraint" on MBO in HEW as ". . . attitude on the part of some managers that the regular attention required of them by such a system is either (a) not consistent with their roles; or

303

(b) not as effective a way to manage as some other approach."[3] Because MBO was seen in whole system terms, Brady apparently saw no opportunity for varying approaches to organizational and managerial problems.

It is fair to say that MBO in HEW did reveal advantages. It was supportive of top management's efforts to control a large, complex organization. The emphasis on objective setting appeared to enhance communication and may have even helped to get a few things on track. Certainly, the persistent query, "Why?" did strip out some useless paper in grants programs. What really emerged was a more elaborated information system (tracking) and a formal review process that supported the leadership in control. There is no evidence that MBO had a significant effect on allocation strategies in the department.

MBO promulgated for the entire government by Malek as deputy director of the Office of Management and Budget in 1973 seemed substantially similar to the HEW effort. With the support of his superior, Roy Ash (another Harvard Business School graduate), Malek gave the allocation dimension emphasis. Goals and objectives were to be proposed upward; decisions reached on proposals were to be the bases for resource allocations. In turn, the tracking was in terms of achievement of the objectives and concurrency of resource usage with levels of accomplishment. Though proclaimed a participative process, government-wide MBO should be more properly identified as a strategy for hierarchical control. Proposals were made from lower to high echelons, but it was up to the boss to decide. It was seen as an advance that the boss now had some clear "options" and could make known to subordinates exactly what he wanted. Furthermore, in the President's case, an elaborate staff activity was established in the OMB to give him support in control and enforcement. A group of "management associates" was recruited, in the main youths out of prestigious business schools, to ensure that agencies observed the process.[4]

In developing a perspective on this period, it is important to realize this was the time of "the manager," defined as someone who gets things done. The manager is in charge. He seeks goal clarity; his system of thinking begins after someone else has told him what is to be done. In no sense can MBO be thought of as an allocation strategy as it suggests no approach to the tough problem of choice. Yet in the objective-setting rhetoric, it was implied that managers were now mystically able to put things on proper course. Essentially, it was a restatement of hierarchical accountability, with ambiguity removed.

In many respects the effort to attach mystique to management was most troublesome. Management is technique, both Brady and Malek imply. It is value neutral, universalistic, applicable in all cases, and best functions when the situation is unambiguous and clear cut. If the situation is not that way, make it so. Demands were made on the Federal Executive Institute, for example, that technical knowledge be taught to the exclusion of discussion of executive values, moorings, and obligations.

As perhaps has already become evident, the way one thinks about MBO is greatly affected by the way one conceives of the world. A basic assumption in MBO is that human behavior is rational. The rational model accepts macro-policy decisions (e.g., goals of "New Federalism" or economic stability without wage and price controls) as the parameters for analysis and decision making about objectives; and value of activities depends on their consistency with, and support for, the broad policies that have been established authoritatively. Behind this commitment to a rational objective-setting process lies several other assumptions: (a) objectives can be stated precisely; (b) organizations are essentially "closed" and participants in the decision (objective setting) process are easily identified; (c) sufficient information is available to administrators to enable objectivity in analysis, decision making, and evaluation of outcomes; and (d) organizational members at all levels will internalize prescribed objectives and cooperate in securing their achievement.

The key question, obviously, is the extent to which such goal clarity can be achieved. Rational behavior, in the instrumental sense, depends on understanding objectives with sufficient specificity to construct behaviors that are consistent with, and supportive of, their achievement.

Yet we frequently cannot even identify the authoritative decision maker in our complex system. While much public policy begins with messages and statements of purpose from executives and legislators, it is clear that those policy statements are not necessarily accepted as national goals. The system of checks and balances, with some exceptions, operates to enforce consensual establishment of major policies. Examples abound in environmental protection, social welfare, and national security. The effect is that an operational macro-goal may be nearly impossible to achieve (or sustain) in the absence of crisis. Further, a national goal or policy may be accepted and supported by a majority but effectively resisted by a particular geographic area or interest group. Civil Rights Act implementation was and is affected by regional variance, manifested in old South and more recently in old and new urban Northern differences.

Indeed, the analogy of MBO to private business seems least applicable in public goal setting. Deep differences in the role and function of public and private organizations exist; and substantive rationality in government may produce behavior that is quite removed from an MBO view of instrumental rationality; as the following conditions illustrate:

1. *Work frequently is allocated to the public sector because lack of knowledge or uncertainty makes it infeasible or too risky for performance in the private sector.*

Risk and infeasibility frequently derive from inadequate knowledge of the nature of a social problem, its incidence and prevalence, and methods for coping. Services initially developed by government (directly or through research grants) have been shifted to the private sector after being developed, tested, and routinized by governmental agencies. Prevention of communicable diseases is an example of an area in which initial government intervention and financial support led ultimately to private performance of essential human services.

2. *The stated objective may not be the real objective.*

C. W. Churchman suggests the management scientist apply a test: Will the system sacrifice other objectives to attain the stated objective?[5] A common fallacy, Churchman notes, is to "emphasize the obvious" in stating objectives. Pressure for precision, quantification, and measurability produces statements of objectives that are susceptible to precise expression though they may not be important. One conceals real objectives when there is questionable legitimacy of the real intent. An agency is pledged to reduce a problem by N percent, though the overriding fiscal policy is to drop expenditures or contain outlays within a dollar ceiling substantially below the amount appropriated for the service. The Congressional Budget and Impoundment Control Act of 1974 was precipitated by such practices.

3. *There are no commonly accepted standards for monitoring performance or measuring achievements of many public objectives.*

Objectives of process, as distinct from output, tend to be particularly resistant to precision, quantification, and valuation of results. How does one measure the value of monthly income maintenance payments to the elderly and unemployable? Devotees of precision and quantification faced with such problems have chosen to concentrate on "quality control" objectives, which monitor and uncover errors in determining eligibility for, and levels of, payments. This process objective presumably improves fiscal accountability, but does not permit assignment of subjective values for products. In the MBO process, one may not establish or defend the objective on a basis of social merit; this is seen as subjective.

Fuzzy objectives may be politically and socially advantageous, just as lack of specificity in expressing statutory purpose frequently is beneficial. Ambiguous objectives frequently are useful products in political compromise. For example, certain health and social service programs of the 1940s and 1950s had a *real* objective of birth control for persons who desired such services. Public funds appropriated annually for birth control were spent covertly in most areas as legal, political, or social considerations weighed against services.

Finally, rationality depends on the technical ability to write objectives that can be operationalized. There has been the rather common complaint that statements of objectives are ambiguous and not amenable to results tracking. It is not a coincidence that most of the literature's examples (a) are easily quantifiable, (b) have face validity in terms of the mission and broad goals of the organization, and (c) are usually routine.

DATA AND OBJECTIVITY

The MBO process evokes the greatest response from persons who value "hard" information and objectivity. High valuation of hard facts runs into difficulty when relevant data are scarce or untimely. A second limitation occurs in meanings or interpretations, which vary from one organization or profession to another. Alienation occurs when an outcome that is cherished by a particular unit is absolutely or relatively devalued by a decision maker who establishes priorities among many objectives.

Problems also arise in the analytical process, at which point judgments have to be made about progress toward goals. Thus, the analyst can have much to say in respect to the valuation of performance. His assumptions and values will affect the outcome. William Capron, former federal budget executive now at Harvard, has advised top executives to be certain that assumptions of the analysts are made explicit and that they employ alternative assumptions.[6]

The essence of instrumental rationality is that the choice of ends (objectives) governs methods to be used in achieving objectives. Methods are presumably neutral and subject to analysis and conclusion. But that is seldom true in the practical situation, and not just because of assumptive analysts. As Watergate has shown, how we do things is as important as what we do. Charles Schultze has written:

> There is no simple division of labor in which the "politicians" achieve consensus on ... objectives while the "analysts" design and evaluate—from efficiency and effectiveness criteria—alternative means of achieving those objectives. . . . Choice of means, particularly among domestic programs, is almost equally as freighted with political values as is the choice ends.[7]

A CLOSED SYSTEM

The MBO process is much more manageable when an organization is perceived as having quite distinct boundaries. Then the setting and tracking of objectives occur within a known arena, subject to control by the leaders. When forces outside the immediate organization are seen as having an increased salience for internal behavior, less viable is the notion of separateness and independence in both the goal-setting and the implementation process.

In terms of their sensitivity to these environmental forces, managers seem to come in two sets. On one side, there is the individual who is practically disabled by the mingling of his concerns with externalities. He tends to reject efforts at a definite statement of objectives for his organization because of the forces outside that he views as massively uncertain. Constitutionally, this person cannot accept MBO even as a managerial tactic.

Conversely, there is the manager who is completely closed—both in respect to his organization and to himself. He ignores the interdependencies of the system with its complex environment, implying that a public agency can set specific objectives, perform its work, and place a value on its products or services without regard for politics (bureaucratic or partisan), economic situation, or public opinion. Such a person is a good candidate to lead the charge for MBO as a whole managerial system. In his view the approach makes good sense because all the variables are subject to leadership control.

In fact, most government organizations are neither fully vulnerable nor invulnerable. The expression, pursuit, and achievement of objectives of a governmental unit are frequently and significantly conditioned by external phenomena. For example, intergovernmental program management (which now occurs at all levels of government) is a continuing experience of the open character of systems. External phenomena include legislators, clientele groups, decisions of other governmental units, mass communication media, economic conditions, courts, special interests, and other private organizations.

With the change in the role imperatives of public managers toward interdependence and collaboration with a wide variety of official and nonofficial organizations, the relatively straightforward MBO view of getting on with the task seems altogether too simplistic. One must exercise influence outside as well as within the system.

LEADERSHIP

It is important to emphasize again that the values and situational factors that operate in the private sector do not necessarily provide a base for thinking about leadership in the public sector. In the necessarily open system of government, the market values of efficiency and effectiveness must always take second place to the maintenance of democratic government, in which the public interest is sought through wide participation in the goal-setting process. If the ideals of democracy are to be taken seriously, it is evident that formal, hierarchical authority will generally have less relevance in the public setting. The system will be subject to more forms of influence; the leader's object will be to support these efforts to influence rather than to make judgments unilaterally.

Thus, it seems fair to say that the personality attributes we may expect of a successful leader in a private sector MBO effort may differ appreciably from his counterpart in the public sector. In a scalar analysis of human behavior, Clare Graves[8] provides a basis for understanding this difference in Table 22-1.

The manager who depends mainly on techniques, including MBO, when there is consensus on fairly routinized activities, would most appropriately be classed at level 4. But public service bureaucracies have neither clarity nor stability of objectives. Their high professionalism requires considerable discretion both in deciding what to do and also in determining how to do it. Professionals can perform well only with leadership corresponding to their behavioral scheme. A level 4 executive attempting to manage a level 6 or 7 work force is a mismatch. Professionals demand more freedom, institutional support, mutual trust, and respect than is likely to be allowed by the "management expert."

Recent initiatives to establish MBO in the federal government reflected inadequate understanding of both leadership and organizational dynamics in public settings. MBO and related managerial controls were inaugurated without necessary understanding of motivation, authority, and power in public organizations.

In a highly professionalized work force, with expertise in specific programmatic specialities, knowledge frequently offsets hierarchical subordination. In-

TABLE 22-1

Nature of Existence	Motivational System	Value System	Appropriate Managerial System
7. Pacificistic, individualistic	Information	Cognitive	Acceptance and support
8. Aggressive, individualistic	Self-esteem	Personal	Goal-setting without prescribing means to goals
4. Aggressive	Master	Amoral	Personal, prescriptive, and hard bargaining
1. Autistic	Psychological	Amoral	Close care and nurturing

crements of program expertise and attendant recognition are major factors in career progression. The manager whose special knowledge is methodological, rather than substantive, traditionally has had lower status than the expert in programs in the U.S. government.

■ 22 ■
Frank P. Sherwood
William J. Page, Jr.

MBO as practiced in the federal government has tended to deny this professional orientation. Emphasis on techniques and procedures, evaluations of unit performance by persons who knew little about programs, and the "top down" allocation of goals and objectives elicited hostility and counterproductive behavior. It was a simplistic, methodological approach that took no account of an organization culture which is, and must be, heavily professionalized. The new bosses sought mastery in order to be prescriptive in their MBO strategy. The civil servants sought recognition for their contribution and support for the values and activities in which they had already invested. The mastery-prescriptive managerial style associated with the MBO effort was not at all compatible with the real organization world in which the strategy was attempted.

It is necessary to assume a world that is knowable, stable, predictable, and compliant in order to conceive MBO as a "whole system" approach to management. The only way a technique such as MBO can claim to deal with the ambiguities that characterize the public sector is to declare them nonexistent.

CONCLUSION: THE FUTURE

MBO continues to have considerable visibility in the federal government partly because of its own merits and also because Malek-Ash people continue to hold important positions. Publicity, such as the Brady article, continues to generate enthusiasm at the state and local level.

The idea of MBO (as distinguished from ritualized process) must always be central to management action and thought. Managers in the public and private sectors alike share common aspirations in their desire to accomplish organizational tasks. The better these can be specified, the more likely the manager is to feel in control.

In the public sector there is a special push toward what is termed accountability. Abuse of governmental powers in the early 1970s and disappointing governmental performance in the 1960s have left legislators and the public skeptical of the intentions and abilities of public officials and organizations. MBO has the potential for reassuring legislators and the polity that government units actually are committed to specifying objectives and to reporting progress achieved toward them.

Though government has traditionally taken on many of the high-risk tasks in society, scarcity of tax dollars is causing decision makers at all levels to become less accepting of "blank check" appropriations. Legislators want more specificity of anticipated outcomes, and they are demanding increased amounts of data on performance in respect to stated objectives. Incrementally, we will undoubtedly be moving to specify intentions and measure achievements in areas such as human services.

It is likely that MBO will find its greatest expression as a tactic in a hierarchical strategy of leadership. Despite pressures for a more humanistic value orientation in society, the fact is that hierarchical patterns of leadership still dominate our organizations. MBO is an advantageous strategy in its goal clarity, in eliciting achievement motivations as objectives become clear, in its tracking wherein high achievers can see results of work, in improved capability to exercise data-based control, and in increased capability to provide rewards (often material benefits in the private sector) in terms of demonstrated performance.

Can we expect that the total system view of MBO will gain greater numbers of adherents? It is altogether likely that the federal push has not yet had its full impact on the governments of the nation. Yet the change in leadership in the OMB and the noticeable disenchantment with MBO as a panacea in the government make it likely that remaining efforts will be tactical within a hierarchical strategy.

Another scenario could be developed, which would assume a greater discontinuity in management action and more acceptance of the philosophy of Douglas McGregor. It might include:

- A seeking of substantive rather than instrumental rationality.
- Recognition that high goal clarity can have the negative effect of enforcing conformity.
- Awareness that the collection and analysis of data are normative acts.
- Acceptance that organizations are open systems and in heavy traffic with their environments, which they influence and which, in turn, influence them.
- Cooperation as a function of interdependence and felt mutual interests.
- Prizing of leaders who help to create environments in which decisions can be made, rather than prescribed.
- A climate in which achievement and affiliative motives dominate, rather than power motivations.

Obviously, this implies a totally different management strategy. The outer trappings of MBO in this circumstance might not appear vastly different, but the dynamics of the process and the "feel" certainly would be. The real task would be to negotiate organizational approaches that reflect multiple interests, in which commitment to a decision or objective would have at least equal importance with its quality. It is in (a) a value—the legitimacy of a diversity of interests in the organization and in (b) a skill—to work collaboratively in interdependent situations—that MBO would find a new home. Whether MBO moves in such a radically discontinuous direction really depends on the degree to which we are prepared to recognize organizational goal structures in their full complexity and are prepared to develop managerial strategies reflective of such understanding and awareness.

NOTES

[1]Clarence Ridley and Herbert Simon, *Measuring Municipal Activities* (Chicago: International City Management Association, 1973).

[2]Rodney H. Brady, "MBO Goes to Work in the Public Sector," *Harvard Business Review* (March–April 1973).

[3]Ibid, p. 71

[4]The recruitment of these management associates showed rather clearly the extent of the Nixon administration bias. In an interview in March 1974, Fred Malek stated that managers in the private sector were preferred because their opportunity to learn managerial techniques was better than that of their counterparts in the public service. The interview, interestingly, was videotaped for presentation to an audience of federal administrators.

[5]C. W. Churchman, *The Systems Approach* (New York: Dell, 1968), pp. 30–31.

[6]William N. Capron, "The Impact of Analysis on Bargaining in Government," in Alan A. Altschuler (ed.), *The Politics of the Federal Bureaucracy* (New York: Dodd, Mead and Company, 1968), p. 201.

[7]Charles L. Schultze, *The Politics and Economics of Public Spending* (Washington, D.C.: Brookings Institution, 1968), pp. 2–3.

[8]Clare W. Graves, "Deterioration of Work Standards," *Harvard Business Review* (September–October, 1966). (Reprint)

23 | The Practical Differences Between Public and Private Sector Collective Bargaining

Lee C. Shaw
R. Theodore Clark, Jr.

The 1960s have rightly been called "the decade of the public employee."[1] While the unionization of employees in the private sector was stagnating, the number of employees who joined unions more than doubled.[2] When viewed in historical perspective, the rapid gains made by unions in organizing public employees in the past several years were probably inevitable. Prior to 1945, public employees, generally speaking, were better off than their counterparts in private industry. Their job security was greater,[3] their wages were comparable, and their fringe benefits were superior. But all of this began to change after World War II, when the unions in the private sector succeeded in winning round after round of wage increases and fringe benefits surpassing those received by public employees.[4]

In an effort to restore the balance, public employees, particularly at the state and municipal levels, have turned to militant union leadership. Many of these union leaders advocate that government is not a benign employer, but an exploiter that must be fought and forced to yield to the union's demand.[5] This militancy presents a direct challenge to public management—a challenge that demands a forthright and positive response. If public managers, who, unlike union officials, are accountable to the public, abdicate their responsibilities, our democratic form of government could be undermined. As A. H. Raskin has observed:

> The essential lesson of New York City's whole experience is that there is no substitute for alertness on the part of the elected officials once they embark on the basically sound proposition that the city's best interests will be served by giving civil service unions negotiating rights comparable to those which prevail in industry. If managerial slackness, ineptitude or politics blunt the relationship, the community will become captive of its unionized employees.[6]

The question is, to what extent are public managers today prepared to offer effective opposition to union militancy?

This article will focus primarily upon the practical differences between private and public sector collective bargaining, including the impact of political considerations upon the latter. It will also offer several suggestions as to how public sector management must approach collective bargaining in order to cope effectively with its relatively new role.

RESPONSIBILITY AND ACCOUNTABILITY FOR COLLECTIVE BARGAINING

Effective collective bargaining in the public sector is dependent upon establishing motivation in public management, determining a basic negotiation philosophy, and realistically preparing for potential public employee strikes. Before motivation, philosophy, or strike preparation can be discussed, however, it is first necessary to decide who should have the responsibility and who should be held accountable for labor relations in the public sector. A brief consideration of the comparable function in the private sector is instructive.

Many successful private corporations have divided their total business activity into several distinct divisions with the head of each division being held responsible for the profitability of his division. Budgets are established by corporate headquarters for each division, and the head of each division is expected to stay within his budget. The management of each division is rewarded according to the profit which that division contributes to the corporation, and if the management does not make a reasonable profit, it is obviously in trouble. Since labor costs form a major proportion of the total costs of any division, it is to the benefit of the head of each division to minimize labor costs.

Toward the end of minimizing labor costs, each divisional executive is assisted by an industrial relations or personnel director who negotiates with one or more unions and administers the contract on a day-to-day basis.[7] The future of the personnel director with the company depends upon how effectively he manages his areas of responsibility. He fully understands that his areas of responsibility are directly related to the profitability of the division. If, in negotiation, the personnel director surrenders those management prerogatives his superiors deem essential, or if he is too lenient with the union in any other aspect, he will more than likely be removed from his position. On the other hand, if he does his job well, he will be rewarded by advancement, and his salary and other benefits will accordingly be increased; he has two positive motivations, and both are important.

In addition to a personnel director, the management group often includes, among others, safety engineers, salary administration experts and employee benefit personnel. Often, legal advice is available from the company's legal department or the company retains outside counsel skilled in labor law and negotiations. The private employer, therefore, orients a sizable portion of management toward personnel and collective bargaining matters and maintains a well-ordered strategy concerning the labor relations function.

Unfortunately, in contrast to their counterparts in the private sector, many public employers have not yet seen the need to establish a distinct labor relations staff function as a permanent part of their organization.[8] All too often the responsibility for collective bargaining has not been fixed with any degree of certainty, a circumstance which promotes at least two unsatisfactory results. First, because responsibility for collective bargaining is not explicitly assigned, no individuals are ascribed the specific obligation to promote and protect management's interests. Second, since labor relations is not recognized as a distinct function, the individuals upon whom this responsibility is thrust are still expected to perform their normal duties, a situation which is often less than satisfactory.

The problems raised above are compounded by the fact that most public employers, and especially those managers charged with the responsibility of administering the medium- and small-sized municipalities, counties, and school districts are not prepared by either training or background to deal with the challenge presented by collective bargaining. In many instances the responsibility for negotiations is assumed by the ultimate policy body, whether it be the school board, city council, or the board of county commissioners.[9] But a school board, for example, composed of a housewife, a sales executive, a plumbing contractor, a lawyer, and a university professor holding office on a part-time, no-pay basis has no business trying to negotiate a collective bargaining agreement with professional union representatives.[10]

Moreover, intense pressures have been generated in the public sector to force the chief executive officer to participate directly in negotiations.[11] While there are always exceptions, in the authors' opinion the chief executive officer should not participate directly in negotiations.[12] Slichter, Healy, and Livernash in their Brookings Institution study of collective bargaining in the private sector offer a similar conclusion:

> [Negotiations by operating officers have] the great disadvantage that operating men can ill afford to take time from their jobs to engage in bargaining, and they are not necessarily capable bargainers. Nothing is more likely to produce bad bargains for employers than impatience on the part of management representatives to get back to their regular jobs. A labor relations staff is selected partly to obtain individuals skilled in the art of negotiations.[13]

The need to establish labor relations as a separate function and to develop the competence of the individuals who staff this function must have high priority if public employers expect to meet the challenge of militant unionism.[14] Establishing a separate labor relations function and holding those who staff this function accountable to high standards of performance is not enough, however. In the public sector the political element must be considered. Prior to the advent of collective bargaining, many groups of public employees, notably postal employees, firemen, and policemen, were very effective in lobbying before legislative bodies to influence changes in wages, hours and working conditions. Collective bargaining, however, contemplates that changes in wages, hours, and working conditions will result from good faith negotiations between representatives of each party in a mutual effort to reach agreement; this process is undermined where the union is able to successfully make an "end run," either during or after negotiations. Such an "end run" involves an attempt by the union to circumvent the collective bargaining process and make a direct appeal to the legislative body that is responsible for making the final decision. Because unions are a potent political force, elected officials tend to be receptive to such approaches.[15] "End runs" have frequently occurred where one or more members of the legislative body have strong political ties to the group in question, and such maneuvers are particularly aggravated where one or more of the members of the legislative body come from organized labor.

If collective bargaining is going to work in the public sector, it is necessary that the "end run" be eliminated.[16] Since the terms and conditions of employment are supposed to result from good faith collective bargaining rather than legislative lobbying, there is no justification for allowing a union to successfully circumvent the bargaining process and make a direct appeal to the legislative body. Moreover, if a union succeeds in making an "end run," the effectiveness of the negotiating team is seriously undermined.

This same problem has been successfully resolved in the private sector. Years ago unions in the private sector frequently made attempts to go over the head of the employer's bargaining team because they believed they could convince higher authorities to grant greater increases than they could get from the bargaining team. Such conduct rarely occurs today because unions apparently understand the corporate structure and are convinced that the company's bargaining team has the necessary authority. Hopefully members of legislative bodies will see the wisdom of confining negotiations to the bargaining table and will resist efforts by union representatives to involve them in negotiations. While there might be some short-term political gains from such intervention, the long-run consequences for stable collective bargaining in the public sector would be disastrous.

THE PROBLEM OF MOTIVATING PUBLIC SECTOR MANAGEMENT

This section of the article will serve to suggest various means by which public employers may foster public management motivation. Since, however, it is apparent that presently private management negotiators are far more motivated than their public counterparts, it will first be instructive to categorize the differences between private and public management motivations.

Differences in Motivation

Whether public sector management meets the militant union challenge will depend in large part on the presence or absence of motivation on the part of public managers. Unlike the private manager who is profit-oriented, the public manager is frequently motivated by political considerations. As a result, the motivations of private and public managers differ considerably. The most important of these differences are:

1. The motivation of the private manager is unaffected by possible concern with direct retribution by his antagonists. In contrast, the public manager may view his union opponents as members of his constituencies. In fact, since a large segment of most constituencies have some union affiliation, the motivation of an elected public manager may be tempered lest he antagonize union members generally. The appointed manager will similarly, but indirectly, be pressured by his elected superior who respects the power of union ballots.

2. The private manager is profit-motivated and his advancement and salary will depend to a degree on how effectively he deals with unions. The public official relies more on his political base rather than on the results of his management. In fact, the viability of his political base is independent of his management expertise or efficiency.

3. The private manager is well aware of the importance of retaining the right to manage from the point of view of the financial success of the business and, more especially, in his personal interest in that success. This profit motivation is missing in the public sector, save perhaps in the desire and ability of the public manager to decrease costs and thereby increase services or reduce taxes.

4. Most companies have a continuous program of training supervisors to think as management and to direct the working force, thereby emphasizing the importance of the management to the success of the business. Such programs are rare and sporadic in the public sector.[17]

5. There is a much sharper line of demarcation between management and nonmanagement employees in the private sector than in the public sector.[18]

6. In some instances the private manager is sensitive to the reaction of other managers in his own company and managers of other companies as to the result of his success in contract negotiations and grievance matters. Again, the political situation plays the dominant role for the public manager. While taxpayer resistance to increased taxes does act as a constraining influence on elected officials, the voice of the taxpayers is frequently not as strong as that of the union in negotiations.

It should be pointed out, however, that public management has to work in a considerably different environment than private management does and that this imposes certain limitations on its ability to express its views adequately. As Frank Zeidler, the former Mayor of Milwaukee, observed:

> Public administration officials are relatively powerless before legislatures in opposing the demands of organized public employees because the public administrators do not represent a bulk constituency or voting bloc. Therefore, the public interest before legislatures must be presented by civic associations, municipal leagues, and other nonpartisan civic groups.
>
> It may be in this area that the greatest weakness for the public lies, and that there may be truly a loss of democracy as some civic groups now fear because no group will consider it its business to protect the public interest in legislation dealing with employee-employer relations in the public service.[19]

Because of the differences in motivation, public managers have often failed to realize that it is their duty to represent management's viewpoint with strength and vigor, not only during contract negotiations but also in day-to-day dealings with the union. This lack of vigor in representing the interests of management is often revealed in the agreements that have been negotiated in the public sector. An analysis prepared by the Michigan Municipal League of 158 contracts negotiated by Michigan municipalities[20] reveals these startling statistics:

a. Over twenty-five percent of the agreements contain either union shop or maintenance of membership provisions, both of which are illegal under Michigan law.

b. Over forty percent of the agreements either contain no management rights clause or only a very brief statement of management rights,[21] such as "the City retains all of its former rights."

c. Over forty percent of the agreements with grievance procedures either contain no definition of the term "grievance" or define the term in rather general and indefinite terms. This is a serious mistake, which is made only by amateurs in the private sector.

d. Over thirty-five percent of the agreements do not have no-strike clauses.[22]

e. Over sixty percent of the agreements make no reference to the employer's right to subcontract. The right to subcontract may be essential in the public sector to reduce costs and to confront unions with this alternative if negotiated increases are too costly.[23]

Suggestions to Motivate

What can be done to properly motivate public managers? Drawing upon the differences outlined above and inferences that may reasonably be drawn, the authors offer the following suggestions.

First, every effort should be made to impress upon public managers that it is their duty to represent and protect the interests of the governmental agency just as it is the duty of unions to represent public employees. In short, the public negotiator must understand that negotiations are a *contest* much akin to the adversary system of litigation. If the public manager fails to do his job, he should be terminated and not enjoy tenure because of civil service or political clout. Of course, if the public manager is not given the authority and support of the executive officer or legislative body he cannot be held accountable. Toward this end, management training programs should be expanded and put on a *permanent* basis. Private industry has learned that such training programs are an invaluable way to motivate managers. One of the purposes of such programs is to sell the manager on his responsibility to manage efficiently.

Second, negotiators in the public sector should be imbued with the need to retain the right to manage. In the long run this is of primary importance. In the private sector, successful companies have recognized the need to retain the right to operate efficiently, to utilize technological change to reduce labor costs, and to avoid restrictive work rules.[24]

Derek Bok and John Dunlop have observed that the problem of preserving the right to manage in the public sector is compounded since:

> The potential for uneconomic work rules . . . is much greater in public employment because budgetary pressures are much less direct and effective than market forces in exerting pressure for efficiency and survival. Many public authorities, moreover, are inexperienced in negotiating with employee organizations over workplace issues. As a result, they are often not alert and enterprising enough to prevent or buy out restrictive rules before they become too wasteful and deep-rooted.[25]

Public managers must therefore be motivated to detect and avoid restrictive and inefficient work practices.

Third, all persons who hold supervisory positions should be considered part of the management team. Although this matter is firmly settled in the private sector, there is a considerable difference of opinion as to whether persons with supervisory authority should be excluded from employee bargaining units in the public sector.

The problem in large part results from the fact that certain professional associations such as the National Education Association and the International Associations of Fire Fighters have historically included supervisory personnel within their ranks. Indeed, the leadership of these professional associations until recently was more often than not composed of individuals who held high supervisory positions. Initially formed for the broad purpose of advancing the general interests of the profession, these professional associations are now actively assuming the role of collective bargaining representatives. Despite this basic change in purpose, these professional associations have continued to insist, sometimes adamantly, that the collective bargaining unit include supervisory personnel. The transformation of these professional associations from all-inclusive groups of supervisory and nonsupervisory employees seeking to advance their professional interests to bargaining representatives requires that the status of these supervisory employees in the collective bargaining unit be reexamined.

Some commentators have argued for the inclusion of supervisory personnel within the ranks of employee bargaining teams.[26] The authors strongly oppose such a view; supervisory employees must be considered part of management if collective bargaining is to succeed.[27] Morris Slavney, the Chairman of the Wisconsin Employment Relations Commission, accurately summarized the reasons why supervisors must be considered part of management:

> In order to have meaningful collective bargaining in public employment, there must be not only an identifiable managerial but also a supervisory community because the collective bargaining process, whether it be in public or private employment, does not terminate when the collective bargaining agreement is reached at the bargaining table. It is a continuing process throughout the term of the agreement, resolution or ordinance covering the bargain. Someone must direct and supervise the employees in the performance of their function; someone must make day-to-day decisions affecting working conditions; and someone must process employee grievances, which are bound to arise as a result of such decisions. Permitting supervisory employees to be included in bargaining units along with the rank and file employees weakens not only the managerial community but has an adverse effect upon the bargaining agent as an employee organization.[28]

Fourth, an attempt should be made to provide public managers some of the financial rewards for outstanding performance which their counterparts in private industry receive. Bonus plans for successful private managers are widely used and very effective. When private industry was organized in the 1930s and 1940s, the personnel director was low on the management totem pole and companies suffered as a result.[29] Public agencies should profit from this experience.

At the minimum, serious considerations should be given to providing different salaries and working conditions for management personnel. At present, it is commonplace in the public sector to extend to management personnel the benefits negotiated for in bargaining with employees. The authors question whether it is desirable for bargaining unit employees to negotiate, in effect, the salaries and working conditions of their superiors.[30] The advent of collective bargaining requires that a system under which the salaries of administrators are directly tied to the salaries of bargaining unit personnel be carefully reexamined, if not entirely eliminated.

THE NEED FOR A BASIC NEGOTIATING PHILOSOPHY

Apart from establishing responsibility and accountability for negotiations and providing sufficient motivation, it is important that public sector negotiators have a firm philosophy to guide them in the formulation of their proposals and in evaluating union proposals. In the private sector, management negotiators have generally relied on the *reserved rights* or *management rights* doctrine as the guiding philosophy. Briefly stated, the reserved rights doctrine can be defined as a rule of construction whereby management retains all those rights which it does not surrender in negotiations.

Labor relations experts[31] and even union spokesmen[32] have acknowledged the vital role which the management rights doctrine plays in the private sector. Moreover, private arbitrators with very few exceptions have relied on this doctrine to interpret contracts.[33] Vital as this doctrine is in the private sector, it may be even more important in government labor relations, for the functional basis for management rights does not allow any room for the union to acquire rights to manage and slide in as a "joint manager," since unions are not functionally managers of the public authority. But public employee unions are increasingly asserting the right to co-determine matters of public policy. This is especially true with respect to educational policies.[34] These attempts must be resisted, however, if public policy decisions are to be made by the officials who are alone accountable to the public. Since union officials are not similarly accountable to the public, they should not be permitted to have an equal voice in the determination of public policy.

Management is the "Acting" Party

Integral to this doctrine is the concept that it is management's duty to act and it is the union's duty to challenge if the union feels that management's action is contrary to the negotiated agreement. Thus, the union's function under the agreement can best be described as a "watchdog" function—watching the actions of the public employer, the "acting" party—to see whether such actions are in compliance with the agreement. It is readily apparent that a union is going beyond its "watchdog" capacity if it has day-to-day operational responsibilities.

Frequently, however, union representatives insist that they are reasonable and that there will be no problems if they are allowed to participate with management in day-to-day decision making.[35] The inherent fallacy of this view was clearly expressed by William Leiserson, formerly a member of the National Labor Relations Board and the Railway Mediation Board, when he criticized the ill-fated attempt to have the Office of Production Management

319

during World War II jointly directed by Management Representative Knudsen and the Union Representative Hillman. Leiserson especially emphasizes the resulting confused organization and administration attributable to an inadequate analysis and lack of differentiation between policy-making and operating functions.[36] For exactly the same reasons union leaders should not participate in day-to-day decision making under a labor agreement.

The management rights doctrine provides a test by which to analyze union contract demands. Thus, to preserve the public employer's right to carry out its designated public function and to manage efficiently its operations, one fundamental question should be asked as each union demand is placed on the bargaining table: Does the proposal prevent the public employer from taking actions necessary to implement the public policy goals entrusted to it by law in an efficient manner? If it does, the proposal should be resisted. Further, proposals—such as "mutual agreement" or "veto" clauses—that require the public employer to first obtain the union's agreement before acting in such areas as discipline, scheduling of overtime, or subcontracting are contrary to the management rights doctrine and should be avoided.

The Union's Function Under a Collective Agreement

If union representatives should not participate in day-to-day decision making, then what is their function under an agreement? Of course, during the negotiation of a collective bargaining agreement, union representatives must be recognized as having equal bargaining rights with management except as certain subjects are declared by law to be outside of the permissible scope of bargaining.[37] Once the agreement is executed, however, the union representatives' role as negotiators on an equal footing with the management representatives should cease and thereafter they should assume an entirely different role. That role should be the policing of the agreement to determine whether actions taken by the public employer are contrary to the contractual commitments previously agreed upon by both parties.

If being the "watchdog" is the union's proper function under the agreement, then the union must have the necessary rights to perform this function. In the private sector, these rights are contained in a properly conceived grievance and arbitration procedure. Approximately ninety-five percent of private collective bargaining agreements contain such provisions.[38] The new Federal Executive Order allows the parties to negotiate grievance and arbitration provisions to resolve interpretive disputes.[39] It is logically consistent with the management rights approach for public employers to agree to binding arbitration of disputes concerning the interpretation and application of a collective bargaining agreement.[40] But it should not be more. The procedure must be carefully drafted and limited to the question of contract compliance—for otherwise grievance handling and settlement procedures can become a means of eroding the public agencies' rights during the term of the agreement.

THE NEED AND ABILITY TO TAKE A STRIKE IF NECESSARY

In virtually every collective bargaining negotiation, the employer must ask himself how far he will go before taking a strike, how long a strike can he stand, and what will be the result of the strike. A manufacturer may be in a position to take a strike for many weeks with very little long-term loss. The strike may reduce an excess of inventory, for example. And most union leaders would agree that from time to time employee demands are so outlandish that a strike is required to reduce the demands. For the long-term good of the employer, a strike may well be a good investment in the future.

The public employer performs, or believes it performs, an "indispensable" service. The public raises a hue and cry if there is no police or fire service, if garbage piles up at the curb, or if schools are closed because of a strike. A strike of policemen, firemen, sanitation workers, or teachers that lasted one week would have a substantial impact on most public employers, whereas a one-week strike at a manufacturing plant usually would not cause a ripple.

The manufacturing employer, although not wanting a strike, frequently becomes more firm in its resolve once a strike gets underway. The public employer, in contrast, may talk as if it is willing to take a strike but will frequently change its position rapidly once a strike becomes imminent and especially if a strike materializes. Perhaps because of panic or confusion over what is in the "public interest," municipalities and school boards will in many instances make hasty judgments and rush to give the union whatever is needed to prevent or end a strike. This has a cumulative effect, for premature surrender of the public employer teaches the union that it should repeat this process on an annual basis or, at least, threaten to repeat it, in order that the employer will once again compromise good judgment.

Municipalities and school boards, as well as the public, will have to change their views concerning the need and ability to take a strike. In some situations, cooperative arrangements can be made with neighboring communities for temporary police, fire, and sanitation services.[41] A school board could extend the school year well into the summer, if need be, to make up for time lost because of a strike. As unpalatable as these solutions may seem, public employers cannot continue to function if they regularly say "yes" to everything that unions want because of the strike weapon.

The ability to take a strike requires considerable contingency planning.[42] Such contingency planning has a two-fold effect. First, it enables the public employer to make adequate arrangements in advance of a strike to provide for the continuation of essential services and to dispense with nonessential services during such a strike. Second, the fact that a public employer indicates that it is prepared to take a strike reduces the possibility of a strike occurring. Unions are less likely to strike an employer that is prepared to take a strike than an employer who is caught unprepared.

The ability to take a strike also requires that a public employer face a strike situation in a rational, nonemotional manner. Public employers must neither panic nor, in the opposite extreme, take retaliatory action such as withdrawing recognition in those states that do not require mandatory bargaining. In either situation, the goal of ending the strike on terms that the employer can live with is ignored, and disastrous long-term consequences may result.

Public employers who do not panic or take retaliatory action are in a better position to cope successfully with a strike. A good example is the manner in which an Illinois junior college board handled a strike called by its faculty members on the day the summer session was scheduled to commence. The initial reaction of the board was to withdraw recognition. Outside counsel was successful in counseling against such action, pointing out that it would convert the strike into one of principle in which the college would in all likelihood lose. This conclusion was influenced in part by the fact that the college was located in an area that included many union members. Counsel also advised against refusal to resume negotiations until the admittedly illegal strike ceased. While this approach has its advantages in other situations, they did not feel that it would work in this situation. Moreover, they doubted whether the public would have supported such an approach for very long. The pros and cons of seeking injunctive relief were also considered but such action was decided against for two reasons. First, if an injunction were granted, the chances were quite good that the union would not obey the injunction. Second, even if the injunction had been obeyed, the underlying dispute would not have been settled. The approach that was finally decided upon was to advise the union that the college was willing to continue negotiations in the hopes that negotiations would lead to an early agreement, but that if negotiations did not result in an agreement within two days the college would have to take into account the paramount interests of the students who had enrolled for the summer session and advise them that they should begin to consider applying to other junior colleges in the area. The union accepted the offer to resume negotiations, and the strike was settled within two days on terms fairly close to the college's final offer prior to the strike.

We do not suggest that all strikes should be handled in this same way. Indeed, they cannot be because each strike must be assessed in light of its own peculiar circumstances and issues, as well as the context within which it occurs. We do suggest, however, that the ability to avoid hasty decisions made in an atmosphere of panic is a prime prerequisite for resolving a strike on a basis that is in the long-term interest of the public employer.

CONCLUSION

There are undoubtedly differences between collective bargaining in the private sector and collective bargaining in the public sector. The nonprofit nature of most public services and the political atmosphere in which bargaining often takes place are two of the most significant differences. Nevertheless, public sector management can learn a great deal from the private sector experience in labor relations over the past thirty-five years. This is especially true with respect to the need for establishing clear-cut responsibility and accountability for labor relations, the need to motivate public management, the need to establish a basic negotiating philosophy, and the need to take a strike if necessary. In this article we have attempted to point out some of the deficiencies that we have detected in these four areas in the public sector and to suggest how the experience in the private sector is relevant in correcting these deficiencies. In the authors' opinion, correction of these deficiencies along the lines suggested would go a long way in preparing public management to meet successfully the challenge of militant unionism.

NOTES

[1] D. Bok & J. Dunlop, *Labor and the American Community* 312 (1970).

[2] The public employee ranks have increased from a little over one million in 1960 to 2.2

million in 1968. Cohany & Dewey, "Union Membership Among Government Employees," *Monthly Lab. Rev.* 15–20 (1970). The size of the largest unions representing public employees, such as the American Federation of State, County and Municipal Employees (AFSCME), the American Federation of Government Employees (AFGE), the National Education Association (NEA), and the American Federation of Teachers (AFT) grew accordingly. AFSCME, for example, saw its membership grow from under 185,000 in 1960 to approximately 460,000 in 1970. L. Kramer, *Labor's Paradox—The American Federation of State, County and Municipal Employees, AFL-CIO* 261 (1962); *Proceedings of the 18th International Convention, AFSCME,* Denver, Colorado, May 4–8, 1970. And between 1964 and 1970, AFSCME moved from the eighteenth largest affiliate of the AFL-CIO to the seventh largest. Stieber, "Remarks to Public Employment Symposium on Employee Organization in State and Local Government," in *Government Employee Relations Report* [hereinafter cited as *GERR*] No. 400, E-1, E-2 (May 10, 1971).

[3]For the most part, government employees were not subject to the periodic layoffs common in many private sector industries. In addition, widespread adoption of the merit system had substantially reduced the incidence of the spoils system under which continued tenure in a public job was contingent upon faithful support of the party in power. See generally E. Banfield & J. Wilson, *City Politics* 207–10 (1965).

[4]In the period from 1948 to 1963, wages in the manufacturing industries, for example, rose a total of eighty percent. See L. Reynolds, *Labor Economics and Labor Relations* 414 (1964). The extent to which these wage gains can be attributed to union power has been the subject of continuing academic debate, see, e.g., id. at 503, nonetheless it is doubtless true that unions were popularly perceived to be the primary cause. As the Advisory Commission on Intergovernmental Relations noted: "The effectiveness of labor unions in the private sector, notably in salary and fringe benefit matters, has also influenced public employee organizations at the state and local levels" (*Labor-Management Policies for State and Local Government* 10 [1969]).

[5]Consider, for example, the following excerpt from an editorial, entitled "Public Employees vs. 'Petty Dictators,'" which appeared in the monthly newspaper of the Laborers' International Union: "Government employees are no longer accepting the arbitrary conditions which 'Stone Age' administrators have imposed on them. The Post Office strike, the Newark Teachers strike, and hundreds of less well-publicized situations testify to the growing militancy of public employees" (*Government Employee,* April 1971, at 2, col. 1).

[6]Raskin, "Politics Up-Ends the Bargaining Table," in *Public Workers and Public Unions* 122, 144 (S. Zagoria ed. 1972).

[7]Normally, the personnel director is also responsible for recruitment, supervisory development, safety, and security.

[8]"[I]t is often unclear, especially in the early stages of new collective bargaining systems, as to who bears the decision-making responsibility on which an agreement with an employee organization may be reached." 1968 *Supplement to Report of Task Force on State and Local Government Labor Relations* 10.

[9]See L. Perry & W. Wildman, *The Impact of Negotiations in Public Education: The Evidence from the Schools* 118 (1970).

[10]Robert Bendiner, in his recent book, has pointedly observed:

Unlike those labor-relations men hired by private enterprise to do their collective bargaining, the hapless members of a school board are by no means free to sit at the bargaining table all hours of the day and night. Engaged full time in earning a living or raising their families, they cannot devote themselves exclusively to negotiations until fatigue sets in or a settlement is reached. Neither can a board use public funds to match those available to private corporations or, for that matter, to the teachers themselves, for publicity and demonstration purposes. And, worst of all, rarely has experience equipped a board's members for the subtleties and "gamesmanship" of collective bargaining. Unfamiliar with the jargon and stratagems of the game, they often misread the signs of their opponents, mistaking a "maybe" for a "no" and a "no" for a "never." It is a field, says Dr. Wesley Wildman of the University of Chicago, in which "the curse of amateurism is rampant." (*The Politics of Schools* 98 [1969]).

A seldom-noted side effect of school boards becoming directly involved in negotiations is that citizens who would otherwise willingly serve on school boards pass up the opportunity to do so because of the vast amount of time that negotiations take.

[11]An example of the kind of pressure that has been generated in this area is evidenced in the following statement of the president of the Cook County Teachers Union, Local 1600, protesting the refusal of Prairie State College to include board members and the president on the negotiating team: "The Union is appearing before the March 5 meeting of the Prairie State College Board to protest the Board position and to demand that the Board demonstrate its respect for the faculty by appointing Board members as well as the college president to the Board Negotiating Committee" (*Chicago 1600 Union Voice,* Jan.–Feb. 1970, at 2, col. 1).

[12]As one commentator has written: "The problems arising from the delegation of bargaining to staff personnel are far outweighed by greater proficiency, objectivity and continuity. Elected officials are rarely trained in personnel matters. . . . Further, elected officials offer no guarantee of continuity for future bargaining sessions. (Mulcahy, "A Municipality's Rights and Responsibilities under the Wisconsin Municipal Labor Law," 49 *Marq. L. Rev.* 512, 515 [1966]). As Mulcahy also noted, "[Elected officials] are subject to numerous pressures which make rendering impartial decisions extremely difficult." Id.

[13]S. Slichter, J. Healy, & R. Livernash, *The Impact of Collective Bargaining on Management* 923 (1960).

[14]The following observation of the Twentieth Century Fund Task Force on Labor Disputes in Public Employment underscores this need:

> In government today, especially below the federal level, there is a paucity of experience in dealing with unions and administering labor agreements. Unless the costly and embittering mistakes made in industry at an earlier time are to be repeated in public employment, *something must be done to provide those who act for government-as-employer and those who act for government employees with the knowledge and sophistication necessary to negotiate and administer labor agreements capably.*
>
> While nothing can match actual experience, its best possible substitutes in this area are training and utilizing expert assistance that may be available from outside. (Report and Recommendations of the Twentieth Century Fund Task Force on Labor Disputes in Public Employment, Pickets at City Hall in GERR Ref. File 51:151, 157 [1970] [emphasis in original]).

Herbert Haber, New York City's Director of Labor Relations, commented as follows concerning the need for establishing a separate labor relations function in the public sector:

> [D]ealing with the unions is a full-time job requiring professional help. Anyone who has authority over a given agency is well-advised to secure full-time professional help or regular professional consultations, whatever he can manage. In running a large scale public operation, he has innumerable responsibilities of which only one small part is dealing with the union. The union, on the other hand, devotes its full time to representing its members and can therefore concentrate on the specifics of each individual matter. Professional assistance from people who can work exclusively on collective bargaining problems is a must for dealing effectively with the unions. ("The Relevance of Private Sector Experience to Public Sector Collective Bargaining," in *Proceedings of the Conference of the Institute of Management and Labor Relations, The State University of New Jersey* 7 [May 23, 1968]).

[15]The case of the Hartford, Connecticut, firefighters' union presents what is probably the extreme example of the "end run" phenomenon. Until recently, the firefighters refused even to seek official recognition for collective bargaining purposes because of the tremendous political influence they enjoyed with the city council. See H. Wellington & R. Winter, *The Unions and the Cities* 121–22 (1971).

[16]In a number of states, the National Education Association and the American Federation of Teachers have adopted the policy of encouraging their members to run for the board of education and in numerous instances their candidates have been successful. Because of the obvious problem which this presents in collective negotiations, one state, Pennsylvania, included the following provision in its public sector bargaining statute: "No person who is member of the same local, State, national or international organization as the employee organization with which the public employer is bargaining or who has an interest in the outcome of such bargaining which interest is in conflict with the interest of the public employer, shall participate on behalf of the public employer in the collective bargaining processes with the proviso that such person may, where entitled, vote on the ratification of an agreement" (Pa. Stat. Ann. tit. 43, § 1101.1801(a) [Supp. 1971]).

[17]See D. Stanley, *Managing Local Government Under Union Pressure* 29–30 (1972). Among the exceptions to the general rule are the cities of Detroit and Milwaukee, both of which have carried on fairly extensive training programs for supervisors. Id. at 153.

[18]Morris Slavney, the Chairman of the Wisconsin Employment Relations Commission, pointed out one of the reasons why the line between supervisors and nonsupervisors is blurred in the public sector:

> The difficulty has arisen [because] many supervisory employees have been long-time members of such employee organizations. This is especially true in the organizations affiliated with the American Federation of State, County and Municipal Employees and affiliates of the National Education Association. Many of the individuals who are now holding high supervisory and managerial positions may very well have been employees who were instrumental in creating the local organizations in the first place. (Advisory Commission on Intergovernmental Relations, *Labor-Management Policies for State and Local Government* 147–48 [1969]).

[19]Zeidler, "Rethinking the Philosophy of Employee Relations in the Public Service," in *Sorry . . . No Government Today: Unions vs. City Hall* 198, 209 (R. Walsh ed. 1969).

[20]Michigan Municipal League, *Labor Contract Analysis for Michigan Municipalities* 1970 (Information Bull. No. 117, April 1970).

[21]For further discussion of management rights, see text accompanying notes 31–36 *infra*.

[22]Public employees are forbidden to strike in Michigan. Mich. Comp. Laws Ann. § 423.202 (1967). However, the law provides no penalty in the event of an illegal strike. Further, in School Dist. v Holland Educ. Ass'n, 380 Mich. 314, 157 N.W.2d 206 (1968), the Supreme Court of Michigan intimated that public employee strikes could not be enjoined unless it was first demonstrated that the strike threatened the public health and safety. It is thus important for public employers in Michigan to insist on no-strike promises from the unions with which they negotiate.

[23]See Wellington & Winter, "Structuring Collective Bargaining in Public Employment," 79 *Yale L.J.* 805, 819–22 (1970).

[24]The following comments of George Morris, the Director of Labor Relations for General Motors, are particularly relevant in this regard:

> [An] important consideration is too often over-looked in evaluating the results of collective bargaining settlements. It is the effect of the resolution of all the union's demands—not just wage demands—on the ability of the company to realize the full benefits of technological change and to operate its plants efficiently.
> The results of a particular settlement cannot be fairly evaluated simply by computing the annual percentage increase in wage and benefit costs.
> Restrictive, featherbedding provisions can be as costly in the long run and even more damaging to the company or industry and the economy as wage increases that exceed the national productivity advance. Experience is overpowering that once unwise concessions are made, they are considered by union leaders and members alike as vested rights never to be relinquished.
> In General Motors, the unions with which we bargain, at the International Union level at least, have recognized and accepted the need for technological change. . . .
> General Motors in its approach to collective bargaining has always maintained as an objective of highest priority the retention of management's freedom and the responsibility to make decisions in areas vital to the continued success of the business. ("Controls on Collective Bargaining—Restraints and Realities," *Daily Labor Report No. 108*, F-1, F-2 [June 4, 1971]).

[25]D. Bok. & J. Dunlop, *Labor and the American Community* 328 (1970).

[26]See, e.g., White, "Rights and Responsibilities in Municipal Collective Bargaining," 22 *Arb, J.* 31, 32 (1967).

[27]As the Advisory Commission on Intergovernmental Relations stated:

> A persistent and perplexing problem is the failure of many key middle-management and supervisory officials to act like "management," even when their role and responsibilities clearly put them on that side of the table. A clear legislative denial of employee rights to such personnel will prompt a clarification of this attitudinal confusion.
> . . . Allowing supervisors to organize and to present proposals perpetuates the vocational ambivalence that this group has long exhibited. The need at the present time is for management to identify its members and to develop a healthy community of interest.

(*Labor-Management Policies for State and Local Government* 95–96 [1969]).

While some states, such as Michigan and New York, continue to permit supervisors to organize, Exec. Order No. 11,491, governing labor relations in the federal service, specifically excludes supervisors, with only limited exceptions, from appropriate bargaining units. Exec. Order No. 11,491 § 10(b)(1), 3 C.F.R. 516 (Supp. 1971).

President Nixon's study committee stated the underlying reasons:

> We view supervisors as a part of management, responsible for participating in and contributing to the formulation of agency policies and procedures and contributing to the negotiation of agreements with employees. Supervisors should be responsible for representing management in the administration of agency policy and labor-management agreements, including negotiated grievance systems, and for expression of management viewpoints in daily communication with employees. In short, they should be and are part of agency management and should be integrated fully into that management. ("Report and Recommendations of President Nixon's Federal Labor Relations Study Commission," in *GERR* Reference File 21:1011, 1018 [1969]).

[28]Slavney, "Representation of Public Employees," in *GERR* No. 269, E-1, E-4 (Nov. 4, 1968).

[29]See L. Reynolds, *Labor Economics and Labor Relations* 155–57 (4th ed. 1964).

[30]Commenting on the index system used by many school boards to tie the salaries of administrators to the beginning or maximum teacher salaries, M. Lieberman and M. Moskow stated: "If the salaries of administrative personnel are directly correlated to the salaries of teachers, administrative objectivity [in negotiations] will be much more difficult to obtain.... As a matter of public policy, it appears that school boards would get more objective recommendations from administrative personnel if salaries of the latter were not tied directly to the salaries of teachers." (*Collective Negotiations for Teachers* 383–84 [1966]).

[31]See, e.g., Chamberlain, "The Corporation and the Trade Union," in *The Corporation in Modern Society* 122, 137 (E. Mason ed. 1966).

[32]See, e.g., Goldberg, "Management's Reserved Rights: A Labor View," in *Management Rights and the Arbitration Process* 118, 120–21 (J. McKelvey ed. 1956).

[33]See generally Loomis & Herman, Management's Rights and the NLRB—An Employer's View, 19 *Lab. L.J.* 695, 712–19 (1968).

[34]For example, the past president of the American Federation of Teachers, Charles Cogen, asserted: "Class sizes, number of classes taught, curriculum, hiring standards, textbooks and supplies, extra-curricular activities—in fact, anything having to do with the operation of the school—is a matter for professional concern and should thus be subject to collective bargaining." ("Collective Negotiations in Education," in *Sorry ... No Government Today: Unions vs. City Hall* 141, 148 [R. Walsh ed. 1969]).

Matters such as class sizes, student discipline, and curricular innovation have become subjects of negotiations in several major cities. See Selden, "Teacher Workload and Teacher Dropout," in *The Teacher Dropout* 61, 71–72 (T. Stinnett ed. 1970); Wellington & Winter, "Structuring Collective Bargaining in Public Employment," 79 *Yale L.J.* 805, 852–57 (1970).

[35]One commentator, in urging that teachers should have the right to codetermine school policies, stated: "The fundamental premise and the future promise of cooperative determination is that men and women of reasonableness and good will on all sides can ultimately reach agreement in their mutual interest where sufficient moral intention exists." (Robbins, "The Decision-Making Apparatus in Public Education," in *The Teacher Dropout* 31, 57 [T. Stinnett ed. 1970]).

[36]In his very pointed, yet analytical and sound criticism, Leiserson said:

> President Roosevelt was asked what would happen if they disagree. He answered they would work together and make joint decisions. This was taken as an indication that the government intended the business of defense production to be a joint cooperative enterprise of employers and workers on an equal partnership basis.... There developed a confused organization and administration.... The arrangement had to be discarded....
>   In retrospect it is easy to see the mistake that was made in establishing the double-headed directorship of the Office of Production Management. It was due to inadequate analysis of the job that was to be done and failure to distinguish functions. We do not have to be versed in the philosophy of management to understand that it is not practical to mix the policy-making functions of an organization with the operating functions.

It does not work and it satisfies no one. It leads to maneuvering and argument about policy among operating officials whose sole duty should be to carry out promptly and efficiently the operating orders.... It turns a production organization into a debating society. (Quoted in Clark, "Negotiating the Public Sector Agreement," in *Collective Negotiations in Public Administration* 32 [Univ. of Iowa Conference Series No. 15, 1970]).

[37]Most state laws authorizing collective bargaining for public employers do little to define the proper scope of bargaining beyond enumerating that bargaining shall extend to "wages, hours and other terms and conditions of employment" as provided in the Labor-Management Relations Act § 8(d), 29 U.S.C. § 158(d) (1970). There are exceptions however; for instance, the Wisconsin law covering state employees provides: "Nothing herein shall require the employer to bargain in relation to statutory and rule provided prerogatives of promotion, layoff, position classification, compensation and fringe benefits, examinations, discipline, merit salary determination policy and other actions provided for by law and rules governing civil service" (Wisc. Stat. § 111.91(2) [1969]).

[38]Unresolved grievances are submitted to arbitration under ninety-four percent of current contracts—down slightly from ninety-six percent in 1966. *Bureau of National Affairs, Labor Relations Yearbook—1970,* at 38.

[39]Exec. Order No. 11,491 §§ 13–14, 3 C.F.R. 516 (Supp. 1971).

[40]The question of the legality of entering into an agreement providing for the binding arbitration of disputes concerning the interpretation or application of the provisions of the agreement is still open to question in a number of jurisdictions. In several cases, the courts have held that such an agreement constitutes an illegal delegation of authority and is, therefore, null and void. See, e.g., School City v. Local 4, AFT, 78 L.R.R.M. 2404 (Ind. Super. Ct. 1971). In an increasing number of jurisdictions, however, the courts have upheld the legality of binding arbitration of grievances concerning the interpretation and application of the agreement. See, e.g., City of Auburn v. Nash, 34 App. Div. 2d 345, 312 N.Y.S.2d 700 (1970); Rockland Professional Fire Fighters Ass'n v. City of Rockland, 261 A.2d 418 (Me. 1970); Local 1226, AFSCME v. City of Rhinelander, 35 Wis. 2d 209, 151 N.W.2d 30 (1967).

[41]That some municipalities are already beginning to take this step is illustrated by recent events in Sacramento, California. During a strike by the Sacramento city firemen, California State Division of Forestry firemen from the San Diego area were deployed to Sacramento to provide the necessary fire protection. See *Sacramento Bee,* Oct. 8, 1971, § A, at 1, col. 1.

[42]See C. Saso, *Coping with Public Employee Strikes* (1970).

PART SEVEN

PERFORMANCE CRITERIA: IS THERE A "BOTTOM LINE" IN GOVERNMENT?

In this book's first selection, Woodrow Wilson identified the two primary objects of the study of public administration: "to discover, first, what government can properly and successfully do, and, secondly, how it can do these proper things. . . ." The public management approach recognizes that, operationally, a manager must give relatively equal attention to these two objectives. Attempting to achieve this balance requires the manager to identify criteria associated with the successful performance of his or her organization.

The literature on organizational performance reflects a belief that organizations differ in the extent to which they achieve their goals and meet the demands placed upon them. Two principal schools of thought emerge from research on organizational effectiveness: the goal approach and the systems approach.

The goal approach assumes that an organization has a limited and definable number of goals. The degree to which such goals are achieved becomes the degree to which that organization is "effective." Measures are developed to assess how well various goals are being met, and evaluation of the relative success of the organization vis-à-vis goal achievement follows naturally.

Proponents of the systems view believe that complex and dynamic organizations support a variety of goals that are too numerous and too elusive to submit to definition. Schein puts the systems view succinctly when he writes: "Acknowledging that every system has multiple functions, and that it exists within an environment that provides unpredictable inputs, a system's effectiveness can be defined as its capacity to survive, adapt, maintain itself, and grow, regardless of the particular functions it fulfills" (1970, p. 118). Thus, the systems view is primarily concerned with the successful performance of various types of activities, regardless of the goals the organization pursues. It is apparent from the behavior of business organizations that their performance can be more accurately judged using the goal approach than the systems approach.

The ultimate measure of business performance is profitability, the oft-cited "bottom line." A good example of the clarity and importance of the bottom line in business involves the firing of NBC President Fred Silverman in June 1981. Silverman's prowess as a TV programmer had become legend after his successful tours of duty as chief programmer for CBS and ABC. However, after three years as chief executive officer at NBC, which had been mired in last place in the prime-time ratings for two years preceding his arrival, Silverman was fired by Thornton Bradshaw, Chairman of the Board of NBC's parent company, RCA. The malady that precipitated Silverman's departure—declining profits—was a result of poor audience ratings, which directly affect network advertising revenue. A former network executive identified the unmistakable performance implications of the "ratings game": "There's no such thing as a poor programming executive with good ratings or a good programming executive with poor ratings. The only measurement of a programming executive is the A. C. Neilsen Company. You'll be hired or fired on that basis" (Rustin, 1981, p. 1).

Complex public organizations, on the other hand, appear to require a more complex approach to the measurement of their effectiveness; thus, government organizations are better judged by means of a systems approach. In all such organizations, multiple constituencies and multiple concerns demand the simultaneous pursuit of several goals. External goals are of concern to a number of diverse interest groups, including legislative bodies and the serviced public. Internal goals, i.e., the outcomes sought by organization members, may or may not complement the external goals, and even internal goals may differ for different organizational subunits. The goals of top management, for example, cannot be expected to conform in all instances to those of the work force at large or to those

of organized labor. In short, what constitutes "effectiveness" in public organizations depends largely on one's frame of reference. In the public sector, frames of reference are particularly diverse, because there are diverse legitimate claimants to the fruits of organizational action.

The four selections in this section reflect the fact that the decisions businesses make about diverse matters—allocation of resources, new technologies or processes, and product or program continuation—are usually related to the profit criterion. What may be more important, the predominance of this single performance measure helps to assure a consistent rationale for decisions. Thus, when a business is faced with a tradeoff between improved operational efficiency and increased market penetration, it has a ready yardstick against which to measure the tradeoff before making a decision.

In contrast, government organizations must often choose between competing criteria, for example, citizen satisfaction versus efficiency, without an overarching criterion, such as profit. These types of value decisions frequently intensify the organization-environment conflicts discussed in the introduction to Part Four.

The first reading in this section, authored by economist Robert Spann, investigates the comparative efficiency of public and private enterprises. Profit maximization requires that costs be minimized, and thus efficiency is a critical concern for businesses. Spann poses an apparently simple (but, in reality, difficult) question: Does the substitution of a private firm for a government producer lower the costs of providing such services? We note that the question is "apparently" simple, because these types of comparisons are often difficult due to the lack of comparable organizational units in the two sectors.

After comparing five activities—airlines, garbage collection, hospitals, fire protection, and electric utilities—Spann concludes that private enterprise can provide the same services at the same costs (for electricity and health care) or lower costs (for airlines, garbage collection, and fire protection) than public producers. He suggests that the extent to which government is less efficient than private producers is a function of four factors:

1. Whether government services are sold at a price that restrains inefficiency
2. Whether a governmental entity can produce enough units of output to achieve economies of scale and to avoid diseconomies of scale
3. Whether the government as a supplier must compete with other sources of supply, which serve to restrain costs
4. Whether citizens are able to move to other jurisdictions, i.e., vote with their feet, to express dissatisfaction.

Given Spann's conclusions (and supportive results in other economic literature), why have we not seen a rush to substitute private for public producers of goods and services? There are at least two compelling reasons. First, many of the goods and services that governments offer, particularly the federal government, are, as Spann recognizes, monopoly public goods that must be provided to all citizens at the same price. Thus, these services are not subject to many of the efficiency-inducing incentives discussed by Spann. Second, as A. J. Cervantes emphasizes in the second article in this section, "government is more than a business," and, therefore, government producers should not necessarily be expected to be "cost minimizers" like their private sector counterparts.

The story that A. J. Cervantes shares about his experiences as mayor of St. Louis is engaging. Cervantes, a businessman-turned-mayor, campaigned for office on a theme reminiscent of Woodrow Wilson's exhortation to bring business methods to government. Like the practitioners whose views are expressed in Part Two, Cervantes came to recognize the futile, quixotic nature of his goals. He learned that government, in addition to its function as a producer of goods and services, "presides over a way of life." Insofar as this function of government is concerned, the bottom line is clear: "If efficiency suffers because the people's will must be followed, our system favors following the people's will."

The last two articles in this section focus broadly on a third gauge of an organization's performance—its ability to adapt itself. The long-run performance of any organization depends both on its short-term efficiency and effectiveness and on its long-term adaptability. An organization's ability to react to changes in its environment reflects a readiness to deal with unusual problems, initiate improvements in operations, and try out new ideas and suggestions.

The first of these two articles, by J. David Roessner, explores the relative ability of public and private organizations to innovate, i.e., to introduce new products or processes to a particular organizational situation. Like the authors of several of the other readings in this book, Roessner attempts to debunk a myth—that public organizations are relatively less innovative than private organizations. This myth is partly attributable to the assumption that innovation and efficiency go hand-in-hand; because public producers are presumed to be less efficient, they are also less innovative. Roessner presents comparative diffusion rates of productivity-improving innovations to refute the view that the public sector is inherently less receptive to efforts to innovate.

In the final article of this section, Zeithaml, Lamb, and Crompton investigate the relative ability of public organizations to adapt to changing circumstances by terminating part or all of their activities. Most businesses are able to employ the profit-maximization criterion to resolve termination issues. The constraints on government are considerably more severe, and the rationales for termination, until recently,

have usually been noneconomic. Substantial constraints must be overcome to terminate a public program. In attempting to meet this challenge, Zeithaml et al. suggest several strategies that can be used in program contraction or termination.

REFERENCES

Rustin, R. E. Troubled NBC seeks a revival by trusting a program whiz kid. *Wall Street Journal*, August 28, 1981, pp. 1; 15.

Schein, E. H. *Organization psychology* (2nd ed.). Englewood Cliffs, N.J.: Prentice-Hall, 1970.

24 | Public Versus Private Provision of Governmental Services

Robert M. Spann

Society chooses to consume many goods and services on a collective basis. Examples of such goods and services include garbage collection, education, police protection, fire protection, and in some areas the provision of electric power. The fact that such goods and services are financed by tax revenues (in whole or in part) and consumed in some type of collective fashion does not mean that such goods must be produced by the government. Many cities, instead of having their own sanitation and fire departments, contract private firms, via competitive bidding, to provide such services. Some hospitals are privately owned, some are publicly owned. Electric utilities may be either publicly or privately owned.

An important question is, does the substitution of a private firm for a government producer lower the costs of providing such services? There are reasons to suspect that private ownership of supplying units may reduce the costs of providing local government services. As Professor A. A. Alchian [2] notes, the rewards and costs of an activity are more directly concentrated on each individual responsible for decisions in private enterprise. An individual will take more care in making decisions when his own wealth is at stake than when the wealth of others is at stake. Private firms must meet the pressure of the marketplace. Inefficient firms can be underpriced and driven out of business by more efficient firms.

The case of public firms is somewhat different. Government decision makers (especially tenured civil servants) have much less of their own wealth at stake in decisions made in governmental agencies.

The average stockholder can monitor the activities of any firm in which he owns an interest by examining the firm's profit and loss statement. The owners of government enterprises (the electorate) are not provided with any such balance sheet. The individual voter can scan newspapers, city budgets, and legislative hearings in order to determine the efficiency of governmental endeavors. However, this information is costly to obtain (if only in terms of the time involved), and the reduction in one's tax bill due to discerning such information may be small.

The stockholder in a private firm has another advantage over the owners of government enterprises (the voters). If a stockholder in a private firm is dissatisfied with management's performance, he can sell his stock in the enterprise. The only way in which a voter can "sell his stock" in a public enterprise is by moving outside the boundaries of that political jurisdiction. While this might be an effective long-run constraint on state and local governments, it is expensive for the average voter to express his dissatisfaction in this manner in the short run. With regard to federal governments, this option is virtually infeasible for the average voter.

On the grounds of the direct incentives inherent in private enterprise but lacking in governmental enterprise, and on the basis the differences in options open to the "stockholders" of the two enterprises, one would expect private firms to be more efficient than governmental enterprises.

There may, of course, be some incentives within the political structure that act to counterbalance these effects. Different candidates and different political parties compete for government office. One way in which these candidates or parties may compete for voter support is by offering to provide the same services at lower cost (in terms of taxes).[1] In some areas of government enterprise, the output of the government is sold at a price, and any "profits" can be used to reduce local taxes. One example is municipal utilities. In other areas government suppliers might compete directly with private suppliers of the same services. An example of this type of competition is hospitals.

In what follows, I shall discuss the conditions under which government supply of goods and services may be efficient or inefficient relative to private suppliers. Then some examples will be presented that illustrate these points and serve as base points for estimates of the efficiency of public versus private supply of government services. These examples will be in the areas of Australian airlines, fire protection, electricity, hospitals, and garbage collection. In all of these cases, private firms are more efficient or at least no less efficient than publicly owned enterprises.

FACTORS AFFECTING THE EFFICIENCY OF GOVERNMENTAL PROVISION OF SERVICES

In this section, four factors[2] that might affect the efficiency of government provision of goods and services are discussed. They are: (1) whether the output is sold at a positive price; (2) the size of the political unit versus the optimum scale of operation for governmental services; (3) how much competition there is from alternative sources of supply; and (4) the mobility of citizens between alternative governmental units. Each will be discussed individually.

Pricing of Governmental Outputs

Governments at all levels provide a variety of services under various "terms of sale." Police protection is provided to all members of the community. The amount an individual pays for police services is dependent on his tax bill, not on the amount of police services he consumes.[3] Municipal electric companies sell electricity at a price. The amount one pays for electricity is dependent on the amount of electricity he uses. When an output is sold at a price that must cover costs, a limit on governmental inefficiency is automatically determined. In addition, consumers can directly compare the price they pay for such a service to the prices charged in other localities. The easier it is for voters to compare costs, the easier it is for them to press, at election time, for efficient operation of such services.

That an output is sold at a positive price also means that consumers can choose to consume less of that output if the price is too high or the quality of service is too low. This subjects governmental enterprise to at least some of the same pressures that the marketplace imposes on private firms. Most non-priced outputs are sold on an all-or-nothing basis. A person either receives police protection or he doesn't. One's children either receive an education or they don't. The average voter can change the quantity of police protection or education he (or his children) receive only at election time. A voter cannot continuously decide how much police services he desires based on the cost to him of alternative levels of police protection. A voter can continuously decide on the amount of electricity he will consume based on the costs of alternative levels of consumption.

It is true that many of these market forces can be circumvented by tax subsidization. In many municipal water systems, the revenue collected via water bills does not cover the costs of providing water. This might reduce some of the market forces operating to increase efficiency in government enterprise. But, by the same token, excess revenues (i.e., revenues that exceed costs) from government enterprise can be used to subsidize other governmental activities. Thus, opportunities for subsidization work two ways, and it is still possible that the pricing of government-produced goods and services, with the opportunities for citizens to quantity adjust, will lead to more efficient production of these outputs.

Size of Political Unit Versus Optimum Scale of Operation

For any particular product, there is some scale of operation (or level of output) at which the unit cost of producing that output is minimized. In some production processes, the cost minimizing size of plant may be fairly small. For others, the optimum size of plant or operation may be very large. This is true of government-produced goods and services also.

In competitive markets, firms and plants generally operate at the optimum scale for that particular output. Profit maximization requires that one minimize the costs of producing any given output. This does not occur in the case of goods and services provided by governments. The scale of operation for most government-produced goods and services is identical to the size of the political unit corresponding to that government. There is no reason to believe that political units are set up so as to minimize the costs of government-provided goods and services. Even if political units were set up in such a fashion, it still does not follow (except by chance) that all the goods and services provided by a particular governmental unit have the same optimum scale of operation.

335

One good example of this problem is municipal electric systems.[4] The optimum scale of operation for both electrical generating plants and electrical companies as a whole is fairly large. Municipal electrical systems are generally restricted to one municipality plus some surrounding areas. If this area or size of operation is small, the costs of electricity produced by small municipalities may be fairly high even if there are no inefficiencies in operation because of bureaucratic behavior and so on. The high cost of producing electricity in this system would be due to the fact that the size of the system is controlled by political boundaries, not by the forces of the marketplace.

The optimum scale of operation for other government-produced goods and services may be much smaller than the political unit. In many local governments the optimum size school may be smaller than the total number of children in the community. In this case, it is true that several schools, each of optimum size, can be built. However, there may be diseconomies of scale in the management and administration of many schools. The optimum number of schools per school board (optimum in the sense of minimizing per unit administrative and managerial costs) may be fewer than the number of schools in the community. In this case, cost inefficiencies will be introduced due to an administrative system that exceeds the optimum size.

Competition from Alternative Sources of Supply

In some areas government enterprises compete directly or indirectly with private suppliers. Hospitals may be privately or publicly owned. In many areas of the country, doctors and patients have a choice of using either a public or private hospital. Many universities run on-campus hotels that compete, at least indirectly, with privately owned hotels and motels. Some areas of the country are served by municipal electric companies and privately owned gas companies. These two firms, one government, one private, compete directly for heating customers.

One would expect competition to exert some market pressure on government enterprises to hold down costs (since customers can always opt for the privately produced output if they desire) and to eliminate some of the opportunities for discretionary behavior on the part of bureaucracies.[5]

Competition from private firms may also lead to a higher quality of government services. A government enterprise cannot survive long if its customers can get a product more to their liking from a privately owned firm in the marketplace. Privately owned firms must produce what consumers desire or they go out of business. Thus, privately owned firms have a strong incentive to produce the type of output the public desires (measured by the fact that the public is willing to pay for it). Government enterprises, when in competition with private firms, must be able to produce a product of similar quality or they will have no customers.[6]

Mobility of the Citizenry

One way citizens can exert an important restraining force on governmental inefficiency is by "voting with their feet." If citizens are dissatisfied with the performance of the government, the level of services or the level of taxes, they always have the option of moving. People moving into a new locality often have the choice of living in any one of several communities. Suburban areas, in which there are numerous political units, offer a good illustration. An individual moving to the New York City area has the option of living in any one of several communities in three states (New Jersey, Connecticut, or New York) all with similar commuting distances to New York City. The individual can "shop around" for the community with the level of services, degree of taxation, and general atmosphere most to his liking. The opportunity for citizens to "vote with their feet" places many governments in a position similar to firms in a competitive market. These governmental units must be at least as efficient as neighboring units or they will lose residents (customers).[7]

Since citizens are more mobile between local governments than between states, we would expect local government services to be provided more efficiently than state government services. The costs of moving from one nation to another are extremely high, so we would not expect citizen mobility to exert much pressure on efficiency in the federal government.[8]

EMPIRICAL EVIDENCE ON THE EFFICIENCY OF PUBLIC VERSUS PRIVATE PROVISION OF GOODS AND SERVICES

In this section several empirical studies of the relative costs of government enterprises versus private enterprises are summarized. These studies are in the areas of Australian airlines, electric utilities, fire protection, hospitals, and garbage collection.

Australian Airlines

Australia[9] has two trunk airlines (equivalent to interstate airlines in the U.S.A.): TransAustralian Airways (TAA), a government firm, and Ansett Australian National Airways (Ansett ANA), a private firm. Government policy is purposely designed to make these airlines similar in many important aspects. The government requires that the airlines fly similar routes, make similar ports of call, be treated equally with respect to airport facilities, charge equal prices, and use similar aircraft.

D. G. Davies has compared the efficiency of these two airlines using three productivity measures: tons of freight and mail carried per employee, passengers carried per employee, and revenue earned per employee. These three productivity measures for the two airlines are listed in Table 24-1. In order to determine the relative efficiency of the two airlines, Davies divides the productivity measure for Ansett ANA (the privately owned firm) by the productivity measure for TAA (the government airline). These figures are listed in Table 24-2 in percentage terms.

The data clearly indicate that the private airline is more efficient than the public airline. In terms of freight and mail, the private airline is twice as efficient as the public airline; in terms of passengers, the private airline is 22 percent more efficient than the public airline; and, in terms of revenue per employee, the private airline is 13 percent more efficient than the public airline.

TABLE 24-1
Productivity of Australian Trunk Airlines

Year	Tons of Freight and Mail Carried per Employee	Passengers Carried per Employee	Revenue Earned per Employee
		TAA	
1958–59	4.42	217	$ 6104
1959–60	4.57	259	7016
1960–61	4.52	228	7052
1961–62	4.64	246	7367
1962–63	4.69	255	7726
1963–64	4.83	274	8093
1964–65	5.02	287	8553
1965–66	4.88	294	9072
1966–67	5.11	316	9954
1967–68	5.41	337	11033
1968–69	5.34	356	11734
Mean	4.86	279	8428
	ANSETT TRANSPORT INDUSTRIES, AIR GROUP		
1958–59	10.69	282	$ 7172
1959–60	10.77	309	7758
1960–61	10.96	337	8679
1961–62	10.84	331	8425
1962–63	11.09	316	8510
1963–64	11.06	324	9071
1964–65	12.14	352	9705
1965–66	11.08	354	10479
1966–67	10.34	348	10829
1967–68	9.57	363	12080
1968–69	9.54	392	13185
Mean	10.73	337	9627

Source: D. G. Davies, "The Efficiency of Public versus Private Firms, The Case of Australias's Two Airlines," *Journal of Law and Economics* (April, 1971). Copyright © 1971 by the University of Chicago.

TABLE 24-2
Ansett Productivity Measures as a Percentage of TAA Productivity Measures

Year	Freight and Mail	Passengers	Revenue
1958–59	242	130	117
1959–60	236	119	111
1960–61	242	148	123
1961–62	234	135	114
1962–63	236	124	110
1963–64	229	118	112
1964–65	242	123	113
1965–66	227	120	116
1966–67	202	110	109
1967–68	177	108	109
1968–69	179	110	112
Mean	204	122	113

Source: Davies, "The Efficiency of Public versus Private Firms." Copyright © 1971 by the University of Chicago.

Davies's study would probably indicate an even stronger indictment of public ownership if Australian law did not require the two airlines to be similar in every respect. The pricing, routing, and service levels required by the government are not necessarily the most efficient pricing, routing, and service levels. If the private airline were allowed to determine its own routing and service levels, it is possible that the measured inefficiency of public ownership relative to private ownership would be even greater.

In any event, Davies's study is strong evidence that private ownership and production is more efficient than public ownership. According to Davies's study, substitution of private production for public production would reduce costs by at least 13 percent.

Electric Utilities

Electricity is produced and sold by both publicly owned and privately owned firms. In this section, two studies of electric utility costs by mode of ownership are presented.

Wallace and Junk [12] have examined the costs of electrical generating systems by mode of ownership. They computed both operating costs on a per kilowatt hour basis and capacity costs on a kilowatt basis for eight regions of the country for municipal and investor-owned utilities.[10] The results of that study are listed in Table 24-3.

As can be readily seen, municipal generating systems have both higher operating costs and higher investment costs than do private firms. Unfortunately, the Wallace and Junk study confounds two effects in its measurement of the relative costs of municipal versus investor owned utilities. The municipal utilities could have higher costs because they are smaller than the investor-owned utilities or they could have higher costs because they are publicly owned (or both).[11] The optimum scale of operation for an electric company is fairly large. Therefore, the Wallace and Junk results could indicate that municipal electric systems are costly because of their small size alone. Alternatively, their results could indicate not only inefficiencies because of small size,

TABLE 24-3
Steam Generating Investment and Operating Cost Comparisons:
Selected Municipal and Private Electric Systems

Region	Operating Cost per KWH (Mills)		Investment per KWH ($)	
	1. MUNICIPAL	2. PRIVATE	3. MUNICIPAL	4. PRIVATE
I	8.61	4.30	209	145
II	5.88	2.96	166	126
III	6.67	3.31	202	104
IV	6.21	3.79	179	137
V	4.82	2.65	157	94
VI	4.87	3.99	156	151
VII	—	2.79	—	145
VIII	5.25	3.75	129	116
All systems	6.09	3.49	172	124

Source: Based on data reported in Federal Power Commission, *Statistics of Electric Utilities in the United States': Publicly Owned* (Washington, D.C.: U.S. Government Printing Office, 1964 and 1965).

but additional inefficiencies in the operation of municipal electric systems because of public ownership.

In order to eliminate the effect of size on cost comparisons between municipal and privately owned electric companies, I examined two large municipal electric companies, one in Los Angeles and one in San Antonio, and compared them to two similar privately owned companies, San Diego Gas and Electric Company and Dallas Power and Light.[12] For each company, I calculated the operating costs (net of taxes) and net electric plant per 1000 KWH for both 1969 and 1965. These results are listed in Tables 24-4 and 24-5.

In 1965, the privately owned companies (San Diego and Dallas) had lower operating costs and smaller amounts of investment per 1000 KWH than did their publicly owned counterparts (Los Angeles and San Antonio, respectively). In 1969, Los Angeles appears to have lower costs than San Diego. San Antonio had higher investment costs but lower operating costs than did Dallas. In order to obtain a direct cost comparison for the two Texas utilities, average costs were computed for each company. Average costs were defined to be investment costs per 1000 KWH times the cost of raising funds plus operating costs per 1000 KWH. Average cost estimates were made using interest rates or cost of funds estimates of 4, 6, and 8 percent. These cost estimates are listed in Table 24-6. As can be seen, Dallas Power and Light (the private firm) has lower average costs at every interest rate.

In Table 24-7 costs per kilowatt (KW) of capacity for each of the four firms are listed. In both years the privately owned firms, Dallas Power and Light and San Diego Gas and Electric, have smaller investment costs per KW of installed capacity. The fact that San Diego's cost per KW of installed capacity is much less than that of Los Angeles is due to differences in capacity

TABLE 24-4
Cost Comparisons for Private and Publicly Owned Electric Utilities—1965

	Los Angeles	San Diego	San Antonio	Dallas
Net electric plant per 1000 KWH	$77.25	$65.49	$68.62	$53.91
Operating costs per 1000 KWH	10.65	10.64	8.17	7.50

TABLE 24-5
Cost Comparisons for Private and Publicly Owned Electric Utilities—1969

	Los Angeles	San Diego	San Antonio	Dallas
Net electric plant per 1000 KWH	$74.60	$77.67	$60.65	$50.05
Operating costs per 1000 KWH	9.98	10.27	6.86	7.20

TABLE 24-6
1965 Average Cost Comparisons at Various
Interest Rates—Dallas and San Antonio

Interest Rate or Cost of Funds (%)	Cost per 1000 KWH ($)	
	SAN ANTONIO	DALLAS
4	9.46	9.20
6	10.76	10.21
8	12.07	11.21

TABLE 24-7
Net Electric Plant per KW of Capacity: 1965 and 1969

	1965	1969
Los Angeles	$342.48	$352.08
San Diego	205.47	214.18
San Antonio	172.17	161.93
Dallas	153.44	160.79

utilization between the two firms. One measure of capacity utilization is the system load factor. The system load factor is the amount of KWH actually generated divided by the number of KWH that could have been generated had the system operated at full capacity all year long. The maximum KWH that could have been generated if the system always operated at full capacity is computed by taking the kilowatt capacity of the firm and multiplying it by 8760, the number of hours in a year. Load factors for each of these four firms are listed in Table 24-8.

As can be seen Los Angeles has a much higher load factor than San Diego. This load factor difference could be because of differences in the characteristics of the customers served by the two systems or the fact that Los Angeles is able to use its existing plant more efficiently than is San Diego.

The data do allow us to draw some tentative conclusions concerning the efficiency of public versus private supply of electric power. The high cost of many municipal electric systems (as indicated by the data in Table 24-3) is due partly to their small size. When systems of similar size are compared, private firms may still be less expensive to operate. There are too few observations for valid statistical inferences, however. San Antonio's municipal power company has higher costs than Dallas Power and Light. Depending on how one treats the problem of capacity utilization, the Los Angeles Municipal

TABLE 24-8
Load Factors: 1965 and 1969

Los Angeles	.5212	.5212
San Diego	.3953	.4187
San Antonio	.3065	.3065
Dallas	.3468	.3508

electric company may or may not be less efficient than San Diego Gas and Electric, a privately owned firm. Los Angeles and San Diego have similar costs per KWH but Los Angeles has much higher costs per KW of installed capacity.

The weakest conclusion allowed by the data is that the costs of government services would be no more if private producers were substituted for public firms of equal size in this sector.[13] It is possible, however, that private firms are more efficient.

Fire Protection

Fire protection is provided by almost every local government via publicly owned fire departments. One city, Scottsdale, Arizona, has elected not to have a public fire department but to contract with the Rural-Metropolitan Fire Protection Company for the provision of fire services. The city's contract with the firm is for four years. If the city is not satisfied with the service it receives, it can always form its own fire protection company or seek out an alternative supplier of fire protection services. The difference between the amount Scottsdale pays for fire protection presently and what it would cost to operate an equivalent public fire department has been examined in a recent paper by Ahlbrandt [1].

In order to determine the costs of publicly owned fire departments, Ahlbrandt estimated cost relationships for 44 publicly owned fire departments in the state of Washington. Cost equations were estimated in which costs per capita were dependent on population, area served, assessed value, percentage of housing units lacking plumbing, a wage index, fire insurance rating, number of aid cars, number of volunteers, number of fire stations, number of full-time personnel and a set of variables to distinguish volunteer from paid fire departments.[14]

Ahlbrandt then used the cost function to predict costs for some Arizona cities with public fire departments. It predicted these costs accurately. He then made cost predictions for Scottsdale, Arizona. Predicted fire protection costs per capita (assuming a public fire department) were $7.10, whereas the cost of the services of the Rural-Metropolitan Fire Protection Company was $3.78.[15] In other words, were Scottsdale to establish its own fire department and operate it at the same level of efficiency as other public fire departments, the costs of fire protection to the residents would double. Thus, in this sector, private firms appear to be much more efficient than public firms.

Garbage Collection

Garbage collection services are provided both by public sanitation departments and by private contractors. Some cities use their own sanitation departments whereas others contract private firms to provide garbage collection services. In this section, several studies of the costs of solid waste disposal are presented and reviewed.

The Planning Board in Monmouth County, New Jersey, conducted a survey of garbage collection costs in the communities in that county [10]. The results of that study are reproduced in Table 24-9.[16] As can be seen, communities using private contractors have significantly lower costs than commu-

TABLE 24-9
1965 Average per Capita Cost of Refuse Collection and Disposal—Monmouth County

	Services Provided by	
	MUNICIPALITY	CONTRACTOR
Average per capita cost	$8.33	$5.84
Residential communities with a small business district		
Two residential collections/week	6.06	5.29
Three residential collections/week	(None)	6.84
Residential community with a large business district		
Two residential collections/week	9.61	5.76
Three residential collections/week	(None)	4.67
Residential community with a large summer population influx		
Three summer residential collections/week	10.40	8.49

nities with public sanitation departments. The average per capita cost of garbage collection is $8.33 for cities with municipal sanitation departments and $5.84 for cities using private contractors.

W. Hirsch, in a paper published in the *Review of Economics and Statistics* [7] examined the costs of garbage collection in 24 St. Louis suburbs. Hirsch found that costs were lower in communities that used private contractors (see Table 24-10).[17] This effect is not statistically significant.

One explanation of the fact that Hirsch found private collection less costly but not significantly so, is the small size and relative proximity of the cities in

Table 24-10
Cost Function for Garbage Collection[a]

$$X_1 = 6.16 + 0.000\ 0890\ X_2$$
$$(0.000\ 195)$$
$$-0.000\ 000\ 000\ 436\ X_2^2 + 3.61\ X_3$$
$$(0.000\ 000\ 000\ 832)\quad(1.14)$$
$$+\ 3.97\ X_4 - 0.000\ 611\ X_5 - 1.87\ X_6$$
$$(1.50)\quad(0.000\ 442)\quad(2.40)$$
$$+\ 3.43\ X_7$$
$$(1.10)$$

where,

X_1 = 1960 average annual residential refuse collection and disposal cost per pickup in dollars,
X_2 = number of pickup units,
X_3 = weekly collection frequency,
X_4 = pickup location, where curb pickup is 0 and rear of house pickup is 1,
X_5 = pickup density, i.e., number of residential pickups per square mile,
X_6 = nature of contractual arrangements, where municipal collection is 0 and private collection is 1, and
X_7 = type of financing, where general revenue financing is 0 and user charge financing is 1.

Source: W. Hirsch, "Cost Functions of Government Service: Refuse Collection," *Review of Economics and Statistics* (February 1965).
[a]Standard errors of estimate are in parentheses.

his sample. All the observations are from neighboring suburban communities. One might expect a high degree of mobility between communities. Residents of the entire St. Louis area are able to choose among different communities based on the attributes of those communities and the level of services provided by the governments in those communities.

This competition between communities forces public firms to behave more like private firms and should reduce the costs of publicly provided services to somewhere near the costs of private provision of those services.

Health Care

Cost considerations may not be the only relevant variable in comparison between public and private provision of goods and services. One might also be concerned with the quality of services provided. This is especially true in areas that involve human life[18] and in areas in which consumers may have difficulty in making accurate a priori quality comparisons. A good example of such a good or service is health care. In this section cost and quality differences[19] between public, nonprofit, and profit hospitals and nursing homes are examined.

Accurate cost and quality comparisons in the health care sector are difficult to obtain. Several studies have been conducted which attempt to make such comparisons. Unfortunately, it is impossible to hold all the important variables constant in such studies, and, as a result, these studies must be interpreted with care.

A study of 118 Minnesota nursing homes [3] attempted to discern quality differences by mode of ownership. Four categories of nursing homes were examined: corporate taxables, noncorporate taxables, nongovernment nontaxable, and government.

Only four quality variables (out of a possible 96) were found to differ significantly between the four modes of ownership. They were:

1. Nongovernment nontaxables have more registered nurses per each licensed practical nurse than do all taxables;

2. Corporate taxables have a greater variety of physician specialities than do all nontaxables;

3. Corporate taxables have more therapeutic services than do nontaxables; and,

4. All nontaxables have fewer patients per room than do corporate taxables.

The study also found that nonprofit hospitals have somewhat more physician hours per patient than do profit hospitals. However, no other quality indicators were found to differ by mode of ownership.

A study by Schuyler Kohl [8] examined cases of perinatal mortality in New York City hospitals for the period 1950–1951 by mode of ownership. Once the relevant adjustments are made to the data, there was little difference in the percentage of preventable deaths (one index of quality) between proprietary (profit) and nonproprietary hospitals.[20] Both these studies would indicate that the quality of health care, as measured by various variables, differs little among ownership modes.

Another, quasi-quality characteristic of health care might be participation in state and local health care programs and the willingness of various hospitals to take high-risk, expensive patients who might not be able to pay their bills. A recent Ph.D. thesis by Lloyd L. Cannedy [5] found that investor-owned hospitals and nonprofit hospitals participated equally in local, state, and county health insurance programs. This implies that profit hospitals are not more likely to exclude high-risk patients who are typically sponsored by the local, county, state, and federal government.

Another way of comparing health care facilities is to ask potential customers to rate various institutions. Such a study of New York nursing homes was conducted using potential nursing home customers. Both proprietary and other nursing homes were found in the group of highly rated nursing homes. Similarly, the group of homes rated lower by potential customers included both proprietary and nonproprietary hospitals.[21] Thus, potential consumers feel that there are some good hospitals in both types of ownership and some bad hospitals in both types of ownership. No general inferences about quality can be drawn based on mode of ownership alone.

Cost and price comparisons by mode of ownership are shown in Tables 24-11 and 24-12. Average construction costs per bed from a 1969 nursing home study are shown in Table 24-11. The data indicate construction costs are much higher in voluntary hospitals than in profit hospitals. This study did not adjust for quality differences so exact cost inferences may not be appropriate. In Table 24-12 mean charges and costs per patient day from the Minnesota nursing home study indicate that profit hospitals have slightly higher prices but slightly lower costs. In Table 24-13 costs per inpatient day for various size hospitals are compared by mode of ownership. It appears that nonprofits are cheaper in the small size categories while profit hospitals are cheaper in the larger size classes.

The data in Tables 24-11–24-13 might be construed to imply that profit hospitals have lower costs than nonprofits. Even though evidence was presented earlier to the effect that there are no quality differences systematically related to ownership, the costs in Tables 24-11–24-13 are not quality adjusted. Thus, one cannot be sure that the cost comparisons are completely accurate.

The overall picture generated by the results cited in this section is important. Quality differences in health care institutions are not systematically re-

TABLE 24-11
Construction Costs for Nursing Homes

	Average Cost per Bed	
Size in Beds	VOLUNTARY[a]	PROPRIETARY[b]
300 and over	$24,959.00	$11,811.00
200–299	19,350.00	9,181.00
1–199	18,230.00	8,888.00

Source: "Planned Capital Formation in Nursing Homes in New York City," Inquiry (Dec. 1969).
[a]Does not include land costs.
[b]Includes land costs.

TABLE 24-12
Mean Charges per Month and Estimated Costs per Patient Day by Nursing Home type—1967

	Proprietary	Nonproprietary
Charge per month	$298.60	$270.84
Cost per day	7.47	7.91

Source: Nursing Home Care, ibid.

TABLE 24-13
Mean Expense per Inpatient Day for Community Hospitals in 1968

Number of Beds	Nonprofit	For-profit Chain	For-profit Nonchain
Under 50	$44.73	$60.78	$51.55
50 – 99	47.64	67.73	52.42
100 – 199	55.23	66.20	46.77
200 and over	67.44	58.72	56.33

Source: "Study of For-Profit Hospitals Chains," mimeographed, May 22, 1970.

lated to mode of ownership. We observe both good and bad profit hospitals and both good and bad nonprofit hospitals. Although there is some indication that profit hospitals may have lower costs than nonprofits, any such conclusion is tenuous at best due to quality adjustment problems. The implication of this study is that the substitution of private provision of health care for the public provision of health care will not lower health care quality but might lower health care costs slightly.

CONCLUSION

The costs of public versus private provision of goods and services have been compared for five activities: airlines, garbage collection, hospitals, fire protection, and electric utilities. For the majority of activities, private producers can provide the same services at the same, or lower costs than can public producers. In some cases, the costs of private firms are half that of governmental agencies for producing the same good or service.

In the case of electricity, a major portion of the cost differences between publicly owned and privately owned utilities is due to size differences. Most municipal electric systems are simply too small to be efficient. Even for similar sized electric firms, there is some evidence that private producers may be more efficient than public firms. In the case of hospitals and nursing homes, there are little cost or quality differences between profit, nonprofit, and government hospitals.

These results also indicate that market forces are an important means of encouraging efficiency. The two services for which private and public production have similar costs, at similar sized scales of operation, electricity and health care, are both services in which governmental suppliers must compete (indirectly or directly) with private firms. In addition, the output of these sectors are sold on a per unit basis and consumers can quantity adjust.

Size of community and competition between communities appears to affect costs also. Hirsch, in his refuse collection cost study, found that suburban communities close to each other have costs similar to those of private firms, probably resulting from competition between communities for new residents, which leads to a more efficient provision of public services.

The results also indicate that a number of governmental functions can be taken over by private producers with an attendant reduction in the costs of government (or at least no increase). Public provision or consumption of a good or service does not imply public production of that good or service. As indicated in this study, garbage and fire services may be provided more cheaply by contracting with private firms rather than by using city-run sanitation or fire departments. There is no reason why similar results would not be true of education, police, and other services. Even in areas where quality may be very important, such as health care, there is no reason to prefer government producers over private producers.

The savings due to the use of private contractors as opposed to public firms can be imputed to two factors: (1) private profit-maximizing firms have an incentive to minimize costs whereas public firms or agencies do not (except under the circumstances noted above); and (2) the size of private firms is not restricted by political boundaries as is the size of governmental producers; private firms are able to reach the maximum efficient size, an opportunity necessarily not allowed public firms.

NOTES

[1]Competition between political parties may not lead to increased efficiency because of factors inherent in the democratic process. Voters are faced with numerous complex issues, and the returns to any one voter of becoming informed on these issues may be small. See Tullock [11].

[2]One factor that is omitted in this discussion is competition between political parties as a source of governmental efficiency or inefficiency. Empirical estimates of the degree of competition between political parties are hard to come by. Even in states with only one political party (such as in the South before the rise of Republicanism in that area) there may be substantial political competition. The primaries in such states may offer as many, if not more, contrasting philosophies and methods of running the government as the general elections in two-party states.

[3]If police protection is a pure public good, each citizen's level of consumption is the same. For some estimates of the degree of "publicness" of many state and local services, see Borcherding and Deacon [4]. That paper argues that many of the services provided by state and local governments may be much closer to private goods than public goods.

[4]For more on municipal electric systems, see the section on electric utilities below.

[5]That competition from private, profit-maximizing firms eliminates some of the opportunities for discretionary behavior on the part of bureaucracies may explain why professional educators are the most vocal opponents of voucher systems in local education.

[6]This is the reverse of the often-cited argument in the public press that government producers set quality standards which must be followed by private firms in order for those firms to stay in business. This argument reverses the causation in the text. It is also erroneous. A private firm can stay in business only if the public is willing to buy its product. As noted in the introduction, the reward structure in private enterprise is such that the costs and benefits of decision are borne by those who make decisions. This is not always true in the public sector. Therefore, there are much stronger incentives for private firms to be "in tune" with what the public desires. This proposition is difficult, if not impossible, to test empirically. Some casual empiricism seems to confirm it, however. Ralph Nader to the contrary, we observe far more complaints about the quality of service in local education, garbage pickup, and police services than the quality of American

automobiles. We observe families willing to pay substantial sums of money to send their children to private instead of public colleges. At the height of complaints about phone service in New York City, no one suggested that the situation could be improved by allowing New York City to take over the operation of the New York Telephone Company.

[7]It is true that the reward structure in public enterprise, even with this mobility, is not as keyed to the actual costs and benefits of decisions as the reward structure in private enterprise. However, this mobility will increase the efficiency of local governments per se.

[8]Tullock, in some as yet unpublished work [11], has argued that local governments show fewer signs of bureaucratic behavior than do other governmental units.

[9]This section is based on Davies [6].

[10]State lines were followed in setting up the regions. Region 1 includes Maine, Vermont, New Hampshire, Massachusetts, Connecticut, Rhode Island, New Jersey, Delaware, New York, Maryland, Pennsylvania, and the District of Columbia. Region II includes Michigan, Indiana, Ohio, West Virginia, and Kentucky. Region III includes Virginia, North Carolina, South Carolina, Georgia, Florida, Alabama, Mississippi, and Tennessee. Region IV includes Wisconsin, Minnesota, Iowa, Missouri, and Illinois. Region V includes Kansas, Oklahoma, Arkansas, Louisiana, Texas, and New Mexico. Region VI includes North Dakota, South Dakota, Nebraska, Wyoming, and Colorado. Region VII includes Washington, Oregon, Idaho, Montana, and Utah. Region VIII includes California, Nevada, and Arizona. The averages were also computed for states and a finer regional breakdown based on the 16 National Power Survey study areas. The results were similar to those presented in Table 24-1 and hence were excluded from this paper.

[11]Wallace and Junk explicitly recognize this in their paper. They state that their primary purpose is to derive estimates of the inefficiency of municipal generating systems due to their small size. As such they eliminated seven municipal generating systems with KWH sales in excess of 200,000 KWH annually.

[12]The private companies chosen for comparison (Dallas Power and Light in the case of San Antonio and San Diego Gas and Electric in the case of Los Angeles) were chosen on the following grounds. Fuel costs and capacity costs are the major components of electrical generating costs; by comparing companies in similar areas of the country I am able to hold these factors constant. Second, the cost of transmitting and distributing electric power is generally higher in rural areas than in urban areas. Urban-rural cost differences are recognized in the rate structure of many investor-owned companies. One large municipal system. Jacksonville, Florida, was not used because of the lack of a comparable urban privately owned system in Florida. Preliminary work indicated that Jacksonville has lower operating costs than the two large investor-owned companies in Florida, but it could not be determined whether this was due to actual efficiency or urban-rural cost differences.

[13]That the privately owned utilities pay federal income taxes presents no problem. Suppose the sole difference in rates between a private and a publicly owned firm is federal income tax. Then taxpayers in other sections of the country are subsidizing the customers of the municipal electric system. If this subsidization is what the electorate actually desires, it could be accomplished through a direct transfer of income.

[14]For a more detailed discussion of this cost function and why each variable was included, see Ahlbrandt [1].

[15]Some of Rural-Metropolitan's overhead is allocated to other cities it serves. Even if one allocates all this overhead to Scottsdale, that city's fire protection charges would increase only to $5.12. This is still less than the estimated costs of a public fire department.

[16]No tests of statistical significance were reported in the Monmouth County study.

[17]Hirsch finds that user cost pricing raises costs, contrary to our expectations. However, he notes that this may be due to the small number of cities with such pricing.

[18]Much of this section is based on "Proprietary and Non-Proprietary Health Care" [9].

[19]Comparing cost and quality independently is not quite correct. Under competitive conditions, one would expect differences in quality to be compensated for by price differences.

[20]For a more detailed discussion of the Kohl study, see [9].

[21]See [9], p. 20.

REFERENCES

1. Ahlbrandt, Roger. "Efficiency in the Provision of Fire Services." *Public Choice* (Fall 1973).

2. Alchian. A. A. "Some Economics of Property Rights." Paper delivered at the 15th General Meeting of the Mont Pelerin Society, Stresa, Italy. (Mimeographed, Sept. 1965).

3. American Rehabilitation Foundation, *Nursing Home Care: A Minnesota Analysis*. Minneapolis, Minn.: The Foundation, 1968.

4. Borcherding, T. E., and R. T. Deacon. "The Demand for the Services of Non-Federal Governments: An Econometric Approach to Collective Choice." *American Economic Review* (Dec. 1973).

5. Cannedy, Lloyd L. "A Heuristic Inquiry Into the Variability of Investor Owned For-Profit Hospital Chains: An Exploratory Consideration of Social Impact and Public Policy." Ph.D. thesis, University of Iowa, 1971.

6. Davies, D. G. "The Efficiency of Public versus Private Firms: The Case of Australia's Two Airlines." *Journal of Law and Economics* (April 1971).

7. Hirsch, W. "Cost Functions of Government Service: Refuse Collection." *Review of Economics and Statistics* (Feb. 1965).

8. Kohl, Schuyler G. *Perinatal Mortality in New York City*. Cambridge, Mass.: Harvard University Press, 1955.

9. *Proprietary and Non-Proprietary Health Care*. Washington, D.C.: ICF, Inc., 1970.

10. *Study and Plan of Refuse Collection and Disposal—Monmouth County*. Monmouth County, N.J.: Monmouth County Planning Board, June 1966 (reprinted May 1971).

11. Tullock, Gordon. "On the Social Costs of Eliminating Social Costs." Unpublished paper, Virginia Polytechnic Institute and State University, 1972.

12. Wallace, R. L., and P. E. Junk. "Economic Inefficiency of Small Municipal Electrical Generating Systems." *Land Economics* (Nov. 1970).

25 | Memoirs of a Businessman-Mayor

A. J. Cervantes

"Business gave birth to the American cities; businessmen can restore life to the American cities."

Ten years ago, I believed that Puritan thesis as an article of civic faith. With the self-righteousness of a successful businessman, I preached this doctrine of the cities' salvation: "Put government back into the hands of men who know the meaning of the tax dollar, the balanced budget, business methods, and a successful city."

The City of St. Louis bought my thesis. Twice they elected me as their mayor.

The cities of Missouri bought my thesis of the mystical power of business as applied to city governance. Twice they elected me as their head of the State Municipal League.

The media—if they did not unreservedly buy my thesis—acted as though they did. Publications from the *Neighborhood News* to the *Harvard Business Review,* TV stations from the sparse communications "laboratories" of the junior college to the lush network studios of New York and Los Angeles gave me as the "businessman's mayor" a klieg-lighted and camera-laden platform to spread the good word and saving doctrine of the computerized city and the system analysis budget.

Even the executive office of the President of the United States, at the invitation of the Office of Management & Budget, had me, as "the businessman turned mayor," address the chief administrators of major governmental agencies of our country on how a successful businessman approaches and subdues the standard urban crisis problems of our seething cities: poverty, discrimination, social tension, strikes, riots, and impending bankruptcy.

REEVALUATION

Now that I have withdrawn from the clang and stress of public life and retired to the more placid tenor of the university lecturer and professor-student dialogue, I realize that the "business" answer is not always the answer to the question of "good government." The good business executive is not necessarily a good government executive. On the contrary, the good business executive by that very fact may well be a poor government executive.

Government is a business. The largest in our country. But government is more than a business. Government presides over a way of life. And if the government executive applies only the priorities and goals of business to the American government and to the American people, he will inevitably destroy the purpose of the American government.

Business methods can be applied by the government executive to the common housekeeping functions of government: computerizing records, regularizing contracts, systematizing inventories, bidding purchases, cultivating public relations, professionalizing budgets, etc.

But as a mayor in the 1960s, I came to realize that these methods would not adequately solve the major urban problems of discrimination, poverty, riots, and social tension. Yet one of the more appealing panaceas to be put forth was that business should become more involved in solving "urban problems."

In fact, my experience as a businessman led me to campaign on that very theme of bringing "business methods to government" and "getting business involved in the problems of the city." We computerized many city records, secured industrial cooperation in job training programs, induced many businesses to hire young people for summer jobs, and laid the groundwork for the major building boom now occurring in downtown St. Louis.

But, as one becomes more involved in governing a large city, one learns that in many cases "business methods" cannot be translated into political reality. To take a word from business, let's give some "practical" examples:

- St. Louis has two city hospitals, one traditionally serving black patients and one traditionally serving white patients. Although no racial restrictions are imposed (indeed, positive steps are taken to ensure patient integration), the public still views one hospital as black and one as white. An efficient businessman would merge the two: But any effort to do that in St. Louis requires that one or the other be closed. And in a city half black and half white, each racial group refuses to allow "its" hospital to close.

- St. Louis has a large number of recreation programs operating in school playgrounds and parks. Some programs have many participants, but others have few. An efficient businessman would say, close those programs that have relatively few participants. But this would mean that some neighborhoods would have no programs for those who do use the facilities. Recreation centers must be reasonably close to everyone, so all of them stay open.

- On a larger scale, I wished to move the St. Louis area forward by building a modern airport suitable for the needs of the twenty-first century. Federal officials and airlines agreed that the best location would be in Illinois, just across the river from St. Louis. Jobs would have been created, the area's economy given a boost, and the city's tax base improved. But Missouri interests—unions and business—wanted the contracts and jobs that would flow from the new airport. Even though Missouri did not have a site or funds for the land, they blocked the Illinois airport. Would a businessman have turned down an investment opportunity because one group of workers or subcontractors received the benefits rather than another? Not one who wanted to survive. Yet the political reality forced other government leaders to oppose the Illinois site.

I give these examples to show that government is not a business: It is people. Government serves people, and in a democracy it must listen to people. If efficiency suffers because the people's will must be followed, our system favors following the people's will. And I—and every other person who believes in our system of government—want it always to be that way.

HORSETRADING

In politics and government, unlike business, intermediaries exist between the ultimate consumer (the citizen) and the provider of services (the government). The intermediaries are the neighborhood political leaders, the neighborhood association leaders, the representatives of labor and business, and the representatives of many other groups. Without the support of these interests, one cannot govern; indeed one cannot get elected. Even the "new politics," which attempts to bypass these intermediaries, creates its own set of representatives. John Kenneth Galbraith, an advocate of the new politics, is said to have played an instrumental role in blocking the nomination of former Boston mayor Kevin White to the Vice Presidency under George McGovern.

A mayor cannot continually bypass these intermediaries. But a businessman can. If he is told that a particular type of tomato soup or bar of soap will not sell, he can try to sell it anyway. But in politics a mayor needs the approval of the legislative body to even try to sell his product—to implement a new policy. To get that approval, he must secure the assent of the representatives of many interests in the community. Sometimes he must give on one matter to get approval for another policy. One may call this horsetrading and deplore it, but in a democracy it is the way things get done.

Thus a mayor may face the dilemma of appointing his third or fourth choice to a job in order to get an important program passed. Should he not make the appointment, bask in his righteousness, and forget about his important program that would benefit the citizens generally? Surely no one faced with that choice would hesitate. Yet a mayor who makes the trade is not being businesslike.

Business methods where possible, yes. Computerize your tax records. Use systems analysis to schedule your trash collections (but make sure everyone gets at least two pickups a week whether they need it or not!). Hire experts.

But if you want to be mayor, be prepared to drop that great gem of efficiency if it arouses the anger of the citizens or of any significant group of citizens. You may win that one victory—although you probably will not—but you won't win many more. The business of government is government, not business.

26 | Incentives to Innovate in Public and Private Organizations

J. David Roessner

New York City's fiscal crisis has dramatized in highly visible form the possible consequences of the two-way pinch that many governmental jurisdictions experience: increased demands for public services coincident with increased costs for supplying those services. At best, citizens grumble about the tax increases required to pay for increased services, thus jeopardizing the tenure of elected officials. At worst, cities find themselves with insufficient revenues to pay debts under any feasible tax increase, thus facing the specter of bankruptcy New York style. Baumol (1967) argues that the gap between wage levels and service levels in the public sector (and in cities in particular) will continue to widen inexorably because of conditions endemic to what he calls the "nonprogressive" sector of the economy. He argues that this sector, because it is intrinsically labor-intensive, is largely denied the usual routes to productivity increase—capital accumulation, economies of scale, and technological innovation—and therefore the possibility is reduced that wage increases will be offset by increases in productivity. Baumol is not alone in his belief that public sector organizations (and many private services as well) are relatively immune to significant productivity increases, especially increases that result from innovative behavior.[1] Yet there is growing evidence that substantial increases in productivity can be made in public sector organizations through innovative management techniques, procedures, and hardware products (National Commission on Productivity, 1974, 1975; Hamilton, 1972). In the words of a *National Journal Reports* article on the subject, productivity is "the 'hottest' new word in public administration circles" (Peirce, 1975: 533). Is there something inherent in public organizations that dooms this movement to failure because of built-in disincentives not present in the private sector?

I propose in this paper to explore why public organizations should be expected to be, and whether they actually are, less innovative than private

Reprinted from *Administration and Society,* 9 (November 1977), pp. 341–365, Sage Publications, Beverly Hills, by permission of the publisher.

ones. Using the different perspectives offered by economic theory, organization theory, public administration, and political science, I will first describe the predictions and explanations each of these theoretical approaches offers with respect to the incentives to innovate in public versus private organizations, and then synthesize the limited empirical evidence that exists to support these predictions and explanations. Finally, I will discuss some of the possible public policy implications of the evidence.

The inquiry will, of necessity, be conducted on a gross level. Relationships among organizational innovativeness, efficiency, and productivity have been explored inadequately at the conceptual level and, accordingly, empirical evidence is indirect at best. As will become evident, one of the weakest links is understanding the relationships between innovativeness and either efficiency or productivity. Moreover, one recent analysis has questioned the validity of *any* comparative study of innovation in public and private organizations, citing the inadequacies of available measures of innovativeness as a key reason for such a pessimistic conclusion (Meyer and Williams, 1976). This article promises no resolution of these thorny issues; rather, its purposes are, hopefully, to illustrate the convergent and divergent conclusions about public and private sector innovativeness reached by different disciplines, to present some suggestive empirical data that bear on the question, and to identify some of the policy implications these varying perspectives suggest.

REASONS FOR STUDYING DIFFERENCES IN INNOVATION PROCESSES IN PUBLIC VERSUS PRIVATE ORGANIZATIONS

One might legitimately ask, why bother to study public-private differences in organization innovation? In the first place, one rationale for the creation of quasi-public corporations such as the U.S. Postal Service is the belief that such organizations will be more efficient (i.e., "businesslike") than a purely government agency. This belief might be questioned, if only to flush out into the open other, more basic, rationales that are perhaps less politically palatable. Second, lack of innovation in the railroads, for example, has contributed significantly to this industry's current financial situation (National Commission on Productivity, 1973b); what do proposals to nationalize part or all of the railroad system imply for future innovation? Third, proposals to shift responsibility for the supply of urban services such as solid waste removal from government to private contractors continue to be made. What are the theoretical bases for such proposals, and what evidence exists to suggest that a change in ownership will improve productivity via innovation or other means? Finally, comparative studies of innovation in public and private organizations may produce useful insights into the incentive systems that induce organization members to generate, adopt, and implement innovations, thus improving our understanding of how innovation occurs. This article's focus on incentives to innovate rests not so much on compelling theory (e.g., the implication of Baumol's thesis that technological innovation may be the only possible route to public sector productivity) as on current federal program emphasis on the application of scientific and technical resources to problems of the cities and states.

PREDICTIONS DERIVED FROM ECONOMIC THEORY

Economists' predictions of the innovativeness of public versus private organizations are based on reasoning that begins with models for judging the efficiency of economic institutions. The ideal, competitive, free market economy has been shown (theoretically) to be optimally efficient for translating resources into products and services, but the static models used to reach these conclusions require that technology, consumer preferences, and resources remain constant. Many economists extended their faith in the competitive market structure to conclude that technological innovation will flourish best under conditions of free and full competition among firms. These leaps of faith were challenged by Schumpeter and, subsequently, by Galbraith, who argued that an oligopolistic market structure provides the best impetus for innovative activity (Kelly and Kranzberg et al., 1975, Vol. 1: 83–85). As monopolistic suppliers of goods and services, government organizations depart from the fully or even partially competitive situation that this theoretical approach predicts will lead to efficient—and possibly optimally innovative—behavior.

An alternative perspective, that of property rights[2] theorists, rests upon the implication that certain market imperfections have for innovative behavior. In particular, inappropriability—the inability to capture and retain the full marginal gains resulting from an action—is used as one basis for arguing that public sector organizations will be less efficient than private sector ones. McKean (1972: 180), for example, notes that inappropriability will lead to inefficiencies in both public and private sectors, but that "the nature of right assignments in the public sector . . . seem certain to limit appropriability there severely." In government, nothing is owned in the sense that shares can be bought and sold and the proceeds retained; no one has a well-defined claim on any increases in the value of government output; and few individual voters feel they can capture sufficient gains from increased government efficiency to warrant expenditures of their time and effort to gather information, form pressure groups, or take similar action. The result is, using this line of argument, that officials in public organizations are not rewarded or penalized for using their resources to change the efficiency of activities for which they are responsible (McKean, 1972: 181). Niskanen (1971) argues that this kind of incentive structure will lead bureaucrats to emphasize rewards such as prestige and personal satisfaction rather than improved organizational performance. Bureaucrats therefore will attempt to maximize the budgets of their bureaus, not the efficiency with which they operate (Niskanen, 1971: 114). To the extent that innovative behavior is a means to improved performance—particularly via increased productivity or efficiency—it will therefore occur less often in public organizations than in private ones.

Public choice theorists (of whom McKean and Niskanen are examples) combine these and other perspectives in order to explore the set of incentives that act upon bureaucratic (usually government) decision makers. Bish and Nourse (1975) focus explicitly on the incentives acting on public officials to be efficient and responsive to their constituents. They note that public officials are rarely subject to the kind of external competition that stimulates private firms to cut costs and/or improve performance, and that rewards for improved performance frequently are lacking or weak because of the difficulty and costs of monitoring the outputs of public agencies. Not only is there limited external pressure for improved performance, but substantial negative sanctions await the public official who attempts to improve performance and fails. Since innovation involves some risk of failure, and since continuing to use past procedures probably will not invoke criticism, few officials will find it worth their while to innovate (Bish and Nourse, 1975: 185). Finally, Bish and Nourse argue that the nature of public goods[3] is such that their value cannot easily be measured and used as a mangement tool. As a consequence, public managers try to manage employee behavior directly rather than to manage by output measure (e.g., profit) as is common in the private sector. Economically based theories therefore span a range of conditions both external and internal to organizations in order to predict the relative efficiencies of public and private organizations and, indirectly, their relative rates of innovativeness.

ORGANIZATION THEORY

Although organization theory has a rich literature that addresses the question of innovative behavior within organizational contexts, these theories rarely incorporate the influence of variables external to the organization, such as ownership (Zaltman et al., 1973; March and Simon, 1958; Blau and Scott, 1962; Roessner, 1974a). Theories of bureaucratic behavior are more relevant since bureaus usually are defined such that all government agencies and some parts of private firms are included. But Downs (1967), for example, does not address the relative efficiency of public versus private organizations, or bureaus versus nonbureaus, much less the relative innovativeness of these types of organizations. He argues that the two kinds of organizations (bureaus and nonbureaus) perform different functions and therefore cannot legitimately be compared—one operates in a free market, while the other operates in a nonmarket (Downs, 1967: 39–40). He approaches the question of innovation when he analyzes the sources of, and incentives to, change in bureaus. For Downs, the basis for change in bureaus is the perception of a "performance gap," but this discussion of the sources of these gaps does not distinguish between public and private organizations. For that matter, it does not appear that the sources of performance gaps Downs mentions are unique to bureaus (Downs, 1967: 191–210).

In a similar vein Thompson (1969) draws on organization theory and the decision-making literature to analyze the incentives and disincentives to innovate that exist in Weberian bureaucracies. The bureaucracy's monocratic structure, reliance on extrinsic rewards, and emphasis on predictable behavior inhibit innovative behavior (he argues), though these influences could be mitigated through provision of slack resources, increased professionalism, and creation of interdisciplinary teams. Like Downs, Thompson does not directly address the impact of external influences such as ownership on innovation.

POLITICAL SCIENCE AND PUBLIC ADMINISTRATION

Brief discussions of the differences between public and private organizations can be found in some of the basic texts in public administration. Simon et al. (1950: 9–11) argue that the administrative problems of governmental and nongovernmental organizations are the same, and that such differences as do exist are ones of degree rather than kind. Corson (1952), in a review of current business administration texts, lists the peculiarities of the public administration "trade," including the lack of performance measures, the need for equitable treatment of clients, and the high degree of accountability to external groups, such as legislatures, interest groups, and the press. More recently, Rainey et al. (1976) identified and systematically arrayed propositions about differences in public and private oganizations, and Wamsley and Zald (1973) analyzed public organizations from a political-economic perspective that included discussions of the difference public ownership makes.

In a relatively extensive analysis of public-private distinctions, Gawthrop (1969) examined the problems of control and decision making in governmental and nongovernmental bureaucracies. For Gawthrop, the key feature of a private organization is the centralization and monopolization of de facto authority at the top of the organization. In public organizations the leadership must share the allocation of rewards and sanctions for what are basically managerial decisions with a variety of external organizations and groups such as legislative bodies, clientele groups, "good government" groups, and other committees. In addition, government bureaucracies (vis-à-vis private ones) are characterized by the absence of a tangible product and by a high rate of turnover among leaders. Public organizations, unlike private ones:

1. lack a high degree of control by top executives due to the existence of multiple appeal routes to external organizations;
2. lack operational measures of effectiveness such as profit;
3. lack clear goals; and
4. need to demonstrate immediate results because of short terms of office and high leadership turnover. (Gawthrop, 1969: 249–260)

Although Gawthrop does not draw out the implications of these features for the existence and strength of incentives to innovate in public versus private organizations, the reasoning is straightforward: lack of top-level control means that the uncertainties associated with introducing and implementing innovation are less likely to be tolerated by organization members or by heterogeneous agency clientele groups; lack of clarity of goals and measures of effectiveness favors highly visible but superficial change over change that might significantly affect long-run performance; high leadership turnover means that low-risk, quick payoff programs will be favored, usually not the attributes of innovative activities (Roessner, 1974b: 11–12).

While some authors (Downs, 1967; Murray, 1975) dismiss the question of comparative efficiency between public and private organizations, others such as Fitch (1974) introduce important and useful distinctions that permit meaningful comparison. Fitch would probably agree that one cannot usefully compare the relative efficiency of public and private organizations without distinguishing between *allocation* efficiency and *production* efficiency. Public organizations have different goals from private ones so that, with respect to the efficiency with which resources are allocated: "The political process acts to bring public, quasi-public, and private interests together for the purpose of

357

securing larger allocations of resources for particular purposes than would be dictated by consumer preferences operating in the market" (Fitch, 1974: 504). The two kinds of organizations can be legitimately compared with respect to production efficiency and Fitch (1974: 503) suggests two reasons for believing that public sector production is inherently less efficient than private: (1) tendencies to expand are not constrained by the level of consumer (taxpayer) demand because of lack of competition and lack of identity between taxes paid and services rendered; (2) bureaucracies tend to be governed by bureaucratic routine and the convenience of bureaucrats rather than by the demand of consumers in the marketplace.

Political scientists stress the unique, politically based features of government agencies and thereby tap a totally different dimension from the economists. The key concept in this approach seems to be public accountability—nearly all the factors hypothesized to affect innovation in public agencies derive from legal and institutional manifestations of accountability. Frequent elections, legal and other sanctions against misfeasance and malfeasance, responsibility to a heterogeneous clientele (including unions), and the expectations of "fish bowl" decision making all derive from the requirement that public agencies be accountable to the electorate for a wide range of their activities (Redford, 1969: 147–153; Freeman, 1965; Woll, 1963).

To sum up: Economists begin with theories of market efficiency; organization theorists begin with analyses of bureaucratic behavior; and political scientists begin with the ways citizen demands for democratic accountability are translated into institutional arrangements and legal constraints, which in turn affect the behavior of government officials. Each approach leads, via tortuous, deductive links weakened by questionable assumptions about relationships among organizational efficiency, productivity, and innovativeness, to a consistent conclusion: Public organizations are less efficient, and probably less innovative, than private organizations. What empirical evidence exists to confirm or disconfirm these predictions?

PRACTITIONER AND EXPERIENTIAL ANALYSES

While not particularly tuned to questions concerning the relative innovativeness or efficiency of public and private organizations, observers of government activity have reported on factors they believe inhibit innovation in government agencies. Their conclusions tend to support the theoretical predictions just described. A former budget director of New York City described state and local governments as "not designed to be highly efficient, responsive, flexible, or innovative" (Hayes, 1972: 8). Another former New York City official laid out the factors in municipal government that inhibit change (Costello, 1973); his list contained those brought out by organization theorists and analysts of public administration. In particular, it is the political dimension—leadership turnover, heterogeneity in constituency goals and values, and external constraints on autonomous decision making—that makes the process of change in municipal government different from other types of organizational change. Finally, a recent conference on productivity in state and local government, attended by 50 public officials and experts, concluded that productivity improvement was inhibited in government in part because:

(a) bad performance is penalized more than good performance is rewarded; (b) the lack of clarity of public objectives makes changes in performance difficult to observe and reward; and (c) political survival means emphasis on short-run results (National Commission on Productivity, 1973a).

RESEARCH-BASED EMPIRICAL EVIDENCE

The "innovativeness" of an organization has different meanings, depending upon whether the organization is a producer of innovations, a consumer (user), or both. Most innovations intended for use by industry and government are developed by private firms as a product of their investment in R&D. While the manufacturing industries are both producers and consumers of innovations, service industries and state and local governments[4] tend to be primarily consumers of innovations. It is therefore appropriate to measure innovativeness in producing industries (manufacturing) by using data such as R&D expenditures as a proportion of sales and number of scientists and engineers as a proportion of total employment, since these are indirect indicators of the level of a firm's investment in innovative activity. These kinds of measures are used in studies of the relationship between market structure and innovation, but they are clearly inappropriate for organizations that are primarily users of innovations. For these latter kinds of organizations, the various measures of innovativeness drawn from the diffusion literature are applicable (Rowe and Boise, 1974). For the purposes of this paper, a useful measure of innovativeness is the speed with which user organizations adopt new products and processes. As recent critiques of the innovation literature have noted, however, measures based on speed of adoption ignore variations in organizational need and in the consequences of innovation adoption for organizational performance (see Rogers, 1975; Downs and Mohr, 1976).

Efficient use of resources has no necessary relationship to the adoption of appropriate, cost-saving innovations when they appear on the market; but, as pointed out earlier, the assumption is often made and will be made here that efficiently run organizations will also tend to be innovative. It thus becomes appropriate to include any evidence of the relative efficiency of public and private organizations because of the indirect link between innovativeness and efficient operation. A similar argument can be made for using productivity differences as crude indicators of relative innovativeness, since innovation can be a major contribution to productivity change.

Ever since Schumpeter challenged the prevailing assumptions about the relationship between market structure and innovation, economists have attempted to test the hypothesis that perfect competition will produce maximum innovative activity. But a recent assessment of the literature on market structure and innovation found no consensus among research results (Kamien and Schwartz, 1974). Conceptual and methodological problems have plagued these investigations, so it is impossible to know the extent to which the findings represent the actual state of affairs. As noted earlier, technological innovation is one of a number of means to productivity growth, so that differential rates of productivity growth could reflect in a crude fashion differential rates of innovation. Industries with some of the highest rates of productivity growth are also highly oligopolistic (and heavily regulated): gas and electric

359

utilities, telephone communications, and air transportation (National Commission on Productivity, 1974: 7). (To the extent that firms in a monopolistic or oligopolistic industry enjoy greater organizational "slack," greater productivity increases may be due in part to the greater innovativeness that organizational theorists hypothesize will result.) This approach thus adds little to the inconclusive findings of research directly focused on market structure and innovation.

In the crude sense just employed, productivity change data can be used to compare the performance of public and private sectors and to draw inferences about the effects ownership has on innovation. Productivity growth varies widely across industries, though the average rate of productivity growth in manufacturing has been consistently and significantly greater than in private service industries such as finance, real estate, wholesale and retail trade, and other sectors. For the period 1948–1969, the average annual percentage change in output per weighted man-hour was 1.8 for the private services sector and 3.0 for the industrial sector (Kendrick, 1973: 24). Efforts to measure government productivity are just beginning and are beset with monumental conceptual problems, but a recent study of productivity in the federal government found that the annual percentage gain in output per man-hour averaged 1.8 for the 1967–1972 period, similar to the figure for private services (National Commission on Productivity, 1974: 8; Kendrick, 1973: 30).

Trends in employment in public and private sectors also may provide some indirect evidence for rates of innovation in the two sectors, because it has been argued that employment in state and local government is growing faster than total national employment at least partially because technological change in the labor-intensive public sector does not keep pace with change in the private sector. But available data do not support this assertion: though over the period from 1962 to 1970 state and local government employment changed at an average annual rate of 4.6 percent, and total employment changed at an average annual rate of 2.7 percent, employment in the nongovernment service industries changed at an average annual rate of 4.7 percent. "If this is the major explanation, then the disparity observed here suggests not a comparison between the public and private sectors, but rather a comparison between the service and production sectors" (Bahl et al., 1972: 817–818).

Few studies have set out to compare the relative performance of public and private organizations that provide the same or similar products or services, and fewer still to investigate the relative innovativeness of the two types of organizations. Scherer (1970: 421) notes with respect to relative performance that "we possess only scattered case study evidence varying widely in both quality and implications." On the basis of such varying experiences as the Tennessee Valley Authority, the U.S. Postal Service, U.S. Army arsenals, and the differing performances of nationalized and private firms in the same industries in Britain, France, and Italy, Scherer (1970: 421–422) concludes that, "The evidence is presently insufficient to support a sharp choice between the alternatives on straightforward economic performance grounds, and so the decision may perforce continue to be made mainly on the basis of ideology."

More recent evidence does little to challenge Scherer's conclusion, but some of the newer studies give a flavor of the analytical problem and more directly address the question of private versus public responsibility for the provision of urban services. At the national level, Davies (1971) studied the performance of the two interstate airlines in Australia, which between them have a monopoly of air transport. The development of these airlines is so closely regulated by the Australian government that competition between them is restricted to peripheral comforts and slight variation in schedules. Using basically a property rights framework, Davies (1971: 151) hypothesized that the private airline would be more efficient than the public one because "In the case of public ownership, the costs and/or rewards of a decision are less fully borne by the decision maker than under a scheme of private property rights." Davies found that on all three of his measures of efficiency —tons carried per employee, number of paying passengers carried per employee, and revenue earned per employee—the private airline exceeded the public one.

Hospitals in the United States provide similar services yet exhibit three kinds of control: for-profit (proprietary), nonprofit (voluntary or community), and government. One study compared the efficiency of these three types of hospitals using measures such as percent occupancy rate and total expenses per adjusted average daily census (Roos et al., 1974). The authors tested the prediction that private hospitals will emphasize efficiency and revenue-producing operations, voluntary hospitals quality, and government hospitals access to the community regardless of ability to pay. They found that:

> The actual rankings [of goals] derived from the performance indicators generally bear out these predictions. . . . [But] the total pattern of goal emphasis by hospital type predicted in the models is not strongly supported. . . . Overall, the data suggest that, although the nature of the power field may influence an organization to emphasize one particular goal, this emphasis need not come at the expense of performance on other goal dimensions. (Roos et al., 1974: 88, 91)

In an interesting effort to study the effect competition has on the efficiency with which urban services are delivered, Ahlbrandt (1973) compared the efficiency of a private fire protection company supplying fire services to the Scottsdale, Arizona, area with the predicted costs for a (hypothetical) bureaucratic producer supplying the same area. Using a regression model based on data from cities and fire districts in the state of Washington to predict the per capita costs of equivalent service for Scottsdale, Ahlbrandt found that the estimated cost for a bureaucratic producer was $7.10 per capita, while actual cost was only $3.78 per capita. He argues that the cost difference is due largely to incentives to reduce costs that act on the private supplier because potential competition exists in the form of the threat of Scottsdale supplying its own fire services or contracting with another private supplier. (Scottsdale owns the fire stations and most of the rolling stock.) Ahlbrandt also reports that at least some of the lower costs of the private producer are due to innovative behavior: the company invests a small portion of its profit in R&D and has developed a number of new devices such as a low cost, low maintenance "attack truck."

Savas (1974) reports the results of a study of refuse collection by New York City's Office of Administration. The study compared the performance of the Department of Sanitation with that of the competitive, private carting industry serving New York's commercial customers. After classifying private carting operations to improve the validity of the comparison, the study concluded that it cost the city twice as much as the private sector to collect a ton of garbage. Savas (1974: 477–479) accounts for the difference in costs as follows: (1) the city used three men per truck versus two in the private firms; (2) wages and fringe benefits were 24 percent higher in the city; and (3) management and supervision seemed far superior in the private firms. However, no mention was made of possible differences in the two sectors' willingness to adopt new products or processes as a means of reducing costs.

COMPARISON OF RATES OF DIFFUSION OF TECHNOLOGY IN PUBLIC AND PRIVATE SECTORS

Mansfield (1968) has noted the importance of diffusion rates in industry as a determinant of rates of productivity increase, and has studied the diffusion of major process innovations in a number of different industries. The diesel locomotive was first used in the United States in 1924, and eleven years later was in use by 50 percent of the major railroads in this country. In another ten years it had achieved widespread acceptance. Upon studying diffusion rates of twelve process innovations in four different industries, Mansfield (1968: 113–117) concluded that diffusion was generally slow: it took 20 years or more for four innovations to achieve 100 percent diffusion among major firms only, and between 10 and 20 years for five innovations to achieve this level of diffusion among major firms. The number of years it took before half the major firms had introduced an innovation varied from 0.9 years to 15 years. In a separate study of the diffusion of numerical control in the tool and die industry, Mansfield et al. (1971: 188) found that it took 13 years from commercial introduction before 20 percent of all firms in the industry had adopted.

Comparison of these figures with diffusion rates of arbitrarily selected (from the perspective taken here) innovations in the public sector is meaningless in anything more than a suggestive sense. Nonetheless, it is instructive to take a look at some data for diffusion rates in the public sector to get a general feel for the numbers involved. Feller and Menzel (1976) obtained diffusion curves for 43 innovations in four different areas of urban services: traffic control, fire services, solid waste collection, and air pollution control. Although some of these innovations were introduced as early as 1935, many are so recent that they have not yet diffused beyond 20 percent of the potential adopters (generally, all cities and towns of about 50,000 in population). For the seven technologies that had diffused to 50 percent or more of the potential adopters as of 1974, the time from commercial introduction to the 50 percent diffusion point varied fairly uniformly from 10 years to 23 years.[5]

More appropriate for present purposes are diffusion rates of the same technologies in the public and private sectors, though at this stage there is only enough data to provoke interest rather than provide definitive findings. Feller and Menzel's survey of technology adoption by cities covered the solid waste area, which in some cities is provided by a public agency and in others by private firms under contract. Feller and Menzel's respondents included 220 cities with publicly provided solid waste collection service and 123 cities with private collection service, so that diffusion rates of the same technologies among the two types of service suppliers can be compared. Since most of the technologies have not been widely diffused, diffusion times must be compared from introduction of the technology to different cumulative adoption levels.[6] Table 26-1 shows the findings for four technologies.

This area of urban services is characterized by exceptionally slow diffusion rates relative to others, and private sector collection services tend to be much smaller operations than city agencies; these and probably other factors contribute to the uncertainty of any implications drawn from these data.

A new study of the diffusion of technology in the hospital sector provides a different data base for comparing diffusion rates. Russell and Burke (1975) studied the diffusion of "high technology" facilities among U.S. hospitals. Data from American Hospital Association surveys, covering 1949–1974, were analyzed by size of hospital and type of control. It proved to be difficult to cumulate findings systematically with respect to diffusion rates because for many of the technologies selected either data were not available over the entire period, diffusion was just beginning, or diffusion was virtually complete. Russell and Burke found that it was difficult to generalize about the innovativeness of state and local government hospitals relative to the other types.

> Depending on the facility, they may come out lower, the same, or higher. For example, state and local hospitals are consistently less likely than comparable voluntary and for-profit hospitals to report intensive care units, but large state and local hospitals report two of the more exotic facilities—renal dialysis and burn units—much more frequently than do hospitals in the other groups. (Russell and Burke, 1975: 42)

Although comparison of diffusion rates between public and private organizations appears to be a useful method of testing for differences in innovative behavior between the two types of (consumer) organizations, the sketchy data reported here do not add up to a firm conclusion other than that there is no dramatic or obvious difference in innovativeness between public and private organizations. With the exception of a small number of case studies, this appears to be the conclusion reached with respect to both of the indicators likely to be correlated with innovation: production efficiency and productivity change.

TABLE 26-1
Diffusion Rates of Four Solid Waste Technologies, by Sector

	Public Sector	Private Sector	Extent of Diffusion as of 1975
Packer trucks	27 yrs.	28 yrs.	40%
Container trucks	18 yrs.	20 yrs.	20%
One-man crews	13 yrs.	21 yrs.	10%
Transfer stations	20 yrs.	14 yrs.	10%

Source: Data courtesy of Irwin Feller, Pennsylvania State University.

CONCLUSIONS AND IMPLICATIONS FOR PUBLIC POLICY

The answer to the question of whether there is anything intrinsic to public sector organizations that relegates them to lives less innovative than their private sector counterparts appears to be, theoretically, yes; empirically, maybe and maybe not. But in any event there is little reason to give up hope of significant productivity improvements. The significant differences between public and private organizations—goals, expectations, legal constraints—lead one to expect that different sets of incentives act upon organization leaders and members. Whether these are differences of degree or kind is less important than the recognition that the differences do exist and have implications for policies intended to affect organizational change and innovation. The different theoretical approaches to innovation in public versus private organizations can be usefully explored with an eye toward the implications each has for public policy.

When economists address the question of public versus private ownership, they do so with an interest in the comparative efficiency of the two types of organizations. Their theoretical interest in innovation seems restricted to business firms, though most seem willing to extend the theoretical implications of free market competition for organizational efficiency to public organizations as well. For most economists, then, the absence of a competitive environment implies that public organizations will be less efficient, less responsive to demand, and less innovative than private ones. Their response to this situation—to recommend introducing competitive elements into the delivery of public goods and services—suggests a belief that the problem is inherent but not intractable. Some degree of competition may already be present in large metropolitan areas, where citizens move from central city to suburb and from suburb to suburb to obtain improved services or lower taxes. Competitive elements could be introduced into the delivery of public services, for example, by publicizing differences in service quality and cost among jurisdictions, contracting out some services to private firms, contracting with other political jurisdictions (e.g., the county or state), or letting the private sector completely take over certain functions (Council on Municipal Performance, 1974; Bish and Nourse, 1975: 134–135, 208–210; Savas, 1974; Fitch, 1974). It will be interesting to observe the outcomes of efforts to accomplish this, such as Scottsdale's private fire company and Lakewood, California's service contracts with Los Angeles County. An alternative strategy, based in part on the property rights approach, is to introduce a form of "profit-sharing" in municipal agencies, whereby employees share partially in the savings (via bonuses) that result from productivity increases in their agencies. This strategy has been initiated in several local governments, although careful analyses of the results have yet to be done.

The organization theorists and students of bureaucratic behavior have little to say about public-private differences. Bureaus are bureaus, and the routes to increased innovation include encouraging professionalism among organization members, applying "diversity" criteria in hiring and periodically shifting assignments of personnel, and supporting the development of improved performance measures (Roessner, 1974b; 13).

In contrast to the economists, who suggest changes in the structural arrangements under which public agencies operate, political scientists and practitioners suggest relatively minor alterations in the inputs to the incentive system. Thus, recommendations derived from this perspective frequently involve either reducing the risk of innovation or educating public officials about the potential rewards of innovation. Examples of the first type of strategy (risk reduction) include subsidizing the dollar costs of new products, providing improved information about the performance of particular innovations via demonstration or certification by professional groups, fostering greater exchange of information among officials from different jurisdictions, and introducing greater technical expertise into government decision making. The educational strategy is exemplified by efforts of the National Commission on Productivity[7] to convince elected officials that their political survival increasingly will depend on their ability to demonstrate improved performance in the delivery of government services (National Commission on Productivity, 1974, 1975). Since the productivity increases that are the goal of the commission's activities are often accomplished through innovation, the educational strategy, if effective, will also influence innovation in government.

At this stage in our knowledge of innovation processes in organizations it is not possible to predict with assurance which of the many strategies for stimulating innovation in public organizations will be more effective. But the empirical evidence concerning the relative innovativeness of public versus private organizations, coupled with numerous recent examples of improved productivity in government through innovation, give reason to doubt the validity of hypotheses that the public sector is inherently immune to efforts to increase innovative behavior there.

NOTES

[1]Baumol does not define the split between progressive and nonprogressive sectors by type of industry, but one can infer that, in his view, manufacturing is most progressive and that the personal services and government are least progressive. This is clearly not analogous to a public-private distinction, but the "inherently" nonprogressive elements would presumably be maximally present in the public sector (government).

[2]Property rights may be defined as the effective rights a person has to do things and his effective claims to rewards (positive or negative) that result from his actions. See McKean (1972: 177).

[3]Public goods are goods or services with the characteristic that consumption by one person does not reduce the consumption by others (i.e., clean air).

[4]The federal government is obviously a large-scale producer of innovations for its own use as well as a consumer of innovations.

[5]These figures covered only traffic control and the fire services, because with one exception none of the technologies in the other two fields had reached the 50 percent adoption point. Diffusion rates in the solid waste field appear to be significantly slower than in the other three fields. This may be due to a slower rate of capital equipment replacement, on the average, in solid waste than in other services areas.

[6]Introduction dates differed for the two sectors for most technologies, with the public sector tending to be first.

[7]Now called the National Center for Productivity and Quality of Working Life.

REFERENCES

Ahlbrandt, R. S., Jr. (1973). "Efficiency in the provision of fire services." *Public Choice* 16 (Fall): 1–15.

Bahl, R. W. et al. (1972). "Intergovernmental and functional aspects of public employment trends in the United States." *Public Admin. Rev.* 32 (November/December): 815–832.

Baumol, W. J. (1967). "Macroeconomics of unbalanced growth: The anatomy of urban crisis." *Amer. Econ. Rev.* 57 (June): 415–426.

Bish, R. L., and R. O. Nourse (1975). *Urban Economics and Policy Analysis,* New York: McGraw-Hill.

Blau, P. M., and W. R. Scott (1962). *Formal Organizations.* San Francisco: Chandler.

Corson, J. J. (1952). "Distinguishing characteristics of public administration." *Public Admin. Rev.* (Spring): 120–126.

Costello, T. W. (1973). "Change in municipal government: A view from the inside," in L. W. Rowe and W. B. Boise (eds.), *Organizational and Managerial Innovation: A Reader.* Pacific Palisades, CA: Goodyear.

Council on Municipal Performance (1974). *Municipal Performance Report* 1 (August).

Davies, D. G. (1971). "The efficiency of public versus private firms: The case of Australia's two airlines." *J. of Law and Economics* (April): 149–165.

Downs, A. (1967). *Inside Bureaucracy.* Boston: Little, Brown.

Downs, G. W., Jr., and L. B. Mohr (1976). "Conceptual issues in the study of innovation." Discussion Paper No. 76. University of Michigan Institute of Public Policy Studies.

Feller, I., and D. C. Menzel (1976). *Diffusion of Technology in Municipal Governments.* Final report on NSF grant DA-44350. Pennsylvania State University Center for the Study of Science Policy.

Fitch, L. C. (1974). "Increasing the role of the private sector in providing public services," pp. 501–557 in W. D. Hawley and D. Rogers (eds.), *Improving the Quality of Urban Management.* Beverly Hills, CA: Sage.

Freeman, J. L. (1965). *The Political Process: Executive Bureau–Legislative Committee Relations.* New York: Random House.

Gawthrop, L. C. (1969). *Bureaucratic Behavior in the Executive Branch.* New York: Free Press.

Hamilton, E. K. (1972). "Productivity: The New York City approach." *Public Admin. Rev.* 32 (November/December): 784–795.

Hayes, F. O. (1972). "Innovation in state and local government," pp. 1–23 in F. O. Hayes and J. E. Rasmussen (eds.), *Centers for Innovation in the Cities and States.* San Francisco: San Francisco Press.

Kamien, M. I., and N. L. Schwartz (1974). *Market Structure and Innovation: A Survey* (July). NTIS Document #PB-235-585/AS.

Kelly, P., et al. (1975). *Technological Innovation: A Critical Review of Current Knowledge.* NTIS Document #PB-242-550/AS. Georgia Institute of Technology.

Kendrick, J. W. (1973). "Technology and productivity trends in the U.S. economy: sectoral trends and shifts." *Application of Technology to Improve Productivity in the Service Sector of the National Economy.* National Academy of Engineering: 15–34.

Mansfield, E. (1968). *The Economics of Technological Change.* New York: Norton.

———— et al. (1971). *Research and Innovation in the Modern Corporation.* New York: Norton.

March, J. G., and H. A. Simon (1958). *Organizations.* New York: John Wiley.

McKean, R. N. (1972). "Property rights within government and devices to increase governmental efficiency." *Southern Economic J.* 39 (October): 177–186.

Meyer, M. W., and R. O. Williams (1976). *Comparison of Innovation in Public and Private Sectors: An Exploratory Study.* Final report to the National Science Foundation under grant PRA 75-19967. Riverside: Univ. of California; Los Angeles: Institute for Social Science Research, UCLA.

Murray, M. A. (1975). "Comparing public and private management: An exploratory essay." *Public Admin. Rev.* 35 (July/August): 364–371.

———— (1973a) *Productivity in State and Local Government. Report on the Wingspread Conference* (July).

———— (1973b). *Improving Railroad Productivity: Final Report of the Task Force on Railroad Productivity*.

———— (1974). *Third Annual Report*.

National Commission on Productivity (1975). *Fourth Annual Report*.

Niskanen, W. A., Jr. (1971). *Bureaucracy and Representative Government*. Chicago: Aldine.

Peirce, R. (1975). "State-local report/'productivity' is slogan for taming spiraling expenses." *National J. Reports* (April 12): 533–540.

Rainey, H. G., R. W. Backoff, and C. H. Levine (1976). "Comparing public and private organizations." *Public Admin. Rev.* (March/April): 233–244.

Redford, E. S. (1969). *Democracy in the Administrative State*. London: Oxford Univ. Press.

Roessner, J. D. (1974a). "Innovation in public organizations." Presented at the National Conference on Public Administration, Syracuse, New York.

———— (1974b). "Designing public organizations for innovative behavior." Presented at the Thirty-Fourth Annual Meeting of the Academy of Management, Seattle, Washington.

Rogers, E. M. (1975). "Innovation in organizations: New research approaches." Presented at the Annual Meeting of the American Political Science Association, San Francisco.

Roos, N. P., J. R. Schermerhorn, and L. L. Roos, Jr. (1974). "Hospital performance: Analyzing power and goals." *J. of Health and Social Behavior* 15 (June): 78–92.

Rowe, L. A., and W. B. Boise (1974). "Organizational innovation: current research and evolving concepts." *Public Admin. Rev.* 34 (May/June).

Russell, L. B., and C. S. Burke (1975). *Technological Diffusion in the Hospital Sector*. Prepared for the National Science Foundation, Office of National R&D Assessment, Grant No. PRA 75-14274. National Planning Association.

Savas, E. S. (1974). "Municipal monopolies versus competition in delivering urban services," pp. 473–500 in W. D. Hawley and D. Rogers (eds.), *Improving the Quality of Urban Management*. Beverly Hills, CA: Sage.

Scherer, F. M. (1970). *Industrial Market Structure and Economic Performance*. Chicago: Rand McNally.

Simon, H. A., D. W. Smithburg, and V. A. Thompson (1950). *Public Administration*. New York: Knopf.

Thompson, V. A. (1969). *Bureaucracy and Innovation*. University: Univ. of Alabama Press.

Wamsley, G. L., and M. N. Zald (1973). *The Political Economy of Public Organizations*. Lexington, MA: D.C. Heath.

Woll, P. (1963). *American Bureaucracy*. New York: Norton.

Zaltman, G., R. Duncan, and J. Holbek (1973). *Innovations and Organizations*. New York: Wiley-Interscience.

27 | Public Program Termination: Conditions, Constraints, and Management Strategies

Valarie A. Zeithaml
Charles W. Lamb, Jr.
John L. Crompton

Until the mid-1970s, public sector managers performed under growth conditions characterized by increasing population, burgeoning financial resources, and an expanding role for government. Public service delivery strategies were most often predicated on the assumption of continuing enlargement of public resources and expenditures. In the 1980s, however, many public service managers are confronted with a shift in this growth trend, and are assuming a new responsibility—that of determining which of their services can be reduced or terminated with the least harm to their clientele and with the lowest threat to their agencies' viability. Instead of expanding programs, public sector organizations are being forced to contract them because of rising costs and declining allocations. Instead of emphasizing the introduction of new programs, managers must concentrate on program termination. Because the 1980s challenge is to manage in the face of shrinking resources, the process of program contraction and termination will become pivotal.

A MODEL OF PROGRAM ELIMINATION

The purpose of this paper is to present a model of public sector program termination that integrates relevant literature on organizational decline with what is known about managing in the public sector. The model describes the process of program termination and contractions, and acknowledges impediments to effective termination that are unique to the public sector. This model also acknowledges that managerial attitudes toward the need for contraction and elimination relate to the strategies that managers select in the face of cutbacks. The model, shown in Figure 27-1, contains five elements: (1) environmental conditions stimulating program termination; (2) public-sector con-

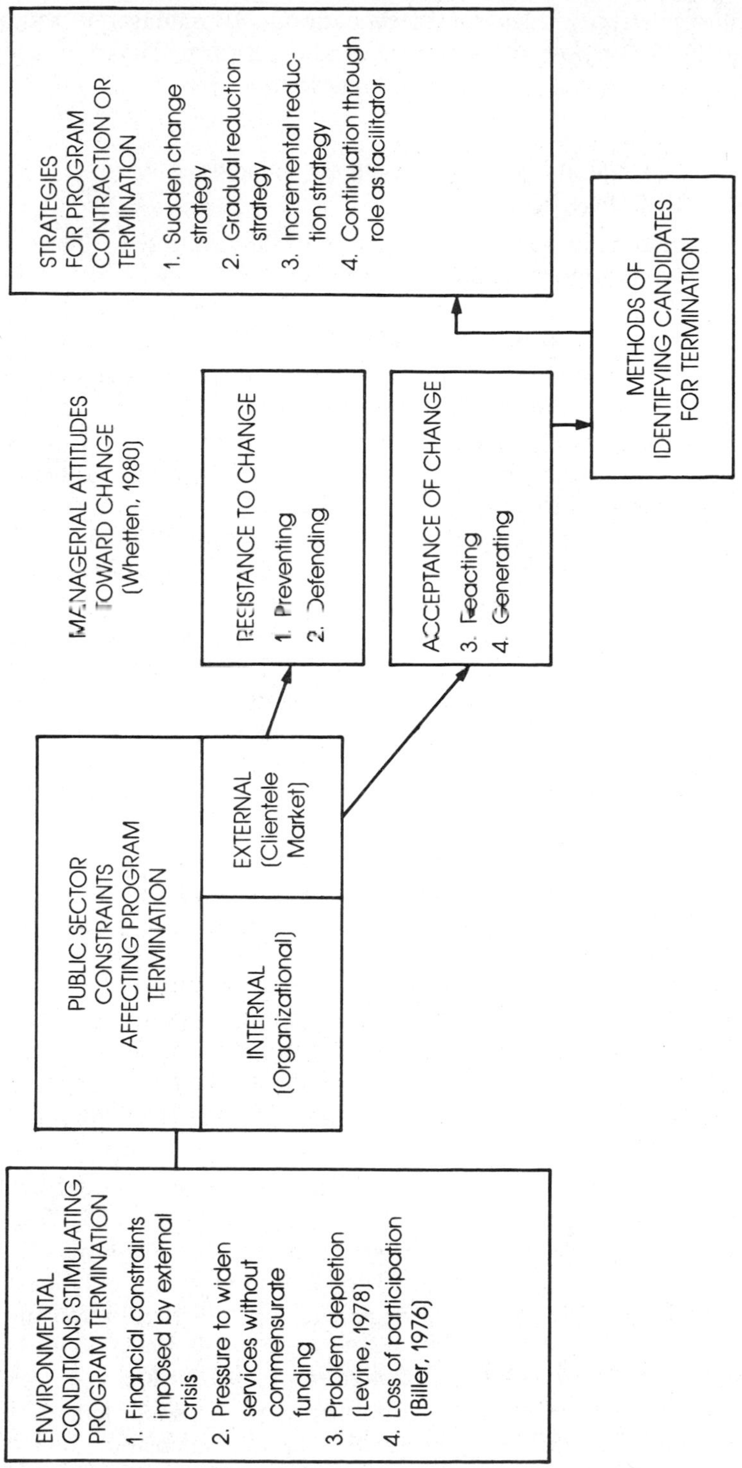

FIGURE 27-1.
A Model of Public Program Termination

straints limiting effective program termination; (3) managerial attitudes toward change; (4) methods of identifying candidates for termination; and (5) strategies for program contraction or termination.

ENVIRONMENTAL CONDITIONS THAT STIMULATE PROGRAM TERMINATION OR CONTRACTION

Action to eliminate an existing program is usually initiated when one or more of the following four conditions arises.

Financial Constraints Imposed by External Crises

The first and most significant stimulus for elimination occurs when an external crisis imposes financial constraints that force an agency to reduce its range of services. Cutbacks in government funds leave public sector managers no choice but to reduce the quality of some services, terminate others, and reject legitimate requests to support new services.

For example, President Reagan's budget cuts will slash about $50 billion of federal funding that affects nearly three hundred public programs. Agencies that provide food stamps and food for the indigent, agencies that compensate victims of black-lung disease, agencies that find jobs for the unemployed, and many others will be forced to reduce or eliminate their services. The administration has also proposed reduction in federal grants to municipalities, which could reduce spending on about one thousand urban projects across the country.

Two other reasons account for reductions in funds to the cities. First, in many large cities, the population has declined with the movement to the suburbs so that fewer people pay property taxes, thus reducing the primary source of local government revenue. Manufacturers and vendors have followed the population to outlying areas, further reducing the tax base for municipalities. New York City provides an excellent example of a city in which substantial personnel and program cuts were enacted as a result of tax base erosion. In the two years from June 30, 1975, to June 30, 1977, the New York City work force declined by 20.8 percent. Reductions in budget allocations for the seven largest functions in the city were: higher education 28.6 percent; environmental protection (including sanitation) 15.8 percent; and social services 13.7 percent (Glassbery, 1978). Second, citizen dissatisfaction with high levels of taxation (and with the lack of commensurate benefits accruing from this taxation) contributes to a reduction in funds. The "tax revolt," most dramatically manifested by the passage of Proposition 13 in California, has reverberated across the nation and impacts not only local and state governments but also the spending policies of the federal government.

Pressures to Widen Services Without Commensurate Funding

Program termination may result when an agency is subjected to strong pressures to broaden its range of services without a commensurate increase in its budget. For example, many communities now require their leisure-service agencies to assume a much broader range of social programs. Food programs for children and senior citizens, general counseling services, and delinquency and drug abuse programs may be added to an agency's domain without proportional increases in funding. In order to accommodate these demands, agencies must reexamine their priorities and determine which of their existing programs should be contracted or deleted to allow resource allocation to the new programs.

■ 27 ■
Valarie A. Zeithaml
Charles W. Lamb, Jr.
John L. Crompton

Problem Depletion or Alleviation (Levine, 1978)

A political institution identifies a problem and commits resources in an effort to resolve it. If the problem is solved, alleviated, or redefined, these resources are contracted and the program is reduced or eliminated (Levine, 1978). As an example, the movement to deinstitutionalize the mentally ill has led to reduced funding of the agencies responsible for treating these populations in institutions. And the Civil Aeronautics Board, the forty-year-old federal regulator of aviation fares and routes, is scheduled to terminate its operations in 1985 because the deregulated airline industry no longer requires its services.

Loss of Participation

Finally, termination may be initiated when participation in a program falls to such a low level that continuation becomes a conspicuous embarrassment to the agency (Kotler, 1965). The presence of stagnant programs to service people's wants and needs results in a poor agency image, which may lead to budget cuts. Stagnant programs may result because the agency's offerings suffer in comparison with competitive programs, especially those from the private sector. Alternatively, changing tastes or lifestyles may lead to a program's stagnation.

Each of the four conditions that stimulate termination in the public sector has its counterpart in the private sector. Problem depletion, for example, is analogous to a decline in industry demand in the private sector. Declining industry demand may occur when new technology supplants existing products (e.g., computers virtually eliminated the slide rule industry) or when the perceived need for a product dissipates due to changing consumer attitudes or environmental conditions (e.g., demand for fallout shelters declined radically as Americans became less fearful of nuclear attack). Loss of participation is the public-sector counterpart to declining firm or product sales in the private sector; both occur when demand decreases because competitive "brands" are perceived as superior or when changing tastes or life styles lead consumers to seek other ways to fulfill their needs. The third condition, financial constraints imposed by external crisis, also occurs in the private sector: Environmental circumstances, such as high interest rates and the unavailability of credit, often lead companies to trim product lines. Finally, the fourth condition, namely, pressure to widen services without commensurate funding, is analogous to the situation that occurs in highly regulated industries. Product termination frequently occurs when private sector firms are forced to comply with costly product improvements while preserving operating efficiencies. As an example, firms in the automobile industry discontinued models requiring extensive improvements to meet the mile-per-gallon standards imposed by the EPA.

PUBLIC-SECTOR CONSTRAINTS AFFECTING PROGRAM TERMINATION

In the public sector, unique organizational and external constraints exist that mediate the impact of environmental conditions on managerial actions. Levine et al. (1980) itemize six organizational constraints that operate in the public but not in the private sector to limit managers' ability to handle retrenchment effectively. First, the plurality of interests that characterizes most public sector organizations limits the authority of managers to redirect resources. Multiplicity of interests usually results in "hesitant, fragmented, and inconsistent" policy making (Caiden, 1981). In contrast, private-sector managers typically possess the necessary authority to cut budgets, products, or employees and to plan cutbacks in an organized and unified manner.

Second, lack of continuity in top management—the normal rather than exceptional condition due to political appointments—leads to immobility, delay, and changes in direction. Whereas continuity in management is a goal in private-sector organizations, it rarely occurs in the public sector. Turnover in politicians results in turnover in political appointees, i.e., managers of most public-sector agencies.

Third, feedback from served markets in the public sector is "sluggish and often insufficient" (Behn, 1981). Organizations rarely know when clients are satisfied, and usually obtain feedback only when clients are exceptionally dissatisfied. In business organizations, formal or informal management information systems provide regular and current feedback on sales, costs, consumer tastes and preferences. The widespread acceptance of the marketing concept in the 1970s led businesses to the realization that success is derived from an understanding of the consumer. Because of the difficulty in obtaining feedback in the public sector, the marketing concept is rarely implemented.

Fourth, because accounts are rigidly segregated in many public budgets, because funds cannot be supplemented by borrowing, and because budgets must be balanced annually, management does not possess the flexibility in budgeting that is present in private-sector organizations.

Fifth, public managers are neither motivated nor trained to conserve resources because incentives are tied to growth and increased spending rather than to contraction. In contrast, many successful private sector managers (e.g., Lee Iacocca at Chrysler) specialize in assuming command of declining organizations and reversing decline by improving internal efficiency.

Sixth and finally, managers can rarely target budget cuts because of legislative or judicial mandates and rigid rules. The private-sector manager possesses the capacity to target cuts so that "programs, departments, personnel, and clients can be affected by the retrenchment according to the organization's goal and priority structure" (Levine et al., 1980). The public-sector manager, in contrast, faces legal or judicial constraints that proscribe cuts in many areas.

In conclusion, these six factors tend to constrain public-sector managers to less effective strategies of program termination and to encourage attitudes of resistance to the changes. In addition to the organizational constraints itemized above, several external constraints also tend to be more pivotal in the public sector (Rainey, Backoff, & Levine, 1976). Vehement resistance from clientele almost always develops because clients feel they have a right to a service that has been provided in the past. Next, public programs are more subject to political influences in the environment than are their counterparts in the private sector.

■ 27 ■
Valarie A. Zeithaml
Charles W. Lamb, Jr.
John L. Crompton

MANAGERIAL ATTITUDES TOWARD CHANGE

When environmental conditions stimulate the need for retrenchment in public service offerings, managers' attitudes toward change affect the type of strategic actions they select (Whetten, 1980). According to Whetten (1980), management responses to environmentally induced change range along a continuum from preventing (the most negative attitude) through "defending" and "reacting" to "generating" (the most positive attitude). This conceptualization is similar to one proposed by Miles, Snow, and Pfeffer (1974), which categorized managers as defenders, reluctant reactors, anxious analyzers, or enthusiastic prospectors.

Preventing

This category embraces unyielding and inflexible attitudes and manipulative efforts to prevent change. Strategies such as buying political influence (Perrow, 1972), price fixing, and other illegal practices (Staw and Szwajkowski, 1975) demonstrate the "preventing" response. Rather than respond to change, organizations direct all their energies and resources to preventing the change.

Defending

The defending attitude involves responses whereby the manager either justifies the existence of the institution or program on ideological grounds (e.g., insisting that the program remain because it "ought" to exist), or uses facts and figures to defend the efficacy of the organization (Whetten, 1979; Pfeffer and Salancik, 1978). According to Whetten, this response is typically found in highly bureaucratic settings or in ideologically based institutions—situations that characterize many public-sector organizations. The defending attitude represents a denial that change is necessary; the manager resists, rather than responds to, the need for elimination.

Reacting

The reacting attitude implies an acceptance of the change and a desire to carry it out in the most appropriate manner. This attitude, as described by Whetten (1980), involves a passive acceptance of the mandate to change, rather than an active effort to seek change.

Generating

The final attitude represents a proactive orientation toward environmentally invoked change; the manager "embraces the enemy" (Whetten, 1980) and welcomes change as an opportunity to create new solutions. This attitude is prescribed by academics but is rarely employed by actual public-sector managers in response to decline.

As shown in Figure 27-1, any of these four attitudes may characterize public-sector managers faced with the need to retrench. However, two of the attitudes—preventing and defending—result in resistance to change rather than in responses to change. They may have succeeded during the 1970s when public funds were plentiful enough that persuasion and inflexibility could be effective strategies to retain programs. However, they are no longer appropriate in the 1980s when shrinking funds and essential cutbacks demand the more adaptive attitudes of reacting and generating.

METHODS OF IDENTIFYING CANDIDATES FOR TERMINATION

One of the essential steps in the contraction or elimination process is the correct identification of programs for elimination. Several different methods for this identification process have been proposed and executed in recent years. The first two methods, zero-base budgeting and sunset legislation, represent efforts to enforce systematic evaluation of public service programs. Zero-base budgeting demands annual justification for existing programs through the requirement that agencies develop a new budget and new priorities each year. This approach requires an agency to systematically evaluate all of its existing and proposed programs on the basis of output or performance criteria. Sunset legislation establishes a timetable for review of a program or agency by automatically terminating it on a predetermined date unless its existence is positively reaffirmed before that date. In the absence of affirmative action, then, the status quo is elimination rather than continuation.

Zero-base budgeting and sunset legislation are usually imposed on an agency by external political or administrative forces. However, other techniques may be self-initiated by the managers, usually by those with a generating attitude—those willing to embrace change in a positive manner. Examples include program life cycle audits (Clifford, 1971), indices of efficiency measures (Hatry et al., 1977), and direct respondent input from surveys (Kotler, 1980). In each of these methods, a program's performance is compared to some predetermined, objective performance criteria; if it does not meet its objectives, the program is changed or discontinued. The use of these and other self-initiated methods results when managers voluntarily perceive the opportunity costs and benefits accruing from termination.

STRATEGIES FOR PROGRAM CONTRACTION OR TERMINATION

Figure 27-2 illustrates four alternative strategies for program contraction or termination. The first three (Easton, 1976) represent different rates of contraction or termination: (1) sudden change strategy; (2) gradual reduction strategy; and (3) incremental reduction strategy. The type of strategy selected by managers is dependent on a number of factors. To avoid conflict, many public-sector managers may prefer the sudden change strategy. In that way, they reduce client resistance to as short a period of time as possible. However, such action may be perceived by citizens as high-handed, arrogant, or as failing to meet a moral obligation to assist those adversely affected by the service cuts. Many may perceive the agency as having an obligation to do as much as possible to help those most directly and adversely affected by the service reductions and not to discontinue support abruptly. These client groups may have come to depend upon the services provided, and those services represent—or at least they will be perceived as representing—a commitment to a clientele (Behn, 1978).

For this reason, many public-service managers seek to inform participating clientele of the elimination or reduction intent far enough in advance to permit them to make arrangements to participate in a similar alternate program if one is available in the community. Hence, they adopt either the gradual reduction (b) or incremental reduction (c) strategy. These strategies permit evaluation of the results of each cutback and provide affected parties with time to adjust to the change and to protect themselves against possible adverse psychological or economic effects (Banville and Pletcher, 1974). Efforts to minimize the impact of terminating a service may decrease the short-run savings from the maneuver but offer benefits of reduced client group and political resistance.

In the fourth strategy, organizations continue the program by assuming the

■ 27 ■
Valarie A. Zeithaml
Charles W. Lamb, Jr.
John L. Crompton

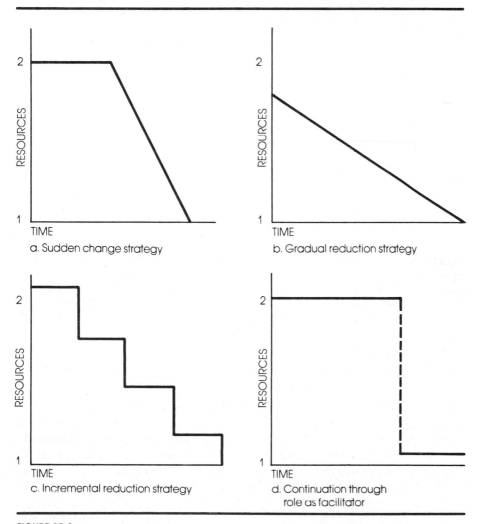

FIGURE 27-2.
Alternative Strategies for Program Contraction

role of facilitator or enabler, rather than of provider. This strategy may involve the cosponsorship of programs with other public sector agencies, the intitiation of referral systems, or the offering of technical and consultative services to private groups who desire to provide the service. Although many agencies have entered into cooperative agreements with other agencies and private organizations (Howard and Crompton, 1980), one Huntington, Long Island, agency is an ideal example. The Huntington Recreation and Parks Department sees itself as a catalyst rather than as a permanent provider. Once the popularity of a recreation or park program has been demonstrated, it is turned over to private groups—profit or nonprofit—for operation. The facilitative function can be expanded further to include the agency assuming the role of a referral agent. In this instance, the agency would act as a broker, providing a connection between the needs of its clientele and the supply of private services available to satisfy them. For example, a recreation and parks staff may act as liaison between community residents and the supply of recreation and park opportunities available in the area. If the manager believes that the program should be maintained, the facilitation strategy offers a creative technique for maintaining the program, although it requires cooperation among different organizations and limits the organization's control over provision of services.

SUMMARY AND IMPLICATIONS

In the future, public agencies will need to manage strategically for stability and decline. The growth management of the past will increasingly be replaced by "cutback management" (Levine, 1978). Decision makers must adjust to managing services with declining capital and reduced operating expenditures.

Decline demands innovation because it is a new phenomenon to the public sector. Although scholars have only begun to consider innovative and responsive methods of dealing with decline, several unique ideas have recently been presented. These include:

- Developing and training a new cadre of leaders who will aggressively respond to declining resources (e.g., Glassbery, 1978). These leaders would likely adopt a generating attitude toward change and would be most open to novel and adaptive methods of handling contraction and elimination.

- Redesigning the structure of public service organizations to make them more flexible. Biller (1976) recommends that public organizations adopt matrix designs so that expendable programs can be eliminated without jeopardizing the viability of the agency.

- Encouraging a marketing orientation on the part of public-sector managers. Adoption of the well-known marketing concept, which emphasizes sensitivity to clientele and anticipation of needs, may encourage public-sector managers to be more attuned to predicting the programs that will be accepted and rejected by clientele and sponsors.

The model of public-program termination presented in this paper illustrates the similarities and isolates the differences between public-program and private-sector product termination. Environmental conditions stimulating termination were revealed to be analogous to conditions stimulating product termination in the private sector. Likewise, strategies for program termination were modeled after product termination strategies. However, the internal and external constraints unique to public-sector organizations interfere with managers' abilities to terminate programs successfully and lead to attitudes of resistance, rather than acceptance, of change. If public-sector managers are to adapt to "cutback management," these constraints must become less limiting. Ultimately, managers need to develop reacting or generating attitudes to deal with public-program termination in the 1980s.

■ 27 ■
Valarie A. Zeithaml
Charles W. Lamb, Jr.
John L. Crompton

REFERENCES

Alexander, R. S. The death and burial of "sick products." *Journal of Marketing,* 1964, *42,* 1–7.

Banville, G. R., & Pletcher, B. A. The product elimination function. *Journal of the Academy of Marketing Science,* 1974, *2,* 432–446.

Behn, R. D. Closing a government facility. *Public Administration Review,* 1978, *38,* 332–338.

Behn, R. D. Can public policy termination be increased by making government more business-like? In Levin and Rubin (Eds.), *Fiscal stress and public policy.* Santa Monica, Calif.: Sage, 1981.

Biller, R. P. On tolerating policy and organizational termination: Some design considerations. *Policy Sciences,* 1976, *7,* 133–149.

Caiden, N. Negative financial management: A backward look at fiscal stress. In Levine and Rubin (Eds.) *Fiscal stress and public policy.* Santa Monica, Calif.: Sage, 1981.

Clifford, D. K. Managing the product life cycle. In R. Mann (Ed.), *The arts of top management: A McKinsey anthology.* New York: McGraw-Hill, 1971.

Easton, A. *Managing for negative growth.* Reston, Va.: Reston Publishing Company, 1976.

Glassbery, A. Organizational responses to municipal budget decreases. *Public Administration Review,* 1978, *38,* 325–332.

Hatry, H. P., Blair, L. H., Fisk, D. M., Greiner, J. M., Hall, J. R., & Schaenman, P. S. How effective are your community services? In *Procedures for monitoring the effectiveness of municipal services.* Washington, D.C.: The Urban Institute, 1977.

Howard, D. R., & Crompton, J. L. *Financing, managing, and marketing recreation and park resources.* Dubuque, Iowa: Wm. C. Brown, 1980.

Kotler, P. F. Phasing out weak products. *Harvard Business Review,* 1965, *43,* 107–118.

Kotler, P. F. *Marketing management: Analysis, planning and control* (4th ed.). New Jersey,: Prentice-Hall, 1980.

Levine, C. H. Organizational decline and cutback management. *Public Administration Review,* July–August 1978, *38,* 317–325.

Levine, C. H., Rubin, I. S., & Wolohojian, G. G. Preconditions for managing organizational retrenchment: Deficiencies and adaption in the public sector. Paper presented at the meeting of the Academy of Management, Detroit, 1980.

Miles, R. E., Snow, C. C., & Pfeffer, J. Organization-environment: Concepts and issues. *Industrial Relations,* 1974, *13,* 244–264.

Perrow, C. *The radical attack on business: A critical analysis.* New York: Harcourt Brace Jovanovich, 1972.

Pfeffer, J., & Salancik, G. R. *The external control of organization: A resource dependence perspective.* New York: Harper and Row, 1978.

Rainey, H. G., Backoff, R. W., & Levine, C. H. Comparing public and private organizations. *Public Administration Review,* 1976, *36,* 223–234. [Included in this volume as Chapter 7]

Staw, B. M., & Szwajkowski, E. The scarcity-munificence component of organizational environments and the commission of illegal acts. *Administrative Science Quarterly,* 1975, *20,* 345–354.

Whetton, D. A. Organizational responses to scarcity: difficult choices for difficult times. (Working paper). College of Commerce & Business Administration, University of Illinois, 1979.

Whetton, D. A. Sources, responses and effects of organizational decline. In J. R. Kimberly & R. H. Miles & Associates (Eds.), *Organizational life cycle*. San Francisco, Calif.: Jossey-Bass, 1980.